Quantum Readiness for Leaders

Build quantum strategies, teams, security, and ecosystems to lead in the era of quantum advantage

Robert Loredo

<packt>

Quantum Readiness for Leaders

Portfolio Director: Kunal Chaudhari
Relationship Lead: Denim Pinto
Project Manager: K. Loganathan
Content Engineer: Deepayan Bhattacharjee
Technical Editor: Irfa Ansari
Indexer: Hemangini Bari
Production Designer: Shankar Kalbhor
Growth Lead: Uzma Sheerin

First published: August 2026

Production reference: 1250826

Published by Packt Publishing Ltd.
Grosvenor House
11 St Paul's Square
Birmingham
B3 1RB, UK.

ISBN 978-1-80638-875-2

www.packtpub.com

I would like to dedicate this book to my family, who have always motivated me to keep moving forward and not settle for too long.

Foreword

As early as 1980, Paul Benioff and Richard Feynman published their work that showed that computation could be accomplished using quantum mechanics. This, along with Feynman's MIT talk delivered in 1981 "Simulating Physics with Computers", is widely viewed as the genesis of the field of Quantum Computing. Just like classical computers before quantum, public sentiment of course was what's the point? Richard Feynman had some compelling arguments to answer that "why". One of his primary arguments was that if you are going to simulate nature, which is essentially quantum, you need a computational system that is also quantum. The details within his argument included some aspects of classical computing that for him were fundamental ground truths. The first of these was that classical computers hit an exponential wall when simulating quantum systems. The second was that since nature isn't classical, a realistic simulator of physical processes must use quantum mechanics internally. And the third was that, taking the second into account, quantum computers are not simply faster classical machines – they are unique devices that are capable of simulating quantum phenomena that classical systems cannot do well.

It was not until the late 1990s to early 2000s that we saw the arrival of the first experimental quantum computers. In 2016, IBM launched the IBM Quantum Experience with a 5-qubit device. This was a turning point for quantum computing as it was the point in time when hands-on quantum computing became available to the public. Another milestone occurred in 2017 with IBM's release of Qiskit (Quantum Information Software Kit). The importance of this cannot be unstated. For the first time, developers had a Python SDK they could use to build quantum circuits, with the ability to manipulate quantum operators and then execute these on quantum hardware or quantum simulators.

While this was going on, several vendors continued to press forward with systems of more than 100 qubits along with error mitigation capabilities. By 2024, superconductors and neutral atoms exceeded 1000 physical qubit systems. This signals another milestone; commercial relevance is within sight. Around this time there was more quantum advantage evidence to drive the commercial relevance argument home. This included verifiable evidence of quantum processors solving specific physics tasks faster than the best classical methods, and verifiable advantages seen in out-of-time-order correlation tasks and memory-limited problems constructed that are fit for purpose.

Quantum is here to stay. Quantum disruption is our future. It has and will advance far quicker than classical computing ever did. Vendors that include IonQ, IBM, Quantinuum, Rigetti, QuEra, Oxford Quantum Circuits, Xanadu, and D-Wave all have expanding offerings and they are expanding rapidly. The challenge now is to provide education and enablement not only industry specific, but to bring the enablement to secondary and post-secondary education in order to bring quantum computing mainstream quickly. However, before we do that, the full range of executive and academic leadership needs to be enabled with knowledge beyond just the basics so that we can build this ecosystem demand from the top down that is carefully targeted.

This book serves as a foundation for senior organizational stakeholders to ensure they do not simply move forward in this environment but do so with competitive advantage while navigating the many opportunities and threats. There are perspectives for the CEO, Investor teams, CISO, and CTOs as well as Academic considerations, so that these various leaders can formulate quantum-ready teams specific to the coming challenges and opportunities of quantum computing.

This book is a great jump-start, and I am sure you will thoroughly enjoy it!

Matt Broomhall

Field CTO and Cross Brand Technical Architect

Contributors

About the author

Robert Loredo is a globally recognized technology strategist, innovator, and thought leader who has over 21 years of experience while working at IBM, where he served as an IBM Master Inventor and key contributor to the IBM Quantum team by leading the global IBM Quantum Ambassador program and functioning as a Go-to-Market Global Strategist. With an inventive mind evidenced by more than 280 patents, Robert has consistently pushed the boundaries of what's possible at the intersection of Artificial Intelligence, Quantum Computing, and enterprise transformation. His published work spans high-impact domains including Life Sciences, Finance, AI, and Quantum Computing, cementing his reputation as one of the most prolific and versatile technology thought leaders of his generation. Currently serving as the Founder and CEO of Entangled Solutions Group, Robert advises organizational leaders worldwide on strategic AI and Quantum readiness. He also serves as Executive Director of Quantum Technologies for Florida Atlantic University, where he is helping prepare the future quantum workforce through education for students and industry professionals. In this role, he's building partnerships among universities, national laboratories, and industry from around the world to advance research, workforce development, and practical quantum innovation. He holds Bachelor's and Master's degrees in Computer and Electrical Engineering from the University of Miami, is a graduate of the Chief Technical Officer program at the Wharton School of Business, and is currently pursuing his PhD in Computer Science at FAU with a specialization in quantum. A sought-after speaker and educator, Robert has lectured at Florida International University, Miami-Dade College, and delivered workshops globally on the technologies reshaping our world. His commitment to humanity extends beyond the boardroom. He donated royalties from his previous book, *Learn Quantum Computing using IBM Quantum*, to his favorite charity and will continue to do so with the proceeds from this book. In *Quantum Readiness for Leaders*, Robert brings his rare combination of deep technical expertise, strategic vision, and philanthropic purpose to equip today's leaders with the mindset and tools to thrive in the quantum era. His favorite quote is, *"A leader is not determined by the number of followers they have, but by the number of leaders they create."*

I would like to extend my thanks to my mentors and friends who without their expertise, guidance, and support this book would not be possible. First and foremost, the two people who initially sparked the idea and shaped the original concept for this book: Matthew Broomhall and Steffen Thoβ. I also want to extend my sincere thanks to Tammy Cornell, John Buselli, Pedro Santos Acosta, Antonio Fornaguera, Manny and Melissa Medina, Tony Jimenez, Silvana Roncal, Luciana Carmelino, Travis Scholten, Paul Stimers, David Barkus, Peter Golcher, Marco Facchini, Valerie Chiang, Kevin Stevens, Pete Martinez (Go CANES!), Rafael Sotelo, Hausi Müller, Gaylen Bennett, Hanhee Paik, Rizwan Hussain, Julian Tan, Martin Svik, Petra Florizoone, Voica Radescu, Federico Mattei, Michele Grossi, Walter Riess, Utz Bacher, Will Oliver, Esperanza Cuenca Gomez, Raquel Puente, Enrique Vargas, Charles Chung, Imed Othmani, Bob Parney, Gabe Chang, Charles Robinson, Ray Harishankar, Kenny Heitritter, Jay Gambetta, Jerry Chow, Dario Gil, Scott Crowder, Zaira Nazario, Claudia Rocio Contreras, Oscar Gomez, Ivana Gomez, Karla Gomez, Frank Gaudio, M. Lewis Temares, Joseph Broz, Bob Sutor, Denise Ruffner, Jorge Echenique, JJ Centurion, my Writer's Conference coaches: Rob Hart, Polly Campbell, Paula Rizzo, and to the entire Packt team for their support during the course of writing this book.

About the reviewers

Matt Broomhall has been in IT since the dawn of personal computing – nearly 40 years. The launch of the IBM PC and PC Jr. sent shockwaves through the computing world with the "non-believers" caught completely flat-footed. These systems and "clones" meant that new systems had to be developed and put in place so that these devices could be integrated into business and then contribute to business in a meaningful way. Matt was involved in that journey from the beginning – starting with a couple of small bio-technology companies. Creativity in the software arena was sky-rocketing and he had become a "closet" expert in a new category of software called "groupware". Lotus Notes was incredibly leading-edge in its time, and as a result, Matt got picked up by IBM in a consulting role and hired direct soon after to help IBM Microelectronics leverage this software to streamline parts of its business.

Matt has held many roles in his career with IBM that include leading initiatives within the CIO organization, leading teams within Lotus to enable Lotus ISVs, and leading pre-sales technical architecture discussions with IBM customers. Matt's customers have been in government, financial services, healthcare, defense, and high-tech manufacturing – each bringing their own challenges and each benefiting from Matt's experiences and expertise.

Claudia Contreras is a seasoned business executive with leadership experience at two Fortune 500 global technology companies, HP and Lenovo, where she served in Vice President and Executive leadership roles. Throughout her career, she has built and scaled new business offerings, led large multifunctional teams, and driven growth across services and solutions, sustainability, and supply chain organizations. She is recognized for combining strategic vision with operational execution to deliver sustainable business results, create new market opportunities, and strengthen customer value.

Table of Contents

Chapter 10: Quantum Threat Landscape and Risk Assessment 273

Chapter 14: Building the Quantum Ecosystem 395

Preface

Quantum technology is no longer a subject reserved for physicists and futurists. It has arrived at the boardroom door.

The convergence of quantum computing, artificial intelligence, and advanced cryptography is reshaping the competitive landscape across every major industry: finance, defense, healthcare, logistics, and beyond. Organizations that understand this shift and move decisively will define the next era of technological leadership. Those that wait for quantum to become "mainstream" before engaging will find themselves playing an increasingly costly game of catch-up against adversaries who began preparing years earlier.

This book was written because a dangerous gap exists between where the conversation about quantum technology happens and where the decisions about quantum technologies get made. Quantum research is advancing at extraordinary speed inside universities, national laboratories, and deep-tech startups. Yet in the boardrooms, investment committees, and policy chambers where resource allocation, risk management, and strategic direction are determined, quantum readiness remains poorly understood, inconsistently prioritized, and frequently deferred.

That gap is not a failure of ambition. It's a failure of translation.

Quantum Readiness for Leaders is designed to close that gap. It does not ask business leaders to become quantum physicists. It asks them to become quantum-literate strategists. Executives and policymakers capable of asking the right questions, making sound investment decisions, building the right teams, and constructing the governance structure and security architectures that will carry their organizations safely through the quantum transition.

The quantum era will not arrive as a single dramatic event. It's already unfolding, incrementally and then suddenly, across supply chains, cryptographic standards, sensing capabilities, and national security frameworks. The window for proactive preparation is open now. The cost of inaction compounds with every passing year as "harvest now, decrypt later" attacks accumulate encrypted data, quantum talent concentrates in organizations that started recruiting early, and standards bodies finalize post-quantum cryptographic frameworks that will soon become compliance requirements.

The leaders who will shape the quantum era are not necessarily those with the largest quantum budgets or the deepest technical teams today. They're the ones who begin the strategic journey with clarity, urgency, and the right conceptual foundation.

That foundation begins here.

A simple overview of my process of writing this book

This book was built on a simple foundation that no AI can replicate: real-life experience, original design and thinking, and deliberate creative choices.

The process began long before any AI was involved. The core themes, personal anecdotes, and both technical and business context you'll find here originated from me. Mostly drawn from the many client engagements and over two decades of working with some of the most intelligent and creative people in the world.

From there, I worked interactively with Claude (Sonnet) to help shape the narrative structure and sharpen the language. Imagine it less like "asking AI to create something for me" and more like an effective, efficient, and very patient editorial collaborator. One that only worked with the content and context which I shared with it directly.

After completing the initial draft, I then proceeded to work with the experienced reviewers and Packt editors: reviewing, refining, all while I made sure that every word sounds like me and reflects what I believe.

AI helped in the middle. However, the creation, the intent, the practice-based frameworks, and the conclusions? Those are entirely human.

Who this book is for

Quantum Readiness for Leaders is written for executives: CEOs, CIOs, CDOs, CTOs, and CISOs, as well as investors, startup founders, research directors, and policymakers who are responsible for strategic decisions at the intersection of emerging technology, organizational resilience, and competitive positioning. No prior quantum physics background is required.

What this book covers

Chapter 1, The Strategic Imperative – Why Quantum Demands Executive Action Now, establishes the strategic urgency of quantum technology by examining how quantum computing, AI, and cybersecurity are converging into a single business reality, and frames the competitive risks of delayed action alongside the ROI case for early investment.

Chapter 2, Quantum Economics and Investment Strategy, provides a comprehensive view of quantum technology markets, funding ecosystems, and budget allocation frameworks, including venture capital dynamics, government incentives, export regulations, and geographic considerations across the US, Asia, and EMEA regions.

Chapter 3, Building Your Quantum Leadership Team, guides executives through recruiting specialized quantum talent, structuring advisory boards, and cultivating internal quantum champions, with practical strategies for compensation, retention, and integrating quantum capability into existing organizational environments.

Chapter 4, Governance and Strategic Planning, delivers a framework for establishing quantum governance structures, setting measurable strategic objectives, and navigating regulatory and compliance considerations, with guidance on integrating quantum planning into existing organizational hierarchies.

Chapter 5, Quantum-AI Infrastructure Assessment, offers a technical evaluation methodology for assessing current systems against quantum-AI integration requirements, covering hybrid computing architectures, cloud quantum services, and practical migration planning.

Chapter 6, Workforce Development and Skills Strategy, outlines a systematic approach to building quantum-literate technical teams through training programs, university partnerships, certification pathways, and targeted upskilling of existing staff.

Chapter 7, Prototyping and Proof-of-Concept Development, provides hands-on guidance for launching quantum pilots and hybrid quantum-AI experiments, including vendor selection criteria, development methodologies, and frameworks for measuring early-stage success.

Chapter 8, Data Strategy for the Quantum Era, addresses the architectural and governance changes organizations must make to prepare their data environments for quantum processing, including quantum data encoding, hybrid workflows, and privacy protection considerations.

Chapter 9, Post-Quantum Cryptography Migration, maps the strategic roadmap for transitioning to quantum-resistant cryptographic systems, covering current vulnerabilities, NIST standards adoption, risk prioritization, and realistic implementation timelines.

Chapter 10, Quantum Threat Landscape and Risk Assessment, delivers a rigorous analysis of how quantum computing threatens current security infrastructure, including timeline projections, threat actor capabilities, industry-specific exposure, and approaches to continuous risk monitoring.

Chapter 11, Seamless Security Integration Strategy, presents a methodology for deploying quantum-safe security measures without disrupting ongoing business operations, with phased implementation approaches, legacy system considerations, and change management guidance.

Chapter 12, Future-Proofing Your Security Architecture, establishes a framework for building adaptive security systems capable of evolving alongside quantum technology, addressing emerging quantum security tools, compliance requirements, and the role of strategic security partnerships.

Chapter 13, The Quantum Technology Ecosystem: Sensing, Networking, and the End-to-End Vision, broadens the lens beyond quantum computing to encompass quantum sensing, quantum networking, quantum key distribution, and distributed quantum computing, showing how these technologies interconnect and what their convergence will enable.

Chapter 14, Building the Quantum Ecosystem, provides the strategic frameworks and partnership models that organizations, institutions, and governments need to actively construct the talent pipelines, research-to-commercial pathways, and cross-disciplinary ecosystems that will determine quantum leadership in the 2030s and beyond.

To get the most out of this book

No quantum physics background is assumed or required. Readers should bring a working familiarity with corporate strategy, technology investment, or organizational leadership. A general awareness of cybersecurity principles will be helpful for Part 3. Each part is designed to stand alone for readers with role-specific needs, though reading sequentially will build the fullest strategic picture.

Get in touch

Feedback from our readers is always welcome.

General feedback: If you have questions about any aspect of this book or have any general feedback, please email us at `customercare@packt.com` and mention the book's title in the subject of your message.

Errata: Although we have taken every care to ensure the accuracy of our content, mistakes do happen. If you have found a mistake in this book, we would be grateful if you reported this to us. Please visit `http://www.packt.com/submit-errata`, click **Submit Errata**, and fill in the form.

Piracy: If you come across any illegal copies of our works in any form on the internet, we would be grateful if you would provide us with the location address or website name. Please contact us at `copyright@packt.com` with a link to the material.

If you are interested in becoming an author: If there is a topic that you have expertise in and you are interested in either writing or contributing to a book, please visit `http://authors.packt.com/`.

Free benefits with your book

This book comes with free benefits to support your learning. Activate them now for instant access (see the "*How to unlock*" section for instructions).

Here's a quick overview of what you can instantly unlock with your purchase:

How to unlock

Scan the QR code (or go to `packtpub.com/unlock`). Search for this book by name, confirm the edition, and then follow the steps on the page.

UNLOCK NOW

Note: Keep your invoice handy. Purchases made directly from Packt don't require one.

Join us on Discord!

Read this book alongside other users, developers, experts, and the author himself.

Ask questions, provide solutions to other readers, chat with the authors via Ask Me Anything sessions, and much more. Scan the QR or visit the link to join the community.

`https://packt.link/deep-engineering-quantum`

Share your thoughts

Once you've read *Quantum Readiness for Leaders*, we'd love to hear your thoughts! Scan the QR code below to go straight to the Amazon review page for this book and share your feedback.

https://packt.link/r/1806388758

Your review is important to us and the tech community and will help us make sure we're delivering excellent quality content.

Part 1

Executive Foundation: Building Quantum Business Readiness

Every major technological transition has its moment of decision. Not the moment when the technology arrives fully formed and the path forward is obvious. The moment before that, when the signals re clear enough to act on but early enough that the right moves still make a difference. For quantum technology, that moment is now.

Quantum Readiness for Leaders is your guide to that moment. Across four parts and fourteen chapters, this book delivers the strategic frameworks, technical foundations, security imperatives, and ecosystem perspectives that executives, security leaders, technical directors, investors, and policymakers need to navigate the quantum transition with clarity and confidence. It was written for leaders who understand that quantum is not a technology story for physicists alone. It's a leadership story, and it's unfolding right now.

Part I is where that story begins. These chapters are written for the executives who will be held accountable for whether their organizations enter the quantum era as leaders or as late movers. That means the CEOs weighing whether quantum belongs on the strategic agenda today or can wait another cycle, the CFOs being asked to fund initiatives whose ROI timelines stretch beyond a standard business case, and the board members trying to govern a technology transition they haven't yet had a clear framework to evaluate.

Across these 4 chapters, you'll build the executive foundation that everything else in this book depends on. You'll start with the strategic case for acting now, grounded in market timing, competitive dynamics, and the real cost of delay. From there, you'll move into the economics of quantum investment, including how to allocate capital intelligently, how to read the global funding landscape, and how to build a business case that holds up to scrutiny. The final two chapters address the human and organizational dimensions that determine whether quantum strategy ever leaves the boardroom. You'll learn how to build and retain the leadership team capable of executing a quantum agenda, and how to establish the governance structures that keep quantum initiatives accountable, compliant, and integrated into the way your organization makes decisions.

Each chapter includes various focused assessments. Use them honestly. It will tell you exactly where your organization stands and where to focus first.

The competitive positions in the quantum era are still open. The chapters ahead will help you claim yours.

This part of the book includes the following chapters:

- *Chapter 1, The Strategic Imperative – Why Quantum Demands Executive Action Now*
- *Chapter 2, Quantum Economics and Investment Strategy*
- *Chapter 3, Building Your Quantum Leadership Team*
- *Chapter 4, Governance and Strategic Planning*

1

The Strategic Imperative – Why Quantum Demands Executive Action Now

Picture this scenario: You're in your office when your CTO, a board member, or a key stakeholder places an article on your desk that reads, "A Demonstration of Quantum Advantage in ...", and asks you point-blank what your organization's response will be. Can you confidently articulate your strategic position, or are you uncertain about what quantum advantage actually means and what action, if any, you should take?

When quantum advantage lands on your desk

That exact moment of uncertainty drove me into quantum computing in 2018. Since then, I've systematically documented insights gained while collaborating with leading practitioners and strategists in the field, not merely to understand what quantum advantage is, but to determine what executive preparedness requires: strategic foresight combined with operational agility to assess, navigate, and mitigate emerging risks and opportunities.

Over the years, I've consulted C-suite leaders, investors, and policymakers on a range of topics, including engagements to develop strategic frameworks, educational programs, market entry strategies, and global workforce initiatives around various quantum technologies, not just quantum computing. This book distills those lessons because I believe knowledge becomes most valuable when shared and stress-tested through dialog.

The most rewarding aspect of this work isn't the initial knowledge transfer; it's what follows. When executives, startup founders, or investors grasp a transformative technology for the first time, they inevitably ask sharper questions and surface perspectives I hadn't initially considered. That's where learning transforms into strategic discovery. Fresh understanding liberates us to explore possibilities unconstrained by assumptions about limitations we don't yet know exist.

That exploration, informed yet unbounded, is where competitive advantage begins.

The emerging quantum technology landscape

Before we go any further, it's worth pausing to ask a foundational question: what do we really mean by "quantum"? In boardrooms, at investor briefings, and during conference Q&A sessions, I am frequently asked various questions of the same themes: "Where should we invest in quantum?", "Who is leading the field?", "Where should my team go to learn more about quantum?"

These are important questions, but they are also broad ones. In many ways, they resemble asking, "Where should I invest in computers?" Without context, the answer is incomplete. The quantum domain is not a single market or technology, but an ecosystem of distinct yet interrelated fields, from sensing and communications to networking, computing, and security. Each has its own maturity curve, risk profile, talent requirements, and of course strategic relevance. This naturally leads to the next set of questions: What differentiates these areas? How do they complement one another? And, most importantly for our intents and purposes, where do they create real strategic and economic value?

To set the stage, we'll begin this section with a concise, executive-level overview of the major quantum technologies, where the objective is to provide you with a clear mental map of the landscape, what each technology is, where it is advancing most rapidly, what challenges still remain, and where meaningful opportunities are already emerging. For each domain, we will outline current and near-term applications across key industries, highlight the principal technical and commercial hurdles, and conclude with real-world use cases that illustrate how these capabilities are being deployed today.

The goal is simple: to equip you, as a decision-maker, with enough clarity and context to assess which areas of quantum are strategically relevant to your organization, and how they might fit into your longer-term innovation, investment, and national or corporate competitiveness agendas. Let's dig in!

Overview of quantum technologies today

Quantum technology, which in essence can be thought of as the harnessing of the principles of quantum mechanics for computation, communication, and measurement, is reshaping expectations across a range of industries from finance to logistics to healthcare and defense. While often discussed as a singular paradigm, quantum technology actually encompasses distinct but interrelated pillars: Quantum Sensing, Quantum Networking, Quantum Key Distribution (QKD), Quantum Computing, and Quantum Cryptography.

Understanding how these segments complement each other is essential for executives and leaders making strategic investments or policy decisions. Together, they form a foundation for the "Quantum Internet" (or often referred to as "Distributed Quantum Systems"), a future ecosystem where quantum data moves securely, is processed efficiently, and enables insights beyond classical limits. To simplify how these technologies could interact with each other, I will cover each technology as part of an end-to-end workflow: from data capture (sensing), through communications (network/QKD), through computation (computing), and the overall security (quantum safe). In addition, for simplicity, I will separate each into sections covering an overview of each technology, the opportunities, challenges, and a recent example.

Quantum sensing

Quantum sensing uses delicate quantum states, such as superposition and entanglement, to measure physical quantities (time, magnetic fields, gravity, acceleration) with precision previously unattainable by classical instruments. There are many practical uses, which is why this specific technology has already seen an increase in total attainable market, according to Boston Consulting Group, to reach $170-$200 billion (USD) by 2030, while the expected global quantum-sensing market will reach $3-5 billion (USD) also by 2030. [1]

Opportunities:

For many executives and policymakers, quantum sensing does offer a path to improvements in timing, navigation, and measurement that can be framed as strategic infrastructure, and not just as interesting components. The ultra-precision that quantum sensors provide opens a wide range of opportunities in various industries. For example, inertial sensors and clocks can enhance GPS-denied navigation for aviation, shipping, and defense, while extremely sensitive magnetometers and gravimeters enhance subsurface resource exploration for drilling companies and civil engineering surveys. There are also many dual-use applications such as early-warning systems for environmental risks. Public use case examples include industries like healthcare, quantum-enhanced imaging, and biosensing, which would enable earlier disease detection, which could improve both cost savings to drug manufacturers and improved drug discovery.

As many of these components improve and mature, there are opportunities to define open standards, certifications, and public-private partnerships that lower adoption risk and allow more sectors to benefit and either build or leverage common platforms. This is especially desired in many regulated industries such as energy, logistics, and finance. Early adopter organizations that invest now in these pilot programs and talent will, in essence, be positioning themselves as leaders in their markets that will shape regulation, logistics, and data systems in quantum sensing measurements.

- Healthcare: Ultra-precise magnetic sensors are leading to new forms of non-invasive brain and heart imaging.
- Defense and Navigation: Quantum accelerometers and gyroscopes provide GPS-independent navigation for submarines or aircraft, useful in denied environments.
- Energy and Environment: Gravimetry sensors can detect underground reserves or monitor glaciers and groundwater.

Challenges:

Quantum sensors, similar to most quantum technologies, require extreme isolation from noise and temperature variations. Scaling from laboratory prototypes to field-ready systems remains costly. Quantum sensing platforms are also very fragile, often requiring ultra-stable environments, cryogenic temperatures, or complex laser systems that are quite difficult to deploy outside of the lab environment. Their extreme sensitivity makes them vulnerable to environmental noise, calibration drift, and interference from other co-located electronic components or devices, which complicates usage in real-world settings. These include, but are not limited to, aircraft, hospitals, or industrial plants. A large number of these devices remain bespoke prototypes with very limited manufacturing maturity, supply-chain depth, or agreed interface standards, which usually drives up cost and slows systems integration with existing control, data, and IT infrastructure. Business leaders and decision-makers also face unclear ROI, since much of the performance gains are incremental over classical sensors. These factors create a gap between impressive demonstrations in the various industry use cases and their ability to be certified products that can be purchased, maintained, and audited within general enterprise or defense contractor procurement frameworks.

Example:

Companies like Qnami [2] and SBQuantum [3] are commercializing diamond-based quantum magnetometers capable of nanoscale imaging, a leap beyond current MRI capabilities. Much of the work is around sensitivity and miniaturization of sensors so that they can fit easily onto various platforms such as drones, rovers, or autonomous underwater vehicles (AUVs). Growth of this technology is moving from research to industry and government, recently in dual-use applications.

Quantum networking

Quantum Networking connects quantum devices such as quantum computers, sensors, or nodes, over optical or free-space channels using entangled photons. These networks form the foundations needed for a "quantum internet". The quantum internet is built upon a distributed quantum infrastructure landscape, as described in the following figure. The infrastructure consists of a foundation layer, a distributed computing layer, and the quantum internet application layer. Each layer has its own technology roadmap that shifts quantum computing from an isolated, laboratory system to a macro-level, highly versatile architecture. For a leader, such as yourself, it is essential to understand how these components differentiate and interconnect to each other to navigate both the future of computing and the cyber-risks involved across the stack.

Quantum Networking: The hardware layer that is responsible for transferring quantum information between locations via photons within fiber optic network cables. Current progress is moving from dark fiber experiment sandboxes to commercialized components and systems. Networking leaders such as Cisco have already begun engineering high-rate entanglement chips that integrate directly into existing fiber networks.[4]

Quantum Distributed Computing: The modular collection of Quantum Processing Units (QPUs) linked together seamlessly to operate as a single yet powerful quantum supercomputer. In essence, it's a collection of small QPU systems working together to operate as what seems like a large quantum system. As most quantum systems face severe physical scaling limits due to noise or cost, hardware researchers and vendors are pivoting to horizontal scaling. For example, IBM's Nighthawk and Loon processors include a platform that introduces scaling by connecting qubits to up to four neighbors and introducing c-couplers to link qubits across the chip, respectively. [5]

Quantum Internet, Global Network Ecosystem: The secure global network that connects various heterogeneous quantum systems that run parallel to the current classical internet we use today. Today, the quantum internet is evolving in phases. Current projects rely on Quantum Key Distribution (QKD), which uses quantum properties to share encryption keys securely across classical channels. Global deployment is currently limited to short distances. In order to reach longer distances, advancements in quantum repeaters/transducers must provide secure and error-free communication to distances that can span across many miles (kilometers).

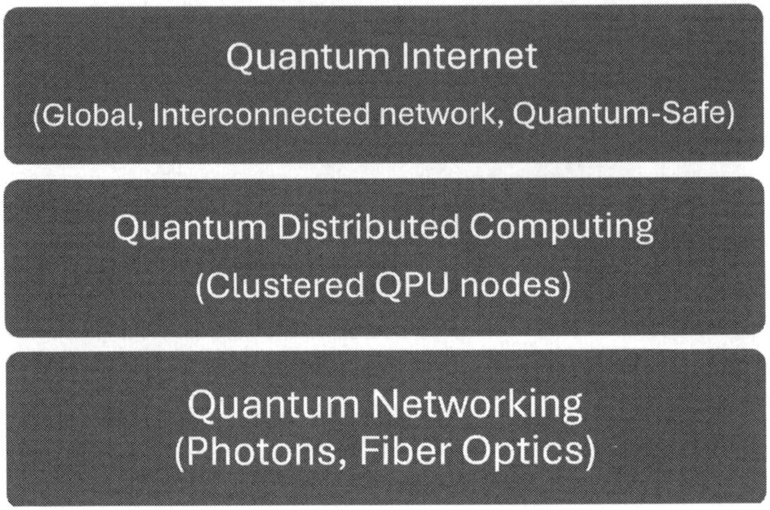

Figure 1.1: The Quantum Internet Infrastructure Landscape

Opportunities:

The main goal of quantum networking is a quantum-enabled communications network, or quantum internet, that can support a distributed quantum computing network, ensure secure cloud services, and generate new models of sensing and synchronization across a plurality of cities, countries, continents, and even into space itself. Initial opportunities exist in the early segments between data centers, national laboratories, and financial institutions. This will initially create a great market for equipment providers, services, and operators. These initial deployments could also serve to provide much operational data that would help organizations create standards for many protocols and performance, which in turn would enable regulators and infrastructure leaders to identify quantum networks as a critical infrastructure path as opposed to a side channel of sorts.

Over time, these hybrid architectures blending classical and quantum networking links may support new services such as ultra-secure interbank settlement channels or quantum sensor grids for weather prediction, space exploration, and secure communications monitoring. Early adopters who work with policymakers and research and development incentives will be the ones accelerating the evolution of the technology and ensuring that there is much interoperability supporting multinational networks to support a global quantum internet that is built upon the current network systems.

- Secure Communications: Sharing entangled particles allows instant detection of eavesdropping attempts.

- Distributed Quantum Computing: Quantum networks will eventually link small quantum processors into cloud-based clusters, amplifying power.
- Scientific Collaboration: Enables synchronized measurements between distant quantum sensors.

Challenges:

Quantum networking has challenges it must overcome before having the capability to provide a quantum internet globally. Challenges include some fundamental physical limits such as loss, decoherence, and the difficulty of storing and routing entangled state information, all while operating on the existing fiber channel links, which are not yet designed for quantum information traffic. Quantum repeaters, quantum memories, and error correction photonic interfaces are still at an early state technologically. Their readiness levels, including quantum network testbeds, are still considered short-range and are custom or heavily engineered on a case-by-case basis rather than a universally scalable infrastructure. There are also many architectural considerations such as interoperability and system management challenges when trying to integrate classical and quantum communication networks and systems.

Current governance and investment models are not clear as to their initial use when quantum networks come online, meaning will they be primarily used as a specialized backbone service, address national security assets, or enterprise overlays, each making it very difficult to build an ROI framework. It's a little different for leaders in academia as there are tensions between rapidly deploying demonstrations and maintaining the rigor, scientifically of course, needed to benchmark true quantum advantage vs. optimized classical secure communications.

Example:

The DARPA Quantum Network Project [6] and China's Micius (or QUESS) satellite [7] have demonstrated quantum communication links over hundreds to thousands of kilometers, which is considered a strong foundational step toward a global quantum network.

Quantum Key Distribution (QKD)

Let's now look at the reality that keeps not only me, but many other CIOs and Risk Committees up at night. Our entire global economy, which includes everything from proprietary information to national defense, is locked behind some very complicated mathematics. The assumption has always been that these encryption keys we use based on these mathematical formulas would be practically impossible to solve, and if so, it would take thousands of years using the fastest supercomputers. However, with quantum computing entering the arena, things are now changing. Enter Shor's algorithm, which is a formula that was described to be able to break the current encryption we have in place today. Granted, with a quantum computer which is not yet large enough to run the algorithm at scale. So, instead of trying to stretch the mathematics further, researchers looked at just changing the way we send keys as digital code and instead use the laws of physics and start sending the keys using photonics, particles of light. Here's where Quantum Key Distribution (QKD) comes in. QKD is a specialized use of quantum networking that provides provably secure encryption keys through quantum mechanisms. Any eavesdropping attempt disrupts the quantum state of photons, alerting users instantly. It's these features for which QKD has the potential to serve as a secured formula that is not limited by a temporary software formula, but by the physics which it derives via each distinct photon.

Opportunities:

Important feature capability for high-assurance communications where secure communications is highly important are required by most industries. Regulated industries such as healthcare, life sciences, finance, and government not only require secure communications for their systems, but also between themselves and third parties or even their clients. Defense command channels, critical utility grids, financial institutions and many others require the highest level of communications. QKD is one of the many layers of a security architecture; other layers include quantum communication and post-quantum cryptography. What QKD offers is an auditable way to ensure that any attempt to intercept the keys will be detected at the physical layer, long before it reaches the application layer. Satellite-based QKD and integration with other emerging quantum technologies related to networking components would be extended from local to a global network. As in other quantum technologies, early adopters serving industries that require highly secure environments in energy, telecom, or financial institutions would be able to offer and support premium secure services to their clients and build an internal workforce ahead of the broader markets. Government leaders can support early standards development and certification frameworks that can be shared among universities to help build the workforce of the future, and can co-invest in pilot programs designed to ensure that QKD is deployed and applied where it's unique to the specified region.

- Critical Infrastructure Security: Energy grids, military communications, and financial transactions can benefit from unhackable key exchanges, including digital currencies.
- Telecom Integrations: Telecom operators like BT and Toshiba have already begun deploying QKD across metropolitan networks. [8]
- Compliance and Sovereignty: Governments view QKD as a part of national cybersecurity frameworks.[9]

Challenges:

QKD promises security for key exchange, albeit competing with post-quantum cryptography that currently runs on existing communication networks, along with regular software updates. [10] One of the main challenges in today's fiber communication networks is that QKD systems have limited range or require a dedicated management team, which are expensive to build, deploy, scale, and manage. There are many offerings available; their reliability and success rely on security scenarios that assume best-case scenario components, which often miss practical issues that can leak side-channel information, raising concerns for security auditors and national security officials. Interoperability is another challenge, where different vendors often deploy proprietary protocols, hardware, and software, which makes connectivity between vendors difficult, especially when crossing regions. For government leaders and executives, this opens up the question as to when QKD could outperform existing classical solutions and how to evaluate the lifecycle of deployment versus regulatory risk and budget availability.

Example:

The EU's EuroQCI initiative [11] aims to deploy a continent-scale QKD network for secure communication across member states by 2030.

Quantum computing

Quantum computing leverages the rules of classical physics and quantum mechanics: superposition, interference, and entanglement, the last of which is quantum mechanical, to form the principles of quantum computing and process information in ways that are fundamentally intractable to classical systems. In general, quantum computing should not be considered a replacement of classical systems but rather as a specialized accelerator or enhancement that has the potential to offer dramatic speedups for a narrow set of problems. These problems include, but are not limited to, simulating nature or complex molecules and materials, optimizing large systems that exist in various industries such as finance, logistics, energy, and, of course, potentially breaking some of our widely used cryptographic algorithms. Current quantum systems are noisy but are continually evolving at a record pace. Some have noted that we could see the earliest examples of quantum advantage and a fault-tolerant quantum system in the next 1-3 years.[12]

I wish it were easy to describe how to build a quantum computer. Just as there are different ways to build an automobile, there are different ways to build a quantum computer. In this case, there are different modalities. Superconducting, Trapped Ions, neutral-atom, and photonics are just a few that are available and pass the DiVincenzo criteria [13] that describe conditions to meet in order to qualify as constructing a quantum computer.

As there are many books, courses, and websites that cover the details of each of these modalities, I'll spare you the details and just cover the opportunities and challenges for each below for you to consider when looking to access these systems. One thing I always recommend my clients do prior to selecting a system to work on. First and foremost, treat "shopping around" no different than you would shop for any high-priced investment. Whether it's a new home, a new car, or selecting an investment, it's always good to do some homework and keep in mind three main criteria to determine the performance of a quantum computer: Scale, Quality, and Speed.

For example, when buying an automobile, if a salesman only discussed how great an engine the vehicle has, then you know as much as I do that this is not enough information for you to consider purchasing it. You'll want to know a few more things. What's the performance regarding fuel consumption? How many passengers or how much room does it have? Are there any quality assurances or safety tests? Why should you not ask the same probing questions when purchasing access to a quantum system? In this case, there are generally three metrics you should consider.

- **Scale**: This generally refers to the number of qubits within each quantum system. Of course, over the past few years, this is what you would most likely see any company talk about, whether it's a startup or a well-established company, the number of qubits is always the main topic. Yes, the number of qubits is important, just as the need that every vehicle have some engine or form to provide power for it to move. However, this is still an important metric, as needing more qubits is what is needed in order to leverage the full power of a quantum system. What you also need to consider is how are these qubits connected? Are they all connected to each other? Can they scale to 500 qubits, and if so, how long will it take to get to 500 then to 1000, and then ultimately 1M qubits? Many modalities can perform well but might be limited to scaling.
- **Quality**: This looks at the quality of not only the qubits, but of the entire system itself. There are many components that are used in order to process a quantum circuit, where a quantum circuit is a series of gate instructions for the quantum computer to run an experiment through a quantum computer. Many of these components themselves might differ from system to system, even if they are using the same modality, whether superconducting, trapped ion, or neutral atoms, the quality could differ very much. Examples of this could be the gate fidelity, which you use to determine how accurate your gates are. How reliable are they at precisely placing your qubits in the correct quantum state, and how often are they calibrated? Another example is the ability to read out the results from each qubit. How accurate are the results and how can I verify that the results are what I expect them to be? There are many other examples, which we will cover in more detail in Part 2 of this book.
- **Speed**: This metric is also very important, particularly when comparing the various quantum system modalities. Early on, when clients would ask me how to choose a quantum computing vendor to collaborate with on their projects, I would always recommend they ask each vendor two simple questions. First, can I run a quantum circuit on your device this very minute from my laptop? Second, if I could run it, then how fast would I get back my results? The first question helps me determine whether

the system has the capability to run any quantum circuit without having to make any changes on the quantum system itself, and not need me to go to a lab to run my quantum circuit (availability). The second question is what we are covering here: speed. There are many quantum systems that offer great quality, but at the expense of speed. Meaning there are modalities which are great at quality, but take a very long time to execute. For example, some can run through a quantum circuit 100,000 times per second, vs others which run a quantum circuit at 3 times per second.

Which is the best? This is probably the most common question I get asked when presenting quantum, whether to industry or government leaders, it all comes down to which one should we pick? And of course, as with most answers, the correct one is always... "it depends". Yes, quantum is no different here. The decision to select a system that is higher in quality but slow on speed, or vice versa, really depends on what's most important to you and the projects you plan to run. If quality is important, then choose the system with the best fidelity and lower error rates; if it's speed then the other. However, there are many things to consider here as well. For example, if the vendor charges by the minute, then you will also likely want to consider the value that the quality will provide compared to the cost it would take to run the quantum circuit over time. Quality and Scale are also important as many vendors offer some information on the quality of their systems, and some include roadmaps on their projected scale of their systems. Here you want to ensure that their roadmap doesn't magically go from 20 or so qubits, up to 100,000 without any insights as to how they plan to get there. Each of the different modalities have their own challenges: noise, scalability, reliability, speed, etc.; therefore, asking how they will address those challenges along the way is also key to knowing whether their roadmaps are realistic or wishful thinking. If the company has had their roadmap out for a while, then this can also serve as a proven track record for the vendor. If they have hit their deadlines each time, then this could also build confidence on the upcoming milestones.

Understanding these metrics and how they impact the overall performance and cost to run your quantum circuits is very important to consider when looking at vendors. Also, be sure to work with your technical leads to help you understand how these metrics apply to your projects so you can make a very educated and financially responsible decision in the long run. As the systems mature over time and new features and advancements are released, it's always a good idea to ensure your technical leads are kept up to date so you can also decide to shift as needed. It also helps the technical team to let them know far in advance if shifts will be upcoming; believe me, they will thank you later for it.

Since I mentioned different modalities, I thought it would make sense to separate each of the modalities when describing both the opportunities and challenges. Not to say that opportunities exist only for one modality over the other. It's more to help understand the sorts of opportunities and challenges that each face in general. This will ensure that you are aware of all, just in case you decide to focus on one modality over the other. I should also stress that these can change at any moment, as research and development are rapidly evolving so much due to the increased activities in each of the following.

Superconducting qubits

Challenges:

Superconducting platforms are limited by 2D chip layout and congestion of microwave wiring, which makes it difficult to add qubits while preserving high gate fidelity and accurate readouts of each qubit. As systems continue to grow, cross-talk between qubits and control lines tends to worsen, which degrades gate quality and pushes error rates high above thresholds needed for efficient and effective error correction. Cryogenic infrastructure such as dilution refrigerators, cabling, packaging, and other components tends to scale poorly. Size, cost, and complexity constrain how many physical qubits can be hosted per system. Maintaining uniform performance across large arrays also becomes difficult, mostly due to the fact that small fabrication variations such as junctions accumulate into significant yield and calibration challenges at the hundreds-to-thousands qubit level.

Opportunities:

Superconducting technology does have some opportunities to address these challenges, which include the maturity of CMOS and RF manufacturing ecosystems, allowing for incremental scaling of larger wafers, 3D integration, and chiplet-based modular architectures. Increased gate speeds support aggressive error-correction cycles, improving the effective use of each physical qubit as many of these systems scale. There are roadmaps for modular quantum modules or tiles linked via microwave or photonic interconnects, making it possible to scale out to multi-module processors instead of relying on a single monolithic chip. As the design and control stacks are already highly automated, further advances in materials, lithography, and cryo-electronics could unlock industrial-style replication of standardized processor modules in the very near future.

Trapped-ion qubits

Challenges:

Trapped-ion systems face scalability limits from slow gate speeds and the need for precise laser control of each ion, which constrains the total computational throughput even if more ions are added. In large chains, motional modes become complex and harder to control, making high-fidelity multi-qubit gates increasingly challenging as systems grow. Architectures that are based on shuttling/moving ions between trap zones add complexity to the architecture in chip design, control electronics, and scheduling, which further complicates scaling to many modules. Optical systems are generally used to route and stabilize laser beams but do not yet scale up toward the thousands of individually addressed channels implied by very large processors.

Opportunities:

Trapped ions do offer excellent qubit quality, such as long coherence and high gate fidelities for single- and two-qubit gates, which reduces the overhead needed for error correction at a given logical qubit count. Modular architectures that are largely based on networking smaller ion-trap chips that use photonic links to entangle ions across modules do provide a nice path to scale. Micro-fabricated surface traps and integrated photonics can miniaturize and replicate ion modules, which in turn gradually tune the laboratories of today into a more compact, easier-to-manufacture unit. This strong qubit performance means trapped-ion roadmaps can focus on scaling engineering of control and interconnects, in lieu of basic qubit quality.

Neutral-atom qubits

Challenges:

Neutral-atom quantum systems rely on the precise trapping and control of large arrays of individual atoms, often numbering in the hundreds of thousands. This is achieved by using advanced tools such as optical tweezers and finely tuned laser fields, which must operate uniformly across the entire array to ensure consistent control and interaction between atoms. While powerful, this approach is technically demanding. Key operations, especially 2-qubit gates, are relatively slow and sensitive to environmental noise, similar to what is seen in trapped-ion systems. As systems scale up, this sensitivity makes it increasingly difficult to run deep quantum circuits before errors accumulate and coherence is lost.

A central challenge is that many of the required engineering breakthroughs are still in development. For example, achieving the very low error rates needed for fault-tolerant operations becomes harder at larger scales, as small imperfections in laser shaping, focusing, and timing compound across big atom arrays. In addition, integrating the necessary high-power, multi-wavelength laser and optical components into compact, reliable, and manufacturable platforms remains at a very early stage of maturity.

Opportunities:

Neutral-atom platforms are naturally well positioned to scale to very large numbers of qubits. Using optical lattices or arrays of optical tweezers, hundreds to thousands of atoms can be arranged in regular, reconfigurable patterns with the same core trapping technology. This makes it possible to increase qubit counts rapidly without redesigning the underlying architecture. An additional advantage is the flexibility that these systems can support a range of connectivity patterns, enabling multi-qubit interactions that are well suited to certain classes of algorithms. At the same time, there is steady progress in integrating optical components and control electronics, which should lead to more compact, repeatable, and manufacturable systems over time.

For leaders, neutral-atom technology represents a credible pathway to very large-scale quantum machines, particularly those for applications such as simulation and optimization, provided that ongoing improvements in gate fidelity, reliability, and system integration continue on their current trajectory.

Photonic qubits

Challenges:

Photonic quantum systems face several challenges that must be addressed as they scale. Key challenges include photon loss, imperfect photon sources, and detector inefficiencies. Each of these factors introduces noise by degrading multi-photon interference, which in turn limits how large and how deep photonic quantum circuits can become.

Building a photonic quantum circuit also requires a large number of components and highly complex routing of optical paths. As the systems grow, this routing quickly becomes intricate, increasing hardware overhead, and engineering complexity. In addition, many photonic gate operations are inherently non-deterministic, which places further limits on gate fidelity and the reliability of computational results.

System integration also remains a significant challenge. High-quality photon sources, interferometers, detectors, and supporting components are often difficult to combine onto a single, tightly integrated processor. Today, these elements are frequently developed separately, sometimes by different manufacturers and across different technology generations, which further complicates interoperability and system optimization. Until these integration and consistency issues are resolved, reducing error rates to the levels required for large-scale, fault-tolerant photonic quantum computers will remain a major focus of ongoing research and development.

Opportunities:

Recent advances in modular networks photonic architectures suggest a promising path forward. In principle, integrated photonic chips can be combined with classical control electronics and fiber-optic networking to form scalable, distributed quantum processors rather than relying on a single, monolithic machine. This modular approach is well aligned with large-scale, monolithic machine and with how large-scale computing systems are already built and deployed today. Progress is also being made on several critical enablers. More deterministic, or near-deterministic, photon sources, error correction codes specifically designed to handle photon loss, and improved software and compilation techniques are all helping to reduce resource overhead and address long-standing scaling challenges. Together, these advances aim to make photonic systems more efficient and predictable as they scale up in size.

A unique advantage of photonics is its ability to leverage the existing global telecom and data ecosystem. Wafer-scale fabrication, mature fiber-optic infrastructure, and well-established supply chains provide quite a realistic foundation for scaling through interconnected modules rather than a single device. As leaders, photonic systems offer a compelling opportunity to align quantum computing growth with existing optical-network investments, particularly for applications that naturally combine computation, communication, and sensing. Once photonic quantum computing reaches commercial reliability, dark fiber networks can evolve into active quantum-classical infrastructure, where fiber is no longer just a transport medium, but a core part of the computing fabric. We'll cover this in more detail in Part 3 of this book when discussing quantum communications and security.

Quantum annealing

Challenges:

Quantum annealers already pack in a lot of qubits, e.g., D-Wave has systems with over 4400 qubits.[14] However, they don't scale as other quantum systems do, where more qubits are better. In this case, it's the connectivity between qubits, at times in a specific pattern, which is where the advantage resides. In order for real-world business problems to run effectively and efficiently on a quantum annealer, they have to be set to fit a specific pattern, which can get complicated as the problems grow over time. To make it work, the system often has to tie several physical qubits together just to represent a single decision variable, which could increase noise and the chances of errors. In practice, this generally means that doubling the number of qubits does not double the size or the accuracy of the problems you can solve. In general, annealers are tuned for a fairly narrow set of optimization-style problems, so their impact is strongest in certain niches rather than across every form of workload or use case.

Opportunities:

There are some good opportunities for quantum annealers, mostly that they are already proving we can build and run machines with thousands of interacting qubits. This makes them valuable for us to figure out how to control large quantum systems, including managing the extreme cooling and packaging into a single commercial unit. Since its inception, there have been many updates to the hardware designs and interesting ways of providing problems to the systems in a way that gradually increases the usefulness of each system. By connecting quantum annealers to classical systems as a form of accelerating existing classical solutions and workflows, organizations can tackle larger logistical problems without having to build out larger classical systems to fit the same problem without them. Finally, what we learn from scaling quantum annealers will help us understand how to engineer the next generation of more versatile quantum processing units (QPUs).

Overall, opportunities exist and are maturing rapidly in the following industries:

- Drug Development: Quantum chemistry simulations accelerate compound design, reducing years of costly experiments.
- Finance and Risk Modeling: Portfolio optimization and Monte Carlo simulations, purely classical AI in optimization and pattern recognition tasks, such as anomaly detection.
- AI and Machine Learning: Hybrid quantum-classical models may outperform purely classical AI in optimization and pattern recognition tasks.

Quantum cryptography

Quantum cryptography broadly encompasses QKD but also extends to quantum-secure algorithms resistant to quantum attacks. This includes post-quantum cryptography (PQC), classical cryptographic methods designed to stay safe even once quantum computers mature. We'll go into details on how these differ in Part 3 of this book.

Opportunities:

- Future-Proof Security: PQC helps governments and companies prepare for a "quantum-safe" future where current encryption breaks easily.
- Standardization Movements: NIST's post-quantum cryptographic standards (expected by the end of 2026) are pushing industries to modernize infrastructures.

Challenges:

Migration to PQC is complex, touching hardware, firmware, and global data systems. Dual deployment of quantum-safe and QKD may be expensive but necessary in critical sectors. Time sensitivity is also a major challenge due to standards such as the CNSA-2.0, which has overall transition end dates for any entities working in certain domains or sectors within the government, with some that have already passed their deadlines back in 2025.[15]

Example:

Companies like ID Quantique [16] and QuSecure [17] already offer hybrid QKD and PQC products for banks and telecom operators.

Integration Across the Quantum Ecosystem

In practice, these technologies will converge into an integrated quantum infrastructure. A potential workflow could look like this:

1. Quantum sensors detect subsurface mineral deposits or physiological signals with unmatched accuracy.
2. The data transmits securely over quantum networks using QKD to prevent interception.
3. Hybrid Classical-Quantum computers process massive datasets from sensors to run optimization or simulation tasks (e.g., energy grid balancing or drug discovery).
4. All communications and stored results employ quantum cryptography protocols, ensuring device-to-device integrity and privacy.

Real-world use case example:

In Pharmaceutical R&D, a distributed quantum infrastructure could link quantum sensors inside bioreactors with cloud-based quantum processors performing live molecular simulations. Quantum Networking ensures data exchange with complete integrity, while QKD secures communication between R&D centers worldwide.

Such an integrated model not only shortens drug cycles but also pioneers a trusted high-performance computing environment, one that could underpin sectors like precision agriculture, climate modeling, or autonomous defense systems.

Why executives must understand the quantum divide

Executives who understand the differences among quantum computing, sensing, communications, and quantum-safe security are better positioned to match technology maturity with the right investment strategy. Just as importantly, they can decide where it makes sense to move early, where a fast-follower strategy may be more appropriate, and which developments should trigger a change in that position.

The timelines below should therefore be viewed as strategic planning horizons rather than fixed predictions. Quantum technologies will not mature according to a single calendar, nor will every application advance at the same pace. Progress will depend on measurable developments in hardware performance, error correction, interoperability, standards, economics, regulation, and demonstrated business value. Organizations should revisit their position as these signals change.

1. Near-term, (now to approximately 3 years), deploy, prepare, and selectively pilot: **Quantum sensing** is currently among the most mature areas of quantum technology. Quantum-enabled sensors already have commercial applications, although readiness

varies considerably by sensor type and use case. Government programs are also moving technologies such as quantum inertial sensing and magnetic navigation toward operational testing, particularly for applications where GPS may be unavailable or unreliable.

Quantum Key Distribution (QKD) is also commercially available and supported by an increasingly developed standards ecosystem, but its deployment remains specialized rather than a universal replacement for conventional cryptography. For most organizations, the more immediate security priority is migration toward post-quantum cryptography (PQC), where standards and government transition expectations are already creating concrete action points.

Executive trigger: Organizations should consider moving beyond observation when a quantum technology can solve a clearly defined operational problem, integrate with existing infrastructure at acceptable cost, or becomes important to regulatory compliance, national security, competitive differentiation, or protection of long-lived data.

Strategic posture: For sensing and selected communications applications, this can be an appropriate period for first-mover pilots. For quantum computing, most organizations can focus on building skills, identifying high-value use cases, experimenting through cloud-accessible systems, and preparing data and computing architectures without making large irreversible infrastructure investments.

2. Mid-term (3-7 years), validate advantage and begin scaling proven applications: During this period, the most important question for quantum computing will shift from *Can the technology perform increasingly sophisticated computation? to Can it create measurable value that exceeds the cost and performance of the best classical alternative?*

   Hybrid quantum-classical computing is already part of today's quantum ecosystem. What remains uncertain is when particular applications will demonstrate reproducible, economically meaningful quantum advantage. Industry roadmaps provide useful signals but should not be treated as guarantees. For example, at the time of this writing IBM and its research partners have reported three demonstrations of quantum advantage that focus on producing results beyond the practical reach of leading classical methods while also showing how those results can be trusted [29] and have plans to deploy a large-scale fault-tolerant system in 2029, the first of which were announced recently[29] and a large-scale fault-tolerant system in 2029. At the same time, NIST cautions that early quantum-advantage demonstrations have not yet established practical usefulness across commercial applications.

   Quantum networking is also likely to advance during this horizon, but its maturity should be measured by capabilities rather than dates alone. Important indicators include improvements in quantum memories and repeaters, longer-distance entanglement distribution, interoperability among network components, standardized interfaces, and successful multi-node network demonstrations.

Executive trigger: A fast follower should consider accelerating investment when independent benchmarks demonstrate sustained advantage for a relevant workload; hardware and software performance can be reproduced outside a laboratory demonstration; vendors can provide credible service-level and cost models; and standards or interoperability begin reducing the risk of technology lock-ins.

Strategic posture: Organizations that invested early in workforce development, partnerships, experimentation, and use-case discovery should be positioned to scale successful pilots. Fast followers can use these technical and commercial milestones to enter with less technology risk while still avoiding the cost of starting from zero.

3. Long-term (Approx. 7-10+ years), prepare for utility-scale and fault-tolerant systems: The longer-term horizon includes the potential emergence of utility-scale and large-scale fault-tolerant quantum computing, more capable quantum networks, and applications that cannot be practically addressed with today's classical or early quantum systems.
There is no universally accepted date for this transition. DARPA's Quantum Benchmarking Initiative,[30] for example, is specifically evaluating whether an industrially useful quantum computer, one whose computational value exceeds its cost, can be built by 2033. DARPA stated in 2026 that such a system by 2033 now appears likely, while still emphasizing uncertainty over which technical approach will succeed. This is an important distinction: the field has credible milestones, but not a single agreed-upon arrival date.

The same uncertainty makes a trigger-based strategy especially important. Organizations should watch for sustained logical-qubit operation, substantial reductions in error-correction overhead, large increases in executable circuit depth, independently verified computational advantage on commercially relevant problems, scalable interconnects, and declining cost per useful quantum computation.

Executive trigger: Major investment becomes easier to justify when quantum systems move from experimental advantage to repeatable business or mission advantage, particularly when they demonstrate capabilities that cannot be economically reproduced using leading classical computing technologies.

Strategic posture: First movers may gain intellectual property, talent, ecosystem influence, and application development experience before the broader market matures. Fast followers may avoid some early technology risk and capital expense, but they should maintain enough internal expertise to recognize when the trigger for broader adoption has arrived.

The more useful executive question is therefore not simply, "When will quantum arrive?" It's "What would need to happen for us to change our level of investment?"

Those triggers will be different for each organization. They could include:

- A demonstrated quantum advantage for a business-relevant problem
- Achievement of fault-tolerant logical computation at useful scale
- Quantum sensing performance that provides measurable operational advantage
- Quantum-network interoperability and repeater milestones
- Regulatory or standards requirements that create mandatory transition dates
- A material reduction in hardware, cloud-access, integration, or operating costs
- Competitors beginning to derive measurable value from a quantum capability

This approach gives both first movers and fast followers a defensible strategy. A first mover can invest ahead of maturity where strategic advantage justifies the risk. A fast follower can establish specific technical and market signals that will trigger greater investment rather than simply waiting for an arbitrary date.

Strategic engagement today, through partnerships, standards bodies, workforce development, use-case exploration, and carefully selected pilots, does not require making a bet on exactly when quantum technologies will mature. It provides the organization knowledge needed to recognize the right moment to move.

With that distinction in place, the discussion can now turn from the individual quantum technologies to an equally important question: how will these emerging capabilities converge with today's classical state-of-the-art systems, infrastructure, and operating models?

Overview of quantum and its convergence with AI, and cybersecurity as a business imperative

Recently, the comfortable distance between emerging technology and business reality that we have been so comfortable with has collapsed. Quantum computing is no longer a theoretical breakthrough confined to research laboratories; it has since entered the strategic planning horizon of every forward-thinking organization, including yours! When IBM first deployed the first commercially available quantum computer on the cloud back in 2016, followed by demonstrations of quantum achievements in many computationally difficult problems, the executive question shifted from "if" to "when" and "how." Today's strategic reality is more complex and urgent than a single technology disruption. What we're witnessing now is the convergence of three transformative forces: quantum computing's exponential processing capabilities, artificial intelligence's pattern recognition and decision-making power, and the quantum threat to current cybersecurity infrastructure. This convergence creates what strategists call a "polycrisis," multiple interconnected challenges that amplify each other's impacts and compress decision timelines.

Consider, for example, a pharmaceutical executive whose competitors are already using quantum simulation to accelerate drug discovery, potentially compressing a decade of research into months.[18] Or the financial services CEO whose encryption infrastructure could become obsolete within five years, exposing decades of archived sensitive data.[19] Or perhaps the logistics leader whose optimization algorithms are reaching computational limits while quantum-enabled competitors are achieving step-function improvements in efficiency. These aren't hypothetical scenarios; they're current strategic realities facing organizations across every sector.

The market signals so far are quite unambiguous. Global quantum computing investments exceeded $35 billion in 2024, with corporate venture capital in quantum technologies growing 340% over three years.[20] Major consulting firms report that quantum strategy inquiries from C-suite leaders increased 500% between 2022 and 2024.[21] Technology leaders including IBM, Google, Amazon, Microsoft, and Alibaba are deploying quantum cloud services, democratizing access, and accelerating adoption curves.

Yet despite this momentum, a dangerous gap persists between quantum's strategic importance and executive preparedness. Most leadership teams lack the framework to evaluate quantum opportunities systematically, assess competitive threats accurately, or time quantum investments strategically. This chapter will address these gaps by establishing the foundational understanding necessary for informed quantum decision-making.

The strategic context we'll explore encompasses three critical dimensions. First, understanding where quantum technologies sit on the maturity curve and what "quantum advantage" actually means for your business, not as a technical achievement, but as a competitive reality. Second, recognizing how quantum disruption manifests differently across industries, requiring sector-specific response strategies rather than generic technology adoption approaches. Third, developing analytical frameworks to build compelling business cases that compete effectively for capital and executive attention against other strategic initiatives.

The evidence increasingly demonstrates that the risks of quantum inaction exceed the risks of proactive quantum investment. Organizations that wait for "quantum readiness" risk discovering that readiness is a moving target, and the cost of catching up, in competitive position, talent acquisition, and strategic partnerships, compounds exponentially over time. Early adopters are already establishing advantage through proprietary algorithms, exclusive hardware access, and quantum-trained workforces that will be difficult for late adopters to replicate.

This section will provide you with the strategic foundation for quantum decision-making by examining market dynamics, investment patterns, and competitive intelligence in detail. By understanding the quantum landscape comprehensively, leaders can move beyond reactive postures and develop proactive strategies that position their organizations to capture quantum opportunities while managing quantum risks effectively.

Quantum computing timeline and market readiness

Understanding quantum computing's evolution from theoretical concept to strategic business tool requires examining specific milestones, current capabilities, and realistic timelines for practical applications. This foundation enables accurate strategic planning rather than decisions based on either excessive optimism or unwarranted skepticism.

The modern quantum computing era effectively began in the 1980s when Richard Feynman and David Deutsch articulated the theoretical foundations, but practical progress remained limited for decades. The timeline accelerated dramatically after 2010 as advances in quantum error correction, improved qubit coherence times, and increased investment transformed quantum from pure research into engineering challenges with solvable pathways.

Several watershed moments define the current quantum landscape. In 2019, Google's Sycamore processor solved a specific problem in 200 seconds that they described would take classical supercomputers 10,000 years, marking a psychological threshold, proving that quantum computers could outperform classical systems in at least narrowly defined tasks with no practical uses to solve real-world problems. IBM followed with quantum volume achievements, demonstrating steady improvements in quantum system capability using a metric that combines qubit count, gate fidelity, and connectivity.

More recently, the field has shifted from demonstrating quantum capability to achieving quantum utility, which is generally defined as solving practical problems with business value with near-term quantum systems.[22] In 2023, IBM announced quantum utility on real-world computational challenges rather than artificial benchmarks.[23] Companies including JPMorgan Chase, ExxonMobil, and E.On reported quantum-accelerated results in portfolio optimization [24], molecular simulation [25], and energy [26], respectively.

The quantum computing landscape currently encompasses three primary technological approaches: scale, quality, and speed, with each maturing at different rates and serving distinct applications. Understanding these differences is crucial for evaluating vendor claims and matching quantum technologies to business needs. Particularly as we have just entered the era of quantum advantage[29].

Gate-based quantum computers, developed by IBM, Google, and IonQ, represent the most versatile quantum computing approach and receive the majority of research investment. These systems manipulate individual qubits using quantum gates to perform universal quantum computation, theoretically capable of running any quantum algorithm. Current gate-based systems operate in the **Noisy Intermediate-Scale Quantum** (**NISQ**) era, in that they have between 50 and 1,000 qubits but limited error correction, restricting practical applications to problems that can tolerate some computational noise. The timeline for fault-tolerant gate-based quantum computers with full error correction remains uncertain, with estimates ranging from 2 to 7 years depending on breakthroughs in qubit quality and error correction schemes.

Quantum annealing systems, pioneered by D-Wave Systems, take a specialized approach optimized for solving optimization and sampling problems. Rather than universal quantum computation, these systems find minimum energy states of problems mapped to quantum physics models. Quantum annealers currently operate with thousands of qubits but with limited connectivity between qubits, making them suitable for specific optimization problems in scheduling, logistics, and machine learning. The advantage for business applications is immediate availability; organizations can access quantum annealing systems today through cloud services and begin exploring practical use cases without waiting for fault-tolerant systems. However, the computational advantage over classical algorithms remains problem-specific and contested for many applications.

Photonic quantum computing, advanced by PsiQuantum, Xanadu, and others, uses photons as qubits and operates at room temperature, potentially offering significant scaling advantage over superconducting approaches that require near-absolute-zero cooling. Photonic systems excel at specific tasks, including quantum simulations and certain machine learning applications. While photonic quantum computing currently lags gate-based approaches in qubit count and connectivity, the technology's compatibility with existing telecommunications infrastructure and room-temperature operation could accelerate deployment timelines significantly if technical challenges around photon generation and detection are solved.

The practical business question isn't which quantum approach will "win"; it's understanding which approach best addresses specific business problems within realistic timeframes. For organizations exploring quantum today, this typically means (at the time of this writing):

- **Near-term applications (1-3 years):** Quantum computing for optimization problems, quantum simulation for chemistry and materials science using gate-based systems, quantum machine learning experiments using hybrid quantum-classical algorithms, and quantum-inspired classical algorithms that deliver some quantum benefits without requiring quantum hardware.

- **Medium-term applications (3-7 years):** More reliable quantum advantage for optimization and simulation as error rates decrease, practical quantum chemistry applications for drug discovery and materials development, quantum-enhanced machine learning showing clear advantage over classical approaches, and early applications of quantum cryptography and quantum key distribution.
- **Long-term applications (7+ years):** Fault-tolerant quantum computing enabling Shor's algorithm for cryptography breaking, large-scale quantum simulation of complex molecular systems and materials, quantum artificial intelligence with demonstrated superiority over classical AI, and broad quantum advantage across multiple problem classes. A good thing to note here is that this would be considered the convergence point for a lot of the concern that is currently being reported, particularly the harvest now, decrypt later. Past this point, you would be considered extremely vulnerable.

The concept of quantum advantage, sometimes referred to as quantum supremacy, though many prefer this less charged term, deserves careful examination because it directly impacts strategic timing decisions. Quantum advantage exists when a quantum computer solves a problem faster, more accurately, or more economically than classical computers, including future classical systems with algorithmic improvements. Critically, quantum advantage is problem-specific, not universal. A quantum system might demonstrate advantage for molecular simulation while offering no benefit for fraud detection.

For business strategy, this means that evaluating all quantum opportunities requires specificity. Rather than asking "Should we invest in quantum?", effective leaders should ask "For which specific business problems might quantum computing offer an advantage, and when will that advantage become practically accessible and economically justified?" This frames quantum as a targeted strategic tool rather than a general technology bet.

The quantum cloud services landscape has matured significantly, lowering barriers to quantum exploration. IBM Quantum, Amazon Braket, Microsoft Azure Quantum, qBraid, and Google Quantum AI provide cloud access to various quantum systems, allowing organizations to experiment without capital investment in quantum hardware. These platforms increasingly offer quantum algorithm libraries, development frameworks, and educational resources that accelerate quantum capability building. The emergence of quantum-computing-as-a-service creates a fundamentally different adoption dynamic from previous computing revolutions; organizations can explore quantum applications immediately rather than waiting for mature, affordable hardware.

Market readiness manifests through multiple indicators beyond hardware capabilities. The quantum software ecosystem has expanded dramatically, with companies including Zapata Computing, QC Ware, and 1QBit developing quantum algorithms and applications for specific industries. Quantum workforce development is accelerating through university programs, professional certifications, and corporate training initiatives, though talent remains scarce. Industry consortia like the Quantum Economic Development Consortium (QED-C) and standards organizations including IEEE and ISO are establishing quantum benchmarking standards, interoperability protocols, and best practices that reduce adoption risks.

Investment patterns provide strong signals about quantum market readiness. Beyond the headline-grabbing investments in quantum hardware companies, we're seeing significant capital flow into quantum applications, quantum cybersecurity solutions, and quantum-classical hybrid systems that bridge current and future computing paradigms. The emergence of quantum-focused venture capital firms, corporate quantum venture arms, and government quantum initiatives totaling billions of dollars globally indicates that sophisticated investors believe quantum's commercial timeline has arrived.

For strategic planning purposes, leaders should understand that quantum readiness operates on multiple timelines simultaneously. Organizations can and should begin quantum exploration now through cloud access, pilot projects, and workforce development while planning for quantum security threats that require multi-year cryptographic transitions. The key strategic skill is matching quantum initiatives to realistic technology timelines while remaining agile enough to accelerate or pivot as the technology matures faster or slower than projected.

Industry disruption scenarios

Quantum computing's transformative potential manifests differently across industries, creating sector-specific disruption patterns that demand tailored strategic responses. Understanding these variations enables leaders to assess their organization's quantum exposure accurately and develop appropriate mitigation or exploitation strategies.

Financial services: the double-edged quantum sword

Financial services face perhaps the most acute quantum timeline pressure, with both existential threats and transformative opportunities converging. The threat is well-documented: Shor's algorithm, once implemented on fault-tolerant quantum computers, will break RSA, elliptic curve, and other public-key cryptography systems that protect virtually all financial transactions, communications, and data storage. While fault-tolerant quantum computers capable of running Shor's algorithm remain years away, "harvest now, decrypt later" attacks are current; adversaries can capture encrypted financial data today and decrypt it when quantum computers become available. For institutions holding decades of sensitive financial data, this creates immediate security imperatives.

The opportunity side is equally compelling. Quantum algorithms for portfolio optimization can evaluate vastly larger solution spaces than classical approaches, potentially improving risk-adjusted returns and enabling more sophisticated hedging strategies. JPMorgan Chase researchers demonstrated quantum advantage for option pricing, achieving results in minutes that would require hours or days using classical methods. Credit risk modeling, fraud detection, and high-frequency trading algorithms all show promise for quantum acceleration. Monte Carlo simulations, fundamental to financial risk analysis, could see exponential speedups through quantum amplitude estimation algorithms.

Leading financial institutions including Goldman Sachs, Wells Fargo, and BBVA have established quantum computing teams, partnered with quantum hardware providers, and begun testing quantum algorithms on real financial problems. The strategic pattern emerging is "defend and advance", implementing quantum-resistant cryptography while simultaneously developing quantum-enabled financial products and services. Organizations that successfully execute both strategies will gain competitive advantages while managing cryptographic risks; those focused exclusively on defense miss offensive opportunities, while those ignoring the threat face potentially catastrophic security exposures, and most importantly, reputational risk for you and your organization.

Pharmaceuticals and biotechnology: quantum-accelerated discovery

The pharmaceutical industry's quantum opportunity centers on molecular simulation, using quantum computers to model molecular interactions with accuracy impossible for classical computers. Drug discovery currently requires screening millions of molecular compounds, with lead candidates spending years in development and billions in investment before reaching the market. Only a small percentage of drug candidates succeed, making the process extraordinarily expensive and time-consuming.

Quantum computers naturally model quantum mechanical systems like molecules, potentially revolutionizing this process. Rather than approximating molecular behavior using classical computers, quantum simulations can directly calculate molecular properties, reaction dynamics, and protein folding with greater accuracy. This could dramatically reduce the costly trial-and-error phase of drug discovery, identify promising candidates faster, and reduce the risk of late-stage failures. Companies including Roche, Biogen, and AstraZeneca are actively exploring quantum applications in drug discovery, protein folding, and personalized medicine.

The strategic implications extend beyond drug discovery. Quantum-enabled personalized medicine could optimize treatment protocols based on individual genetic profiles with unprecedented precision. Materials science applications could accelerate the development of more effective drug delivery mechanisms. The quantum advantage in pharmaceuticals likely arrives earlier than in many other industries because the quantum simulation advantage is fundamental rather than incremental; classical computers struggle with quantum chemistry, while quantum computers excel at it naturally.

Organizations in this sector should be actively building quantum chemistry expertise, establishing partnerships with quantum hardware and software providers, and identifying specific drug discovery problems where quantum simulation could accelerate research. The competitive risk is significant; if competitors achieve quantum-accelerated drug discovery, they could bring products to market faster and more economically, fundamentally altering competitive dynamics.

Logistics and supply chain: quantum optimization at scale

Logistics and supply chain management involve optimization problems of staggering complexity, routing millions of packages through dynamic networks, scheduling thousands of vehicles considering real-time traffic and weather, optimizing warehouse layouts for millions of SKUs, and balancing inventory across global supply chains with thousands of variables and constraints. Many of these problems are computationally intractable for classical computers, forcing organizations to use heuristic approximations that leave significant efficiency gains on the table.

Quantum optimization algorithms show promise for dramatically improving these calculations. Companies including Volkswagen, Airbus, and DHL have conducted quantum optimization pilots for vehicle routing, flight gate optimization, and package routing, respectively. While results vary, several have demonstrated quantum advantages for specific optimization scenarios, achieving better solutions faster than classical approaches.

The competitive implications are substantial. In industries with thin margins where a percentage point of efficiency translates to millions in profit, quantum optimization could create sustainable competitive advantages. Consider a logistics company that achieves quantum-enabled routing optimization, reducing fuel consumption by 5%, improving delivery times by 10%, and increasing vehicle utilization by 8%. These advantages compound: better service attracts more customers, increased volume enhances operational leverage, and improved margins enable greater investment in further optimization. Competitors using classical optimization methods may find themselves unable to match either pricing or service levels.

Beyond pure optimization, quantum machine learning algorithms could improve demand forecasting, anomaly detection, and predictive maintenance, all crucial for supply chain efficiency. The combination of quantum optimization and quantum-enhanced AI could transform supply chain management from a largely reactive discipline to a predictive, self-optimizing system.

Strategic timing matters significantly in logistics. Unlike pharmaceuticals where quantum advantage requires fault-tolerant systems, logistics optimization shows promise with current NISQ-era quantum computers and quantum annealers. Organizations can begin testing quantum optimization algorithms today, gaining experience, and developing hybrid quantum-classical systems that improve incrementally as quantum hardware matures.

Automotive and manufacturing: materials science and process optimization

The automotive industry faces multiple quantum disruption vectors. Battery chemistry optimization for electric vehicles involves quantum mechanical calculations that quantum computers can address more naturally than classical systems. Quantum simulations could accelerate discovery of battery materials with higher energy density, faster charging, and longer lifespans, critical competitive differentiators as the industry transitions to electric vehicles.

Autonomous vehicle route planning involves real-time optimization problems where quantum algorithms could improve traffic flow, reduce energy consumption, and enhance safety. Manufacturing process optimization, quality control using quantum-enhanced machine learning, and supply chain coordination all present quantum opportunities.

Companies including Daimler, BMW, and Toyota have established quantum computing initiatives focused on these applications. Daimler's research on quantum computers for battery simulation demonstrated promising results, while automotive suppliers are exploring quantum optimization for manufacturing logistics and quality control.

The strategic implications for automotive extend beyond individual companies. The industry operates in complex ecosystems where advantages cascade through supplier networks. An automotive manufacturer that achieves quantum-enabled battery improvements doesn't just improve its own competitive position; it potentially reshapes supplier relationships, influences consumer preferences, and affects regulatory compliance strategies. Similarly, quantum-optimized supply chains could enable more customized manufacturing, faster time-to-market for new models, and improved resilience to supply disruptions.

Energy: optimization and simulation across the value chain

Energy sector applications span exploration, production, distribution, and consumption optimization. Quantum algorithms could improve seismic data analysis for oil and gas exploration, optimize power grid operations for renewable energy integration, enhance battery and energy storage system design, and improve climate modeling for long-term energy planning.

ExxonMobil has explored quantum algorithms for molecular simulation relevant to chemical processes and materials development.[27] Utilities are investigating quantum optimization for managing increasingly complex power grids as renewable energy sources introduce variability. The combination of quantum optimization and quantum-enhanced weather forecasting could significantly improve renewable energy economics by reducing uncertainty in solar and wind power generation.

The energy transition from fossil fuels to renewables creates particular quantum opportunities. Grid optimization becomes exponentially more complex with distributed renewable generation, energy storage systems, and demand response programs all interacting dynamically. Classical optimization methods struggle with this complexity, leading to suboptimal renewable energy utilization and higher costs. Quantum optimization could enable higher renewable penetration, lower costs, and improved grid reliability, strategically important for organizations navigating the energy transition.

Cross-industry patterns and strategic implications

Several patterns emerge across industry disruption scenarios. First, quantum advantage arrives at different times for different applications, requiring sector-specific strategic planning rather than generic quantum adoption timelines. Second, early movers in quantum experimentation are building organizational capabilities, talent, partnerships, and algorithm libraries that will be difficult for late adopters to replicate quickly. Third, quantum threats and opportunities often appear together, requiring organizations to develop dual strategies that manage risks while capturing opportunities.

The strategic imperative for leaders is conducting honest assessments of their organization's quantum exposure. Which business processes involve optimization or simulation problems where quantum might offer advantages? When do realistic quantum timelines for those specific applications suggest advantage could materialize? What competitive intelligence exists about competitors' quantum initiatives? How vulnerable is our organization to quantum-enabled competitors or quantum cybersecurity threats?

Organizations that answer these questions systematically and act on the insights will position themselves advantageously. Those who treat quantum as a distant future concern risk discovering that competitive quantum advantages materialize faster than anticipated, with limited catching-up opportunities for late movers.

Competitive intelligence and quantum advantage

Understanding how early quantum adoption creates sustainable competitive advantages requires examining the mechanisms through which quantum capabilities translate into market position. The strategic question isn't whether quantum computing will eventually impact most industries; it's whether early movers can establish advantages that persist even as quantum technologies become widely available.

The architecture of quantum competitive advantage

Competitive advantages from quantum adoption manifest through multiple channels. Proprietary quantum algorithms represent the most direct advantage; organizations that develop quantum solutions for their specific business problems create intellectual property that competitors cannot easily replicate. Unlike classical algorithms where best practices diffuse rapidly through the industry, quantum algorithms remain specialized, and the expertise required to develop them remains scarce. Companies that build quantum algorithm libraries optimized for their operations create moats that widen as these algorithms mature and integrate deeper into business processes.

Exclusive partnerships with quantum hardware providers offer another advantage mechanism. As quantum computing resources remain constrained, organizations that establish strategic partnerships gain priority access to quantum computing time, early access to hardware improvements, and influence over development roadmaps. Several Fortune 500 companies have formed "quantum partnerships" with IBM, Google, IonQ, and other providers, securing dedicated access to quantum systems and collaborative development relationships. These partnerships create information advantages; partners learn about quantum capabilities and limitations through hands-on experience rather than theoretical speculation, enabling more informed strategic decisions.

Quantum-trained workforces represent perhaps the most durable competitive advantage, yet at the moment it's more scarce than any other technology due to its steep learning curve, in particular those with quantum-industry expertise. Talent with quantum computing expertise remains extraordinarily scarce, with demand far exceeding supply.[28] Organizations that invest early in quantum workforce development through training programs, university partnerships, and strategic hires build capabilities that competitors cannot quickly match. The compounding nature of expertise – experienced quantum professionals become more valuable as they develop organization-specific knowledge – means early talent investments yield increasing returns.

Case studies in quantum competitive advantage

JPMorgan Chase's quantum finance initiative demonstrates how financial institutions are positioning for quantum advantage. The bank partnered with the IBM Quantum Network, developed proprietary quantum algorithms for option pricing and portfolio optimization, and built an internal quantum computing team. While the immediate business impact remains limited – current quantum computers cannot yet handle the scale of real trading operations – JPMorgan Chase is accumulating quantum expertise and algorithm intellectual property that will become valuable as quantum systems scale. Competitors starting quantum exploration today face a multi-year gap in institutional knowledge and algorithm development.

In pharmaceuticals, Roche's quantum simulation initiative illustrates the intersection of quantum computing and AI. Roche has established partnerships with multiple quantum computing companies, exploring applications from molecular simulation to drug-drug interaction prediction. The strategic approach combines quantum computing for specific high-value calculations with classical AI for broader drug discovery tasks, creating hybrid systems that leverage each technology's strengths. This hybrid strategy may prove more valuable than pure quantum or classical approaches, as it builds organizational capability to integrate emerging technologies rather than betting exclusively on any single approach.

Volkswagen's quantum optimization projects for traffic flow and vehicle routing demonstrate how manufacturing leaders are exploring quantum applications in their operations. The company has tested quantum algorithms for optimizing traffic flow in cities (benefiting both private vehicles and public transit), logistics route planning, and manufacturing process optimization. While definitive competitive advantages haven't yet materialized and current quantum systems remain limited, Volkswagen is systematically building quantum expertise across multiple business units, creating organizational readiness to capture quantum advantages as technology matures.

These case studies reveal common patterns. Leaders are making quantum investments before clear ROI materializes, treating quantum initiatives as strategic options rather than conventional technology deployments. They're building quantum capabilities broadly rather than making narrow bets, creating organizational flexibility to pivot toward successful applications as quantum technology evolves. They're combining quantum exploration with parallel improvements in classical computing and AI, avoiding over-dependence on quantum timelines while maintaining quantum readiness.

Conducting competitive quantum intelligence

Systematic competitive intelligence around quantum requires monitoring multiple signals. Patent filings provide insights into competitors' quantum research directions; an uptick in quantum-related patents from a competitor suggests serious organizational commitment and potentially valuable intellectual property development. Partnership announcements with quantum hardware providers, quantum software companies, or quantum research institutions indicate strategic commitment and resource allocation. Job postings for quantum expertise reveal workforce development priorities and technical focus areas.

Conference presentations and academic publications from corporate research teams offer windows into quantum strategies. While companies typically don't disclose strategically sensitive information, the problems they choose to discuss publicly indicate strategic priorities. A competitor publishing quantum optimization research for supply chain problems signals their strategic focus without revealing proprietary algorithmic details.

Investment patterns provide strong signals. Organizations that establish dedicated quantum budgets, create quantum-specific organizational units, or assign senior executives to quantum initiatives demonstrate strategic commitment beyond experimental exploration. Conversely, competitors with no visible quantum initiatives may be vulnerable to disruption or strategically confident that quantum won't impact their business model within their planning horizon.

The intelligence analysis challenge is separating substantive quantum initiatives from strategic positioning. Many organizations announce quantum partnerships primarily for marketing value or investor signaling rather than serious capability building. Distinguishing genuine quantum investments from quantum theater requires looking beyond press releases to evidence of sustained commitment, budget allocation, talent acquisition, publications, patents, and executive engagement.

Identifying and exploiting quantum opportunity windows

Quantum opportunity windows, periods where quantum advantage can be established before becoming industry-standard, vary by industry and application. In industries where quantum advantage arrives early and requires substantial expertise to implement, opportunity windows may remain open for years. In industries where quantum solutions can be purchased as packaged software or cloud services, opportunity windows may close quickly once solutions mature.

The strategic challenge is identifying which quantum applications are likely to create durable advantages versus which will commoditize rapidly. Applications requiring deep domain expertise combined with quantum knowledge, like developing proprietary quantum algorithms for firm-specific optimization problems, create more durable advantages. Applications using standard quantum algorithms applied to common problems may create only temporary advantages as quantum solutions become widely available.

Organizations can extend opportunity windows through several mechanisms. Developing quantum intellectual property through patents protects advantages legally. Building quantum-classical hybrid solutions that integrate quantum capabilities deeply into existing systems creates switching costs that protect market position. Establishing quantum partnerships with exclusive or preferential terms secures quantum resources as they remain constrained. Developing quantum expertise that's embedded in organizational processes rather than dependent on individual experts creates institutional advantages that persist despite talent mobility.

The timing dimension requires careful analysis. Investing too early in quantum risks backing technologies that may not deliver practical advantages within strategic planning horizons, wasting resources on capabilities that don't materialize into business value. Waiting too long risks allowing competitors to establish advantages that become difficult to overcome. The optimal strategy typically involves staged investments, early exploration, and pilot projects to build organizational readiness, followed by scaled investment as quantum advantages become clearer and technology maturity reduces risk.

ROI calculation frameworks

Quantifying returns on quantum investments presents unique challenges that conventional financial analysis struggles to address. Traditional ROI models excel at evaluating incremental improvements to established processes but poorly capture the optionality, uncertainty, and potential exponential advantages characteristic of quantum computing. Developing specialized quantum ROI frameworks enables more accurate investment decision-making and more compelling business cases.

The limitations of traditional ROI for quantum

Standard ROI calculations, dividing financial benefits by investment costs to produce a simple ratio or payback period, fail to capture quantum computing's strategic characteristics. Traditional models assume relatively predictable benefits and costs, which doesn't reflect quantum's uncertainty around performance timelines and advantage magnitude. They discount future benefits using constant rates, undervaluing quantum investments where benefits potentially compound exponentially. They struggle to quantify strategic benefits like talent development, partnership opportunities, and organizational learning that often exceed direct operational benefits in quantum's early phases. Perhaps most critically, traditional ROI models evaluate investments independently, missing portfolio effects where quantum investments reduce risk across other initiatives or create synergies with parallel technology investments. A quantum cybersecurity initiative, for example, protects multiple business units and systems simultaneously, with benefits that cascade through the organization. Conventional ROI models undervalue these cross-cutting benefits.

Option value models for quantum investments

Option pricing frameworks from financial economics provide more appropriate models for quantum investment analysis. These frameworks recognize that quantum investments create options, rights but not obligations to make future investments as uncertainty resolves. Early quantum exploration investments create organizational capabilities and relationships that position companies to scale quantum initiatives quickly when advantages become clear, similar to how financial options provide rights to purchase assets at predetermined prices. Option value models for quantum investments consider multiple factors: the potential value if quantum advantages materialize (option upside), the probability that quantum advantages materialize within strategic timeframes (probability of exercise), the cost of quantum exploration and capability building (option premium), and the time until quantum advantages become clear (time to expiration). This framework recognizes that quantum investments create value through strategic flexibility, the ability to accelerate quantum adoption if it proves valuable or minimize losses if it doesn't.

Using this approach, a quantum exploration budget of $5 million annually might be justified not through direct ROI but through the option value it creates. If quantum optimization could improve operational efficiency by $50 million annually, and there's a 30% probability this materializes within five years, the option value significantly exceeds the exploration investment even before considering defensive value against competitive threats or cybersecurity risks.

Portfolio approaches to quantum investing

Portfolio optimization models from investment management offer another framework for quantum ROI analysis. Rather than evaluating each quantum initiative independently, portfolio approaches consider how quantum investments interact with each other and with other strategic initiatives. This framework is particularly valuable for organizations exploring multiple quantum applications simultaneously: portfolio benefits from diversification, correlation effects, and staged investment strategies. A portfolio approach might allocate quantum investment across multiple applications: quantum optimization for supply chain (high probability of near-term advantage, moderate impact), quantum simulation for R&D (lower probability, potentially transformative impact), and quantum cybersecurity (defensive investment, high consequence if needed). The portfolio generates better risk-adjusted returns than concentrating investment in any single application because the applications have imperfectly correlated outcomes; if one application underperforms, others may exceed expectations.

Portfolio models also capture learning effects across quantum initiatives. Organizational capabilities developed for one quantum application often transfer to others; quantum programming skills, partnerships with quantum providers, and understanding of quantum-classical hybrid architectures all create value across multiple quantum use cases. Traditional ROI models miss these cross-application benefits, undervaluing comprehensive quantum strategies relative to narrow single-application bets.

Scenario-based quantum ROI models

Given the inherent uncertainty in quantum technology timelines and competitive dynamics, scenario-based modeling provides another effective framework. Rather than producing single-point ROI estimates, scenario models evaluate quantum investments across multiple plausible futures: an optimistic scenario where quantum advantage arrives early and delivers substantial benefits, a baseline scenario with moderate quantum impact on expected timelines, and a pessimistic scenario where quantum advantages arrive late or prove smaller than anticipated. For each scenario, the model calculates the value of quantum investments considering both direct operational benefits and strategic positioning effects. The scenarios incorporate different assumptions about technology maturity rates, competitive adoption patterns, and quantum advantage magnitude. The overall investment decision considers weighted outcomes across scenarios, with weights reflecting leadership's probability assessments for each scenario. It's good to note that many of the advantages listed may also stack onto one another. Therefore, if you are consistently investing in both the technology and the talent associated with each technology, then you will consistently derive benefits for each slice across the stack as the maturation curves upward.

This approach improves decision-making in several ways. It forces explicit articulation of assumptions about quantum timelines and impacts, enabling better assessment of investment risk. It identifies quantum investments that provide positive returns across multiple scenarios; these robust investments deserve priority over investments that only succeed in optimistic scenarios. It facilitates sensitivity analysis, showing which assumptions most affect quantum investment value and therefore deserve greatest attention in ongoing competitive intelligence and technology monitoring.

Measuring quantum value creation

Beyond financial models, quantum value creation requires appropriate performance metrics. Traditional IT metrics like system uptime or transaction processing speed often don't capture quantum's strategic value. Quantum-specific metrics might include:

- **Solution quality improvements**: For optimization problems, measuring the performance improvement of quantum-enabled solutions compared to classical benchmarks. A supply chain optimization solution that reduces costs by 5% relative to previous methods creates measurable value even if quantum computers only contribute a fraction of that improvement through hybrid quantum-classical approaches.
- **Time-to-solution reductions**: For complex simulations or calculations, quantum advantage often manifests as dramatic time reductions. Drug discovery simulations that complete in hours rather than weeks create value through accelerated R&D cycles and faster time-to-market, even if simulation accuracy remains comparable to classical methods.
- **Problem scale expansions:** Quantum computers can often address larger or more complex problems than are tractable with classical approaches. The ability to optimize across 10,000 variables rather than 1,000 creates strategic value by enabling more sophisticated business processes, even if per-variable processing costs increase.
- **Capability development metrics**: Organizational quantum readiness, measured through quantum talent acquisition and retention, algorithm development progress, partnership maturity, and quantum literacy across the organization, creates value that

manifests in future quantum adoption speed and success probability. While harder to quantify than operational metrics, capability metrics often predict long-term quantum value creation more reliably than near-term operational results.

Quantifying intangible quantum benefits

Quantum initiatives create significant intangible value that traditional models overlook. Talent attraction and retention improve because quantum initiatives signal innovation leadership, particularly to technically sophisticated candidates. Organizations known for quantum exploration recruit more successfully in adjacent technology areas including AI, machine learning, and advanced analytics; quantum signals broad technological sophistication.

Strategic partnerships often accompany quantum initiatives, creating value beyond quantum applications specifically. Quantum partnerships with technology leaders provide access to expertise, early technology access, and collaborative opportunities that extend beyond quantum to other emerging technologies. These relationship benefits compound over time as partnerships deepen and expand.

Innovation culture effects represent another intangible benefit. Organizations that explore quantum computing often report cultural shifts toward greater technological risk-taking, more systematic innovation processes, and improved cross-functional collaboration. These cultural changes create value across the organization, extending well beyond quantum initiatives specifically.

Effective quantum ROI frameworks incorporate these intangible benefits through several mechanisms. Surveying technical talent about organizational attractiveness before and after quantum initiatives quantifies talent effects. Tracking partnership opportunities and technology access improvements resulting from quantum relationships measures partnership value. Assessing innovation metrics across the organization, not just within quantum initiatives, captures cultural effects.

Integrated quantum ROI framework

A comprehensive quantum ROI approach integrates multiple methodologies. Initial investment decisions use option value models to justify exploration investments, recognizing quantum's strategic flexibility value. As quantum projects mature and uncertainty reduces, scenario-based models provide more detailed ROI projections across plausible outcomes. Portfolio optimization ensures balanced quantum investment allocation across applications with different risk-return profiles. Quantum-specific performance metrics track value creation as initiatives progress, with intangible benefit measurements capturing strategic value beyond operational improvements.

This integrated approach acknowledges quantum investment analysis requires greater sophistication than conventional technology investments while providing structured frameworks that enable systematic evaluation and resource allocation. Organizations that develop robust quantum ROI frameworks make better investment decisions, build more compelling business cases, and justify quantum strategies more effectively to skeptical stakeholders.

Strategic risk assessment

Comprehensive quantum risk assessment requires examining both the risks of quantum inaction and the risks of quantum investment, with particular attention to asymmetric risk profiles where quantum threats and opportunities create fundamentally different risk-reward dynamics than conventional strategic decisions.

The quantum cryptography threat

The most immediate and quantifiable quantum risk involves cryptographic vulnerability. Current public-key encryption systems, RSA, elliptic curve cryptography, and Diffie-Hellman key exchange, derive their security from the computational difficulty of certain mathematical problems for classical computers. Shor's algorithm, executable on fault-tolerant quantum computers, solves these problems efficiently, rendering current encryption ineffective.

The timeline uncertainty around fault-tolerant quantum computers creates a risk management challenge. Conservative estimates suggest 10-15 years before quantum computers threaten current encryption, while more aggressive projections suggest 5-7 years. However, "harvest now, decrypt later" attacks are occurring today; adversaries capture encrypted data now with the intention of decrypting it when quantum computers become available. For organizations handling long-term sensitive information, healthcare records, financial archives, government communications, intellectual property, the quantum cryptographic threat is immediate regardless of when quantum computers actually break encryption.

The strategic risk assessment must consider data sensitivity timelines. Healthcare organizations storing patient records that must remain confidential for decades face higher quantum cryptographic risk than retailers storing transaction data with shorter sensitivity windows. Research institutions with valuable intellectual property face harvest-now-decrypt-later threats immediately. Financial institutions with decades of archived communications face both competitive intelligence risks and regulatory compliance challenges if historical data becomes accessible to adversaries.

Mitigation strategies include transitioning to post-quantum cryptography, encryption algorithms believed to be quantum-resistant, though this transition involves substantial technical complexity, testing requirements, and coordination challenges. NIST standardized post-quantum cryptographic algorithms in 2024, but implementation across complex enterprise systems requires years of effort. Organizations beginning this transition today may complete it around the same time quantum computers actually threaten current encryption, making the already urgent timeline even more compressed.

The risk of quantum cryptographic inaction is asymmetric; the downside of data exposure potentially far exceeds the cost of preventive cryptographic transitions. This risk profile argues for aggressive quantum cybersecurity investment even given timeline uncertainty.

Competitive obsolescence risk

Beyond cryptographic threats, quantum computing creates competitive risks through asymmetric capability development. In industries where quantum algorithms provide substantial advantages, quantum-enabled competitors could establish market positions that become difficult to challenge. The risk manifests differently across competitive scenarios.

In optimization-intensive industries, logistics, supply chain, and financial services, quantum advantages in operational efficiency could create cost structures that competitors cannot match with classical approaches. A logistics company achieving quantum-enabled 5% efficiency improvements gains pricing flexibility that forces competitors into loss-making price matching or market share erosion. The feedback effects compound; better economics enable greater investment in further optimization, widening the competitive gap.

In R&D-intensive industries, pharmaceuticals, materials science, and chemicals, quantum simulation advantages could accelerate product development cycles, creating sustained innovation leadership. A pharmaceutical company achieving quantum-accelerated drug discovery doesn't just bring one drug to market faster; it potentially establishes a durable innovation advantage that produces a pipeline of quantum-accelerated products over years.

In data-intensive industries utilizing machine learning, advertising technology, financial trading, and personalized medicine, quantum-enhanced AI could improve prediction accuracy, creating advantages in customer acquisition, trading performance, or treatment outcomes that classical AI struggles to match.

The strategic challenge is that competitive quantum advantages often become apparent only after competitors have established them, limiting response options. By the time a competitor's quantum-enabled supply chain optimization demonstrates measurable market share gains, replicating their quantum capabilities requires not just acquiring quantum computing access but developing quantum expertise, adapting algorithms to specific business contexts, and integrating quantum solutions into operations – processes requiring years. The competitive advantage window widens as late movers struggle to catch up.

Assessing competitive obsolescence risk requires systematic competitive intelligence, industry analysis, and honest evaluation of quantum's potential impact on competitive dynamics in specific markets. Organizations should model scenarios where leading competitors achieve quantum advantages, evaluating the magnitude and durability of those advantages and the difficulty of catching up. This scenario analysis often reveals that the risk of inaction exceeds the risk of premature quantum investment, particularly in industries where quantum applications map clearly to competitive advantages.

Talent acquisition and retention risks

The scarcity of quantum expertise creates strategic risks beyond direct quantum initiatives. As quantum computing becomes strategically relevant across industries, quantum expertise becomes a competitive asset even for organizations not yet implementing quantum solutions. Organizations known for quantum engagement recruit technical talent more successfully because quantum signals innovation, leadership, and technological sophistication.

Conversely, organizations perceived as quantum laggards face talent recruitment challenges with technically sophisticated candidates who view quantum engagement as a proxy for overall technological progressiveness. This talent risk extends beyond quantum specialists to adjacent areas; AI researchers, data scientists, and advanced software engineers increasingly expect employers to explore emerging technologies including quantum computing.

Retention risks compound recruitment challenges. High-performing technical employees often leave organizations they perceive as technologically conservative for competitors offering more innovative technical environments. Quantum initiatives signal technological leadership that improves retention even among employees not directly working on quantum projects.

The strategic implication is that quantum investment creates talent benefits that exceed direct quantum application value, while quantum inaction creates talent risks that extend beyond missing quantum capabilities to broader recruitment and retention challenges. Organizations should quantify these talent effects when assessing quantum investment business cases, recognizing that talent advantages and risks often exceed near-term operational impacts.

Strategic partnership and ecosystem risks

Quantum computing is developing within partnership ecosystems where hardware providers, software companies, cloud platforms, and enterprise customers collaborate on capability development. Organizations that engage early in these ecosystems gain relationship capital, influence over development priorities, and access advantages as quantum technologies mature.

The risk of late ecosystem engagement is limited partnership options. Quantum hardware providers cultivate strategic relationships with select enterprise customers, offering priority access, collaborative development opportunities, and preferential pricing. As these partnerships mature, hardware providers have limited capacity or incentive to replicate relationships with late-arriving organizations. Strategic partnership opportunities that exist today may become unavailable as quantum ecosystems consolidate.

Similar dynamics operate in quantum software ecosystems. Organizations that partner with quantum algorithm developers, quantum cloud platforms, and quantum consulting firms during formative stages influence product development, gain implementation expertise, and build relationships that create advantages as quantum software matures. Late adopters access quantum software as commodity purchasers rather than collaborative partners, reducing flexibility and customization opportunities.

Assessing ecosystem risk requires evaluating the strategic value of quantum partnerships beyond immediate quantum capabilities. Partnership benefits include technology access, expertise development, influence over capability roadmaps, and signals to talent and investors about innovation leadership. Organizations should model scenarios where quantum ecosystem consolidation limits future partnership options, evaluating whether early engagement creates strategic options worth the investment even given quantum technology uncertainty. In Part Four of this book, we will delve into the specifics and value of the quantum ecosystem and the partnership options within the ecosystem to ensure you don't miss any opportunities across the quantum ecosystem itself.

Regulatory and standards risks

As quantum computing advances, regulatory frameworks and industry standards are emerging around quantum cybersecurity, quantum computing standards, and quantum workforce development. Organizations that engage early in standards development influence regulatory outcomes and industry best practices, while late movers adapt to standards developed without their input.

Quantum cybersecurity regulation is advancing rapidly. Government agencies including NIST in the United States and ENISA in Europe are developing post-quantum cryptography standards and compliance timelines. Industry regulators in finance, healthcare, and critical infrastructure are establishing quantum cybersecurity requirements. Organizations engaged in standards development shape these requirements to align with their operational realities and strategic priorities. Late movers face potentially costly compliance requirements developed without their participation.

Industry standards for quantum computing, including benchmarking methodologies, interoperability protocols, and performance metrics, are being established through consortia including the Quantum Economic Development Consortium, IEEE quantum standards initiatives, and ISO quantum computing working groups. Organizations participating in standards development influence measurement frameworks that will evaluate quantum performance, affecting how their quantum investments are assessed by investors, customers, and stakeholders.

Strategic risk assessment should include the value of standards participation and the risk of regulatory requirements developed without organizational input. While standards participation requires resource commitment, the alternative – adapting to externally imposed standards – often proves more costly and operationally disruptive.

Probabilistic risk modeling for quantum decisions

Given the multiple risk dimensions and inherent uncertainties, probabilistic risk modeling provides structured frameworks for quantum risk assessment. Monte Carlo simulation can model quantum investment outcomes across distributions of possible technology maturity timelines, competitive adoption rates, and quantum advantage magnitudes. This approach produces probability distributions of outcomes rather than single-point estimates, better capturing quantum uncertainty.

Decision tree analysis maps quantum investment decisions across sequential stages: initial exploration decisions, subsequent scaling decisions, and final implementation decisions, with probabilities and payoffs at each decision node. This framework explicitly models how quantum investment decisions evolve as uncertainty resolves, enabling better evaluation of staged investment strategies.

Sensitivity analysis identifies which variables most affect quantum investment outcomes, focusing attention on the assumptions deserving greatest scrutiny and ongoing monitoring. If quantum investment value proves highly sensitive to competitive adoption timelines, organizations should invest in competitive intelligence around quantum initiatives. If quantum ROI depends critically on specific technical breakthroughs, organizations should monitor technical progress indicators closely.

Integrated risk-benefit assessment

Comprehensive quantum strategy requires integrating risk assessment with benefit analysis, recognizing that quantum risks and opportunities often correlate. Industries facing the greatest quantum cryptographic threats – financial services, healthcare, government – also often have substantial quantum opportunity in optimization and machine learning applications. This correlation argues for comprehensive quantum strategies addressing both offensive and defensive dimensions rather than narrow approaches focused exclusively on threats or opportunities.

The risk-benefit integration should employ portfolio optimization approaches that balance quantum investments across risk mitigation and opportunity capture, recognizing different risk-return profiles and different timelines. Quantum cybersecurity investments provide defensive value with relatively predictable timelines, while quantum algorithm development offers offensive opportunity with greater uncertainty but potentially higher returns.

Organizations should develop integrated quantum risk dashboards that monitor multiple risk dimensions, cryptographic vulnerability, competitive quantum adoption, talent gaps, partnership opportunities, and regulatory developments, enabling systematic risk tracking and timely strategy adjustments. These dashboards should include leading indicators that signal changing risk profiles before crises materialize, enabling proactive rather than reactive quantum strategy.

The ultimate strategic imperative is recognizing that quantum risk assessment isn't a one-time analysis but an ongoing process that evolves as quantum technologies mature, competitive landscapes shift, and organizational capabilities develop. Organizations that establish systematic quantum risk assessment processes position themselves to navigate quantum uncertainty more effectively than those treating quantum as a distant future concern requiring only periodic reassessment.

Organizations do not need to begin with a consultant or a large quantum program. A sensible first step is to build a small internal working group across technology, cybersecurity, finance, operations, and strategy to identify where quantum could create either material risk or measurable business value. From there, the team can establish a baseline, select a small number of realistic use cases, and ask a straightforward set of questions: What problem are we trying to solve? What does it cost us today? What would improve if this worked? What would happen if we did nothing? And what level of improvement would justify further investment? External advisors can help accelerate the process, especially where internal expertise is limited, but they should support, not replace, the organization's own decision-making.

The next step is to turn those answers into a business case that can stand up to the same scrutiny as any other investment. For a defensive initiative, ROI may come from avoided loss, reduced regulatory exposure, lower remediation costs, or improved resilience. For an opportunity-focused initiative, value may come from cost savings, revenue growth, faster processing, better optimization, or strategic option value. Where outcomes are still uncertain, leaders can use ranges, scenarios, and decision thresholds rather than forcing a precise forecast. The practical goal is to size the risk and opportunity well enough to answer the CFO's core questions: How much are we investing, what do we expect to gain or avoid, what assumptions are we making, and what evidence will tell us whether to continue, stop, or scale?

Summary

The quantum revolution has transitioned from distant possibility to immediate strategic reality. Organizations across industries face quantum-driven disruption timelines compressing faster than traditional technology adoption cycles, creating urgent imperatives for executive action even as uncertainties remain.

Quantum computing technologies have achieved critical maturity thresholds where practical business applications are emerging. Gate-based quantum computers, quantum annealers, and photonic quantum systems each approach commercial viability on different timelines for different applications. The availability of quantum cloud services has democratized access, enabling organizations to explore quantum capabilities without capital-intensive hardware investments. This accessibility accelerates competitive dynamics; quantum advantages are no longer constrained to organizations with massive research budgets but are increasingly available to any organization with strategic vision and appropriate expertise.

Industry disruption manifests through sector-specific patterns. Financial services confront both existential cryptographic threats and transformative opportunities in optimization and risk analysis. Pharmaceuticals approach quantum-accelerated drug discovery that could compress development timelines from years to months. Logistics and supply chain operations see optimization improvements that create sustainable competitive advantages in efficiency-driven markets. Automotive and energy industries explore quantum applications across their value chains, from materials development to operational optimization.

Early movers establish competitive advantages through multiple mechanisms. Proprietary quantum algorithms create intellectual property moats. Strategic partnerships secure preferential access to constrained quantum resources. Quantum-trained workforces develop expertise that competitors cannot quickly replicate. These advantages compound over time as quantum technologies mature and organizational capabilities deepen, creating barriers to entry that late movers struggle to overcome.

Quantifying quantum investment returns requires moving beyond traditional ROI frameworks to specialized methodologies that capture quantum's unique characteristics. Option value models recognize quantum investments create strategic flexibility. Portfolio approaches optimize quantum allocation across multiple applications with different risk-return profiles. Scenario-based modeling addresses timeline uncertainty through weighted outcomes across plausible futures. Quantum-specific metrics measure value creation through solution quality improvements, time-to-solution reductions, and capability development. Intangible benefits including talent advantages, strategic partnerships, and innovation culture often exceed direct operational value in quantum's early phases.

Strategic risk assessment reveals that quantum inaction often carries greater risk than quantum investment. Cryptographic vulnerabilities threaten data security on timelines that argue for immediate post-quantum cryptography transitions. Competitive obsolescence risks manifest as quantum-enabled competitors establish advantages in optimization, simulation, and machine learning applications. Talent acquisition challenges intensify as quantum expertise becomes both scarcer and more strategically valuable. Partnership and ecosystem consolidation limits options for late movers. Regulatory and standards development proceeds with or without organizational participation, affecting compliance costs and operational constraints.

The executive skills developed through mastering this content enable systematic evaluation of quantum opportunities and threats. Leaders gain competency in strategic technology assessment, moving beyond quantum hype to realistic evaluation frameworks. Market timing analysis capabilities improve through understanding quantum maturity indicators and competitive dynamics. Business case development skills strengthen through exposure to quantum-specific valuation approaches and stakeholder communication techniques. Risk-benefit modeling sophistication increases through probabilistic frameworks that address quantum uncertainty systematically. Stakeholder communication improves through practice translating quantum technical concepts into strategic business language.

The path forward requires neither reckless quantum enthusiasm nor complacent dismissal of quantum as a distant concern. Instead, effective quantum strategy combines realistic assessment of current quantum capabilities with systematic preparation for quantum futures. Organizations should begin quantum exploration through pilot projects and workforce development while planning multi-year transitions for quantum cybersecurity and strategic positioning. The key is matching quantum initiatives to realistic technology timelines while maintaining strategic agility to accelerate or pivot as quantum technologies evolve.

That agility depends on knowing what to watch out for. Important triggers include independently validated quantum advantage on commercially relevant problems, sustained improvements in logical qubit performance and error correction, meaningful reductions in the cost of useful quantum computation, advances in quantum networking such as reliable repeaters and multi-node interoperability, and quantum sensing demonstrations that show clear operational advantages over classical alternatives. Just as important are non-technical signals: new regulatory requirements, accelerated cryptographic depreciation timelines, major industry adoption, competitors moving from pilots into production, or vendors offering repeatable solutions with credible performance and cost benchmarks. When several of these signals begin to converge, the window for simply watching the market starts to close. That is the point when organizations should be prepared to move from experimentation and capability-building into more deliberate investment, implementation, and scale.

The organizations that will thrive in the quantum era are those that act decisively today, not with massive irreversible quantum bets, but with systematic, staged investments that build quantum readiness while managing quantum risks. The quantum imperative is clear: executive action cannot wait for perfect information or complete certainty. The competitive landscape is already shifting, and the organizations positioning themselves advantageously are those recognizing that quantum readiness is not a future requirement but a current and necessary strategic priority.

Just as importantly, this book does not stop at explaining why quantum matters. The chapters that follow are intended to move from awareness into action by helping leaders determine what their first practical step should be, how much they should invest, what they should expect in return, and how to justify that investment against other competing corporate priorities.

For many organizations, that first step will not be purchasing quantum technology or launching a large-scale program. It will be developing a clear business case. That business case should answer a small number of practical questions: What business problem or risk is being addressed? What happens if nothing is done? What is the expected financial or strategic value of acting? What level of investment is required? And what evidence would justify increasing, reducing, or stopping that investment?

This becomes especially important in organizations where quantum initiatives must compete with cybersecurity, cloud modernization, AI, workforce, infrastructure, and other strategic priorities for the same investment dollars. Quantum will ultimately face the same test as any other initiative presented to a CFO or investment committee: What is the value, what is the risk, how much will it cost, and why should the organization fund it now?

This book therefore treats quantum business-case development as a practical management discipline rather than an abstract financial exercise. You will be shown how to frame quantum opportunities and risks using measurable business variables such as avoided loss, revenue opportunity, productivity improvement, time-to-solution, cost reduction, regulatory exposure, competitive advantage, capability development, and strategic option value. Where precise estimates are not yet possible, scenario ranges and probability-weighted assumptions can provide a more credible alternative to unsupported forecasts.

A practical quantum business case can begin with a relatively simple structure:

Business problem or opportunity → current baseline → quantum of quantum-safe intervention → investment required → measureable benefit → risk adjusted value → decision trigger

A practical quantum business case does not need to predict the future perfectly. It simply just needs to help leaders decide when an investment is worth making. For a quantum-safe security initiative, that might mean weighing the cost of a migration against the financial, regulatory, and operational impact of waiting too long. For a quantum optimization pilot, it might mean setting a clear performance target that must be met before committing additional funding. This gives executives a sensible way to start small, learn, reduce risk, and invest more only when the evidence supports it. Some organizations will have the internal expertise to do this themselves, while others may benefit from an outside advisor to help establish the baseline, identify realistic opportunities, and build the initial business case. The path is fairly simple: understand the exposure, size the opportunity, fund a reasonable first step, measure what happens, and then decide whether it makes sense to scale. In the end, the goal is to move quantum from an interesting conversation to a business decision that leadership, and the CFO, can confidently support.

Further reading

1. https://www.bcg.com/publications/2023/making-sense-of-quantum-sensing
2. https://qnami.ch/portfolio/quantum-foundry/
3. https://sbquantum.com/our-solutions/
4. https://blogs.cisco.com/news/quantum-networking-how-cisco-is-accelerating-practical-quantum-computing
5. https://www.ibm.com/roadmaps/quantum/2026/
6. https://arxiv.org/abs/quant-ph/0412029
7. https://www.scientificamerican.com/article/china-reaches-new-milestone-in-space-based-quantum-communications/
8. https://newsroom.bt.com/bt-and-toshiba-to-build-worlds-first-commercial-quantum-secured-metro-network-across-london/
9. https://www.ncsc.gov.uk/paper/quantum-networking-technologies
10. https://www.ibm.com/quantum/quantum-safe
11. https://digital-strategy.ec.europa.eu/en/policies/european-quantum-communication-infrastructure-euroqci
12. https://newsroom.ibm.com/2025-11-12-ibm-delivers-new-quantum-processors,-software,-and-algorithm-breakthroughs-on-path-to-advantage-and-fault-tolerance
13. https://en.wikipedia.org/wiki/DiVincenzo%27s_criteria
14. https://www.dwavequantum.com/solutions-and-products/systems/
15. https://media.defense.gov/2025/May/30/2003728741/-1/-1/0/CSA_CNSA_2.0_ALGORITHMS.PDF
16. https://www.idquantique.com/
17. https://www.qusecure.com/
18. https://pmc.ncbi.nlm.nih.gov/articles/PMC12306909/

19. https://www.nist.gov/cybersecurity/what-post-quantum-cryptography
20. https://www.qureca.com/quantum-initiatives-worldwide/#:~:text=October%2015%2C%202025,billion%20by%202040%20%5B1%5D
21. https://www.mckinsey.com/capabilities/tech-and-ai/our-insights/the-year-of-quantum-from-concept-to-reality-in-2025
22. https://www.ibm.com/quantum/blog/what-is-quantum-utility
23. https://www.nature.com/articles/s41586-023-06096-3
24. https://www.jpmorganchase.com/about/technology/blog/quantum-linear-systems-for-portfolio-optimization
25. https://www.qai.ca/resource-library/exxonmobil-and-mitsubishi-chemical-leveraging-quantum-computing-for-industry-advancement
26. https://www.eon.com/en/about-us/digitalization/quantum-computing.html
27. https://corporate.exxonmobil.com/news/news-releases/2019/0108_exxonmobil-and-ibm-to-advance-energy-sector-application-of-quantum-computing
28. https://www.mckinsey.com/capabilities/tech-and-ai/our-insights/tech-forward/enabling-the-next-frontier-of-quantum-computing
29. https://www.ibm.com/quantum/blog/quantum-advantage
30. https://www.darpa.mil/research/programs/quantum-benchmarking-initiative

2

Quantum Economics and Investment Strategy

Quantum technology represents one of the most significant investment opportunities and poses some strategic challenges of the next decade, requiring sophisticated economic analysis and investment strategies that go far beyond traditional technology investments. This chapter provides comprehensive guidance on navigating the complex quantum investment landscape, from understanding global funding patterns and geopolitical considerations to developing portfolio approaches and optimizing funding models.

As executives, venture capitalists, and policymakers stand on the threshold of the quantum era, the investment decisions made today will shape competitive positioning for decades to come. Unlike previous technological revolutions where first-mover advantage was clear and markets developed along predictable trajectories, quantum technology presents a fundamentally different challenge. The path from laboratory breakthrough to commercial application is measured not in months but in years, sometimes as long as decades. The capital requirements are substantial, the technical risks are high, and the regulatory landscape is complex and evolving.[1] Consider the experience of IBM, which has invested billions in quantum computing research since the 1990s. Their quantum journey illustrates both the opportunities and challenges inherent in quantum investment: decades of patient capital deployment, continuous pivoting as technologies matured, and ultimately the creation of new markets. Today, the IBM Quantum Network boasts over 300 partners and has made quantum computing accessible through the cloud, demonstrating how sustained strategic investment can create defensible competitive advantages.[2]

Leaders will learn to evaluate quantum investment opportunities across the entire ecosystem, including hardware companies like IonQ and Quantinuum, software platforms from providers such as Quantum Machines and qBraid, and quantum-enabled applications that promise to transform industries from pharmaceuticals to finance.

In this chapter, we're going to address critical economic factors such as export controls, international competition, and government incentives that shape quantum investment decisions and returns.[3] You'll also see a few frameworks for making these decisions despite fundamental uncertainties about technology trajectories and market development timelines. The quantum investment landscape is not merely about identifying promising technologies or betting on winning approaches. It also requires understanding how government policy intersects with private capital, how geopolitical tensions shape acceptable partnership structures, and how export controls constrain business models. Most of this will demand new valuation methodologies that account for optionality and technical risk, new partnership structures that align incentives across long development timelines, and new due diligence processes that can assess quantum technical claims. The takeaways from this chapter will surely equip you with the frameworks, skills, and strategic perspectives needed to navigate these complexities successfully, whether you're deploying venture capital, setting corporate innovation strategy, or shaping government quantum initiatives or policy.

Main topics covered in this chapter are:

- Global quantum investment landscape
- Quantum ecosystems and strategic positioning
- Optimizing quantum funding models
- Quantum investment frameworks
- Quantum investment landscape examples

Global quantum investment landscape

"I've got a group of investors looking to invest in quantum. What do you suggest?"

This is just one of the common questions I get asked from various venture capital firms, many of which have spent years perfecting the art of evaluating software startups, companies that can scale from small to large sized users with minimal capital. Now they find themselves analyzing quantum technology companies that burn through millions of dollars before producing any commercial customers. Traditional venture capital playbooks offer limited guidance when confronting technologies that might require a decade or more to reach commercial viability. In this section I'm going to cover some fundamentals to help refine your playbooks, including some recent details on the current geographic quantum ecosystems and strategic positioning. I'll also include some notable considerations regarding export controls, regulatory compliance, and national security, particularly as most nations are creating their own sovereign initiatives that stretch from workforce development to economic development. Better safe than sorry, right?

Recently the quantum investment ecosystem has evolved into a multibillion-dollar market with characteristics that fundamentally differentiate it from conventional technology investments. From an overall global quantum technology perspective, funding has exceeded $25 billion (USD), with approximately $4 billion from private venture capital, $20+ billion from government programs, and growing corporate venture investment from technology giants.[4] This does paint an interesting picture that explains how some governments view quantum technology as strategically important enough to warrant sustained public investment at scales typically reserved for defense or space programs. Many of them also view quantum technologies as a "dual-use" critical element with capabilities offering both economic opportunities and existential national security risks that could be as large as existing government defense or space budgets.

Many quantum venture funds have developed recently, led by firms such as Quantonation, [5] 55 North, and NVentures (NVIDIA), all of which bring quantum-specific expertise that general technology investors often lack, such as the ability to evaluate technical claims about qubit coherence times, assess competitive positioning across different quantum modalities, and understand the regulatory landscape shaping quantum business models. Corporate venture arms such as IBM, Google, Amazon, and Honeywell actively invest in quantum startups, but their motivations differ from financial investors. Strategic investors seek quantum capabilities that complement their existing businesses or provide early insight into emerging technologies. When Amazon's AWS invests in quantum networking companies, they're positioning for a future where quantum secure communications become an essential cloud service.

The private sector isn't the only one, of course, playing an unprecedented role in quantum investment, with implications that extend beyond capital provision. Back in 2018, the U.S. National Quantum Initiative authorized $1.2 billion in funding, while the European Union's Quantum Flagship program represents a €1 billion, ten-year commitment.[6, 7] China's investments in quantum technology reportedly exceed $15 billion, though exact numbers remain opaque.[8] Government funding of quantum technology doesn't simply supplement private investment; it fundamentally shapes market development by supporting research priorities, creating workforce pipelines within their regions, and eventually establishing technical standards – standards which may not yet exist but will certainly be needed in the not-so-distant future.

Geographic quantum ecosystems and strategic positioning

Quantum technology development is far from evenly spread around the world. Instead, it tends to cluster in a handful of regional ecosystems, each with its own strengths, priorities, and strategic flavor. Understanding how these regions differ is essential for making thoughtful investment decisions, structuring cross-border partnerships, and navigating the geopolitical undercurrents that increasingly influence the quantum landscape. In the US, much of the momentum sits at the crossroads of software, algorithms, and cloud-delivered quantum services. Activity is heavily concentrated along the East Coast from Boston, down through New York, Washington DC, and just recently reaching as far south as Florida. Across the Midwest into Chicago, Illinois, which is the home of the Chicago Quantum Exchange (CQE), and where the state is in the process of building the Illinois Quantum and Microelectronics Park (IQMP). Out west in the San Francisco Bay Area, where top universities, national labs, and deep pools of venture capital reinforce one another. Institutions like MIT, Harvard, and the University of Maryland not only train a steady stream of quantum specialists but also spin out startups that feed directly into the broader ecosystem.

China, by contrast, has focused enormous state-backed resources on quantum communications and networking. High-profile achievements, such as the Micius quantum satellite and a quantum-secured communication link spanning roughly 2000 kilometers between Beijing and Shanghai, signal a clear national commitment to building quantum infrastructure at scale. These projects are as much about technological leadership as they are about strategic positioning.[9]

The European Union has taken yet another path, emphasizing quantum sovereignty and coordinated progress across its member states. Its Quantum Flagship initiative, launched back in 2018, stands among the EU's most ambitious research programs, supporting work across quantum computing, communication, sensing, and simulations. The aim is not only to advance the science, but to ensure that Europe can develop and retain key quantum capabilities within its own borders.

Canada has carved out an outsized role given the size of its economy, particularly in quantum computing hardware. The University of Waterloo's Institute for Quantum Computing has grown into a major global hub, helping launch companies such as D-Wave Systems and Xanadu, both leading players in quantum annealers and photonic quantum computing, respectively. Together, they showcase how a focused research ecosystem can punch well above its weight on the world stage.

As with most globally geographic ecosystems, there are just as many regulations as there are opportunities. So before you consider globe-trotting across the world looking for partners, let's take a moment to consider the current controls and regulations to ensure you are aware of any potential risks and exposures.

Export controls, regulatory compliance, and national security

As someone who spends free time volunteering, I truly enjoy helping others wherever and whenever I can. The experience becomes even more meaningful when it takes me to parts of the world I've never seen before, not only to lend support where it's needed, but also to immerse myself in new cultures and forge lasting friendships along the way. Yet, as anyone who travels frequently knows, every destination comes with its own protocols and requirements. I've often found myself ticking through lists of vaccines, insurance documents, and visa applications just to gain entry to certain countries. These rules don't end with tourism; they extend deeply into how nations regulate trade, collaboration, and innovation. Export controls, in particular, add another layer of complexity for those seeking to build partnerships or conduct business abroad. The risks associated with these regulations could potentially be significantly underestimated by investors and organizations attempting to grow talent in quantum and its related areas, when the standard mechanisms of talent acquisition, retention, and off-shoring will not apply for the foreseeable future, including investment.

Quantum technology is no exception. If quantum innovation signals the future of computing, sensing, and communication, then export control regulations represent the present reality, the necessary framework that shapes and sometimes limits how quantum enterprises engage across borders. These regulations, intended to keep sensitive technologies out of the hands of potential adversaries, add layers of complexity that can reshape entire quantum investment strategies, partnership structures, and business models.

The export control landscape for quantum technologies is a web of overlapping systems. The International Traffic in Arms Regulations (ITAR) govern items with clear military applications, while the Export Administration Regulations (EAR) cover so-called "dual-use" items, which are technologies that can serve both commercial and defense purposes.[10] Many quantum innovations land squarely in this dual-use category, making compliance anything but straightforward. On top of all this, the Committee on Foreign Investment in the United States (CFIUS) keeps a close eye on foreign investments that might pose national security risks.[11] Quantum companies, given their strategic importance, often draw heightened scrutiny. Since 2018, CFIUS has extended its oversight to include even non-controlling investments in firms working with "critical technologies," a list that explicitly names quantum computing.

For business leaders new to the field, it's very easy to overlook how deeply these controls reach into quantum supply chains. Even components or subsystems that aren't quantum in nature may still fall under export rules if they're specifically engineered for quantum systems.

Another often overlooked challenge lies in talent mobility. Quantum expertise is in short supply worldwide, and companies naturally want the best minds, wherever they may be. Yet export controls don't just govern hardware or software, they also restrict the transfer of controlled technical data. In some cases, that means even sharing what's inside a researcher's head can cross regulatory lines.

While navigating export controls and compliance frameworks can often feel like a maze, these regulatory realities are just one part of the broader challenge facing quantum enterprises. Building and scaling within such constraints also requires smart, adaptive funding strategies. To stay competitive, quantum companies must structure their financing models as thoughtfully as they approach their technology development. In the next section, we'll dive deeper into these funding models and portfolio approaches.

Optimizing quantum funding models

Building a quantum company often feels like navigating a funding puzzle that can only be solved through creativity and collaboration. Because quantum technologies are still maturing, with long roadmaps to commercialization, high technical uncertainty, and significant capital demands, no single funding model fits all. Instead, success usually comes from blending government support, private investment, and strategic partnerships to balance risk and make every dollar count. Government programs remain a vital source of early, non-dilutive funding. U.S. initiatives like the Small Business Innovation Research (SBIR), which was extended back in 2022, and Small Business Technology Transfer (STTR) programs provide grants to quantum startups, typically ranging from $250,000 (USD) for Phase 1 projects up to $1.5 million (USD) for Phase 2.[12] These funds can help founders validate ideas without giving up equity, which we all know is a precious advantage in such a research-intensive field. Of course, other pathways exist beyond government-funded programs.

Collaborating with national laboratories offers another powerful path. Facilities such as Oak Ridge, Los Alamos, and Lawrence Berkeley National Laboratories host some of the world's most advanced quantum infrastructure. Beyond the financial benefits, partnerships with these labs open access to rare technical expertise, experimental platforms, and opportunities to co-develop emerging technologies.

Strategic industry partnerships also play an essential role. When IBM launched the IBM Quantum Network, for example, it created a model where organizations could pay for access to IBM's quantum systems while contributing insights from real-world use cases. This kind of partnership not only spreads development costs and risks but also helps build a thriving quantum ecosystem that advances alongside its participants.

In practice, the most resilient companies use a hybrid approach, mixing capital sources at each stage of growth. A hardware startup might begin with an SBIR grant to fund proof-of-concept work, follow up with venture capital to build prototypes, partner with national labs for testing, and later bring in corporate investors as commercialization nears. In a field defined by uncertainty, this layered funding strategy enables quantum innovators to stay both agile and ambitious.

Now, once a company has pieced together the right mix of funding sources, the next challenge is deciding where to place those resources. In a field as fast-moving and uncertain as quantum technology, success depends not only on how capital is raised but also on how it's deployed. That's where thoughtful portfolio strategies come into play, balancing vision with prudence, and ambition with risk awareness. In the next subsection we will look into portfolio approaches which will guide us to creating our own quantum investment framework.

Portfolio approaches to quantum investing

Quantum investing is less about finding a single winner and more about building a balanced, resilient portfolio. The path forward is full of unknowns: which technological platform will prove most scalable, which applications will reach the market first, and how global regulations will evolve. Diversification isn't just smart, it's necessary for anyone seeking to participate meaningfully in this emerging ecosystem.

Direct investments in quantum companies can yield significant rewards but also come with steep risks. Take the hardware landscape, for instance: IBM, Google, and IQM continue advancing superconducting qubits; IonQ and Quantinuum are betting on trapped ions; Xanadu and PsiQuantum pursue photonics; and Atom Computing explores neutral atoms. Each of these approaches holds theoretical promise but faces unique engineering and commercialization hurdles.

A robust portfolio also balances exposure across hardware, software, and application layers. Hardware investments, while capital-intensive and long-term, build the foundation for tomorrow's quantum capabilities. Software and algorithm investments, on the other hand, may generate earlier returns as they leverage incremental advances in hardware performance. Together, they help investors stay positioned across the quantum value chain.

Strategic partnerships and joint ventures offer another way to engage with quantum innovation while containing risk. Instead of acquiring early-stage startups outright, corporations can structure collaborations with defined milestones, gaining access to quantum technologies, testing potential use cases, and reserving the option to invest more deeply if results warrant it.

Finally, sequencing investments to build capabilities step by step often proves the most sustainable approach. An organization might start by funding quantum education or workforce development, then pilot industry-specific applications, make minority investments in emerging leaders, and eventually pursue acquisitions once the technology reaches maturity. It's not about rushing to stake a claim; it's about pacing progress in sync with the science itself.

Quantum investment frameworks: tools for decision-making

Building a balanced quantum portfolio is just one part of the equation. To make smart decisions within that portfolio, especially in an environment defined by uncertainty, investors need clear, adaptable frameworks that guide how opportunities are assessed and prioritized. These frameworks turn strategic vision into practical decision-making tools, allowing teams to evaluate risk, potential returns, and timing with greater confidence. Leveraging these frameworks in an incredibly complex technical landscape such as this, more than ever you are going to need to make an investment decision which relies on more than a "gut" feeling. The frameworks here will help provide you with answers to real questions such as: what are you trying to solve and for whom? And will you be successful when you do?

While deeper return-on-investment (ROI) models will be covered in later chapters, this section introduces three foundational frameworks designed to give quantum investors a structured way to think about their choices. Each helps translate the intricate mix of technology readiness, regulatory context, and market potential explored in this chapter into clear, actionable investment strategies.

Framework 1: Quantum investment evaluation matrix

Having a quantum investment evaluation matrix offers a practical, structured way to weigh the promise and risk of quantum opportunities. It helps investors and executives look beyond the hype by assessing each opportunity across five key dimensions that capture what truly makes quantum ventures different from traditional tech investments:

Dimension	Key Evaluation Criteria
Technical Viability	• Technology readiness level • Technical team expertise • Competitive technical positioning • Path to quantum advantage • Intellectual property strength

Dimension	Key Evaluation Criteria
Market Opportunity	• Target market size and growth • Customer willingness to pay • Competitive intensity • Time to market adoption • Defensible market position
Regulatory Risk	• Export control implications • CFIUS/foreign investment sensitivity • International market access • Compliance infrastructure adequacy
Capital Efficiency	• Total capital required • Government funding accessibility • Burn rate sustainability • Path to revenue • Scalability economics
Strategic Fit	• Alignment with portfolio strategy • Synergies with existing investments • Exit opportunity potential • Strategic value beyond financial returns

By scoring each dimension according to your organization's goals, risk appetite, and strategic priorities, this matrix brings clarity to an otherwise complex space. It also highlights how these factors are interconnected, ensuring that decisions aren't made in isolation but reflect the broader dynamics of technology readiness, market timing, and collaboration potential.

Framework 2: Quantum portfolio risk-return balance

A Quantum Portfolio Risk-Return Balance framework takes a step back to consider the bigger picture: how all your quantum investments fit together. Since each quantum category, whether hardware, software, or applications, comes with its own mix of technical maturity, capital needs, and time horizons, this approach helps investors spread exposure wisely while managing downside risk. Here, the goal isn't just diversification for its own sake, but balance, building a portfolio that aligns with an organization's objectives, funding capacity, and tolerance for uncertainty. In practice, that might mean weighing investments differently based on shifting market signals or prioritizing areas with faster commercialization potential while keeping long-term bets in play. Note that having the portfolio approach is a simple comparison and it does not cover the technological spread. Similar to that of stock portfolios, it will require some alignment with the ability to scale and remain relevant in the long term.

Framework 3: Regulatory compliance decision tree

The regulatory compliance decision tree helps investors and business leaders translate a maze of export control and national security rules into clear, actionable steps. It brings structure to the question of what's allowed and where, ensuring compliance doesn't become an afterthought.

Decision Point	Key Questions	Actions Required
Export Control Classification	Does technology fall under ITAR or EAR? What export control category numbers (ECCNs)?	• Conduct classification review • Consult export control counsel • Document classification determination
National Security Review	Does investment involve foreign parties? Will CFIUS or equivalent review be triggered?	• Assess CFIUS/foreign investment risk • File voluntary notice if appropriate • Structure the transaction to address concerns
International Operations	Where will the technology be developed, manufactured, or deployed? What cross-border transfers will be required?	• Identify licensing requirements • Establish compliance procedures • Create segregated operations if needed

Decision Point	Key Questions	Actions Required
Ongoing Compliance	How will compliance be monitored as technology and regulations evolve?	• Implement compliance management systems • Train personnel • Conduct periodic audits • Update procedures as regulations change

Ideally, this framework comes into play early, before term sheets are drafted or partnerships formalized, when it can still shape deal terms and prevent costly pivots later. By building regulatory awareness into the decision-making process from the start, organizations protect both their flexibility and their reputation while positioning themselves for sustainable global growth.

Let's now try to bring these frameworks down from the abstract to the real world. In the next section, we will look at a few stories of individual companies to illustrate how different teams interpret the same technical, regulatory, and funding landscape, and still arrive at very different strategies. With that in mind, we can look at a few representative players to see how quantum investment decisions actually unfold in practice and what lessons they offer for anyone thinking about where to place their own bets.

Quantum investment landscape: company spotlights

Understanding the quantum investment landscape means looking closely at how leading companies navigate the challenges and opportunities described herein. The following spotlights highlight different paths to quantum commercialization, funding strategies, and market positioning, each reflecting a distinct way of thinking about risk, timing, and scale. Each example was selected to illustrate the different-sized organizations, from startups to enterprises.

IBM: The long game in quantum computing

IBM is a classic example of patient, long-horizon quantum investment. Having invested in quantum computing research since the 1990s, the company has committed billions of dollars while weathering multiple shifts in technology and market expectations. Their IBM Quantum Network, launched in 2017, has grown to include hundreds of partners across Fortune 500 enterprises, universities, and startups, illustrating the power of an ecosystem-centric approach.[13]

IBM's strategy centers on superconducting qubits and cloud-based access to quantum hardware. By publishing a clear quantum roadmap, with explicit targets for qubit counts and performance, they provide partners and customers with a concrete way to plan their own adoption timelines and experiments.[14]

From an investment perspective, IBM shows how an established technology company can leverage existing strengths, research depth, enterprise relationships, cloud infrastructure, and balance-sheet resilience to pursue quantum opportunities that would be extremely difficult for a startup to tackle alone.

The key investment lesson here is that patient capital over decades can secure defensible positions in emerging technologies: ecosystem strategies that create network effects can matter as much as technical performance; transparent roadmaps help build partner confidence and support thoughtful adoption planning.

IonQ: Pioneering trapped-ion quantum computing

IonQ became the first pure-play quantum computing company to enter public markets when it completed a SPAC merger in 2021 at a multibillion-dollar valuation. The move brought in significant capital for continued development while giving early investors liquidity.[15]

Its business model blends hardware sales to government and research customers with cloud-based access through major cloud providers, including Amazon, Microsoft, Google, and qBraid. This multi-channel strategy diversifies revenue and expands the user base, helping IonQ move toward scale without relying on a single route to market.[16]

Key investment lesson here is that different quantum modalities embody distinct risk and return dynamics; public listings can unlock large capital pools but introduce pressure for transparency and performance; diversified distribution and partnership models reduce dependence on any one customer or platform.

Quantinuum: Strategic merger creating quantum full stack

Quantinuum was created through the 2021 merger of Honeywell Quantum Solutions and Cambridge Quantum Computing, forming one of the largest independent quantum companies. This combination brought together Honeywell's trapped-ion hardware with Cambridge Quantum's software, algorithms, and cybersecurity expertise, demonstrating how strategic mergers can accelerate quantum commercialization by uniting complementary strengths.[17]

The company was set up as a standalone entity rather than fully absorbing one business into another. This structure was designed to preserve the innovative, entrepreneurial cultures that had driven both organizations, while still benefiting from the resources and backing of a major industrial parent.

By owning both hardware and software, Quantinuum pursues a full-stack model that allows tighter integration and optimization across the entire system. That kind of vertical control can create advantages in performance, user experience, and pace of innovation that are harder to achieve for companies focused on only one layer.

Key investment lesson here is that well-designed mergers can assemble capabilities far faster than building them organically; full-stack integration can become a meaningful competitive edge; governance and organizational design matter for preserving entrepreneurial energy while scaling.

Google: Quantum commercial uncertainty

Google's quantum effort drew global attention in 2019 when its Sycamore processor was used to demonstrate so-called "quantum supremacy," a task completed faster than any known classical supercomputer could match. This milestone validated years of sustained research investment and showcased the potential power of quantum devices.[18]

Yet Google continues to treat quantum as a long-term research initiative rather than a near-term business line. Its quantum AI team focuses on foundational advances in hardware, error correction, and algorithms, with an eye toward achieving error-corrected systems capable of running applications that genuinely matter to customers.[19]

The quantum supremacy result highlights both the promise and the limits of headline-grabbing technical achievements. Proving that quantum computers can outperform classical machines on certain contrived tasks is meaningful, but commercial value only emerges when those capabilities align with real-world problems and paying users.

Key investment lesson here is that technical milestones can validate research directions and attract attention without immediately translating into revenue; organizations with deep resources can afford to invest in long-term research horizons; enduring commercial value requires tight alignment between quantum advantage and customer needs.

Quantum Machines: Infrastructure for the quantum ecosystem

Quantum Machines, founded in 2018 and with global offices in the US, Denmark, Germany, France, and Japan, is a company that specializes in developing control hardware and software for quantum computers. Their main product provides a Quantum Orchestration Platform (QOP) and processors for managing quantum computers. This embodies Quantum Machines as a different kind of quantum company. Instead of building quantum computers or designing algorithms, it focuses on the control and orchestration infrastructure that all quantum systems require. Its Quantum Orchestration Platform coordinates the intricate, real-time operations needed to run quantum processors effectively.[20]

This infrastructure-first approach offers several advantages. Quantum Machines does not have to bet on a single winning modality; its technology is designed to work across superconducting, trapped-ion, and other architectures. That enables the company to serve a broad set of customers, including quantum hardware manufacturers, research laboratories, and organizations developing their own systems.

The firm has attracted significant venture investment and built a customer base that spans many of the leading players in the field. Revenue from these early-stage customers helps sustain operations while the broader commercial quantum market continues to mature.

Key investment lessons here are that infrastructure investments can enable the entire ecosystem without committing to one specific technical path; serving a wide range of quantum stakeholders can create more diversified and resilient revenue streams; focusing on tools and controls layers can generate value even before large-scale commercial quantum applications fully arrive.

The companies we've just explored show that there's no single "right" way to invest in quantum, only strategies that fit different strengths, timelines, and risk appetites. What they all share, though, is a deeper set of capabilities behind the scenes: teams that can interpret technical signals, navigate regulations, structure nuanced deals, and stay grounded amid uncertainty. To build lasting success in quantum, investors and leads need to cultivate a specific skill set that goes well beyond traditional checklists and slide decks.

Critical skills for quantum investing success

Thriving in quantum investment and strategy means developing capabilities that stretch beyond conventional financial analysis or standard corporate planning. This section highlights five essential skills that leaders and investors need if they want to navigate quantum opportunities with confidence rather than guesswork.

The following examples describe how these critical skills show up in real-world quantum investment practice, not just in theory. Each section takes one capability – portfolio management, regulatory navigation, financial modeling, partnership negotiation, and market intelligence – and illustrates what it looks like when done well in a quantum context. Together, they offer a practical roadmap for leaders who want to move beyond high-level enthusiasm and build the day-to-day habits needed to make sound, durable decisions in this emerging field.

Investment portfolio management

Managing a quantum investment portfolio is not just a matter of applying familiar tools with a new label; it requires adapting sophisticated financial techniques to a very different environment. Traditional portfolio thinking assumes reasonably predictable timelines, established ways to value companies, and clear views on how and when investors might exit. Quantum routinely breaks those assumptions.

Crafting a thoughtful quantum investment thesis, for instance, demands a deep understanding of technology roadmaps, competitive positioning, and likely adoption trajectories. A strong thesis doesn't just name promising companies; it articulates which quantum approaches are most compelling, which applications are likely to commercialize first, and how the broader market structure might evolve.

Once capital is deployed, portfolio company management becomes an active, hands-on effort. Investors often need to help quantum teams navigate key strategic decisions, attract specialized talent, design partnership structures, and secure follow-on funding. In a field this technical and regulated, simply writing a check and waiting on quarterly updates is rarely enough.

Regulatory navigation

Every serious quantum investment decision now carries a regulatory dimension that cannot be ignored. Export controls, national security reviews, and differing rules across jurisdictions create a moving target that investors must understand in detail. In many cases, export compliance is the first and most pressing hurdle.

Knowing how national security review processes work, such as those that can add months to deal timelines or attach conditions to foreign participation, is critical for structuring transactions efficiently. Failing to anticipate these requirements can derail carefully negotiated deals or limit how investors can engage with a company after the fact.

Staying ahead of these shifts means building a habit of continuous regulatory awareness, monitoring policy changes, participating in industry groups that engage with policymakers, and maintaining relationships with advisors or authorities who understand the nuances of quantum-related rules.

Financial modeling for quantum investments

Financial modeling in quantum requires comfort with uncertainty and tools that can accommodate it. Traditional discounted cash flow models struggle when both the timing and scale of future revenues are highly speculative, as is often the case in quantum.

More suitable approaches treat investments as a series of options – rights, but not obligations – to commit additional capital or pivot as new information emerges. Real options thinking fits naturally here, framing quantum investments as staged commitments rather than all-or-nothing bets.

Techniques like Monte Carlo simulation also become especially valuable. By exploring thousands of potential paths for technical progress, market growth, and competitive responses, these models generate probability distributions instead of single-point forecasts, giving decision-makers a more realistic view of possible outcomes.

Partnership negotiations

Because quantum progress frequently hinges on collaboration between companies, universities, labs, and governments, partnership negotiations are a core skill rather than a side task. These arrangements are often complex, reflecting long timelines, high technical uncertainty, and nontrivial regulatory constraints.

Effective structuring must address multiple dimensions at once: who owns which intellectual property, how it can be licensed or reused, how costs and risks are shared, how decisions get made, and how eventual benefits are divided. Getting these elements wrong can limit flexibility or create friction just when projects need agility.

Negotiating with different partner types adds another layer of nuance. Quantum startups may prioritize capital, customers, and credibility but worry about losing control. Research institutions value scientific impact, publication rights, and student opportunities. Government agencies often focus on national interest and security. Recognizing and respecting these differing priorities is key to building durable relationships.

Market intelligence gathering

Finally, effective quantum investing depends on a very particular kind of market intelligence. Standard market research tools, surveys, historical comps, and mature-industry benchmarking offer limited value when both the technology and its markets are still taking shape.

Instead, investors often look to forward-looking indicators, such as patterns in patent activity, as early signals of where research focus and competitive energy are shifting. Patent filings can reveal technical directions that may not yet be reflected in product announcements or marketing materials.

Equally important is cultivating a strong network across the quantum community. Trusted relationships with researchers, founders, corporate innovators, and fellow investors provide insights and context that never make it into public reports. In a domain where the frontier moves quickly, these informal information channels can make the difference between reacting late and positioning ahead of the curve.

Summary

Quantum technology investment sits at the intersection of extraordinary promise and real complexity. The choices that executives, investors, and policymakers make today will shape who leads in quantum-enabled industries for decades, even though many of the key variables, winning technologies, first breakout applications, and market trajectories are still very much in motion. Throughout this chapter, we've focused on how to move forward confidently in the face of that uncertainty. We've explored how capital flows into quantum, from government programs and research funding to venture capital, corporate initiatives, and strategic partnerships, and how these can be combined into hybrid funding models that match the unique risk profile and timelines of quantum technologies.

We've also looked at the guardrails that quietly but powerfully shape what is possible. Export controls, national security reviews, and cross-border regulations influence how deals are structured, which collaborations are viable, and how technologies can be shared internationally. Alongside this, we've examined how to construct quantum portfolios that balance different technologies, business models, and time horizons, reducing dependence on any single technical bet or market scenario.

Just as important, we've surfaced the human capabilities that underpin successful quantum strategies. These include portfolio management tuned to quantum's long development cycles, regulatory fluency across overlapping jurisdictions, financial modeling designed for deep uncertainty, partnership negotiation suited to complex, long-lived collaborations, and market intelligence practices that keep leaders close to both technical progress and emerging demand.

The broader quantum landscape will continue to evolve. Technologies that appear dominant today may encounter unforeseen limits, while applications that seem distant might reach commercial relevance sooner than expected. Regulatory frameworks will adapt as governments deepen their understanding of quantum's strategic implications. In this environment, advantage rests with leaders who stay curious, cultivate strong networks, and maintain enough strategic flexibility to pivot as the picture changes.

As you move ahead, it's worth acknowledging that perfect information will never be available, and that's not a flaw; it's a feature of frontier innovation. The goal is not to predict a single "winner," but to design portfolios and positions that can benefit from quantum progress across many possible futures. The frameworks, examples, and skills discussed in this chapter are meant to provide just enough structure to support confident decision-making without ignoring the uncertainty that defines the field.

That also raises an important question: who should you surround yourself with as your organization becomes quantum ready? For many organizations, the answer will be a mix of internal leaders, technical specialists, academic partners, vendors, and outside advisors rather than a single consultant or firm. When evaluating external partners, look beyond quantum credentials alone. The strongest partners should be able to connect quantum technology to your industry, business model, risk profile, and investment priorities. Useful competencies include hands-on experience with quantum computing or quantum-safe security, a vendor-neutral understanding of the broader ecosystem, experience building business cases and ROI models, familiarity with regulatory and cybersecurity requirements, the ability to translate technical concepts for executives, and a track record of developing internal capabilities rather than creating long-term dependence on outside expertise.

A good partner should also be comfortable telling you when not to invest. Ask prospective advisors how they evaluate use cases, what evidence they use to distinguish realistic opportunities from hype, how they compare quantum approaches with the best available classical alternatives, and how they measure success at each stage of a program. Look for experience working across technology, strategy, finance, security, and workforce development, as quantum readiness rarely belongs to a single department. References, prior implementations, industry experience, relationships across academia and the vendor ecosystem, and an ability to establish clear decision gates can all be more valuable than affiliation with any particular quantum platform. The objective is not simply to hire someone who understands quantum; it's to find partners who can help your organization build the judgment and skills to eventually make these decisions for itself.

With that foundation in place, the natural next step is to focus on the people who will actually execute these strategies. The next chapter turns from capital and structures to leadership and teams, how to navigate the quantum talent landscape, build an advisory board with the right mix of expertise, choose organizational models that integrate quantum into your core business, and manage the cultural change that comes with embracing a new computing paradigm. Ultimately, success in quantum will depend not only on where you invest, but on whom you empower, how you retain them, and how you support their growth over time.

Further reading

1. `https://quantum-journal.org/papers/q-2018-08-06-79/`
2. `https://www.ibm.com/quantum/blog/ibm-quantum-roadmap`
3. `https://www.ida.org/research-and-publications/publications/all/a/as/assessment-of-the-future-economic-impact-of-quantum-information-science`
4. `https://www.mckinsey.com/capabilities/tech-and-ai/our-insights/tech-forward/quantum-technology-investment-hits-a-magic-moment`
5. `https://quantumcomputingreport.com/quantonation-secures-novo-holdings-investment-in-quantum-venture-fund-ii/`
6. `https://www.congress.gov/bill/115th-congress/house-bill/6227`
7. `https://qt.eu/`
8. `https://itif.org/publications/2024/09/09/how-innovative-is-china-in-quantum/`

9. https://www.nature.com/articles/s41586-020-03093-8
10. https://www.federalregister.gov/documents/2022/12/07/2022-26662/implementation-of-additional-export-controls-certain-advanced-computing-and-semiconductor
11. https://home.treasury.gov/policy-issues/international/the-committee-on-foreign-investment-in-the-united-states-cfius
12. https://www.sbir.gov/sites/default/files/SBA_FY22_SBIR_STTR_Annual_Report.pdf
13. https://www.ibm.com/quantum/ibm-quantum-network
14. https://www.ibm.com/quantum/hardware#roadmap
15. https://www.ionq.com/news/october-01-2021-ionq-listed-on-nyse
16. https://www.ionq.com/quantum-cloud
17. https://www.quantinuum.com/press-releases/introducing-quantinuum
18. https://www.nature.com/articles/s41586-019-1666-5
19. https://quantumai.google/
20. https://www.quantum-machines.co/solutions/quantum-computing-at-scale/

3

Building Your Quantum Leadership Team

Picture this: you're in a boardroom on a Monday morning fresh from a nice relaxing weekend with friends and family. The CTO just announced that your company needs to hire a quantum computational scientist. Your CFO's color then drains as they mentally tally the salary range, and your Head of HR quickly opens LinkedIn, discovering that there are roughly a dozen people worldwide who match the job description. Welcome to the toughest and most strategic part of quantum leadership: building your team.

The quantum talent crunch isn't a distant worry; it's already here! As of 2024, the global quantum workforce amounted to around 30,000 professionals. Projections suggested more than half of the quantum jobs likely remained unfilled by 2025.[1] It's daunting, yes, but understanding the landscape is the first step toward navigating it.

This chapter tackles the question every forward-thinking executive eventually faces: how do you actually build a quantum team when everyone else wants the same talent? We'll look beyond the obvious challenge of recruiting PhDs and get into the deeper structural questions that shape success. How do you prevent your quantum team from becoming an isolated ivory tower? How do you balance centralized expertise with distributed innovation? And how on earth do you pay for it without breaking your compensation model?

Building a quantum team isn't simply about hiring brilliant physicists; it's about constructing an ecosystem where quantum and classical expertise coexist. The organizations that thrive don't just add "quantum" to their job descriptions: they build quantum-ready cultures that merge applied science, product thinking, and business foresight.

Main topics and key insights covered in this chapter are:

- Understanding the quantum talent landscape

- Designing your quantum organization
- Organizational decision trees
- Quantum company spotlights: IBM, Quantum Machines
- Building your quantum advisory board

Understanding the quantum talent landscape

Let's begin with some straight talk about what you're walking into. The quantum job market isn't just competitive; it's arguably the most demanding global talent arena in all of technology right now. Roles with "quantum" in the title have jumped by roughly 180% between 2020 and 2024, with more than 8,400 open positions by mid-2024. The punchline? Only about 10-15% of applicants show up with the specialized skills employers actually need.[2]

The problem goes far beyond raw numbers. Universities are still wired for a world where physics and computer science live in separate silos. In 2019, when 50 quantum researchers from the U.S. and Europe came together, their verdict was blunt: there are physics programs and computer science programs, but very few that truly integrate the two, let alone add business and leadership training on top.[3] The situation has improved only marginally since, and certainly not fast enough to match industry demand.[4, 5]

OK, so now that you have a little insight into the current talent landscape, let's dig into why the quantum talent pool is so hard to find. There are a few compounding factors at play here:

- Deep technical barriers: Quantum computing demands real mastery of quantum mechanics, not just a few online tutorials. You can't bluff your way through superposition and entanglement.
- Interdisciplinary requirements: The strongest quantum professionals blend physics, computer science, mathematics, and increasingly domain expertise in areas like finance, chemistry, or logistics.
- Long training periods: Developing genuine quantum fluency takes years of focused work. There is no three-month bootcamp that turns someone into a quantum architect.
- Global competition: Governments and industry are pouring billions into quantum programs, intensifying the battle for a limited pool of experts and pushing salaries steadily upward.[3]

But wait! There is some good news! The quantum talent landscape is broader than most executives realize. Yes, you'll need a handful of quantum computational scientists, but the real power comes from assembling a portfolio of roles that together form your quantum capability, not just a row of PhD badges. Let's take a look at the broader landscape.

The quantum talent ecosystem: beyond the PhD

One of the most stubborn myths in quantum hiring is that you need a bench full of quantum physics PhDs before you can do anything meaningful. That mindset does two kinds of damage: it shrinks your potential talent pool, and it leads to teams that are brilliant on paper but struggle to ship anything commercially relevant.

Multiple industry analyses now converge on the same insights, where a majority of quantum roles do not actually require a PhD. IBM and others have highlighted that as the field matures, more of the work sits in engineering, software, and product layers where advanced degrees are useful but not mandatory.[6] With that in mind, it's helpful to think of your quantum workforce as a balanced ecosystem. Let's delve into a range of roles that may be ideal for a quantum talent portfolio. Note that all salaries and estimates are based on the time of this writing and in USD; a link to the sources will be provided. However, these salaries seem conservative, particularly as the increase in opportunities grows while the scarcity of talent stays the same.

Quantum research scientists (PhD level)

These are your theory heavyweights, those who live and breathe algorithm design, error corrections, and long-term architectural thinking. They usually come with PhDs in physics, computer science, or mathematics with a quantum focus, and they anchor your most advanced R&D efforts.

Salary range: Typically, in the $200k-$350k+ band, depending on experience and location, with senior staff at leading tech companies sometimes crossing $400k when equity is included.[7]

Reality check: Unless you are a quantum hardware or platform company, you probably need no more than one to three of these roles. Beyond that, you risk overweighting theory while underinvesting in people who can turn concepts into workable and viable products.

Quantum hardware engineers

Hardware engineers are the builders of the actual quantum machines, designing superconducting circuits, trapped-ion systems, or photonic architectures, along with the cryogenic and control electronics that keep everything running. They draw on backgrounds in electrical engineering, cryogenics, RF/microwave engineering, and optics, depending on their chosen qubit modality.

Salary range: Mid-level roles tend to land in the $180k-300k+ range,[8] with demand climbing as more companies attempt to stand up or maintain physical quantum systems. This is particularly true in countries or regions that are focused on building their own quantum systems and not being dependent on other external entities, which coincidentally is where a growing number of my clients are focusing, in an effort to build a strong workforce and an economic powerhouse.

Reality check: If you aren't manufacturing quantum hardware or running a dedicated lab, you probably don't need these roles in-house. You'll consume quantum hardware through cloud access from providers like IBM, IonQ, D-Wave, and many others.

Quantum software engineers

This is where most organizations will find their real hiring leverage. Quantum software engineers write algorithms, build applications, and create the glue that connects quantum backends to classical systems, including integrating these systems into existing workflows and processes. They bring strong programming skills (often in Python, C/C++, or specialized quantum languages), a working understanding of quantum principles, and fluency with SDKs like Qiskit (Quantum Information Science Kit), Cirq, or Amazon Braket.

Salary range: Generally $130k-$200k+ depending on experience and geography, with entry-level quantum developers earning 20-40% more than their classical software peers in many markets.[9]

Reality check: This should be your primary hiring focus. These engineers are the bridge between theoretical capability and business application. In practice, most organizations will benefit more from hiring three to ten quantum software engineers before they add a second research scientist.

Quantum business translators

This is the role that rarely shows up on the headcount plans and quietly determines whether your quantum initiative ever generates ROI. Quantum business translators speak both languages: they understand enough of the technology to be credible with scientists and enough of the business to frame use cases, prioritize investments, and communicate value.

Salary range: Often between $200k-$300k, with many coming from consulting, product management, strategy, or technical business development roles.

Reality check: Treat this as a core hire, not a "nice to have." A world-class technical team without someone to translate their work into business outcomes is just an expensive science experiment. As a rule of thumb, bring in at least one strong business translator before you hire your third quantum researcher.

Framework 1: Quantum talent assessment matrix

Not all quantum candidates are created equal, and the traditional technical interview process often misses critical dimensions of quantum readiness. This assessment framework helps you evaluate candidates across five key dimensions: technical depth, breadth of knowledge, business acumen, cultural fit, and growth potential.

How to use this framework: Rate candidates on each dimension using a 1-4 scale. A candidate should score at least 3 in their primary competency area (e.g., technical depth for research scientists) and at least 2 in all other areas. Total scores provide a quick comparison tool, but pay attention to the pattern; you want balanced strengths, not just high numbers.

Assessment Dimension	**Evaluation Criteria & Questions**	**Score (1–4)**
Technical Depth	Can they explain quantum concepts clearly? Do they understand limitations? Ask: • "Explain quantum superposition to a business executive." • "What problems can't quantum computers solve?" • "Describe a quantum algorithm you've worked with."	
Breadth of Knowledge	"Do they understand the quantum ecosystem?" "Awareness of different approaches?" Ask: • "What are the tradeoffs between different qubit technologies?" • "Name three companies doing interesting quantum work and why." • "How do you stay current with quantum developments?"	

Assessment Dimension	Evaluation Criteria & Questions	Score (1–4)
Business Acumen	Can they connect quantum capabilities to business value? Understanding of practical constraints? Ask: • "How would you identify quantum use cases for our industry?" • "What makes a good quantum computing investment today?" • "How do you balance research exploration vs. business needs?"	
Cultural Fit and Collaboration	Can they work with non-quantum teams? Communication style? Team player? Ask: • "Describe a time you explained complex concepts to non-experts." • "How do you handle disagreements with colleagues?" • "Tell us about a failed project and what you learned."	
Growth Potential	Learning agility? Adaptability > Long-term trajectory? Ask: • "What quantum topics are you currently learning?" • "Where do you want your quantum career to be in 5 years?" • "How do you approach learning new quantum frameworks?"	

Assessment Dimension	Evaluation Criteria & Questions	Score (1–4)
Scoring Guide:	1 = Weak/Concerning 2 = Adequate/Developing 3 = Strong/Proficient 4 = Exceptional/Expert	Total: _ / 20

Interpretation guide:

- 16-20 points = Strong hire for senior roles
- 12-15 points = Solid hire for mid-level roles
- 10-11 points = Consider hiring for junior roles with mentorship
- Below 10 points = High risk, unless specific circumstances justify the hire

Designing your quantum organization: integration models that actually work

Let's assume you've won a few battles in the talent war and brought some quantum professionals on board. The next question is deceptively simple: where do these people actually sit? This just isn't a box on an org chart; it's a strategic design decision that will determine whether your quantum team creates business value or disappears into the "cool science, no impact" bucket.

In practice, I see three primary integration models, each with its own strengths and painful trade-offs. The right choice depends on your stage of maturity, number of quantum staff, and how far quantum has progressed from experimentation to production in your business. Let's now examine each model, when it works and when it doesn't.

Model 1: The centralized quantum centre of excellence

In this model, all quantum professionals report into a single, dedicated quantum organization, often under the CTO or a Chief Quantum Officer (Ah, now THAT's a cool title! Sorry, I digressed). The quantum team operates as a shared service, taking requests from various business units and building quantum solutions centrally.

Advantages:

- Deep technical expertise: Quantum professionals work alongside other quantum experts, accelerating learning and maintaining technical rigor
- Resource efficiency: You can flex quantum resources across multiple projects and business units rather than duplicating expertise
- Clear career paths: Quantum professionals see obvious advancement opportunities within the quantum organization
- Standards and best practices: Centralized teams can establish consistent approaches to quantum development, tooling, and methodologies

Disadvantages:

- Business unit misalignment: Quantum team can become disconnected from actual business problems, building technically impressive solutions that nobody needs
- Ivory tower syndrome: The quantum team becomes viewed as an elite, isolated group that speaks an incomprehensible language
- Priority conflicts: When multiple business units compete for quantum resources, political battles emerge over who gets quantum support
- Slow response time: Central teams often struggle with bureaucracy and ticketing systems that slow down business unit requests

When this model works: Early-stage quantum initiatives (first 1–2 years), small quantum teams (under 10 people), or organizations where quantum applications are still exploratory rather than business-critical or not yet tied directly to P&L.

Model 2: The distributed embedded model

In this approach, quantum professionals are embedded directly within business units, one quantum expert in supply chain, another in R&D, a third in finance, and so on. They report to business unit leaders, not a central quantum organization.

Advantages:

- Strong business alignment: Quantum experts live close to the problems, priorities, and metrics that matter
- Fast iteration: There's no central ticket queue; quantum professionals collaborate directly with their stakeholders
- Cultural integration: Quantum becomes part of how the business unit operates, not an external service
- Clear impact visibility: It's easier to see quantum's contribution to specific P&L lines

Disadvantages:

- Technical isolation: Individual quantum practitioners may lack peers for code reviews, idea exchange, and skill development
- Duplicate effort: Different units may reinvent the same wheels, platform choices, libraries, or even basic tooling
- Inconsistent standards: Each unit might adopt its own frameworks, increasing technical debt and integration headaches
- Career development ambiguity: In some business units, there's no obvious path for someone whose expertise is niche and highly technical

When this model works: More mature quantum programs with clear, repeatable use cases; businesses where individual units already have strong technical cultures, or scenarios where quantum applications are highly domain-specific and need deep local context.

Model 3: The hybrid Hub-and-Spoke model (recommended)

This model combines the best of centralized and distributed approaches. A small, centralized quantum center of excellence (the 'hub') provides technical leadership, platform management, and shared resources. Quantum application developers (the 'spokes') embed within the business units but maintain dotted-line reporting to the central quantum team.

How it works in practice:

- Central hub responsibilities: Selecting and managing platforms, owning advanced algorithm R&D, setting standards, running training, and maintaining shared quantum infrastructure
- Embedded spoke responsibilities: Identifying use cases within their business unit, developing and deploying applications, managing local stakeholders, and tracking ROI
- Connection mechanisms: Regular internal quantum meetups, shared communication channels, quarterly technical working sessions, and rotation opportunities between hub and business units

Advantages:

- Balanced depth and alignment: You gain strong technical coherence without losing proximity to business needs
- Community for practitioners: Embedded staff still feel part of a broader quantum tribe, not isolated specialists

- Natural knowledge sharing: Lessons from one business unit can propagate through the hub to others
- Dual career paths: People can grow either as deep technical experts (hub) or as business-facing specialists (spokes)

Disadvantages:

- ***Matrix complexity***: Dual reporting structures can create tension around priorities and performance evaluation.
- ***Governance overhead***: The hub leaders need real authority to set standards without becoming a bottleneck.
- ***Coordination overhead***: Maintaining alignment between hub and spokes takes time, processes, and sustained leadership attention.

When this model works: Once you have 10+ quantum professionals, multiple active use cases across the business, and a shift from pure experimentation to production pilots and early products. For most organizations past their first year or two of exploration, this is the model I generally recommend.

Framework 2: Organizational integration decision tree

Use this decision tree to determine which organizational model fits your current situation. Start at the top and follow the path based on your honest answers.

Decision Point	If YES	If NO
Do you have 10+ quantum professionals?	Proceed to the next question	Centralized Model (team too small for a distributed model)
Do you have quantum use cases in 3+ business units?	Proceed to the next question	Centralized Model (insufficient demand for the distributed model)
Are quantum initiatives business critical (not exploratory)?	Proceed to the next question	Centralized Model (exploration phase, still discovering applications)
Is your org comfortable with matrix reporting?	Hybrid Hub-and-Spoke Model (best of both worlds)	Proceed to the next question

Decision Point	If YES	If NO
Do you have a strong technical culture in business units?	Distributed Embedded Model (business units can support quantum professionals)	Centralized Model (quantum professionals need stronger central, dedicated technical leadership)

One final point: none of these structures is permanent. Most organizations start centralized in years 1-2, move into a hybrid hub-and-spoke pattern around years 3-5, and may eventually lean more distributed as quantum becomes a standard part of everyday technology operations. Revisit this decision tree at least annually as your quantum portfolio and headcount evolve.

Quantum team building in action

To make all of this a bit more concrete, let's look at how five different players, ranging from incumbents to fast-growing specialists, are building their quantum workforce. Their approaches illustrate how strategy, scale, and history shape very different organizational choices. We'll start with a startup that invested in growing top talent long before the first brick was put down in fabrication.

Quantum Machines: Hardware-agnostic excellence

Quantum Machines, headquartered in Tel-Aviv, represents a different kind of quantum workforce story: a company built around deep expertise in quantum control and orchestration that underpins the entire quantum ecosystem, rather than a single hardware platform. Founded in 2018 by quantum electronics specialists, the company now supports more than half of the world's quantum efforts with its control stack, a remarkable reach for a firm that doesn't build its own quantum processor! That hardware-agnostic stance isn't just a product decision; it's a people strategy.

After closing a $170 million funding round in early 2025, led by PSG Equity and Intel Capital, Quantum Machines made it clear that headcount growth was not an afterthought but a central pillar of its plan.[10] The company is scaling research and development, product, and go-to-market teams in parallel, while expanding its footprint beyond Israel into additional global hubs. That balance between engineering and commercial hiring reflects a simple insight: in quantum, it's not enough to build great tools; you have to bring them into the hands of customers at the right time, in the right way.

Israel's quantum environment amplifies both the opportunity and the competition. A rapidly growing cluster of quantum research groups and startups has turned the country into a dense, high-talent ecosystem, but also into a fiercely contested recruiting ground. Quantum Machines taps into a uniquely Israeli blend of academic excellence and defense-linked systems engineering: many of its specialists bring experience from elite military technology units where complex, mission-critical control systems are the norm. That background maps naturally onto quantum control, where reliability and precision are non-negotiable.

Internally, the company designs its workforce around cross-functional breadth because its products must work across superconducting, trapped-ion, neutral-atom, and emerging architectures. Quantum Machines can't afford engineers who only understand one qubit modality in isolation. Instead, it hires strong generalists in control theory, signal processing, embedded systems, and software architecture, then layers quantum-specific training on top. This approach dramatically widens the talent pipeline and reduces dependence on the time pool of PhD-level quantum physicists, without sacrificing technological rigor.

Key lesson for executives: If you're building platforms, infrastructure, or tooling rather than your own quantum hardware, you can win by hiring top-tier generalist engineers and teaching them quantum, rather than fighting everyone else for the same handful of PhDs. Locating in dense quantum ecosystems can accelerate learning and partnerships, but you'll need a compelling narrative and culture to stand out in competitive markets. Most importantly, invest in commercial talent early: platform success depends as much on adoption and integration as on exquisite engineering.

IBM Quantum: Full-stack quantum ecosystem leader

IBM has been investing in quantum longer than almost anyone, and you can see it in the depth and breadth of their talent strategy. With multiple hardware locations worldwide and dozens of open quantum roles at any given time, IBM has assembled one of the most comprehensive internal quantum teams in the industry.

What stands out is not just size but intentional diversity of roles. IBM's quantum organization spans hardware engineers working on superconducting qubits, software developers extending the Qiskit stack, application scientists building vertical use cases, and business-facing staff who translate those capabilities into customer value. In other words, they've built a full-stack quantum workforce rather than a research-only lab.[11]

Their talent pipeline is equally multi-layered. IBM maintains deep relationships with universities for PhD recruiting and runs formal internship programs that bring students into their labs. At the same time, they use platforms like IBM Quantum Platform [12] and Qiskit education [13] to grow a broader community of quantum-literate developers who can progress into more specialized roles over time.

IBM has also been candid about the talent bottleneck itself. In their 2024 quantum readiness study, they identified talent shortage as the single largest hurdle for enterprises, with average readiness scores still low. That openness reflects a recognition that no single company can solve the talent gap alone; it requires ecosystem-level investment in education and training. [14]

Key lesson for executives: Don't stop at hiring a few star researchers. Think in terms of a full-stack quantum organization, multiple talent pipelines, and broad upskilling. Treat workforce development as a strategic pillar, not an afterthought.

PsiQuantum: Manufacturing-scale ambition through public-private partnerships

PsiQuantum is one of the most ambitious bets on large-scale quantum computing in the United States. Founded in 2016 and headquartered in Palo Alto, the company is building large-scale quantum computing systems using silicon photonics rather than superconducting or trapped-ion qubits. In 2025, Illinois broke ground on the Illinois Quantum and Microelectronics Park (IQMP) on Chicago's South Side,[15] with PsiQuantum as the anchor tenant committed to building what is billed as the first utility-scale, error-corrected photonic quantum computer at the site.[16] This move positions PsiQuantum not just as a research player but as a cornerstone of U.S. quantum manufacturing infrastructure,[17] tying its growth directly to regional economic development and workforce creation.[18]

From a workforce perspective, PsiQuantum operates with a manufacturing-first mindset rather than a pure research lab model. By mid-2025, the company employed roughly 321 people, with about 150 in engineering roles – nearly half the organization – alongside business management, IT, operations, and customer-facing teams.[19] Its technology strategy hinges on a long-standing partnership with GlobalFoundries, where PsiQuantum's silicon photonic chips are fabricated on standard 300mm semiconductor lines, leveraging existing high-volume manufacturing processes instead of bespoke quantum-only facilities. That choice shapes hiring: the company recruits semiconductor process engineers, photonics and packaging specialists, and cryogenic and systems expertise on top of that base. In practice, PsiQuantum is hiring as much from the semiconductor and telecom worlds as from traditional physics departments.

The Illinois project illustrates how public-private collaboration can underpin quantum workforce development at scale. State and local partners are investing heavily in site preparation, shared cryogenic infrastructure, and workforce programs to support IQMP, with the park expected to generate thousands of jobs over time across construction, maintenance, research, and advanced manufacturing. PsiQuantum's planned facility, roughly 300,000 square feet in early phases, will require teams spanning plant operations, health and safety, facilities engineering, and supply-chain management in addition to quantum and photonics specialists.[20] The company is also plugged into a broader Chicago ecosystem that includes IBM, Diraq, Infleqtion, and regional universities, creating shared talent pipelines and giving employees exposure to multiple quantum modalities, not just photonics.

PsiQuantum's dual-geography footprint adds another layer of complexity and opportunity to its talent strategy. While its largest concentration of staff remains in California, with over 150 employees in San Francisco alone, the company already maintains smaller teams in Chicago, the UK, and other U.S. tech hubs, plus more than a hundred distributed staff working remotely. As the Illinois facility scales, PsiQuantum will effectively operate with R&D and design anchored in Silicon Valley and high-volume manufacturing and systems integration rooted in the Midwest.

Key lesson for executives: Manufacturing-scale quantum programs require a different kind of leadership and hiring strategy than research-centric efforts. You need to recruit from semiconductor fabs, complex industrial operations, and large-scale infrastructure projects, then use public-private partnerships to co-invest in the training, shared facilities, and regional ecosystems that make a million-qubit roadmap credible rather than aspirational.[21]

IQM Quantum Computers: European hardware excellence through cross-border collaboration

IQM Quantum Computers, based in Finland, is a case study in how to build a pan-European quantum hardware organization without losing focus. From its headquarters near Helsinki, IQM has grown to more than 300 employees spread across five European countries: Finland, Germany, France, Spain, and Poland, while also extending its presence to Singapore, South Korea, Japan, and the United States. Rather than trying to centralize everything in one city, IQM has deliberately designed a distributed workforce that mirrors Europe's strengths.

The company's late-2025 announcement of a €40 million expansion to its Finnish production facility tells you a lot about its ambitions.[22] The upgraded site, spanning more than 8,000 square meters, is built to assemble over 30 full-stack quantum computers per year, a scale that moves IQM from prototyping into genuine manufacturing territory.[23] Achieving that shift requires more than smart theorists: it demands production engineers, test and validation teams, quality assurance specialists, supply chain leaders, and manufacturing technicians who know how to make complex systems reliable and repeatable.

IQM's "secret sauce" lies in how it maps roles to regions. Quantum algorithm and software research clusters around Munich, Germany, where it can tap into Germany's strong academic ecosystem and industrial base. Customer-facing roles in France and Spain keep the company close to major enterprise and government buyers across southern and western Europe.[24] Meanwhile, Finland remains the heart of hardware development and production, leveraging Nordic strengths in precision manufacturing and engineering discipline. The result is a genuinely integrated, multi-country operation that uses digital collaboration as a standard practice rather than an afterthought.

Beyond its internal structure, IQM has taken a visible public stance on the quantum talent issue. In its 2025 State of Quantum report, produced with Omdia, the company highlighted talent shortages and immature software platforms as two of the biggest structural risks to the industry's progress.[25] By naming the problem so clearly, IQM positions itself not just as a hardware vendor but as a thought leader shaping the broader workforce conversation. That posture helps attract candidates who are motivated to work on the ecosystem as well as the technology itself.

Key lesson for executives: If your quantum strategy is hardware-intensive, build your workforce plan around the entire value chain, not just the lab. You'll need manufacturing, quality, and operations talent alongside physicists and algorithm designers. Multi-country structures can unlock access to specialized regional skill pools and create resilience against local bottlenecks. And sometimes, talking openly about industry-wide constraints, like the talent gap, can strengthen your employer brand by signaling honesty, ambition, and a commitment to solving hard systemic problems.

Pasqal: Rapid scale-up through mission-driven culture

Pasqal, a French leader in neutral-atom quantum computing, shows how a mission-driven scale-up can compete for world-class talent without the balance sheet of a hyperscaler. Founded in 2019 by Nobel laureate Alain Aspect and fellow researchers, the company has expanded from roughly 50 employees in 2022 to more than 300 by 2025. That six-fold growth in just a few years reflects both the momentum of neutral-atom technology and a deliberate strategy for attracting people who are deeply passionate about where quantum is headed.

At the heart of Pasqal's hiring narrative is a simple promise: join us to build the "second quantum revolution."[26] Rather than selling roles purely on salary or prestige, the company consistently frames its work as foundational, something that will reshape computing, industry, and science. That framing resonates with candidates who are motivated by impact and purpose, especially in Europe, where many high-caliber researchers face a choice between joining deep-tech ventures like Pasqal or staying in academic labs. The connection to Nobel-winning science lends credibility: this is not just a startup with a big slide deck; it's anchored in decades of fundamental research.

Pasqal's talent strategy is built around vertical integration. Instead of specializing in a single layer, the company develops much of the stack itself: atomic physics, laser and optical systems, control electronics, classical and quantum software, and industry-specific applications. That means it hires across a wide range of profiles, from experimental physicists and photonics engineers to software developers and application scientists, and encourages movement between teams. For employees, this creates unusual career mobility: you can start close to the lab and later shift toward applications or customer work without having to leave the company.

Fueled by a nine-figure Series B round, Pasqal has also expanded beyond France into the Middle East, Asia, other parts of Europe, and North America.[27] Each new office serves as both a talent magnet and a customer bridge, placing teams near key industrial partners like BMW, BASF, Siemens, and Airbus. Those partnerships are not just logos on a slide; they give Pasqal's staff a steady stream of real-world optimization, simulation, and materials problems to work on. For commercially oriented scientists and engineers, that combination – cutting-edge physics plus direct industrial impact – is a powerful draw.

Key lesson for executives: A clear, authentic mission and a strong scientific foundation can help smaller or mid-sized players attract and retain top quantum talent, even when they cannot simply outbid larger competitors. Building full-stack capabilities in-house creates rich internal career paths and reduces the risk of losing people who want new challenges. Strategic partnerships with major industrial players give quantum professionals meaningful, real-world problems to tackle, turning your company into a place where they can both advance science and see their work matter in the market.

Framework 3: Quantum compensation planning matrix

Now to the question that keeps every CFO and CHRO awake: what does it actually cost to build a quantum team? The reality is that quantum roles command a premium over comparable classical tech positions, and simple salary bands don't tell the whole story.

The matrix below reflects typical 2024-2025 U.S. ranges across roles and levels, drawing on aggregated market data from public salary platforms and specialized quantum job boards.[28] Again, these are all based on the time of this writing.[29, 30, 31]

Role Type	Entry Level (0-2 yrs)	Mid Level (3-7 yrs)	Senior (8+ yrs)	Typical Equity
Quantum Research Scientist	$150K–$250K	$250K–$300K	$300K–$400K+	0.1–0.5%
Quantum Software Engineer	$130K–$150K	$150K–$200K	$200K–$300K	0.05–0.3%
Quantum Hardware Engineer	$140K–$160K	$130K–$180K	$170K–$300K	0.05–0.3%
Quantum Business Translator	$85K–$120K	$110K–$160K	$150K–$220K	0.03–0.2%

Role Type	Entry Level (0-2 yrs)	Mid Level (3-7 yrs)	Senior (8+ yrs)	Typical Equity
Quantum Algorithm Developer	\$95K–\$140K	\$135K–\$200K	\$180K–\$300K	0.05–0.3%

Geographic multipliers: These ranges are anchored to U.S. markets, with the highest level typically in the Bay Area, Boston, and Seattle. As a rough guide, you might apply multipliers of 0.9-1.0x for New York, 0.85-0.95x for hubs like Austin or Denver, 0.75-0.90x for major European cities, and 0.65-0.85x across much of Asia-Pacific.[32]

Beyond base salary: Competitive packages in quantum usually layer in equity, annual bonuses, often in the 10-20% range of base, dedicated budgets for conferences and travel, support for publications, and structured time for research or learning. Put together, these non-cash elements can add 20-40% to the perceived value of an offer, and they speak directly to what many quantum professionals care about: impact, visibility, and growth.

Building your quantum advisory board: strategic guidance that actually matters

Here's a humbling but important reality: even if you've been in technology for decades, you probably don't know enough about quantum to navigate it entirely on instinct. Believe me, after decades of innovation, I too find it difficult myself. That's of course not a knock on your experience, far from it. It's a reflection of how specialized and fast-moving this field is.

A well-constructed quantum advisory board gives you access to hard-won expertise without having to hire every specialist full-time. The trap, however, is treating the board as a branding exercise: a list of impressive names and titles that look good on a slide but rarely show up in the actual decision-making process. To avoid that, you need to be intentional about who you bring in and what you ask them to do, as well as be empowered and agile in order to respond to any technical and market dynamics.

The three pillars of effective quantum advisory boards

An effective quantum advisory board typically blends three kinds of voices, each adding a different lens:

1. Technical thought leaders: Senior researchers or practitioners who understand the frontier of algorithms, hardware, and architecture, and can keep you grounded in what's technically real versus hype

2. Industry and commercialization experts: Leaders who've taken advanced technologies to market before, ideally in quantum or adjacent deep-tech fields, and can advise on business models, partnerships, and go-to-market timing
3. Strategic business advisors: Seasoned executives or board members who can connect your quantum ambitions to corporate strategy, risk appetite, and capital allocation, ensuring quantum doesn't become a disconnected science project

The most effective boards meet regularly, often quarterly, get real materials and metrics in advance, and are treated as working partners rather than ceremonial reviewers. In return, they help you pressure-test your roadmap, avoid costly missteps, and plug into broader ecosystems of talent, research collaborators, and early customers.

Summary

Building a quantum leadership team right now is one of the hardest talent challenges in technology. With an estimated 30,000 qualified professionals worldwide and demand heading toward 1 million roles by 2030, the talent gap is already constraining projects and timelines rather than looming as a distant threat.[33]

But the central message of this chapter is that winning in quantum talent isn't about hoarding PhDs. It's about understanding the full spectrum of roles, from research scientists to software engineers to business translators, and designing a team where technical excellence and commercial relevance reinforce each other. The organizations pulling ahead are not necessarily those with the biggest labs; they're the ones building ecosystems where quantum innovation is tightly coupled to business outcomes.

In this chapter, we've explored three organizational models: centralized centers of excellence, distributed embedded teams, and hybrid hub-and-spoke structures, and how each fits different stages of maturity. Over time, most organizations will move along this spectrum, starting centralized while they're learning, then adopting hybrid models as quantum becomes more tightly integrated with products and P&L.

On compensation, the reality is straightforward: quantum professionals command a premium, and trying to hire at a classical rate is a recipe for unfilled roles and fast turnover. Sustainable strategies pair competitive base salaries with equity, research time, publication support, and development opportunities that align with how quantum experts think about their careers.

Finally, advisory boards can be a quiet superpower when built thoughtfully. By combining deep technical insight, commercialization experience, and high-level strategic guidance, they help you steer through uncertainty, connect to the broader ecosystem, and avoid turning quantum into an isolated science experiment.

The quantum talent challenge is real, but it's far from hopeless. Leaders who approach it with intentional design, clear role definitions, smart org structures, realistic compensation, and the humility to bring in outside expertise when needed can assemble quantum teams that deliver meaningful business results. The key to choosing the right external partner. A strong consultant should bring more than technical quantum credentials; they should understand your industry, business model, risk profile, regulatory environment, and investment priorities, while remaining sufficiently vendor-neutral to recommend what is best for the organization rather than a particular platform. Look for partners who can translate technical complexity into executive decisions, build practical business cases, compare quantum approaches against strong classical alternatives, define measurable success criteria, and transfer knowledge to internal teams rather than creating long-term dependence. Just as importantly, they should be willing to say when a quantum initiative is too early, too costly, or simply not the right fit. As the quantum industry moves from research and development toward a greater commercial and capital intensity, the question is no longer only whether to engge, but how to build the right internal and external capabilities to govern that engagement responsibly. The next chapter will set the stage for treating quantum not as an experimental side effort, but as a strategically managed capability that demands disciplined oversight, informed risk-taking, and sustained stakeholder trust.

Further reading

1. `https://www.mckinsey.com/capabilities/tech-and-ai/our-insights/five-lessons-from-ai-on-closing-quantums-talent-gap-before-its-too-late`
2. `https://www.quantumjobs.us/post/are-quantum-computing-jobs-in-high-demand`
3. `https://www.vectorsynergy.com/post/the-global-quantum-talent-shortage`
4. `https://professional.uchicago.edu/stories/quantum-science-networking-and-communications/high-paying-quantum-tech-jobs-growing-fast?language_content_entity=en`
5. `https://mitsloan.mit.edu/ideas-made-to-matter/building-a-quantum-workforce`
6. `https://medium.com/qiskit/the-hitchhiking-cats-guide-to-getting-a-job-in-quantum-computing-da7e3bb9ff64`
7. `https://www.quantumjobs.us/post/are-quantum-computing-jobs-in-high-demand`
8. `https://www.quantumjobs.us/post/quantum-computing-salaries-a-comprehensive-guide`

9. https://thequantuminsider.com/2026/05/29/quantum-computing-jobs-and-salaries-in-2026/
10. https://www.timesofisrael.com/backed-by-intel-israeli-quantum-control-startup-pulls-in-170-million-investment/
11. https://www.ibm.com/quantum
12. https://quantum.cloud.ibm.com/
13. https://quantum.cloud.ibm.com/learning/en
14. https://www.ibm.com/thought-leadership/institute-business-value/en-us/report/2025-quantum-computing-readiness
15. https://iqmp.org/news/gov-pritzker-breaks-ground-on-illinois-quantum-and-microelectronics-park-iqmp/
16. https://www.forbes.com/sites/moorinsights/2024/08/21/psiquantum-is-closing-in-on-fault-tolerance-and-a-million-qubits/
17. https://news.uchicago.edu/story/groundbreaking-illinois-quantum-and-microelectronics-park-creates-anchor-quantum-innovation
18. https://tsginvest.com/psiquantum/
19. https://www.unifygtm.com/insights-headcount/psiquantum
20. https://thequantuminsider.com/2025/11/09/phase-one-construction-begins-on-chicago-quantum-computing-facility/
21. https://www.sourcery.vc/p/breaking-psiquantums-1b-series-e
22. https://meetiqm.com/press-releases/iqm-to-invest-over-e40-million-to-expand-finland-production-facility-accelerate-innovation-and-fuel-growth/
23. https://www.fairedih.fi/en/2025/11/26/quantum-computing-firm-iqm-announces-e40-million-finnish-facility-expansion/
24. https://iqm.teamtailor.com/
25. https://www.businesswire.com/news/home/20250610552224/en/IQMs-State-of-Quantum-2025-Quantum-Industry-Must-Solve-Talent-Shortage-and-Software-Platforms-Not-Just-Qubits
26. https://careers.pasqal.com/
27. https://www.eu-startups.com/2023/01/paris-based-pasqal-lands-e100-million-to-advance-the-future-of-quantum-computing/

28. https://patentpc.com/blog/quantum-computing-job-market-salaries-demand-and-hiring-trends
29. https://www.glassdoor.com/Salaries/quantum-computing-salary-SRCH_KO0,17.html
30. https://www.quantumjobs.us/post/are-quantum-computing-jobs-in-high-demand
31. https://thequantuminsider.com/2026/05/29/quantum-computing-jobs-and-salaries-in-2026/
32. https://www.quantumjobs.us/post/are-quantum-computing-jobs-in-high-demand
33. https://tietalent.com/en/blog/217/quantum-careers-in-2025

4

Governance and Strategic Planning

If classical IT governance is about keeping a well-run train on time, quantum governance is more like captaining an expedition into a partly mapped territory. You still need structure, discipline, and accountability, but you also need people who are comfortable making big bets under deep uncertainty.

Think of quantum governance as the difference between a startup that burns through venture funding chasing every shiny object and one that steadily builds toward durable competitive advantage. The distinction isn't just about adding another oversight layer; it's about cultivating the organizational intelligence to navigate deep technological uncertainty while still keeping stakeholders confident and regulators satisfied.

Quantum computing does not behave like a new CRM rollout or a cloud migration. It's a multi-year, multi-million-dollar commitment with unknown timelines, shifting regulatory expectations, and exponential potential that could transform industries, or fizzle out if mismanaged. Without deliberate governance, even generously funded quantum programs can buckle under their own ambiguity. Boards lose patience when they cannot see tangible progress, regulators intervene when they discover unapproved technology transfers, and investors walk away when milestones slip again and again.

Effective quantum governance provides the strategic scaffolding and oversight mechanisms that guide quantum initiatives from first investment through implementation and eventually scaling. In this chapter we'll focus on why formal governance structures are indispensable for managing quantum risk, allocating scarce resources wisely, and ensuring quantum efforts remain aligned with corporate strategy and risk appetite. The World Economic Forum's Quantum Computing Governance initiative, which convenes public and private sector experts, underscores that responsible quantum adoption does not emerge organically; it requires intentional, coordinated governance across organizational boundaries.[14]

In this chapter, you will also see how to design quantum governance committees with the right mix of authority and expertise, how to build planning processes that respect quantum uncertainty and extended timelines, and how to install accountability mechanisms that track progress without locking you into rigid plans. We will also look at how these governance structures fit into existing corporate mechanisms and the regulatory demands that shape them. With governments already committing billions of dollars globally to quantum technologies, the pressure on organizations to get quantum governance right has never been higher.

By the end of this chapter, we will cover how leading organizations design governance, which metrics actually matter when progress is anything but linear, how to navigate the increasingly dense web of international regulations, and how to communicate quantum developments to stakeholders who may never learn the physics but absolutely must understand the strategic stakes and risks.

Main topics and key insights covered in this chapter are:

- Quantum governance framework design
- Strategic objective setting and KPI development
- Regulatory compliance planning
- Stakeholder communication and reporting
- Integration with existing corporate governance
- Critical skills for quantum governance

Quantum governance framework design

When IBM reported in December 2025 that quantum computing now absorbs, on average, 11% of R&D budgets among surveyed organizations, up from 7% in 2023, the headline number was striking, but the more revealing insight was buried just beneath it: quantum-ready organizations are the ones struggling most with skills, precisely because they are moving from experimentation to production.[1] That paradox is a warning sign. You cannot simply copy and paste existing technology governance models onto quantum and expect them to work. The more advanced your quantum program becomes, the more nuanced your governance must be.

Quantum governance, at its core, requires structures that marry strategic oversight, technical depth, and operational adaptability. Traditional IT governance benefits from mature best practices and relatively predictable outcomes. Quantum lives in a different rhythm: technical breakthroughs can arrive monthly, competitors reposition quarterly, and regulators revise their expectations annually. Your governance model must be sturdy enough to provide consistent direction, yet agile enough to pivot as the quantum landscape shifts. We'll learn more details on how to be agile in Part 3 of this book.

Committee composition and structure

In practice, effective quantum governance committees tend to share a common pattern. They include board members with technology and risk experience, senior executives from the business units most affected by quantum, and quantum specialists who can offer both technical interpretation and market intelligence. The sweet spot for committee size is usually five to nine members, just small enough to move quickly, yet large enough to bring diverse perspectives to the table. Term lengths of two to three years give you continuity without stagnation, while staggered terms prevent a full reset of institutional memory.

But getting the right mix is more than just ticking representation boxes. The real challenge is depth. Committee members need enough quantum literacy to separate meaningful breakthroughs from marketing spin, yet they cannot disappear into technical details and lose sight of strategic priorities. I've borne witness to many committees that were made up of quantum scientists discussing in much detail about error correction for hours at a time on web conferences, yet they struggled to translate those achievements into board-relevant business narratives.

The fix was a two-tier model: a Quantum Advisory Council, stacked with technical experts who report to a Quantum Steering Committee that has a more business-oriented membership. The Advisory Council focuses on questions like technical feasibility, platform choices, and competitive positioning. The Steering Committee decides where to place bets, how to allocate budgets, and how to manage stakeholder expectations. This separation of concerns lets quantum specialists stay deep while ensuring that strategic control stays where it belongs, with business leaders. In all cases, it's very important not to forget the importance of strategic education of all business leaders, as this helps keep the organization valid and nimble.

Governance processes and decision-making

How often your quantum governance committee meets should reflect both the maturity of your initiatives and the volatility of the environment. During early exploration, quarterly meetings may be enough to keep things on track. As key milestones approach, or when regulatory shifts are on the horizon, monthly or even bi-weekly meetings often become necessary. The ISO/IEC Joint Technical Committee 3 on Quantum Technologies, created in January 2024 to harmonize terminology, benchmarks, and interoperability standards, shows just how quickly the field is moving and why governance rhythms must adjust in response.[2]

Decision-making protocols also need to adapt to quantum's unique uncertainties. Traditional governance leans heavily on ROI calculations and risk-adjusted NPV analyses. Those remain useful, but quantum governance must also incorporate option value thinking, the recognition that early investments can create future opportunities whose eventual payoff may dwarf current costs. This does not mean abandoning financial discipline. It means complementing standard financial measures with assessments of strategic positioning, ecosystem influence, and learning value.

None of this works without reliable information flow. Quantum governance committees need timely, synthesized insight into internal progress, competitor moves, regulatory developments, and overall technology trends and changes. Many organizations address this by building a Quantum Program Management Office. This group pulls all forms of input from technical teams, business units, legal and compliance, and external advisors, then distills them into concise, decision-ready materials for the committee.

Authority, accountability, and charters

Charters are where quantum governance moves from good intentions to actual authority. A well-crafted charter spells out what the committee is responsible for, which decisions it owns, and how its work connects to other governance bodies. Without this clarity, you can end up with a committee that is purely advisory and easily ignored, or with one that overreaches and collides with existing structures. Strong charters explicitly define decision rights around budget allocation, partnership approvals, technology selection, and strategic direction.

Accountability mechanisms must be tuned to quantum realities. In a typical software initiative, you can point to sprint velocity, feature completion, and user adoption as clear markers of progress. Quantum teams, by contrast, may spend months refining algorithms, evaluating hardware, or running experiments without producing visible "features" in production. Effective accountability frameworks therefore track a broader set of indicators: milestone completion, adherence to budgets, quality of partnerships, success in recruiting and retaining talent, shifts in competitive position, and technical progress.

The broader framework also must address quantum-specific governance dilemmas. Leaders must be able to distinguish between healthy technical risk-taking and reckless speculation, and they need guidelines that clarify which experiments the organization is willing to fund and which are out of bounds. As quantum programs spread across multiple business units and technical domains, governance structures must prevent fragmentation, where separate teams unknowingly duplicate efforts, dilute talent, and waste scarce resources, which happens a lot more often than you think.

Framework: quantum governance maturity model

Most organizations do not wake up one day with a fully formed quantum governance system. They evolve through recognizable stages or phases. Understanding where you are today helps you make smart decisions about what to build next and avoid jumping into advanced practices before you have the basics in place. The following framework will help you understand the characteristics and governance focus based on the level of maturity.

Maturity Level	Characteristics	Governance Focus
Level 1: Ad Hoc	• Quantum discussions occur sporadically • No formal governance structure • Decisions made reactively • Limited quantum expertise at the leadership level	• Establish basic quantum literacy among leadership • Designate a quantum champion • Begin market and technology monitoring
Level 2: Initial	• Designated quantum oversight role exists • Informal governance meetings • Basic tracking of quantum developments • Exploratory partnerships initiated	• Formalize governance committee • Develop initial charter • Establish regular meeting cadence • Create basic reporting template
Level 3: Defined	• Formal quantum governance committee established • Clear charter and decision rights • Regular monitoring of technical progress and the competitive landscape • Integration with existing governance bodies	• Refine decision-making processes • Develop comprehensive KPI framework • Establish stakeholder communication protocols • Align with broader corporate governance

Maturity Level	Characteristics	Governance Focus
Level 4: Managed	• Systematic governance processes • Quantitative progress tracking • Stakeholder engagement formalized • Regulatory compliance monitoring active • Resource allocation optimized	• Implement advanced analytics for decision support • Develop scenario planning capabilities • Establish governance performance metrics • Conduct regular governance effectiveness reviews
Level 5: Optimizing	• Continuous governance improvement • Predictive analytics informs decisions • Quantum governance integrated seamlessly with corporate strategy • Thought leadership position established	• Focus on innovation in governance practices • Share governance insights with the broader community • Contribute to industry governance standards • Mentor other organizations

Table 4.1: Maturity level and governance focus

Understanding where your governance maturity stands today gives you a clear starting point. It helps you set meaningful strategic objectives and define the right KPIs to move your organization forward. We'll explore how to do that in the next section.

Strategic objective setting and KPI development

Back in 2021, the European Quantum Flagship's Strategy Advisory Board defined 23 Key Performance Indicators (KPIs) across six pillars: Ecosystem, Quantum Communication, Quantum Computing, Quantum Simulation, Quantum Sensing and Metrology, and Education. [22] By 2024, these KPIs revealed impressive European progress but also exposed the limitations of static metrics in a rapidly changing field, prompting periodic review and adjustment, and transforming the KPI framework into what officials describe as a 'living document' that must evolve alongside the technology.

This European experience illustrates a fundamental truth about quantum strategic planning: objectives and metrics that appear comprehensive today may be irrelevant six months from now. Yet organizations can't plan without objectives, and they can't measure progress without KPIs. The solution lies not in avoiding metrics but in designing adaptive frameworks that provide direction while maintaining flexibility.

Quantum-specific objective setting

Quantum strategic planning calls for its own approach to setting objectives. You are dealing with technologies whose timelines are uncertain, whose performance improvements can be exponential, and whose competitive dynamics are still forming. Conventional tools such as SMART goals (Specific, Measurable, Achievable, Relevant, Time-bound) start to strain under that load. How do you make a time-bound commitment when the enabling breakthrough could arrive next year or five years from now? How do you define "achievable" when the very notion of quantum advantage remains fluid?

The OECD's 2025 review of national quantum strategies illustrates how different jurisdictions are wrestling with these questions. Some, such as the United States, favor broad, flexible objectives that sketch strategic direction but avoid hard numerical targets. Others, like the European Union, South Korea, and the United Kingdom, lean into detailed metrics and KPIs, specifying target performance levels, readiness thresholds, and ecosystem indicators ranging from skills development to market share and international collaboration.[3]

Neither philosophy is inherently superior. Flexible objectives absorb uncertainty but risk becoming so vague that they offer little guidance. Detailed metrics create accountability, but they can lock you into chasing goals that no longer match reality as the field shifts. In practice, the most resilient strategies blend both: enduring strategic themes that hold over multi-year horizons, paired with milestones that can be updated as quantum realities evolve. In essence, neither will offer "defining" insights right away, only guidance as we are still in the early phases. The truth, for now, is somewhere in between.

Typical strategic themes include:

- Building internal quantum capabilities and expertise.
- Securing strategic partnerships and strong ecosystem position.
- Demonstrating business value through pilot and proof-of-concept applications.
- Maintaining sharp competitive and market intelligence.
- Ensuring regulatory compliance and risk management.

These themes remain relevant regardless of which hardware platform pulls ahead or which algorithm wins the next benchmark. The specific milestones inside each theme, whether partners, candidate use cases, or regulatory thresholds, can each flex as opportunities and constraint changes. It's also good to stay agile as changes could shift your existing course.

Comprehensive KPI development

Designing KPIs for quantum initiatives means measuring three distinct but interdependent dimensions:

- Technical performance
- Business impact
- Strategic position

Measuring only one is a trap. Technical metrics in isolation can celebrate engineering feats that never translate into commercial value. Business metrics without technical grounding can misattribute success to "quantum" when in reality it's classical compute doing the work. Strategic metrics without either technical or business validation risk confusing perception with capability.

The German Quantum Technology and Application Consortium (QUTAC) tackled this challenge head-on in 2024 with a KPI framework aimed at standardizing how national progress on quantum computing is measured.[4] Their work addresses inconsistencies in definitions, measurement methods, and data comparability across countries and offers a set of standardized KPIs for meaningful benchmarking and policy decisions. While QUTAC's focus is national ecosystems, its principles translate well to the organizational level.

On the technical side, KPIs track system capabilities and algorithm performance. Common measures include qubit counts and quality metrics such as coherence times and error rates, achievable circuit depth and multi-qubit gate counts, standardized benchmark results, and composite metrics like Circuit Layer Operations Per Second (CLOPS), which is a metric that indicates the number of quantum volume circuits a quantum processing unit (QPU) can execute within a given period of time. But these numbers must be interpreted carefully. A 1,000-qubit noisy device may be less useful than a 50-qubit high-fidelity system, and record-breaking multi-qubit gate counts only matter if they produce meaningful, verifiable results.

Business impact KPIs demonstrate whether quantum is creating value and using resources wisely. They might track cost per useful quantum computation, time-to-solution relative to classical approaches, the number and quality of business processes enhanced or enabled by quantum, documented cost savings or new revenue streams, and the depth of external partnerships. For early-stage programs, it is perfectly reasonable for business impact to be modest, as long as technical and strategic progress justify sustained investment. The key is being honest about which phase of the journey you are in.

Strategic KPIs monitor your position within the broader ecosystem. These include quantum talent acquisition and retention, IP creation (patents filed, papers published), participation in standards bodies and industry initiatives, visibility in quantum thought leadership, and partnerships with leading quantum companies and institutions. IBM's Quantum Network, now encompassing more than 300 members from industry, commercial collaborations, startups, and academic and research institutions, is a valid example of ecosystem participation turning into a strategic asset in its own right.[5] An ecosystem-driven approach will naturally invite thought leadership into the conversation. Once the foundations are set, progress tends to follow. In this way, quantum technologies will evolve much like other transformative technologies have before.

Milestone definition and progress tracking

Defining milestones in quantum requires a careful balance between ambition and realism. You want milestones that stretch the organization and signal meaningful progress, but they must still be credible and achievable enough to sustain momentum. One practical approach is to think in terms of milestone categories:

- Technical achievements
- Partnership developments
- Business application deployments
- Ecosystem contributions

Technical milestones might involve hitting specific coherence thresholds, demonstrating error correction below a critical error rate, successfully executing circuits of a given complexity, or validating algorithms on physical hardware rather than solely in simulation.

Partnership milestones could include joining a major quantum network, forming a strategic collaboration with a hardware provider, or securing cloud access to leading platforms.

Application milestones range from proof-of-concept demonstrations and pilots to fully integrated production deployments.

Ecosystem milestones might involve publishing research, contributing to standards, or securing speaking slots at key industry events.

Sequencing these milestones is as important as choosing them. Organizations sometimes rush to chase high-visibility application milestones before they have sufficient technical depth or the right partnerships in place. The result is often disappointing pilots that damage credibility. A more sustainable sequence is to build literacy and partnerships first, deepen technical capabilities through experimentation, and then layer in business applications as readiness and opportunity converge.

Framework: balanced quantum KPI dashboard

A well-designed quantum KPI dashboard brings all this together by balancing leading and lagging indicators across technical, business, and strategic domains. It is a living tool that senior leaders and governance committees can use to see, at a glance, where the program is progressing, where it is stuck, and where to intervene. Key categories and sample metrics are illustrated in the following framework:

KPI Category	Sample Metrics
Technical Performance (Lagging)	• Quantum volume achieved • Qubit coherence time (T1, T2) • Two-qubit gate fidelity • Circuit depth successfully executed • Error rate (physical and logical) • Benchmark problem performance vs. classical baseline
Technical Progress (Leading)	• Algorithm development pipeline • Hardware access secured (cloud/partnership) • Quantum experiments conducted monthly • Technical publications submitted • Open-source contributions made
Business Value (Lagging)	• Cost per useful quantum computation • Time to solution vs. classical methods • Business processes enhanced • Cost savings documented • Revenue generated from quantum-enabled services

KPI Category	Sample Metrics
Business Development (Leading)	• Proof-of-Concept projects initiated • Use cases under evaluation • Business unit engagement level • Training programs completed • Internal quantum champions identified
Strategic Position (Lagging)	• Quantum job requisitions posted • Patent applications in progress • Standards committees joined • Conference presentations scheduled • Thought leadership content published • Competitive intelligence reports completed
Governance and Risk (Ongoing)	• Governance committee meeting frequency • Budget variance (planned vs. actual) • Regulatory compliance status • Risk assessments completed • Stakeholder satisfaction scores

Table 4.2: Sample metrics

Of course, you and your organization should tailor this dashboard to your own context, maturity, and risk appetite. What matters most is not the precise metric list but the discipline of seeing technical, business, strategic, and governance signals together, so quantum is governed as a strategic enterprise initiative, not as an isolated lab project.

Regulatory compliance planning

Regulatory compliance in the quantum era is no longer a distant concern; it's now arriving on clear timelines with real consequences. In August 2024, the National Institute of Standards and Technology (NIST) released the first **post-quantum cryptography (PQC)** standards after years of work, and the clock immediately started ticking. By January 2027, all new National Security Systems in the United States must be quantum-safe, and the National Security Agency expects the full transition to quantum-resistant algorithms to be completed by 2035, in line with NSM-10.[6] Across the Atlantic, the European Union's Commission Recommendation on Post-Quantum Cryptography builds on its Cybersecurity Strategy for the Digital Decade, with a clear aim to strengthen end-to-end security and resilience of digital infrastructure as quantum threats mature.[7] Monitoring regulations is equally important as the subject matter could change as the depth of quantum understanding and the evolution of the technology progresses over time.

These parallel developments, each with their own timelines, technical requirements, and enforcement mechanisms, show why quantum regulatory compliance cannot be treated as an add-on to existing programs. For globally active organizations, the reality is a messy patchwork: U.S. export controls, European data protection and cybersecurity rules, and Chinese technology-sovereignty policies can pull strategies in different directions. The practical question for leaders here is not whether these regimes will converge neatly, but how to build compliance capabilities that can navigate, and sometimes reconcile, competing obligations.

The quantum regulatory landscape

Quantum technologies sit at the intersection of several powerful regulatory currents, and the overall landscape looks more like a stack of overlapping layers than a single regime. At the top are export-control rules that shape which quantum technologies can be shared, where, and with whom. Beneath that lie industry-specific regulations in areas such as financial services, healthcare, and defense, each adding its own quantum-relevant expectations. Data protection and privacy laws determine how quantum systems can handle sensitive information. Intellectual property frameworks govern the protection and licensing of quantum innovations. National security policies, in turn, influence everything from collaboration partners to deployment environments.

Export control is often the most immediate concern for organizations developing or deploying quantum technologies. In the United States, regulations under ITAR (International Traffic in Arms Regulations) and EAR (Export Administration Regulations) increasingly classify quantum technologies as dual-use items, meaning they can require licenses for transfer to certain countries or entities. Section 234 of the FY2019 National Defense Authorization Act, subsequently updated through later NDAAs, directs the Secretary of Defense to run a quantum research and development program in coordination with industry, allies, and other agencies, but insists that all such coordination respect stringent export-control rules.[8] For leaders, this means that even well-intentioned collaboration can cross into restricted territory if not carefully managed.

The European Union, by contrast, has leaned more heavily into standardization and certification that broaden export restrictions by embedding national security goals directly into its market standardization and product certification systems. Therefore, instead of relying on the usual list of banned goods, it uses technical rules, compliance certificates, and regulatory approvals to monitor and restrict trading. Its Digital Decade Strategy set aggressive goals: deploy the first European supercomputer with quantum acceleration and put Europe at the cutting edge of quantum capabilities by 2030. The European Chips Act complements this with measures to encourage low-cost, high-volume manufacturing of quantum chips within the EU. For companies, this creates attractive opportunities in European markets, but some of these initiatives may not align cleanly with U.S. export frameworks, forcing nuanced structuring of partnerships and supply chains.

China's approach is driven by technology sovereignty and state-directed development. A national venture fund on the order of RMB 1 trillion (approximately $138 billion USD) for quantum and other frontier technologies signals a long-term strategic commitment.[9] Organizations with Chinese operations or partners must navigate tight technology-transfer rules and data-sovereignty requirements, which can clash with Western regulations and corporate policies. In practice, this often means structuring separate technical stacks, data flows, or collaboration models for China-related work.

Industry-specific quantum compliance

On top of national and regional rules, sector regulators are beginning to articulate quantum-specific expectations, particularly in heavily regulated industries such as finance, healthcare, and defense.

- ***In finance***, regulators are increasingly focused on the risk that quantum computing poses to cryptographic infrastructure, especially for digital assets and high-value transaction systems. The Post-Quantum Financial Infrastructure Framework (PQFIF), designed specifically for digital asset ecosystems, is an early glimpse of how regulators may express quantum-specific requirements.[10] Banks and financial institutions must plan their transactions to use quantum-safe cryptography while still complying with an already dense web of prudential, conduct, and cybersecurity regulations across multiple jurisdictions.
- ***Healthcare*** organizations face a different set of challenges. Protected Health Information processed through quantum algorithms must retain confidentiality, integrity, and availability under HIPAA and equivalent regimes abroad. At the same time, the prospect that quantum computers could eventually break today's encryption introduces a forward-looking risk; data captured and stored securely today might be vulnerable to decryption in the future. As a result, healthcare quantum initiatives need to examine not just current safeguards, but also how and when to introduce post-

quantum cryptography into their data-protection strategies. We'll cover details on how to do this effectively in Part 3 of this book.

- ***Defense and aerospace*** contractors operate under some of the strictest requirements. Quantum technologies developed under defense contracts typically involve security-cleared personnel, accredited facilities, and tight restrictions on foreign-national access. The Defense Science Board's view that quantum sensing is the most mature military application, "poised for mission use," has sharpened regulatory and security attention on how quantum technologies are shared and deployed.[11] For companies in this space, quantum governance and compliance are inseparable from broader security and export-control practices.

Understanding your existing governance structure is important for keeping your compliance office aligned and informed. It enables them to anticipate changes, communicate effectively with stakeholders, and establish processes that keep the organization on track. We'll explore this in more detail in the next section.

Building effective compliance programs

Given this complexity, quantum compliance programs must do two things at once: ensure adherence to current rules and prepare the organization for regulations that have not yet fully materialized. Building such a program involves several core components.

First, a *structural regulatory landscape analysis* is essential. This is more than a one-off legal memo; it's an ongoing process to identify which existing regulations apply to your quantum activities and to track emerging laws, guidance, and standards. Second, you need *internal policies* that translate those external requirements into concrete do's and don'ts. These should cover everything from who can access what systems to how cross-border research collaborations are vetted. Third, *training programs* must equip relevant teams – technical, legal, compliance, and business leaders – with enough quantum-specific understanding to recognize when a project or partnership might raise regulatory issues. Finally, *monitoring and audit mechanisms* are needed to detect non-compliance early, before it leads to investigation or penalties.

International coordination adds another layer of difficulty. Some researchers and policy experts argue that voluntary global standards may be a better early-stage governance tool for quantum technologies than strict regulation, at least until the technology matures further.[12] The ISO/IEC Joint Technical Committee 3 on Quantum Technologies reflects this mindset, bringing together experts from the U.S., Europe, China, Japan, and South Korea to coordinate terminology, benchmarks, and interoperability standards. For companies, participation in or alignment with such standards can provide a common reference point when navigating multiple legal regimes.

Just as importantly, quantum compliance cannot live in a silo. It needs to be woven into the broader compliance architecture that already covers export control, privacy, and data protection, sector-specific obligations, and corporate-wide ethics and risk programs. When quantum is managed in isolation, it can inadvertently create gaps. Projects that are compliant from a narrow quantum perspective are misaligned with broader organizational obligations. Integrating quantum compliance into enterprise risk management and compliance committees helps prevent these blind spots.

Not all compliance risks deserve equal attention. An effective program starts with a risk assessment that ranks potential violations by both likelihood and impact. Export-control breaches can trigger large fines, revocation of export privileges, and even criminal liability. Data-protection failures may carry steep financial penalties and reputational damage. Sector-specific violations can cost licenses, contracts, or market access. Mapping quantum-related activities onto this risk landscape helps you decide where to focus limited compliance resources and where to build the strongest controls.

Company spotlight: IBM's quantum governance and strategic planning

IBM's experience provides a concrete example of how a large, diversified organization can operationalize quantum governance. With a dedicated quantum team of roughly hundreds of people, and a Quantum Network that includes industry members, commercial partnerships, and academic and research institutions, IBM has had to design governance structures that serve both cutting-edge research and real-world deployment.

At the center of IBM's approach is transparent roadmapping and active stakeholder engagement. The company publishes detailed quantum roadmaps that now extend through 2033 and refreshes them regularly, openly discussing progress as well as setbacks. For partners and customers, this level of transparency is not just a communication nicety; it's a planning tool that allows them to align their own quantum strategies with IBM's trajectory. When IBM pivoted from pursuing single-chip processors such as the 1,121-qubit Condor to multi-chip architecture like Heron and recently Nighthawk, the roadmap update clearly explained both the technical insights and strategic rationale behind the shift, illustrating governance that is responsive to learning rather than locked into prior commitments.

IBM's Quantum Readiness Index, released by its Institute for Business Value in December 2025, highlights how governance and strategy are tightly coupled. The index assesses organizations across three dimensions: strategy, technology, and operations, and found that quantum now accounts for 11% of R&D budgets on average among surveyed organizations, up from 7% in 2023. At the same time, the data showed that quantum-ready organizations face the steepest skills pressures, with 61% citing a shortage of quantum skills as a primary concern. IBM used these insights to recalibrate its own talent-development and partnership strategies, reinforcing the idea that governance must be informed by candid, data-driven self-assessment.

Perhaps the most distinctive feature of IBM's governance language is the concept of "quantum utility", the point at which quantum systems can perform useful computations that classical systems cannot easily match, even if the field has not yet reached broad commercially viable quantum advantage. This intermediate target offers a realistic, motivating goal for teams and stakeholders who might otherwise be waiting for an all-or-nothing breakthrough. In a recent State of the Union address, IBM highlighted candidate advantage experiments in three areas: observable estimation, variational algorithms, and problems with efficient classical verification, demonstrating how governance priorities can steer technical work toward commercially relevant experiments rather than purely academic milestones.

Stakeholder communication and reporting

If governance is the brain of a quantum program, communication is its voice. The Google Willow episode underscores both the power and the peril of quantum narratives. When Google announced its Willow processor in December 2024, it reported that the chip had completed a benchmark computation in under five minutes that would have taken a conventional supercomputer 1,025 years.[13] The claim created enormous buzz, and equally enormous confusion. Months later, CEO Sundar Pichai felt compelled to clarify that practical quantum computers are likely still about a decade away, a reminder that spectacular performance numbers do not automatically translate into near-term business impact.[22]

This example captures a central tension in quantum communication: how to generate legitimate excitement and support without overshooting on promises. Effective stakeholder communication must sustain interest over long development arcs, avoid short-term hype that erodes credibility, and translate deeply technical progress into strategic implications that decision-makers can act on. At the same time, it must be precise enough that quantum experts inside and outside the organization do not dismiss it as empty marketing.

Audience-specific communication strategies

Different stakeholders experience your quantum journey from very different angles, and your communication strategy has to reflect that. Boards are primarily concerned with strategy, risk, and timing. They care less about gate fidelities and more about questions like: How does this development affect our competitive position? What level of investment will be required to stay credible in quantum? What regulatory or reputational risks arise if we move forward, or if we choose not to? When can we reasonably expect to see business value from these investments? What is the cost of being left behind or late out of the gate?

Investors, especially in public markets, need a careful balance of ambitions and realism. Securities regulations require accurate disclosure of material information, but deciding what counts as "material" progress in a still-emerging field can be tricky. Partnership announcements, technical milestones, and competitive moves all can influence investor perceptions. Over-communicate minor advances, and you risk desensitizing investors or creating an impression of spin. Under-communicate, and you may fail to capture the strategic upside of your quantum program.

Employees form another critical audience, and they are far from monolithic. Technical employees want to understand the specifics of the technology and what it means for their careers. Business staff want to know how quantum affects their products, customers, and performance metrics. Everyone benefits from a clear explanation of why quantum matters to the organization's strategy, but that explanation must be accessible, free of unnecessary jargon, and respectful of their existing expertise.

For customers and partners, quantum communication demands particular care. Aggressive marketing about future quantum capabilities can backfire if those capabilities are delayed or never materialize. Yet staying silent can create the impression that competitors are more advanced. The sweet spot is usually open, honest communication about what you are exploring, what you can do today, what you hope to do tomorrow, and what guardrails you are using to avoid over-promising.

Communication frameworks and reporting systems

To avoid ad hoc, inconsistent messaging, many organizations adopt explicit quantum communication frameworks. These frameworks define a small set of core messages that remain consistent across audiences, outline how these messages should be tailored for different groups, and link communication timing to key milestones and external events. They also include crisis-communication playbooks so that if setbacks occur, as they inevitably will, the organization responds with clarity rather than improvisation.

Core messages typically answer five questions:

1. Why does quantum matter to the organization's long-term strategy?
2. What are the capabilities that the organization is building?
3. How do quantum initiatives align with existing business objectives?
4. When can the stakeholders expect tangible outcomes?
5. What risks is the organization managing as it moves forward?

With these anchors in place, teams can adjust tone and depth for boards, investors, employees, customers, or regulators without drifting into contradiction.

Reporting systems translate quantum progress into formats that stakeholders can actually use. Dashboards for governance committees might display KPIs across technical, business, and strategic dimensions, while board-level materials may lean more heavily on trend lines, milestones, and competitive benchmarks. Narrative reporting is equally important. It adds the "why" behind the numbers, explaining why some milestones arrived early, why others slipped, and how competitive or regulatory shifts are influencing priorities.

The World Economic Forum's Quantum Computing Governance initiative illustrates the power of narrative-rich reporting. Rather than focusing solely on numeric indicators, the initiative frames discussions around how quantum ethics can contribute to a better society, explores risks and social implications, and pilots governance frameworks in concrete applications.[14] This kind of narrative structure pulls in stakeholders who might otherwise disengage from a conversation dominated by technical metrics.

Thought leadership and crisis communication

Thought leadership is a powerful tool in quantum. It can position your organization as a serious player, attract talent, and open doors to high-value partnerships. Activities range from publishing peer-reviewed research and presenting at conferences to participating in standards bodies, consortia, and public education efforts. Done well, these efforts demonstrate not just technical strength but also a willingness to help shape the broader ecosystem.

However, thought leadership is not risk-free. If an organization aggressively promotes its quantum capabilities but cannot back claims with real technical achievements or credible roadmaps, it invites skepticism and reputational damage. The antidote is grounding public statements in verifiable progress and being candid about uncertainties and open questions. IBM's practice of publishing detailed roadmaps, including aspirational targets, and honest discussions of obstacles, is a good example of how transparency can actually reinforce, rather than undermine, thought leadership.

Crisis communication planning deserves just as much attention as day-to-day messaging. Quantum programs will inevitably encounter setbacks. A promising algorithm fails to scale, a partnership unravels, a competitor announces a breakthrough, or a new regulation disrupts a carefully laid plan. Effective crisis communication protocols address four basic issues in advance:

1. How quickly to inform different stakeholder groups?
2. How much detail to share about causes and impacts?
3. How to acknowledge problems without eroding confidence?
4. How to describe the corrective actions underway?

The UK-Google partnership around the Willow processor offers a nuanced case study. When Google granted UK researchers access to Willow in December 2025, UK officials framed the agreement as an accelerator for British quantum ambitions. Soon after, analysis from the Bloomsbury Intelligence and Security Institute argued that the partnership highlighted a core tension: gaining access to world-leading capabilities while potentially sacrificing strategic autonomy.[15] The gap between official messaging and independent critique shows why quantum communication cannot simply celebrate the upside; it must also anticipate and address likely lines of criticism, ideally before they dominate the public narrative.

The following spotlight highlights a strong example of public-private governance that goes beyond a single funding source, bringing together multiple interests under a unified approach.

Company spotlight: PsiQuantum's public-private governance model

PsiQuantum's story shows how an ambitious startup can use public-private partnerships not just as a funding source, but as a governance instrument to manage risk, expectations, and national interests all at once. In April 2024, the company secured a 620 million AUD package from the Australian and Queensland governments to build what officials described as the world's first utility-scale, fault-tolerant quantum computer in Brisbane.[16] This came on top of a $750 million funding round in March 2025 that blended private venture capital from BlackRock with government grants and equity, creating a capital stack that inherently demanded careful, multi-stakeholder oversight.

The governance structure around this partnership is deliberately dual in nature. On one side, PsiQuantum answers to private investors through a conventional board model that focuses on commercial returns, defensible IP, and competitive positioning. On the other, it is accountable to government stakeholders via milestone-based funding tranches, formal reporting requirements, and regular performance reviews tied to national strategic objectives. That dual accountability naturally produces tensions: private investors want speed, differentiation, and optionality; public stakeholders place more weight on national capability, ecosystem spillovers, and long-term technological sovereignty.

PsiQuantum's strategic communication is designed to meet each audience where it is. For investors, the company leads with its photonic quantum architecture as a potential scaling advantage over rival modalities, underpinned by its manufacturing partnership with GlobalFoundries as a credible path to volume production.[17] For Australian federal and state stakeholders, the emphasis shifts: local headquarters presence, deep links with domestic quantum startups and advanced manufacturing clusters, joint programs with universities and research institutes, and the creation of doctorate-level positions and internships that build local human capital and strengthen the broader digital supply chain.[18]

The company's emergence as the first quantum startup to achieve a $1 billion USD valuation is one visible marker that this governance model resonates with markets. Yet PsiQuantum also illustrates how complex international governance becomes when quantum operations span multiple jurisdictions. Founded by Australian academics, headquartered in Palo Alto, dependent on a New York-based manufacturing partner, and financially tied to Australian governments, the firm operates at the intersection of U.S. export controls, Australian technology-sovereignty imperatives, and the confidentiality demands of high-stakes commercial R&D. Its governance framework addresses this by carefully structuring IP ownership, implementing facility security protocols that satisfy multiple regulators, and applying stringent personnel screening where sensitive technology is involved, all while trying to preserve the agility and focus of a fast-moving startup. Of course, this will likely get more complex as export controls update restrictions while quantum technologies evolve over time.

Integration with existing corporate governance

The most frequent failure mode in quantum governance is not poor intent or lack of effort; it's isolation. When quantum committees operate as self-contained islands, disconnected from core corporate governance, the result is often conflict, duplication, or unmanaged risk. A European multinational learned this the hard way when its newly formed Quantum Innovation Committee approved a partnership with a Chinese quantum company without involving the corporate compliance function. The collaboration inadvertently breached export-control restrictions the committee did not realize applied, because it was working outside existing compliance structures. Unwinding the deal cost the company the partnership, strained regulatory relationships, and nearly derailed its entire quantum program.

To avoid that pattern, which I assume we all would, quantum governance has to plug directly into the corporate governance fabric rather than sit apart from it. That means integrating with risk management, technology governance, strategic planning, compliance, finance, and HR, while still preserving dedicated attention to quantum's unique risks and opportunities. At the heart of this integration is clarity: who decides what, who reports to whom, and how information flows between quantum-focused bodies and existing committees. Without this clarity, organizations either waste energy on overlapping processes or, worse, leave critical decisions in a governance vacuum.

Defining governance relationships and authorities

Integrating quantum governance starts with explicit decisions about reporting lines, authorities, and coordination routines. Reporting lines answer a simple but powerful question: where does the quantum governance committee sit? Some organizations route it directly to the full board, while others connect it to a technology or innovation committee; still others create a hybrid, where different dimensions of quantum oversight (strategy, risk, investment) report into different committees. Direct board reporting maximizes visibility and authority but can consume scarce board time and risk over-focusing on technical detail. Routing through technology governance leverages existing expertise but may underweight strategic and geopolitical considerations. Multi-channel reporting can give a more complete picture, but only if the coordination overhead is managed intentionally.

Decision rights must be equally clear. A typical pattern might give the quantum governance committee final say on quantum technology selection, major quantum partnerships, and research roadmaps, while the enterprise technology committee retains authority over core architecture and IT standards that quantum systems must plug into. The risk committee continues to own enterprise-wide risk frameworks that quantum efforts must respect. The audit committee oversees the financial control environment around quantum investments, and the compensation committee ensures that quantum-specific incentives sit coherently within the broader remuneration philosophy. Encoding these boundaries explicitly avoids turf battles and reduces the chance that crucial quantum decisions fall between institutional cracks.

Coordination mechanisms then turn structure into practice. Chairs of key committees might meet monthly to review quantum developments and flag cross-cutting issues early. Shared governance dashboards can give all relevant bodies real-time visibility into quantum progress, risk indicators, and resource use. Agreed escalation paths help resolve conflicts when, for example, a high-value quantum partnership conflicts with existing cybersecurity policies or a time-sensitive quantum opportunity bumps up against export-control constraints.

Policy development and risk management integration

Speaking of policy, the task here is to weave quantum-specific requirements into existing frameworks without creating a parallel universe of exceptions. Technology policies need to specify where and how quantum computing fits into the enterprise architecture, what security controls apply to quantum workloads, and which standards govern quantum software and hardware choices. Procurement policies must address how the organization acquires quantum hardware and services, whether via cloud access, on-premise systems, or consortia, how vendors are evaluated, and how contracts handle IP, data rights, and compliance. Financial policies should define who can approve quantum budgets, what thresholds apply, and how quantum investments are evaluated over time. HR policies need to reflect the realities of the quantum talent market, covering recruitment channels, compensation bands, and specialized training.

Here, the tension is between necessary flexibility and organizational coherence. Quantum talent, for example, often commands a premium. Offering significantly higher salaries or bespoke packages may be essential to attract key hires, but unconstrained exceptions risk undermining internal equity and morale among other technical teams. Many organizations resolve this by establishing clearly defined "quantum bands" that sit within, but slightly above, existing technical ranges, coupled with transparent criteria for placement. In this way, quantum is treated as a strategic exception, not an unfettered outlier.

Risk management must likewise absorb quantum in a structured way. Quantum initiatives introduce familiar risk types – financial, regulatory, reputational – but also intensify or reshape them. Technical risk is higher because outcomes are uncertain and timelines long. Competitive risk can spike if organizations allow marketing narratives to outpace real capability. These quantum-specific dimensions need to be mapped into the enterprise risk taxonomy, with consistent assessment methods and regular reporting.

Tensions between quantum innovation and traditional risk management are inevitable. Established risk frameworks often privilege proven technologies, incremental change, and tight control, while quantum innovation demands tolerance for uncertainty and investment in unproven approaches. The integration work lies in distinguishing which risks can and should be handled through existing processes, such as financial exposure or regulatory compliance, and which require specialized quantum governance judgment, such as technical feasibility or ecosystem positioning. Escalation protocols then define when a disagreement between a quantum committee and a risk function must be brought to the board or a joint forum for resolution.

Governance performance measurement

Finally, integrated governance has to evolve and requires measurement. Organizations need to track both quantum initiative outcomes and the performance of the governance structures themselves. On the initiative side, indicators include technical milestones achieved, business value created, talent recruited and retained, and shifts in competitive position. On the governance side, leaders look at decision quality (how often decisions lead to desired outcomes), decision efficiency (how quickly issues move from identification to resolution), stakeholder satisfaction with governance processes, and how effectively conflicts between committees are identified and resolved.

Periodic governance reviews, annually or when quantum programs hit significant inflection points, create disciplined opportunities to ask whether the current structure still fits. Lightweight governance may be sufficient in early exploratory phases, but as quantum investments grow and deployments approach production, more formal and frequent oversight is usually warranted. The quantum governance maturity model presented earlier in this chapter offers a structured way to decide when and how to advance from one governance level to the next.

Framework: governance integration assessment

To make integration tangible, organizations can use the following assessment framework to evaluate how well quantum governance has been woven into existing corporate mechanisms and where gaps still exist.

Integration Dimension	Assessment Questions
Reporting Relationships	• Is the quantum governance reporting structure clearly defined? • Do relevant board committees receive appropriate quantum updates? • Are reporting frequencies aligned with quantum initiative maturity? • Is the escalation path for quantum issues clear?
Decision Authorities	• Are quantum decision authorities explicitly delineated? • Do quantum and existing governance authorities overlap appropriately? • Are conflicts between quantum and existing authority resolved efficiently? • Can a quantum governance committee make binding decisions?
Policy Alignment	• Do quantum initiatives comply with existing corporate policies? • Are quantum-specific policy exceptions documented and justified? • Are existing policies updated to address quantum requirements? Do policy conflicts get identified and resolved proactively?

Integration Dimension	Assessment Questions
Risk Management	• Are quantum risks incorporated into enterprise risk frameworks? • Do quantum risk assessments use consistent methodologies? • Are quantum risk appetites aligned with overall risk tolerance? • Is quantum risk monitoring integrated with enterprise risk reporting?
Resource Coordination	• Are quantum budgets integrated with overall capital planning? • Do quantum talent initiatives align with HR strategy? • Do quantum infrastructure needs coordinate with IT planning? • Are quantum dashboards accessible to appropriate stakeholders? Do governance meetings address cross-cutting quantum issues? • Is quantum competitive intelligence distributed appropriately?
Information sharing	• Do governance committees share relevant quantum information? • Are quantum dashboards accessible to appropriate stakeholders? • Do governance meetings address cross-cutting quantum issues? • Is quantum competitive intelligence distributed appropriately?

Integration Dimension	Assessment Questions
Governance Effectiveness	• Are governance structures reviewed periodically? • Do governance participants understand their roles and authorities? • Are governance decisions implemented effectively? • Is governance overhead proportionate to quantum initiative scale?

Table 4.3: Governance integration assessment

As with any framework, keep these questions dynamic and focused on your own business processes. This is not intended to be an exhaustive list of questions, but it should give you a practical starting point without adding unnecessary complexity, especially when integrating with another entity. The next company spotlight highlights a strong use case that delivered meaningful value for both parties.

Company spotlight: Quantinuum's merger-based governance

Quantinuum's origin story is a governance case study in itself. Formed in November 2021 through the merger of Honeywell Quantum Solutions and Cambridge Quantum Computing, the company had to stitch together two very different organizational DNA strands: Honeywell's large-enterprise processes and control mindset, and Cambridge Quantum's startup agility and software-centric culture. At the same time, it had to reconcile hardware-heavy and software-heavy roadmaps, navigate U.S. and UK regulatory regimes, and present a unified strategic story to customers and investors.[19]

The company's strategic planning illustrates how this governance model plays out in practice. Quantinuum's H-Series trapped-ion systems reached a quantum volume over 1M in April 2024.[20] But the governance narrative did not stop at raw performance metrics. Instead, Quantinuum's leadership emphasized integrated quantum-classical workflows and real commercial deployments as the yardsticks that mattered most. In November 2024, the company introduced a commercial quantum system with 12 logical qubits, the largest number of entangled logical qubits yet demonstrated at the time, integrated directly into Microsoft's Azure Quantum platform.[21]

The emphasis on production-grade integration and customer value reflects a governance philosophy that prizes usable capability over vanity metrics. Investors have responded accordingly: Quantinuum has raised roughly $600 million from a syndicate of leading investors, validating both its technical vision and its governance approach. Its partner ecosystem, with over 85 organizations such as investors, enterprise users, research centers, and governments, shows how governance that deliberately cultivates an ecosystem can amplify internal R&D efforts and accelerate learning, rather than treating partnerships as a secondary concern.

Critical skills for quantum governance

All of these structures and case studies point to a simple truth: effective quantum governance depends on a set of leadership skills that go well beyond traditional technology oversight. The following five skills form the core toolkit for leaders, including quantum oversight and strategic planning, and are as follows:

1. Governance Framework Development
2. Strategic Planning Execution
3. Compliance Management
4. Board Reporting and Communication
5. Process Integration

Skill 1: Governance framework development

First, leaders need the ability to design and evolve governance frameworks suited to a technology whose trajectory is inherently uncertain. This includes deciding who sits on governance committees and why, how often they meet, what information they receive, and how decisions are made when technical and commercial considerations collide. With mature technologies, organizations can lean on established templates; with quantum, they often have to create those templates from scratch, knowing they will have to adjust them as the field moves.

Developing this skill starts with understanding what makes quantum different: much higher technical uncertainty, timelines that can stretch across multiple planning cycles before business value appears, and a scarcity of board-level quantum expertise. Effective frameworks give teams enough autonomy to explore and learn while still imposing clear guardrails on risk, investment, and strategic fit.

Over time, leaders must also learn when and how to adapt these frameworks. Early in a quantum program, a lightweight, exploration-focused structure may be appropriate. As investments grow and projects approach deployment, governance often needs to become more formal and integrated with enterprise processes. That might mean changing meeting frequency, expanding or refocusing committee membership, revising charters, or tightening reporting expectations as quantum moves from R&D curiosity to strategic asset.

The most reliable way to build this skill is through practice and exposure: helping to stand up new governance structures, facilitating governance meetings, studying models from other organizations and industries, and working with mentors who have navigated similar transitions. Rotating emerging leaders through quantum governance roles and board-facing forums can accelerate this learning process.

Skill 2: Strategic planning and execution

Second, quantum leaders must become adept at strategic planning in an environment where both the upside and the uncertainty are unusually high. That means mastering scenario-based planning, option-value thinking, and milestone-driven execution that remains flexible as new information emerges.

Quantum scenario planning stretches further than typical strategy exercises. One plausible scenario features rapid breakthroughs and meaningful quantum advantage within three to five years, compelling aggressive investments, and a race to secure ecosystem position. Another assumes a slower curve, where quantum remains primarily a research and experimentation tool for a decade, suggesting more measured exploration and targeted bets. Good plans acknowledge both, and design portfolios that create value regardless of which scenario, or combination, materializes.

Resource allocation under quantum conditions similarly demands a different mindset. Traditional NPV-driven models often produce "no" answers because they discount uncertain, long-dated returns. Quantum leaders need to weigh not only direct ROI, but also learning value, strategic positioning, talent magnetism, and ecosystem influence. The question then becomes: which investments create options and capabilities we will want in multiple plausible futures, even if the near-term P&L impact is modest?

Finally, strategic planning execution involves harmonizing quantum work with day-to-day business realities. That includes sequencing initiatives so capability building precedes large-scale deployment, aligning pilots with business unit priorities, and setting expectations about when and how quantum will start to show up in products, processes, or cost structures. It also requires building in review points where leaders decide whether to persist, pivot, or pause based on evidence rather than hope, or just crossing your fingers. It's important to keep in mind that this is a long play, so ensure the planning and execution sticks to realistic expectations throughout its course.

Skill 3: Compliance management

Third, leaders need a deep and evolving grasp of the regulatory environment that surrounds quantum technologies. This is not a one-time legal briefing; it's an ongoing management discipline. Quantum compliance spans export controls, data protection, sector-specific rules, and national security considerations, and it varies widely by jurisdiction.

A particularly critical area is export control. As quantum moves closer to mission-critical and defense-relevant applications, controls under regimes such as ITAR and EAR are tightening.[6] Leaders must stay current on classification decisions, understand how they apply to specific hardware, software, and know-how, and structure collaborations and data flows accordingly. What was permissible for a proof-of-concept exchange last year may require a license, or be prohibited, this year.

Beyond export controls, effective compliance management means building and running a formal program: drafting policies that translate abstract legal requirements into concrete rules of behavior, developing training that gives technical teams and managers enough literacy to spot issues early, and deploying monitoring and auditing mechanisms that catch problems before regulators do. Quantum adds its own wrinkles, from handling data that might be subject to multiple legal regimes simultaneously, to protecting sensitive IP while meeting transparency expectations tied to public funding.

Risk assessment sits at the center of this skill. Leaders must be able to identify where quantum activities carry the highest regulatory exposure, prioritize mitigation efforts, and decide when to seek pre-emptive guidance from regulators. Constructive relationships with oversight bodies, grounded in transparency and early engagement, can turn ambiguous requirements into navigable pathways rather than constant sources of fear.

Skill 4: Board reporting and communication

Fourth, quantum governance rises or falls on communications. Leaders must be able to translate highly technical developments into clear, decision-ready narratives for boards and executive audiences. Slides, dashboards, and talking points need to answer the questions directors actually have:

- What have we achieved?
- How does it affect our competitive position?
- What risks are we taking?
- What options are we creating?
- What decisions do you need from us?

This skill begins with thoughtful stakeholder analysis. Boards often include a mix of technology-savvy members and those whose expertise is primarily financial, operational, or sectoral. Effective quantum communication layers information: concise executive summaries that spell out strategic implications for everyone, supported by appendices and optional deep dives for those who want to examine coherence times, error-correction thresholds, or benchmark results in more detail.

Equally important is how leaders talk about uncertainty and risk. Quantum timelines are not just long; they are variable. Competitive dynamics can change with a single external announcement. Some promising avenues will fail. Boards need to hear this clearly, without sugar-coating, but they also need to see evidence that leaders are managing these uncertainties rather than being at their mercy. Scenario-based narratives, explicit risk-mitigation strategies, and regular strategy refreshes are all part of maintaining that confidence.

Board reporting and communication also encompasses crisis communication and opportunity framing. Leaders must know when a setback, such as a failed experiment, a lost partnership, or an adverse regulatory development, warrants immediate board attention versus inclusion in routine reporting. They must also be able to explain competitive threats without panic and frame time-sensitive opportunities in a way that supports high-quality, rapid decision-making.

Skill 5: Process integration

Finally, leaders must become architects of integration, ensuring that quantum governance is not a parallel universe but a fully connected part of how the organization makes decisions. This is as much about organizational design and change management as it is about quantum itself.

Process integration starts with mapping existing governance workflows, how technology decisions are made, how risks are escalated, how budgets are approved, how partnerships are vetted, and then designing touchpoints where quantum committees and stakeholders plug in. The goal is to create clear, predictable interfaces rather than ad hoc workarounds.

Change management is essential. New quantum governance structures can easily be perceived as encroaching on existing authority or adding bureaucracy. Leaders need to communicate the purpose and benefits of quantum governance, provide training on new processes, and listen to concerns from affected groups. Addressing resistance through engagement, rather than top-down mandates, makes it more likely that quantum governance will be used as intended rather than bypassed.

Conflict resolution is part of this skill as well. There will be real philosophical differences between those pushing for quantum innovation and those charged with protecting the firm from risk. Effective integrators can distinguish between conflicts that reflect incompatible goals and those that are simply misaligned incentives or misunderstandings. They facilitate structured conversations that move the organization toward workable compromises, rather than allowing entrenched positions to stall progress.

Finally, process integration requires ongoing measurements and refinement. Leaders should track indicators such as governance overhead, decision cycle times, the rate at which decisions are implemented as intended, and feedback from participants about process effectiveness.

Where integration creates bottlenecks or leaves gaps, governance structures and workflows can be adjusted so that quantum oversight remains both robust and efficient.

Summary

This chapter brought together these themes into a coherent blueprint for governing quantum initiatives with the same intentionality organizations apply to their most strategic business decisions. It shows that effective quantum governance depends on specialized structures that blend strategic oversight with deep technical understanding, while still remaining agile enough to adapt as technologies and markets evolve. From committee design and decision protocols to compliance frameworks and communication systems, the chapter outlines the institutional scaffolding needed to navigate high uncertainty without losing control.

We also made clear that strategic objective setting for quantum cannot simply reuse classical IT playbooks. With timelines uncertain and performance gains potentially exponential, organizations must combine durable strategic themes with adaptive KPIs and maturity models that track technical, business, and strategic progress without locking them into obsolete goals. Those that excel in quantum strategic planning learn to pair ambition with realism, using milestones as tools for learning and course correction, not just as reporting artifacts.

Regulatory compliance emerges as a core governance competency, not a peripheral concern. As post-quantum cryptography standards roll out and national and regional strategies harden into concrete rules, organizations must monitor evolving requirements across export controls, sector regulations, data protection laws, and national security policies. The chapter emphasizes that reactive compliance is no longer sufficient; proactive, integrated programs are now essential for any serious quantum effort.

Stakeholder communication sits alongside compliance as a key enabler of sustainable quantum investment. The frameworks and examples in this chapter show how to craft messages that resonate with boards, investors, employees, customers, and partners, making quantum progress understandable without oversimplification, and exciting without exaggeration. Organizations that get this right will build durable support, even through inevitable setbacks.

Perhaps the most underappreciated lesson is the importance of integration with existing corporate governance. Quantum cannot be allowed to drift outside established structures, nor can it be smothered by frameworks designed for mature, low-uncertainty technologies. The integration tools and assessment framework presented here help leaders avoid fragmented efforts, conflicting decisions, and governance gaps that can derail promising programs.

By investing in the five critical skills outlined – governance framework development, strategic planning execution, compliance management, board reporting and communication, and process integration – leaders equip themselves and their organizations to steer quantum initiatives toward genuine competitive advantage rather than short-lived experiments. These capabilities are learned, not inherited, and they grow through deliberate practice, structured learning, and exposure to real governance challenges.

The path forward is demanding but clear. As global quantum investment accelerates, through at least $10 billion in government funding by April 2025 and billions more in private capital, organizations that treat governance as a first-class capability will be far better positioned to convert technical promise into durable value. Governance, in this sense, is not friction; it's the operating system that allows quantum innovation to scale safely, strategically, and sustainably.

That governance model should also reflect an important reality; not every organization needs to be a quantum first mover. The right posture depends on the industry, the business problem, the level of competitive exposure, and the organization's ability to absorb technical and financial uncertainty. For some companies, particularly those in sectors where quantum could materially reshape core products, security, optimization, simulation, or intellectual property, early capability-building may be strategically important. For others, a fast-follower approach may be the better choice, allowing the organization to watch for technical and commercial milestones, learn from early adopters, and enter once the value proposition is clearer. Still others may never need substantial in-house quantum expertise at all and may instead consume quantum capabilities through trusted technology providers, cloud platforms, consultants, or industry partners. In those cases, the strategic advantage comes less from building the technology and more from knowing where to adopt it, which problems are worth solving, and which partners can be trusted to deliver.

This distinction also changes how quantum should be treated inside the organization. In many cases, quantum belongs initially in an incubation environment where experimentation, learning, and capability development are valued even before conventional ROI can be demonstrated. But it should not become a protected laboratory with no connection to business outcomes. Unlike a typical incubation effort, quantum can create both opportunity and enterprise risk at the same time, particularly where cybersecurity, long-lived data, regulation, supply chains, or competitive positioning are involved. A better model is disciplined incubation; give teams room to explore, but establish clear learning objectives, spending limits, decision gates, and triggers for when an initiative should be expanded, partnered, paused, or stopped. The goal is not to force every early experiment to generate immediate returns, but to ensure that each one answers a useful strategic question and improves the organization's ability to make the next investment decision.

This brings us to the close of Part 1. Here, we focused on the "what," the key steps needed to begin preparing your organization for quantum readiness. In Part 2, we turn to the "how."

While many discussions outline what should be done, far fewer take the next step of describing how to actually do it. We'll begin that journey in the next chapter with the foundation of it all: workforce development and skills strategy.

Further reading

1. https://www.ibm.com/thought-leadership/institute-business-value/en-us/report/2025-quantum-computing-readiness
2. https://thequantuminsider.com/2025/08/23/researchers-promote-global-standards-over-regulation-as-a-more-flexible-path-to-quantum-governance/
3. https://www.oecd.org/en/publications/an-overview-of-national-strategies-and-policies-for-quantum-technologies_5e55e7ab-en.html
4. https://doi.org/10.1140/epjqt/s40507-024-00245-x
5. https://www.ibm.com/quantum/ibm-quantum-network
6. https://www.congress.gov/crs-product/IF11836
7. https://qubip.eu/
8. https://www.congress.gov/crs-product/IF11836
9. https://www.reuters.com/world/china/china-set-up-national-venture-capital-guidance-fund-state-planner-says-2025-03-06/
10. https://www.sec.gov/files/cft-written-input-daniel-bruno-corvelo-costa-090325.pdf
11. https://www.congress.gov/crs-product/IF11836
12. https://thequantuminsider.com/2025/08/23/researchers-promote-global-standards-over-regulation-as-a-more-flexible-path-to-quantum-governance/
13. https://www.datacenterdynamics.com/en/news/google-ceo-practical-quantum-computers-likely-still-a-decade-away/
14. https://www.weforum.org/projects/quantum-computing-ethics/
15. https://bisi.org.uk/reports/uk-google-quantum-collaboration-implications-of-the-willow-chip-partnership
16. https://www.mckinsey.com/capabilities/tech-and-ai/our-insights/the-year-of-quantum-from-concept-to-reality-in-2025

17. https://www.spinquanta.com/news-detail/quantum-computing-funding-explosive-growth-strategic-investment-2025
18. https://www.spinquanta.com/news-detail/quantum-startups-disrupting-the-future-of-computing
19. https://www.quantinuum.com/press-releases/introducing-quantinuum
20. https://www.quantinuum.com/blog/quantinuum-extends-its-significant-lead-in-quantum-computing-achieving-historic-milestones-for-hardware-fidelity-and-quantum-volume
21. https://blogs.microsoft.com/blog/2024/09/10/microsoft-announces-the-best-performing-logical-qubits-on-record-and-will-provide-priority-access-to-reliable-quantum-hardware-in-azure-quantum/
22. https://qt.eu/media/pdf/KPI_booklet_2025.pdf?m=1744347631&

Part 2

Building the Quantum-Ready Enterprise: From Strategy to Execution

You've aligned your leadership, articulated your quantum strategy, and secured a seat at the table. Now comes the hard part, actually building something.

Part II is where quantum readiness gets real. The chapters ahead are written for the technical leaders who will be held accountable for turning quantum ambition into working systems: the CTOs fielding architecture questions they've never had to answer before, the CIOs wondering whether their infrastructure can survive the transition, and the CDOs quietly realizing their data pipelines weren't designed for any of this. If that sounds familiar, you're in exactly the right place.

Across Chapters 5 through 8, you'll work through the four pillars of quantum-era technical readiness; infrastructure, talent, prototyping, and data, in the sequence that matters for execution. You won't find abstract theory here. You'll find assessment frameworks you can apply to your current environment this quarter, vendor evaluation tools grounded in real performance metrics, workforce strategies that acknowledge just how scarce quantum talent is, and data architecture guidance that will save you from costly retrofitting down the road.

Think of this section as your technical implementation playbook. Each chapter builds on the last, moving you from understanding what your organization currently has, to building the teams capable of using it, to running the pilots that will tell you whether quantum investment is genuinely warranted, and finally, to ensuring your data infrastructure is ready to deliver when production quantum systems arrive.

The gap between organizations that assess and modernize now versus those that wait is widening every month. The chapters ahead give you the frameworks to act with precision, not panic.

This part of the book includes the following chapters:

5

Quantum-AI Infrastructure Assessment

If you stripped away the buzzwords/jargon, most quantum-AI conversations with infrastructure teams boil down to a deceptively simple question: "Can our stack handle this without breaking?" You are not being asked to build a quantum computer; you are being asked to make your infrastructure a competent host for quantum resources that live in someone else's data center, or in time could live in our own. For a CTO, CIO, or CDO, that is a very different challenge than "doing quantum research."

Now, mix that with the experience you have if you've lived through at least one major technology wave: cloud, big data, mobile devices, or deep learning (happy to report I lived, and survived all of the above), then you already know the pattern: the organizations that benefit early are rarely the ones that bet the most money; they are the ones whose infrastructure and teams are ready when the technology crosses from interesting to useful. I recall the time, after joining the AI team at IBM, when I was sitting with clients interested in using this fresh new commercial technology. The first question I would ask is, "could I sit with your data scientists to discuss use cases." Almost every single one had a similar answer, "What's a data scientist?"

Of course, Quantum-AI will follow a similar trajectory. The hard truth for technical executives, startup founders, or research directors is that near-term advantage is mostly in learning and integration readiness, not immediate ROI. The headline wins will be rare; the quietly compounding advantage will sit inside teams who already know how to plug quantum services into their existing pipelines the day they matter.

In practice, "being quantum ready" is not about buying quantum hardware or signaling a flashy cloud contract. It's about much more mundane things:

- Do you know the latency from your core data centers to the major quantum clouds?
- Can you spin up a reproducible environment where developers can safely experiment with quantum SDKs?
- Do your data pipelines and feature stores serve the kinds of structured problems quantum-AI will likely touch first? For example, routing, optimization, anomaly patterns, molecular representations?

Readiness lives in these details, not in strategy decks.

I wrote this chapter for you with that same practical spirit. You and I will treat quantum-AI as a hybrid extension of your current stack and walk through how to evaluate your architecture for that reality. We will look at vendor platforms through the lens of integration fit, not hype. We will spend most of our time on the unglamorous but critical work: assessing your infrastructure, designing migration patterns, and enabling your teams so that, when you decide to run a quantum pilot in supply chain routing, fraud/anomaly detection, or drug discovery, you are not starting from zero.

We'll of course stay conversational and concrete as we have been throughout this book. Instead of just listing requirements, we'll walk through scenarios such as:

- What it looks like when your head of infrastructure runs a six-week readiness sprint
- How a pharma data platform team might wire a quantum chemistry workflow into their existing pipelines
- How can a manufacturing CIO frame a quantum-AI roadmap so it supports current AI and spotlights Pasqal, IonQ, QBlox, and several hyperscalers not as heroes, but as examples of patterns you can adapt?

By the end of this chapter, you should be able to do three things. First, look at your current systems and roughly score their quantum-AI readiness with a maturity model that makes sense to both engineers and board members. Second, turn that score into a prioritized migration path that aligns with your existing modernization programs. Third, lead conversations with vendors, partners, and your own teams from a position of calm, informed confidence: you are not buying magic, you are investing now to be prepared for the not-so-distant future.

Main topics and key insights covered in this chapter are:

- Hybrid computing architecture evaluation
- Cloud quantum services: vendor landscape and integration requirements

- Infrastructure readiness assessment methodology
- Migration planning and phased integration roadmaps
- Assessment tools, benchmarks, and evaluation frameworks

A quick note before we dive in: what is Quantum-AI?

Before we get into the meat of this chapter, I want to take a moment to address something you may have already noticed: the term "quantum-AI." It deserves a proper explanation, because if you are going to invest your time and organizational energy in the ideas ahead, you should know exactly what I mean by it.

Here is the honest truth: if you look around your organization right now, AI is already there. Maybe it's a scheduling assistant quietly optimizing your calendar. Maybe it's a developer platform your engineering team uses to accelerate code reviews. Maybe it's something far more sophisticated, woven into the products you ship or the decisions your operations depend on. Whatever form it takes, AI has already made itself at home in your infrastructure, and frankly, if it has not yet, then that is a conversation worth having sooner rather than later!

So, when I use the term "quantum-AI" throughout this chapter and those that follow, I'm not referring to quantum machine learning or some exotic fusion of quantum physics and artificial intelligence, tempting as that might be. That said, it is a space I'm actively exploring, and I'll be sharing more on LinkedIn and through an upcoming project, so stay tuned. But for now, let's stay on track.

What I mean by quantum-AI is much more practical and immediate. It's simply a way of describing the integration of your existing classical computing systems and AI workflows with quantum computing capabilities, what the field sometimes calls quantum-classical computing, hybrid computing, or quantum-centric supercomputing, etc. I simply use "quantum-AI" because it more accurately reflects the reality of where modern infrastructure is headed. Plus, it's easier to say and it uses a lot less ink.

Hybrid computing architecture evaluation

Modern quantum and classical computing is no longer a single architecture; it's a design pattern, classical-quantum-classical loops orchestrated across heterogeneous resources. In practice, your architecture's readiness depends on how well it can support that loop under real workloads, with realistic data sizes and latency constraints.[1]

How Quantum-AI actually lands in your stack

This may come as a surprise to a lot of firms, but almost every realistic near-term scenario for quantum-AI has the same basic shape. Quantum does not show up as a brand-new platform sitting off to the side. It shows up as a special step inside a workflow you already run.

A supply chain routing system, for example, might use classical ML models to forecast demand and capacity, then call out to a quantum subroutine to solve a particularly tough routing or packing problem, then return to classical code to update schedules and trigger logistics actions. A Fraud or anomaly detection platform might use quantum routines to explore alternative clustering boundaries in an offline model improvement process, while day-to-day scoring stays entirely classical.

These scenarios share an iterative classical-quantum-classical loop. Data is cleaned and transformed on CPUs and GPUs. Certain pieces are encoded into quantum-friendly representations and sent to a quantum processing unit (QPU) via an SDK. Results come back and are integrated into optimization or learning steps. The loop may run thousands of times in a single job, especially for variational algorithms. That raises practical architecture questions about latency, throughput, and orchestration: can you feed the QPU efficiently, and can you make good use of the results without stalling the rest of the system?

If you sketched this on a whiteboard, you would probably draw three zones: a classical compute zone (CPUs, GPUs, containers, microservices), a quantum service zone (cloud QPUs or simulators behind APIs), and a control or orchestration zone that coordinates the dance between them. The joins between these zones are where your readiness really lives. It's often not the quantum component that fails a pilot. It's the brittle Python script that nobody can redeploy, the unexpected 200+ milliseconds of latency to a quantum endpoint, or the missing observability that leaves your SRE team blind when a hybrid pipeline misbehaves.

Evaluating topology: where hybrid lives

Your first design decision is deceptively simple: where does hybrid logic live?

Do you embed it in your existing data science platform, inside your MLOps workflows? Do you treat quantum jobs as a new kind of HPC workload scheduled by the same engine that runs simulations today? Or do you build a separate "quantum sandbox" that is loosely coupled to production until you feel comfortable? These questions will help determine the right path, as illustrated in the following workflow diagram.

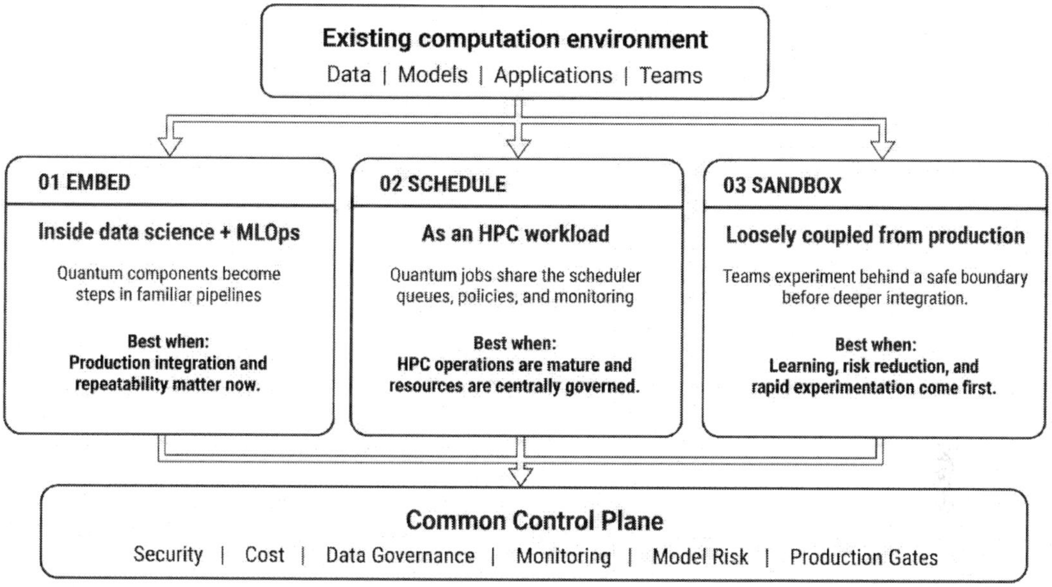

Figure 5.1: Workflow diagram

There is no single right answer, but there are patterns that make your life much easier.

Many organizations start by co-locating hybrid workloads as close as possible to their quantum providers. If your primary cloud also hosts your quantum platform, that might mean running your classical control code in the same regions and virtual networks where the QPUs are exposed. This minimizes latency and networking complexity and lets your team reuse identity and security patterns they already understand. Over time, as you move from experiments to pilots, you may bring the control layer closer to your core systems, integrating hybrid pipelines into your existing orchestrators (Kubernetes, Airflow, managed workflow services) and treating quantum calls like any other external service dependency with SLAs, retries, and fallbacks.

In order to properly evaluate your topology, you need to ask a few very straightforward questions. Do we know the network paths between our control and orchestration systems and the quantum endpoints? Do we have enough GPU and CPU capacity near that control plane to run the heavy classical parts of the hybrid algorithms? Do we have clear boundaries where we can insert quantum calls without ripping apart existing applications? A simple practical exercise is to take your current training and inference pipelines, draw them on a whiteboard, and mark where a quantum call could logically fit. That simple exercise alone often surfaces missing APIs, inconsistent data formats, or observability gaps that you can fix long before you run your first quantum job.

Hybrid architecture readiness scoring

To move beyond what most call, "this feels good" toward something you can track and monitor, it helps to adopt a small hybrid architecture readiness scoring framework. Think along these three dimensions: latency tolerance, parallelism capacity, and orchestration maturity. For each, you assign a score from 1 (nascent) to 5 (production-ready) based on evidence, not gut feel. The following Table illustrates a Hybrid Architecture Readiness Scoring Matrix for you to get started and build upon:

Dimension	Score 1-2: Nascent	Score 3: Emerging	Score 4: Advanced	Score 5: Production Ready
Latency Tolerance	No consistent quantum endpoint testing. Latency unknown or based on ad hoc manual pings	Some measurements to at least one endpoint. Basic P95 latency known, but no colocation strategy	Regular latency measurements to multiple endpoints Co-location of control workloads in at least one region that meets target latency.	Latency SLOs defined for hybrid workloads Endpoints and control code placed intentionally to meet those budgets, with dashboards and alerts
Parallelism capacity	Only a single hybrid job runs at a time, often manually No concept of concurrent scheduling	Small batches of jobs run concurrently, but orchestration is script-based and fragile	Workflow tools or orchestrators manage dozens of concurrent hybrid jobs with basic quotas or backpressure	Autoscaling and policy-driven orchestration for hybrid workloads Hundreds of thousands of concurrent jobs supported with predictable behavior
Orchestration maturity	No hybrid-aware orchestration Individual scripts handle submission and result handling	Basic workflows exist, but monitoring and error handling are partial or inconsistent	Integrated workflows with proper logging, retries, and basic tracing of quantum calls	Unified orchestration and observability across CPU, GPU, and QPI steps with clear ownership and runbooks

Table 5.1: Hybrid Architecture Readiness Scoring Matrix

Keep in mind that you don't need to obsess over precise numbers. The real value here is in creating a shared language with your organization. This way, when your head of infrastructure says, "for hybrid quantum-AI we are at about a 2 on latency measurement and a 3 on orchestration," everyone on the team knows what that means, and most importantly, where to invest.

Company spotlight: NVIDIA CUDA-Q as a hybrid platform

One useful reference pattern that comes to mind is how NVIDIA CUDA-Q approaches hybrid computing. CUDA-Q is designed to let you express quantum kernels alongside classical code in a single, coherent programming, and execution model, with GPUs and QPUs treated as peers in the same workflow. For your teams, this can feel like an extension of familiar CUDA and HPC practices: you write classical and quantum pieces together, package them into containers or jobs, and let the underlying runtime handle dispatch across CPUs, GPUs, and QPUs, and quantum backends.[2]

From an architecture evaluation perspective, this is attractive because it gives you a clear, code-level pattern for heterogeneous execution without forcing you to reinvent orchestration from scratch. You can imagine a supply chain or anomaly detection workload where GPUs handle heavy numerical work while QPUs are called for specific optimization or sampling steps, all coordinated in one CUDA-Q program. At the same time, it raises important questions you should address early. How will you monitor these multi-backend workflows from your existing observability stack? How does CUDA-Q integrate with your current job schedulers, Kubernetes clusters, and security controls? If you rely on CUDA-Q abstractions, then how portable are your workloads across different quantum providers or hardware generations?

Using these questions to evaluate the CUDA-Q pattern, and not just NVIDIA as a vendor, teaches your organization how to think about hybrid architecture in a way that blends accelerators and quantum cleanly. Even if you later use different tools or platforms, you will have a concrete example of what "good heterogeneous integration" looks like: a model where CPUs, GPUs, and QPUs are orchestrated together, with data movement, observability, and governance treated as first-class design concerns.

Cloud quantum services: vendor landscape and integration requirements

Cloud quantum services are increasingly where your organization will first encounter practical quantum capabilities, yet the differences that matter to you as a technical leader are rarely the ones highlighted in glossy announcements. In this section, we will zoom out from individual algorithms and look at the broader vendor landscape through a very specific lens: how will each platform best fit into your existing stack. You will see how to think beyond qubit counts and benchmark headlines and instead focus on SDK ergonomics, hybrid runtimes, network and regional alignment, identity and access integration, observability, and data handling. The goal is not to crown a "winner," but to give you a structured way to compare platforms, ask sharper questions in vendor meetings, and design proof-of-concepts that test real integration friction. By the end, you should be able to look at any cloud quantum offering and quickly assess whether it supports the kinds of hybrid workflows, governance expectations, and migration paths your organization needs over the next few years. Let's start by shifting the question out of just what's the best qubit.

Shifting the question: from "Best Qubits" to "Best Fit"

It is tempting to treat cloud quantum platforms like a benchmark race that looks to see who has the most qubits, who's faster, or cleaner. That contest changes every few months and is largely out of your control. What you can control, and what will matter most in the next few years, is integration fit. A good example of what a "best fit" for the financial industry means is the platform that lives closest to your trading and risk systems, uses authentication methods your security team already approves, and integrates cleanly with your logging, metrics, and deployment pipelines. For a pharma company, it might mean a platform that offers deep integration with HPC schedulers and supports the chemistry-focused tool chains your researchers rely on. In both cases, immediate benefit comes from being able to run realistic experiments without rearchitecting half your environment.

What your stack must do

Regardless of which vendor you pick, your environment needs to do a handful of things well. First, you must be able to host hybrid control code near the quantum service. That means reproducible environments: containers, images, standard development setups, where your team can install quantum SDKs, connect securely to APIs, and run both classical and quantum portions of hybrid workloads. If spinning up such environments today requires manual work or special permissions, that is a readiness flag.

Second, your identity and access management systems must treat quantum services as first-class citizens. In practice, this means having a way to create and manage service identities for quantum workloads, assign appropriate permissions, and log access for audit. If your Identity Access Management (IAM) and security teams have never been asked to review quantum-related services, now is the time to start that conversation!

Third, your data pipelines must be able to serve and capture the data involved in quantum experiments. For a supply chain use case, this might mean feeding compact but structured problem instances into hybrid jobs and storing results in existing databases or data lakes. For drug discovery, it might involve generating molecular representations from cheminformatics platforms and capturing outputs for downstream analysis. The goal is to avoid isolated "quantum side projects" that live outside your normal data and governance patterns.

Practical vendor evaluation matrix

If you've been in the quantum industry as long as I have, you've probably heard the various vendors talk about their quantum systems and how great each one is with respect to other vendors. However, most of these vendors don't use the same cloud platform for you to select and access. So when choosing a vendor, you don't have to just look at the quality of these systems; you need to also consider how you would integrate them into your own system. Thankfully, there are a few qualifying questions you may consider asking, where each could provide you with the information needed to determine whether their systems are "best fit" for your immediate and long-term needs. The following simple vendor evaluation matrix should help you keep your focus on what matters most for integration.

Dimension	Guiding Questions	Score (1-5)	Weight (Low/ Med/High)	Notes
Hybrid runtime quality	How easy is it to write, deploy, and operate hybrid workflows? Are these concepts like sessions or job containers that simplify iterative algorithms?		High	Consider sample complexity and developer experience
SDK and tooling alignment	Does the platform support the languages, frameworks, and CI/CD tools your teams use today? Can you manage it with your infrastructure-as-code approach?		High	Look at documentation quality, testing patterns, and library stability
Network and regional alignment	Where are the quantum services hosted relative to your main regions and data centers? Are private connectivity options available if needed?		Med	Note any regions where latency or policy constraints could be a problem
Operational transparency	Do you have visibility into queue times, error rates, resource usage, and failures? Can you integrate these signals into your existing observability stack?		Med	Consider both real-time monitoring and historical reporting
Error mitigation and reliability	What mechanisms exist for error mitigation or correction? How often is hardware calibrated? How stable are services over time?		Med	Evaluate both technical features and track record
Portability and lock-in	How easily can circuits, workflows, or intermediate formats move to other providers if needed? Are you tied to proprietary abstractions?		Low to Med	Higher scores mean more flexibility and standards-based approaches

Table 5.2: Cloud Quantum Vendor Integration Evaluation Matrix

You do not need to be perfect here. This is a rough scoring exercise, anchored in a small proof of concept, which will give you far better insight than any marketing deck.

Company spotlights: IonQ and a Hyperscaler

IonQ offers a useful example because it has a clear hardware identity, trapped-ion qubits, and a growing focus on enterprise integrations. For you, the interesting part is how their services are wrapped: accessible through major cloud ecosystems, with tools aimed at real workloads in chemistry, optimization, and machine learning. If your organization already uses those clouds heavily, IonQ can be a low-friction way to explore quantum while staying within familiar operational boundaries.[3]

On the other hand, a hyperscale cloud's own quantum platform may appeal to some, mostly due to the depth of integration. You get the same IAM patterns, the same network constructs, the same logging and monitoring sinks. That really makes life easier for your security and operations teams and for any pilot that needs to touch production-like data or pipelines. The tradeoff is that you may find it harder to compare or move workloads elsewhere later.

Your vendor matrix helps you see these tradeoffs clearly. Instead of "which brand is the best this year," the question becomes "which platform is the best fit for how we build and operate systems today, and how easily could we switch if the landscape shifts?"

Infrastructure readiness: assessment methodology

This is one of the anchor sections of this chapter, because it's where abstract readiness turns into something you can actually do over the next few months. Think of it as a playbook for a six-to-eight-week quantum-AI readiness sprint led by your infrastructure and platform teams, with support from security, data, and a handful of forward-leaning applied researchers or data scientists.

Four domains, one story

We'll start by organizing your assessment around four domains: network and connectivity, compute and memory, storage and data pipelines, and security and governance. Each domain tells a different part of the story, but together they will provide you with a nice full picture of how well your environment can support hybrid quantum-AI workflows. Let's get started with the first domain.

In the *network and connectivity* domain, you care about basic but critical facts. What is the latency from your main regions or data centers to the quantum services you might use? Do you have private connectivity options? Where are the possible bottlenecks, legacy firewalls, overloaded links, or odd routing that could make hybrid workflows act flaky? For a supply chain use case, where an optimization engine runs in a specific region, you want to know what it would actually cost, in milliseconds, and reliability, to call out to a quantum service from there.

For *compute and memory*, your focus is the classical side of hybrid algorithms. Do you have enough GPU capacity and scheduling flexibility to support optimization and simulation loops around quantum calls? Are those resources accessible to the teams likely to experiment, or reserved for unrelated jobs? In a drug discovery scenario, your quantum chemistry researchers may already be using CPU/GPU clusters. Part of your assessment is understanding whether those environments are ready to host hybrid workflows or need modernization first.

Storage and data pipelines tell you whether you can feed and capture quantum workloads cleanly. Are the data sources relevant to your target use cases, supply chain networks, sensor or transaction telemetry, molecular libraries, available in standardized, governed formats? Do you have feature stores, data marts, or APIs that serve structured problem instances suitable for quantum optimization or simulation? If the only way to assemble a routing problem today is through a series of manual queries and spreadsheets, that is a clear readiness gap.

Finally, *security and governance* ensure that quantum-AI does not become an exception to your normal standards. Can you create identities and roles specifically for quantum services? Are network paths locked down appropriately? Do you know where quantum outputs will land and how they will be classified? For anomaly detection pilots that touch production telemetry, for example, you will want any quantum-enhanced pipelines to inherit the same logging, monitoring, and incident response patterns as your existing analytics systems.

Quantum-AI infrastructure readiness maturity model

To make this concrete, it helps to define a maturity model with four levels. The labels in the following table will help keep it simple and easy to discuss.

Level	Label	Network Connectivity	Compute & Memory	Storage & Data Pipelines	Security & Governance
0	No Quantum Awareness	No measurements to quantum endpoints No architecture diagrams mention quantum	No GPU or accelerator capacity earmarked for AI or quantum experiments	Data relevant to potential use cases is fragmented and accessed manually	Quantum services are not recognized in IAM, risk, or governance processes
1	Experimental Curiosity	Best-effort connectivity using public internet	Small GPU nodes exist and are used for AI proofs of concept, often informally	Prototype scripts exist to build small quantum-ready datasets for experiments	Ad hoc cloud accounts or trial access used for experiments with minimal oversight
2	Structured Pilot Ready	Latency and jitter measures to at least one quantum endpoint Basic dashboards exist	Dedicated GPU pools available for hybrid ptimization and simulation	Standardized data formats and regular ETL into feature sets for target use cases	IAM roles and policies define quantum APIs Basic audit logging is in place
3	Scalable Pilot & Pre-Production	Private links or optimized routing in place for key regions Latency SLOs for pilot workloads	Elastic scaling for hybrid workloads Resource managers can schedule and prioritize hybrid jobs	Streamlined, scalable pipelines that can feed hybrid applications without manual steps	Quantum projects integrated into security review and continuous monitoring
4	Production-Grade Hybrid Pipelines	Hybrid latency is monitored and managed like any other critical dependency	Unified resource management across CPU, GPU, and QPU Capacity planning includes quantum	Data quality checks and lineage tracking explicitly cover quantum-enhanced workflows	Quantum pipelines are fully folded into governance, risk, and compliance frameworks

Table 5.3: Quantum-AI infrastructure readiness maturity model

In your readiness sprint, you can score each domain against these levels. The important rule to keep in mind is to ground scores in evidence. Meaning, if there are no metrics, documentation, or configurations to point to, then the level is probably lower than people think.

How to run a six- to eight-week readiness sprint

You can run a meaningful readiness sprint in one or two months if you keep the scope focused. There are many patterns you can use; however, of all the various patterns I have tried, the following pattern seems to work the best:

- ***Weeks 1-2: Discovery and inventory***
  In the first two weeks, assemble a small cross-functional team: someone from infrastructure or platform engineering, network, security, data engineering, and an applied industry lead. Together, identify two or three target use cases you care about over the next two to three years, such as supply chain routing, anomaly detection, and a drug discovery exploration. For each, sketch how things work today. Where does data come from? What systems process it? What compute resources are used? This yields a handful of honest architecture diagrams that capture reality, not wishful thinking. To help you get started, you can find useful examples on either the Qiskit or qBraid learning platform.
- ***Weeks 3-4: Measurement and scoring***
  Next, run a few simple tests. Measure latency from key regions to at least one quantum endpoint. Spin up a test environment with a quantum SDK and run a tiny hybrid-style job to see how hard it is. Exercise your GPU clusters with workloads that resemble the classical parts of hybrid algorithms. Then, as a group, score each domain in the maturity model for each use case, ensuring that you document why you picked those levels.
- ***Weeks 5-6 (and possibly 7-8): Gap analysis and options***
  In the final phase, consolidate what you found into a gap register. Group gaps by domain and tag them as pilot blockers, pre-production constraints, or "nice to fix." Then brainstorm a small set of readiness moves you could accomplish in the next six to twelve months. These might include "add quantum endpoints to our IAM catalog," "standardize a container image for hybrid workloads," or "instrument latency dashboards for outbound calls to candidate regions." Wherever possible, choose moves that also benefit your broader AI, data, or cloud modernization programs.

The output of this sprint should not be your final quantum strategy, far from it. It's something better: a grounded view of where you stand and a short list of improvements that will make your infrastructure healthier regardless of how fast quantum evolves.

Company spotlight: Pasqal and hybrid HPC readiness

Pasqal's work with European high-performance computing centers offers a concrete example of what hybrid readiness looks like in practice. In those collaborations, quantum processors are integrated alongside large classical HPC systems.[4] The centers do not abandon their simulation and modeling stacks. They extend them to include Pasqal's neutral-atom devices as specialized accelerators.

HPC operations teams must answer very practical questions. How will quantum jobs be scheduled through existing batch systems? How are they metered and accounted for? How are results stored, and how do they appear alongside classical simulation outputs? Where are the security boundaries? None of this is abstract. It's the same kind of integration work you face, just in a different environment.

The pattern is instructive even if you don't run an HPC center. Rather than building a separate "quantum island," look for your most mature platform, maybe your AI platform, maybe your analytics environment, and ask how it could treat quantum resources as a new type of accelerator. Your readiness assessment would then have a clear anchor in real systems, rather than floating in a separate quantum bubble.

Migration planning and phased integration roadmap

If the readiness assessment tells you where you are, then the migration roadmap tells you how to move from there in a sane way. This is the second anchor of the chapter: combining infrastructure modernization, technical enablement, technical debt, and practical quantum-AI pilots into a coherent journey. It does bear reminding you that the level of process of validation/verification and technical debt needs to always be addressed during the migration process.

Three phases you will recognize

Across industries, migration patterns tend to fall into three overlapping phases as illustrated in the following diagram:

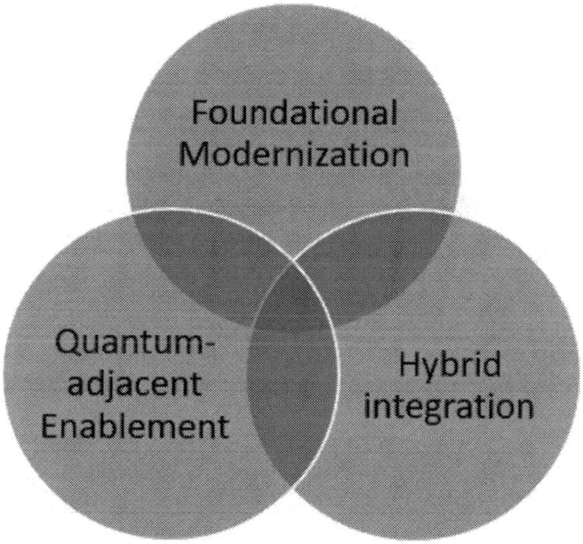

Figure 5.2: Phases of migration patterns

These phases are not strictly sequential. You might have some teams at phase three while others are still at phase one. But the structure is useful for aligning stakeholders and budgets.

In *foundational modernization*, your investments look familiar. You modernize APIs for key systems, expand containerization, strengthen CI/CD, consolidate or upgrade GPU and AI infrastructure, and clean up data pipelines and feature stores. None of this is unique to quantum. All of it is necessary for quantum-AI to sit comfortably in your environment.

In *quantum-adjacent enablement*, you begin adding quantum-specific capabilities. You create standardized environments that include quantum SDKs. You set up controlled access to one of two quantum platforms. You instrument basic network paths to those endpoints. You identify a small number of realistic use cases and start running experiments on real or simulated quantum backends. These experiments motivate and validate the modernization work.

In *hybrid integration*, you start wiring quantum into live workflows, carefully. This might mean adding a "quantum-enhanced" branch to a planning system that runs in parallel with a classical baseline or incorporating quantum kernels into an offline model improvement loop. Your focus here is not just technical. It's operational reliability, observability, and stakeholder trust. All of which should be very important at all times.

Migration patterns for supply chain, anomaly detection, and drug discovery

Let's put the rubber to the road here and visualize how these phases play out in specific domains.

In *supply chain routing and planning*, you may already have engines built on mixed-integer programming, heuristics, or vendor systems. A sensible path is to start with offline experiments. Take real historical routing problems, run quantum or quantum-inspired solvers against them in a lab environment, and compare solution quality and runtime to your current approach. At the same time, clean up the data and APIs required to serve these problem instances from your source systems.

If those experiments show promise, then you can move on and design a hybrid pilot where a subset of planning scenarios is routed through a hybrid service. Importantly, you keep your existing solver as a reference and fallback. On the infrastructure side, your roadmap includes building a stable API for submitting problems, ensuring hybrid jobs are scheduled and monitored like other batch jobs, and deciding where to run the control layer.

For *anomaly detection in financial services, energy, or operations*, a good starting point is to treat quantum-AI as a "second opinion" system. Simply create a pipeline that periodically samples telemetry or transactional data, runs it through a quantum-enhanced model in an offline environment, and compares the anomalies it finds with those from your existing models. This lets you study whether quantum-flavored approaches discover interesting patterns without putting them directly in production.

If the results are encouraging, you might then integrate a hybrid branch into your alerting pipeline. For example, certain classes of suspicious events could trigger a quantum-enhanced analysis step before escalation. To support this, your migration plan will include making sure the data used for these decisions flows through your governed pipelines and that any new infrastructure is visible to your operations teams.

In *drug discovery*, the path often begins in research rather than production. Computational chemists might start by running quantum chemistry algorithms on cloud QPUs and simulators under controlled conditions. Your foundational work here is to provide secure access to these services, adequate classical compute nearby, and data management so that results are stored with proper metadata. As certain workflows prove useful, you can refactor them from notebooks into repeatable services or pipelines. Over time, some of these may become candidates for more integrated hybrid workflows tied into your broader R&D platforms.

Across all three domains, you are not promising an immediate transformation. You are quite simply structuring a journey where each step delivers value on its own: better data, cleaner pipelines, more flexible infrastructure, even before quantum provides unique computational gains. That is how you justify investments now as preparing for the not-so-distant future.

Embedding Quantum-AI into governance and risk

One migration challenge is not technical at all. It's about how quantum-AI fits into your existing governance and risk frameworks. Boards, regulators, and internal risk committees are already asking hard questions (believe me I'm hearing them more and more nowadays) about AI, data, and model risk. Quantum-AI will naturally attract the same attention. Your roadmap should therefore include a governance track.

You might adapt your current model risk framework to include quantum-AI experiments and pilots. For each project, you document what data is used, what decisions or recommendations the hybrid system influences, how you validate performance, and what fallbacks exist. For regulated industries, you also make sure any new cross-border data flows or third-party dependencies introduced by quantum cloud services are visible to compliance teams. As you can imagine, this could turn into a big issue for obvious reasons surrounding export controls, regulation, compliance, and other factors we covered in the previous chapters.

Operational risk matters as well. If your anomaly detection pipeline gains a quantum-enhanced branch, do your incident playbooks reflect this? Do operations teams know how to recognize and handle issues specific to the hybrid portion, such as spikes in quantum job failures or degraded performance? Do you have criteria for switching off the quantum branch or reverting to classical-only behavior if needed?

Building these patterns into your roadmap makes the difference between impressive pilots and systems that stakeholders actually trust.

Company spotlight: QBlox and modular controls

QBlox focuses on modular quantum control hardware and software, but the architectural idea behind their work is more general. They treat quantum control systems as modular, rack-level assets that can be integrated into data center environments much like other specialized hardware. There is a consistent control plane, standard interfaces, and clear separation between device-level details and system-level orchestration.[5, 6]

That mindset is exactly what you want to bring into your own migration plans. When you think about wiring quantum into your infrastructure, imagine quantum endpoints, whether physical devices or managed cloud services, as components in a broader control plane. You want consistent ways to configure, monitor, and update them. You want the ability to plug in new quantum capabilities without rewriting all the upstream logic. You want your operations teams to see them in their dashboards and treat them as part of the overall fleet.

Designing your own roadmap around this kind of modularity makes it far more likely that early experiments will evolve into maintainable, scalable systems rather than dead-end prototypes.

Assessment tools, benchmarks, and evaluation frameworks

Even with solid story and clear phases, you still need tools and metrics to ground your decisions. This section stays practical: what helps you decide whether your infrastructure can support realistic experiments and whether a given platform is suitable for your workloads.

Simulators and small-scale benchmarks

Before you commit serious time or budget to quantum hardware access, you can learn a lot by running realistic workloads on simulators and small-scale benchmarks inside your existing environment.

For hybrid algorithms, much of the heavy lifting, such as data preparation, classical optimization, and objective evaluations, happens on CPUs and GPUs. That means you can stress-test those parts today. If a prototype hybrid algorithm chokes your current GPU cluster or reveals painfully slow data access, that is valuable information, even before you touch a real QPU.

A practical approach is to choose one representative problem per use case. For supply chain routing, pick a set of realistic graphs with constraints that matter to you. For anomaly detection, choose slices of your telemetry or transaction data with known anomalies. For drug discovery, select a small set of molecules and target properties. Implement prototype hybrid workflows using simulators, measure runtime, resource consumption, data movement, and failure models, and note where the friction lies.

The goal is not to prove or disprove quantum advantage. It's to uncover infrastructure weaknesses while the stakes are low.

Internal frameworks and checklists

Alongside technical tools, internal frameworks and checklists help you standardize how different teams approach quantum-AI. You might create a one-page "Quantum-AI Experiment Checklist" that every pilot has to fill out. It would ask a few questions such as:

1. Which data sources are involved, and how are they accessed?
2. Which environments are used (development, test, staging)? Are they reproducible?
3. How are results stored, and who will access them?

4. What metrics will you collect for performance and reliability?
5. How will you compare the hybrid approach to a baseline?

You could pair this with a "Hybrid Pipeline Design Template" where teams sketch their architecture: data inputs, classical steps, quantum calls, outputs, and integration points. Over time, you will build a catalog of patterns. New teams can borrow from prior designs rather than start from scratch.

You can also extend your existing architecture review process with a simple quantum-AI section. That section might prompt reviewers to ask about quantum endpoints, data residency, and failure modes. The point is to route quantum-AI efforts through the same governance machinery as any other significant change.

Interpreting benchmarks

Eventually, you will have to look at vendor benchmarks and decide how much they matter for you. The trick is to keep two simple questions in mind. First, what does this benchmark tell us about circuits that look like our workloads?[7] Second, under what conditions were these numbers measured?[1]

If a provider shows an impressive circuit depth or a particular speed, ask whether those circuits resemble the kind of problems you care about. A grid optimization problem in energy might have very different structure from a small chemistry example. Similarly, ask whether performance numbers were measured with or without error mitigation and what variability looks like.

Often, the most useful benchmarks are the ones you design for yourself. A modest-sized routing problem, a small anomaly detection subtask, or a constrained molecular example can serve as a bespoke "fitness test" across platforms. You run the same workload through each provider, collect the results, and compare not just speed and quality, but also developer effort and operational friction.

Example: an energy utility's readiness journey

Consider a large energy utility that wants to explore quantum-AI for grid optimization and anomaly detection in sensor networks. The CIO is not expecting to slash costs in year one. The aim is to build capacity before grid complexity and regulation make that capacity essential.

The utility starts with an eight-week readiness sprint. They map out their current telemetry pipelines, forecasting tools, and grid simulation systems. They discover that their best-managed platform is an internal data and analytics environment in a major cloud, with reasonable GPU capacity but weak network observability.

Using simulators, they prototype hybrid workflows that simulate small sections of the grid and detect anomalies in sensor data. This surfaces practical issues: data models are inconsistent across regions, environment provisioning for experiments is slow, and monitoring for outbound calls is patchy.

Rather than jumping straight into production quantum pilots, they spend four to six months on foundational work. They standardize data models, improve CI/CD for analytics workloads, and integrate basic network and job observability. In parallel, a small team runs occasional experiments on a quantum cloud platform, building hands-on experience.

A year later, when a new generation of quantum hardware becomes available and a vendor offers a targeted optimization service, the utility company is in a very different position. Their data is cleaner. Their orchestration tools are modern. Their teams know how to evaluate and integrate a new compute resource. The investment they made early was not speculative; it was preparation for a future that is now arriving!

Skills learned

The last part of this chapter focuses on leadership skills. These are not about writing circuits. They are about steering your organization as quantum-AI moves from idea to reality.

Hybrid architecture design evaluation

Hybrid architecture design evaluation is the ability to look at a proposed design and quickly see whether it stands on solid ground. When a team presents a diagram for a supply chain pilot that includes a quantum optimization step, you should be able to ask: Where does the data enter, and how is it validated? Where does the hybrid control logic run? How do we authenticate to the quantum service? What happens if the quantum call is slow or fails? How does this integrate with monitoring and alerting?

You develop this skill by becoming comfortable with building blocks of hybrid workflows, classical pre- and post-processing, orchestration, network paths, IAM, and observability, and by insisting that quantum-AI architectures be held to the same standards as any other critical system.

One practical way to build this muscle is to ask teams to bring early sketches to a regular design review. You can use a short checklist based on the readiness domains and scoring dimensions: are latency expectations defined and plausible? Is the environment reproducible? Are there clear fallbacks? Over time, teams internalize these questions, and the quality of designs improves.

Vendor technical due diligence

Vendor technical due diligence is about shifting the conversation from "what can your hardware do in theory" to "what can we actually run in our environment, at what cost, and risk."

This means preparing integration-focused questions, not just physics-driven ones. Rather than asking "how many qubits do you have," you might ask, "show us how a typical hybrid job is authored, deployed, monitored, and debugged in practice." And instead of "what is your benchmark score," a more practical question is, "what performance can we expect on workloads structured like ours, and how consistent are those results?"

You also test claims by doing small joint experiments. Ask a vendor to spend a few days with your engineers to stand up a simple hybrid pipeline in your experiments. Observe how many manual steps are required, where documentation is unclear, and how often you need support. This gives you a real sense of integration friction.

Over time, you will build a sense for which vendors are aligned with your way of working and which are likely to generate friction, regardless of their latest performance numbers.

Infrastructure gap analysis

Infrastructure gap analysis turns your maturity model and readiness sprint into an action plan. It starts with bringing domain experts together to share their findings from measurements and experiments. Network leads, platform engineers, data engineers, security, and applied AI come to the table with concrete observations. Together, you list gaps. Maybe environment provisioning is slow and manual. Maybe network monitoring does not cover outbound paths to quantum services. Maybe data for a high-priority use case is still scattered across legacy systems.

Your role is to structure these into a gap register with clear descriptions, severity levels, suggested owners, and rough effort estimates. Then you guide the group through prioritization, identifying which gaps must be addressed before pilots and which can wait until you aim for pre-production or beyond.

The most important part is how you communicate this to your peers and to the board. You are not saying "we need a big quantum budget." You are instead saying "here are three infrastructure moves that will benefit AI, data, and future quantum work, and here is why they are worth doing now."

Migration roadmap development

Migration roadmap development is the art of weaving quantum-AI readiness into your broader technology story, rather than presenting it as a separate track. You start by overlaying the gaps and readiness moves you identified on your existing roadmaps: cloud migration, data platform consolidation, AI platform upgrades, security programs. In other words, you look for alignment. For instance, if you are planning to modernize your MLOps platform, you make sure that roadmap explicitly includes hybrid workload support and external accelerator integration. If network upgrades are on the table, you include requirements for monitoring and controlling outbound traffic to specialized services.

Then you frame quantum-AI as a practical motivator and beneficiary of these investments. It provides compelling use cases and pilot projects that can validate new capabilities. At the same time, the infrastructure improvements you make for quantum-AI also support more conventional AI and data work.

The result is a roadmap that does not depend on speculative quantum timelines. It makes sense even if quantum hardware advances more slowly than expected, and it positions you well if it advances faster.

Quantum benchmark interpretation

Quantum benchmark interpretation is your tool for navigating vendor claims and internal enthusiasm with a clear head. You do not need to master every technical detail. What you need is a habit: whenever you see a benchmark, you ask what it tells you about circuits that resemble your workloads and under what conditions it was measured.

If a provider reports an impressive throughput on a particular suite, you ask whether those circuits are similar in depth and structure to your optimization or anomaly detection tasks. If a vendor showcases high fidelity scores, you ask whether those numbers hold when error mitigation is applied at the levels you would need.

You strengthen this skill by working closely with a small group of technical leads who understand both the hardware and your business problems. Ask them to translate benchmarks into simple, decision-relevant language: "for our use case, here is what this device likely can and cannot do this year." Over time, you will accumulate your own reference points and be able to anchor conversations in those, rather than in marketing headlines.

Summary

Quantum-AI is not going to transform your organization overnight. Its early impact will depend less on sudden breakthroughs and more on how ready your infrastructure, teams, and governance processes are to treat quantum as one more specialized resource in an already complex landscape.

In this chapter, you saw how to evaluate your current hybrid computing architecture, how to focus vendor conversations on integration fit, how to run a structured readiness assessment across network, compute, data, and security, and how to design migration patterns that align with your broader modernization efforts. We grounded these ideas in concrete scenarios around supply chain routing, anomaly detection, and drug discovery, and we drew lessons from early movers like Pasqal and QBlox as well as major cloud platforms.

Most importantly, you now have a way to turn an abstract design to "be ready for quantum" into specific moves you can start right away: measure key metrics, standardize environments, improve data and orchestration, and enable your teams to run meaningful experiments without drama.

Those investments are not blind bets; to the contrary, they are investments in preparing for the not-so-distant future, where quantum-AI becomes just another powerful tool in your technology portfolio, and you are one of the leaders who can use it with confidence and judgment.

Further reading

1. https://mrmgroup.cs.princeton.edu/papers/tomesh-supermarq.pdf
2. https://developer.nvidia.com/cuda-q
3. https://www.ionq.com/news/ionq-to-advance-hybrid-quantum-computing-with-new-chemistry-application-and
4. https://www.pasqal.com/newsroom/with-two-100-qubits-quantum-computers-from-pasqal-fzj-and-genci-boost-hpcqs-the-pan-european-hybrid-hpc-quantum-infrastructure/
5. https://ui.adsabs.harvard.edu/abs/2022APS..MARM78001D/abstract
6. https://quantware.com/articles/quantum-utility-block
7. https://www.osti.gov/biblio/1969005

6

Workforce Development and Skills Strategy

Let's start with a confession that most quantum enthusiasts don't like to make: the hardware is almost the easy part. Quantum processors are becoming more accessible by the month. IBM's quantum systems are available on the cloud, and DWave, IonQ, Quantinuum, and a growing roster of others are opening up access through APIs that any developer can call either directly from their local system or via a third-party platform such as qBraid that has built-in features to easily connect to many hardware vendors. The hardware problem, while far from solved, is yielding to engineering and capital. The problem that keeps CTOs, CIOs, and CDOs awake at night is different. It's the *talent problem*.

The quantum skills gap is not a minor hiring inconvenience. It's a structural constraint on the pace at which organizations can realize quantum value. Universities are graduating quantum-trained people at a tiny fraction of the rate industry demand is growing. Analyses from groups like QED-C and the EU Quantum Flagship point in the same direction: a looming shortfall of quantum-capable workers measured in multiples, not percentages. The pipeline won't magically fix itself, and the companies that wait for the "next market" to sort it out will be watching fast movers disappear over the horizon.

Here's the good news, and it's genuinely good news: most of the quantum workforce you need already works for you! They just don't know quantum yet. The data scientists, software engineers, cloud architects, security engineers, and IT operations staff who populate your technical organizations today are the raw material for the quantum-capable team you'll need tomorrow. The question is not where to find quantum talent; it's how to build it, systematically, at a pace that matches your quantum roadmap without disrupting the day job.

This chapter gives you a way to do exactly that. We'll walk through a structured quantum skills taxonomy that maps concrete competencies to specific roles, a training architecture that sequences learning so it sticks, partnership models with universities that build a long-term talent pipeline, certification pathways that give you external benchmarks, and knowledge-transfer frameworks that keep quantum expertise inside the organization instead of trapped in a single person's head. By the time you reach the skills section at the end, you'll have the building blocks of a practical quantum workforce development plan tuned to where your organization is today.

One framing point before we dive in: this chapter is about near-term, practical reality. We're not staffing for some abstract, fault-tolerant quantum future in 2035. We're building teams for the hybrid quantum-classical era that's already here. NISQ devices, quantum-enhanced optimization on cloud platforms, post-quantum cryptography, migrations, and quantum computing experiments woven into classical pipelines. The skills for this era are real, learnable, and needed now, not in ten years. Now, let's not ignore the elephant in the room. This will require real investment, and there are no shortcuts. The most effective way to approach this is to start early, when it can be treated as a single investment, rather than waiting until it becomes a far too costly effort to catch up.

In this chapter we'll cover the following topics:

- Quantum skills taxonomy and role architecture
- Training programs and internal upskilling architecture
- University partnerships and talent pipeline development
- Certification pathways and professional development
- Knowledge transfer and institutional memory architecture
- Critical skills for technical leaders
- The quantum workforce development maturity model

Quantum skills taxonomy and role architecture

Before you can build a quantum workforce, you need to know exactly what you're building. That sounds obvious, but one of the most common mistakes technical leaders make in early quantum workforce planning is treating "quantum skills" as a monolithic requirement, as if every person on the team needs to understand quantum error correction before they can contribute. That's the equivalent of saying every software engineer needs to understand semiconductor physics before they write a line of code. It's not true, and planning as if it were wastes resources and demoralizes talent.

The more useful framing is a tiered taxonomy, a structured map of quantum competencies organized by depth and breadth, linked to specific organizational roles. Here's a three-tier framework that has proven practical for enterprise quantum workforce planning.[1]

Tier	Label	Target Roles	Core Competencies	Typical Timeline to Achieve
Tier 1	Foundational Quantum Literacy	All technical staff, product managers, IT staff, business analysts	Quantum computing concepts (qubits, superposition, entanglement, measurement), difference between quantum and classical computing Awareness of quantum use cases in relevant industries Quantum threat awareness (cryptography) Basic cloud quantum access Linear algebra, probability	4–8 weeks of structured learning
Tier 2	Quantum-Adjacent Proficiency	Data scientists, ML engineers, software architects, security engineers, cloud engineers, DevOps leads	Quantum circuit basics Variational quantum algorithms (VQE, QAOA) at conceptual level Quantum-classical hybrid architectures Post-quantum cryptography standards (NIST, PQC) Quantum SDK exposure (Qiskit, PennyLane, Ocean SDK) Quantum cloud platform operation	3–6 months of targeted upskilling
Tier 3	Deep Quantum Specialization	Quantum algorithm developers, quantum software engineers, quantum research leads, quantum hardware liaisons	Quantum algorithm design and complexity theory, error mitigation techniques, full SDK proficiency (Qiskit, Cirq, PennyLane, Q#), quantum linear algebra, variational and adiabatic optimization methods, domain-specific quantum application development, quantum error correction fundamentals	1-3+ years (often requires an advanced degree foundation)

Table 6.1: Quantum Skills Tiered Taxonomy

A few things are worth emphasizing about this taxonomy.

First, most of your quantum workforce need only reach Tier 1 or Tier 2. For most enterprises in 2024–2025, Tier 3 specialists are needed in small numbers – think of a quantum center of excellence team of three to eight people, not a department of fifty. The leverage in workforce development lies at Tier 1 and Tier 2, where you can build broad organizational awareness and practical capability without the multi-year development timelines of deep specialization.

Second, Tier 2 is where the real business value lies in the near term. The data scientists and ML engineers who can discover or identify feasible quantum use cases based on your organization or client's industry or domain, the security engineers who can execute post-quantum cryptography migrations, and the software architects who can design hybrid quantum-classical systems are the ones who will move quantum from proof-of-concept to production. Targeting Tier 2 development in your highest-leverage technical roles is the single highest-ROI workforce investment you can make right now.

Third, don't overlook the operational layer. IT administrators, help desk staff, cloud operations teams, etc. These roles need Tier 1 quantum literacy plus some targeted skills in quantum cloud platform management. Tasks such as provisioning quantum jobs, managing access controls on quantum systems, and supporting quantum development environments. As quantum platforms become embedded in enterprise infrastructure, you'll need people who can keep the lights on operationally, and that skill set is different from the algorithm development skills at Tier 3.[2]

Conducting a quantum skills gap analysis

Once you have the taxonomy, the next step is mapping it to your current workforce to produce a quantum skills gap matrix. This is simpler than it sounds, if you approach it systemically. Start with a self-assessment survey administered to your technical population, structured around the Tier 1 and Tier 2 competency areas, and supplement it with a short set of validation questions that prevent overconfidence bias, which is a chronic problem in self-assessment. This will help you set a foundational element across all existing and future tiers.

Layer in manager assessments for your highest-priority roles, the Tier 2 target population, and calibrate across your organization by running a small set of structured technical conversations with volunteers across skill levels. This calibration exercise helps you anchor the self-assessment scale to real competency levels and dramatically improves the reliability of your gap analysis results.[3]

The output of the gap analysis is a skills gap matrix: a heatmap of your organization's quantum readiness by role family and tier, with explicit quantification of breadth gaps, such as Tier 1 literacy missing across large populations, and depth gaps, such as Tier 3 specialization missing in critical roles. This matrix becomes the input to your training prioritization, hiring specifications, and organizational design decisions. It's also the document you bring to your CHRO and CFO when you're making the case for quantum workforce investment, we'll talk about how to frame that conversation later in the skills section.

Training programs and internal upskilling architecture

Designing an effective quantum training program is harder than it looks, and the difficulty is not primarily about quantum; it's about adult learning design. Quantum concepts are genuinely challenging. Most software engineers don't use linear algebra, complex numbers, or probability theory every day. Quantum computing in general requires new ways of thinking about resolving problems. Concepts such as superposition, entanglement, and interference, take repeated practice and exposure to become second nature. A Friday afternoon webinar is helpful but it's not going to get you there.

Effective quantum training architecture is built on three design principles that the learning science literature consistently supports:

- ***Sequence before you accelerate***. Mathematical foundations before quantum abstractions. Conceptual understanding before circuit design. Circuit design before algorithm development. Organizations that rush to the "interesting" quantum content without building the mathematical and conceptual foundations produce learners who can talk the language but can't do the work.
- ***Simulate before you build***. Quantum simulation tools (Qiskit's Statevector simulator, PennyLane's default qubit device, Cirq's simulators and DWave's Ocean SDK) allow learners to run quantum circuits on classical hardware and observe quantum behavior without queuing for scarce quantum hardware time. Simulation-first learning dramatically accelerates concept acquisition because learners can iterate rapidly, make mistakes cheaply, and build intuition through experimentation without increasing costs.
- ***Apply before you generalize***. Project-based learning anchored in your organization's specific application domains is consistently more effective than generic quantum curricula. A quantum optimization module built around your specific logistics routing problem will embed learning far more durably than a generic traveling salesman problem or max-cut example. Domain-relevant applications are the difference between training that transfers to job performance and training that stays on the laptop.

Evaluating external training providers

The market for quantum training has matured considerably in the past three years. Even though most are generally focused on "what is quantum/a qubit," the different quantum modalities and vendors, and of course the general overview of algorithms and use cases, details from experts in the field outside of algorithm researchers are seldom available and in growing demand. Here's a general evaluation of the leading external options, organized by target learner tier:

Provider/Program	Best For	Format	Approximate Cost	Strengths	Limitations
IBM Quantum Learning[4]	Tier 1–3 developers; Qiskit practitioners	Self-paced online Labs on real hardware	Free (hardware access tier)	Real hardware access Regularly updated Excellent documentation	IBM-ecosystem-centric Limited domain-specific content
MIT xPRO Quantum Computing Courses[5]	Tier 2–3 technical	Online cohort-based 6–10 weeks	$2,500–$3,500 per learner	Rigorous foundational content Strong network MIT brand for retention	Limited hands-on coding More conceptual than applied
Coursera: Quantum Computing Specializations (St. Petersburg/MIT)	Tier 1–2; self-paced learners	On-demand video Graded assignments	$49–$79/month subscription	Flexible schedule Solid fundamentals Accessible to non-PhDs	Variable quality Outdated in some areas Limited applied focus
Q-Next/National Quantum Initiative Learning Resources	Tier 1–2 industrial workforce	Free online modules Workshop programs	Free to low-cost	Vendor-neutral US government-backed Accessible	Less technically advanced More awareness than proficiency
Quantum Computing Inc. (QCI) / IonQ Academy	Tier 2 with specific hardware targets	Online + Consulting	Vendor-negotiated	Hardware-specific depth Industry-focused use cases	Vendor bias Variable curriculum maturity
Internal Curriculum Development	All tiers Domain-specific training	Instructor-led + self-paced hybrid	High upfront, low marginal	Maximum customization Business context IP retention	Significant resource investment Expertise required to build

Table 6.2: List of External Training Providers

For most enterprise CTOs, the practical answer is a blended approach: IBM Quantum Learning or Coursera for Tier 1 broad rollout (high scalability, low cost), MIT xPRO or targeted vendor programs for Tier 2 high-priority roles, and a custom internal curriculum for the organization-specific application context that external providers simply cannot deliver. Many institutions are already focusing on creating executive/leadership courses to complement their technical courses. You're already off to a great start if you're reading this book.

Quantum champions and centres of excellence

No training architecture is complete without a human acceleration layer. Quantum champions, internal practitioners who have achieved Tier 2 or Tier 3 proficiency, are your highest-leverage force multipliers in workforce development. A single engaged quantum champion running a monthly "quantum office hours" session, contributing to an internal Slack channel, and pairing with colleagues on their first quantum experiments can do more to build Tier 1 and Tier 2 capability across a team than three months of online coursework.

How do these work? Well, glad you asked! The quantum center of excellence (QCoE) model formalizes this by creating a small team of quantum specialists (typically three to eight people at early stages) charged not only with driving quantum projects but also with developing the broader workforce. A well-designed QCoE explicitly includes knowledge transfer, peer learning facilitation, and internal curriculum development as core accountabilities, not afterthoughts. Microsoft, IBM, and a growing number of enterprises have published case studies on QCoE design that are worth reviewing before you build your own model.[6]

Company spotlight: Airbus SE, quantum workforce at scale in European aerospace

Airbus SE, the European aerospace giant headquartered in Toulouse, France, has emerged as one of the most instructive examples of systematic quantum workforce development at enterprise scale. Beginning around 2020, Airbus established a dedicated quantum computing team within its central R&D function, but the more interesting strategic move was their simultaneous investment in quantum literacy across their broader engineering workforce, not just their quantum specialists.

Airbus's approach combined several elements that map directly to the frameworks in this chapter. They established a formal partnership with several European universities, including TU Delft in the Netherlands and Sorbonne University in Paris, to access emerging quantum talent and co-develop quantum algorithms relevant to aerospace optimization problems such as aircraft loading, route optimization, and structural simulation. Simultaneously, they invested in internal training programs targeting engineers in their fluid dynamics, structural analysis, and operations research teams: precisely the Tier 2 quantum-adjacent practitioners most relevant to Airbus's application priorities.[7]

What makes Airbus particularly instructive is how they handled the domain-specificity challenge. Rather than sending engineers through generic quantum courses, Airbus built problem-framing workshops where quantum specialists worked alongside domain engineers to translate existing optimization problems into quantum-amenable formulations. The learning was embedded in real work, a far more effective approach than abstract training, and one that produced both competency development and progress on actual business problems simultaneously.

Key lessons from Airbus: Start with a domain-relevant problem framing before planning the abstract quantum education. Co-invest in university partnerships early; Airbus's academic relationships took a few months to produce their first internship cohort, and longer to produce research outputs. Build quantum literacy in your domain experts, not just your IT and software teams, because the people who understand your hardest problems are the ones who'll be able to recognize quantum-amenable formulations when they emerge.

University partnerships and talent pipeline development

Here's the hard truth about quantum talent recruitment: by the time quantum PhDs land on your job board, fifteen other companies are already calling them. The academic quantum talent market at the deep specialization level is extraordinarily competitive. Simply posting roles on career websites and waiting for applicants to respond is unlikely to succeed. The organizations that consistently attract top quantum talent are the ones who have been cultivating relationships with quantum researchers and their advisors for years before any specific role opens.

University partnerships are the infrastructure for those relationships. They're not just about research outputs or internship pipelines; they're about building organizational visibility and credibility in academic quantum computing communities, so that when promising students are evaluating their post-graduation options, your organization is already on the list.

Evaluating and selecting university partners

Not all quantum programs are created equal, and your partnership investment should be concentrated where it will produce the highest return. The following framework structures university evaluation across four dimensions:

Evaluation Dimension	Key Questions	High-Value Signals
Research Quality	• What is the faculty's publication record? • Are they contributing to top quantum venues (Nature, Physical Review Letters, QIP, APS, IEEE Quantum – peer-reviewed)?	• Faculty in top 20 quantum programs globally • Active NSF/DOE/EU grants • Recent high-impact publications
Research-Application Alignment	• Does the faculty's research focus overlap with your quantum application priorities (optimization, ML, cryptography, simulation)?	• Faculty working on variational algorithms • Quantum optimization • AI for Quantum • Post-quantum security • Or your specific domain applications
Geographic Proximity	• Is the university accessible for regular relationship management and co-location of interns?	• Within commuting distance of major org hubs • Willing to support remote/ hybrid internship models
Partnership Track Record	• Has the university successfully managed industry partnerships before? • Are there existing IP frameworks?	• Active industry advisory boards • Established sponsored research infrastructure • Existing corporate partners in tech/science

Evaluation Dimension	Key Questions	High-Value Signals
Graduate Talent Volume	• How many quantum MS/PhD students graduate annually? • What is their post-graduation placement pattern?	• Programs graduating 10+ quantum-focused students annually • Strong placement in industry (not only academia)

Table 6.3: University Partnership Evaluation Framework

Partnership models: from engagement to integration

University partnerships exist on a spectrum of depth and investment. The most effective quantum talent strategies layer multiple partnership models simultaneously rather than committing exclusively to one:

Sponsored Research Agreements fund specific research projects aligned with your quantum application roadmap, typically for one to three years. In exchange for funding, usually $100K–$500K per year depending on scope, you receive access to research results, student talent exposure, and often IP licensing rights for jointly developed methods. The key to making these productive is tight alignment between your program managers and the faculty PI.

> **Tip**
>
> Vague research mandates produce academic outputs that don't translate into organizational value.

Internship Programs are your most reliable recruiting pipelines for Tier 3 talent. Structure them as genuine technical projects, and not as "interim projects" that sit outside the real work, mentored by your quantum specialists. Conversion rates from quantum internship to full-time offer typically run 40–70% when the experience is well-structured, making quantum internship programs among the most cost-effective recruitment investments available.

Curriculum Developed Partnerships allow you to co-design course content that includes real-world application context from your domain. These are lighter touch than sponsored research, often requiring only faculty time contribution and some problem framing from your side, but they build significant goodwill and often result in instructors directing strong students toward your internship program organically.

National quantum initiatives provide a powerful framework for multi-institution partnership development. In the United States, the National Quantum Initiative Act[8] funded many National Quantum Information Science Research Centers that actively seek industry partners.[9] In Europe the EU Quantum Flagship program similarly provides structured frameworks for industry-academic collaboration.[10] Engaging with these initiatives as an industry partner gives you access to multiple institutions simultaneously and signals organizational quantum commitment in ways that attract talent.

Company spotlight: JPMorgan Chase, University Partnerships as quantum talent engine

JPMorgan Chase's quantum computing program, led by their Global Technology Applied Research Center, represents one of the most sophisticated enterprise approaches to quantum talent pipeline development through academic partnerships. Rather than relying on competitive market recruitment for quantum specialists, JPMorgan Chase built a multi-institutional university engagement strategy that has made them one of the most visible quantum employers in academic quantum computing circles.

Their approach includes sponsored research collaborations with MIT, Caltech, and several European quantum research groups on topics directly relevant to financial services quantum applications such as portfolio optimizations, Monte Carlo simulation acceleration, and a quantum machine learning model for risk modeling.[11] Critically, JPMorgan Chase structured these relationships not just as research contracts but as talent development pipelines: PhD students and postdoctoral researchers working on JPMorgan-funded projects receive visibility into real financial applications, exposure to JPMorgan's technical teams, and often internship placements that anchor recruiting relationships well before graduation.[12]

Certification pathways and professional development frameworks

Certifications serve several functions in a quantum workforce development strategy that go beyond the obvious "does this person know quantum computing." They provide externally validated benchmarks that support more objective hiring and promotion decisions. They create a structured training roadmap with clear milestones that help learners navigate the quantum knowledge landscape without getting lost in the depth and breadth of available content. And they signal organizational commitment to quantum development in ways that attract quantum-interested talent during recruitment.

The certification landscape for quantum computing is still maturing compared to, say, cloud computing certifications, but there are now enough credible options to build a coherent certification strategy around. The following is the current certification landscape as of 2024–2025:

Certification	Provider	Level	Focus	Recommended For	Maintenance Req.
IBM Certified Associate Developer: Quantum Computation using Qiskit	IBM	Associate (Tier 2)	Qiskit programming, quantum circuits, quantum algorithm basics	Developers, data scientists moving to Tier 2 quantum proficiency	Recertification every 2 years, updates with Qiskit releases
Microsoft Certified Azure Quantum Developer	Microsoft	Associate (Tier 2)	Q# language, Azure Quantum Platform, hybrid quantum-classical development	Azure-ecosystem developers targeting Tier 2–3	Annual renewal with platform updates
Quantum Computing Foundation (QCF) Certificate	Coding Dojo / Multiple providers	Foundation (Tier 1)	Quantum fundamentals, qubit concepts, quantum computing awareness	Broad Tier 1 literacy rollout across the technical population	No expiry, awareness level
AWS Braket Quantum Computing Practitioner	Google/ Coursera	Intermediate (Tier 2)	Cirq framework, quantum ML fundamentals, TensorFlow Quantum	ML engineers targeting quantum-enhanced machine learning	No formal renewal, course-based completion

Table 6.4: Quantum Certification Landscape (as of 2024–2025)

Note that the certifications listed may change by the time you read this, so I strongly encourage you to monitor their certification sites regularly. Most of the certification providers also provide documentation or courses for exam preparation.

Integrating certifications into talent systems

Certifications are most effective when they're embedded in the talent management systems that shape day-to-day career behavior such as performance management, compensation, and career laddering. Without this embedding, certifications become check-the-box activities that learners complete and then promptly forget, rather than milestones in sustained capability development.

The most effective integration model we've observed ties quantum certification to compensation bands through a quantum skills premium, a salary supplement for Tier 2 or Tier 3 certification that reflects the market value of quantum competency. For Tier 2 certifications (IBM Quantum, Azure Quantum Developer), a premium of 5–10% above the base compensation band has proven sufficient to create genuine motivation without distorting compensation equity. For Tier 3 specialists, market premiums are often much larger and need to be benchmarked against academic and national laboratory alternatives that are your primary competitive reference points.[13]

Career laddering integration means defining explicit quantum competency requirements at each level of your technical career tracks. An engineer advancing from L4 to L5 might require demonstrated Tier 1 quantum literacy; L5 to L6 might require Tier 2 certification in the SDK most relevant to the organization's stack. This creates a clear line of sight between quantum skill development and career advancement that intrinsically motivates sustained learning investment across the technical population.

Internal recognition: hackathons, paper groups, and algorithm challenges

Formal certification and compensation structures drive the extrinsic motivation for quantum skill development. Equally important is the intrinsic side, creating a culture where quantum curiosity and quantum contribution are celebrated and visible. Internal quantum hackathons are one of the most effective tools for this. Run quarterly or biannually, a well-structured quantum hackathon gives Tier 1 and Tier 2 practitioners a structured opportunity to apply their learning to real (or at least realistic) business problems, compete constructively, and get organizational visibility for quantum work that might not yet be part of their day job. The social energy of hackathons such as the late nights, the impromptu collaboration, the moment when someone's quantum circuit does something useful, is disproportionately effective at building community and sustaining learning motivation. Ever since I launched my first hackathon in 2018 at IBM, along with the great Bob Sutor (which if you haven't picked up his book, Dancing with Qubits, you really should), two consistent reactions emerge the moment the non-technical participants complete running their first circuit:

1. "Wow! That was quick!"
2. "Ok, so what do these results actually mean?"

To leadership, this moment represents far more than engaging workshop exercise. It's a calculated talent-retention and risk-mitigation strategy designed to drastically shorten the Time-to-Value (TTV) for non-technical stakeholders.

In highly complex sectors, on-boarding non-technical hires such as product managers, legal counsel, policymakers, and sales executives traditionally suffers from a steep, intimidating learning curve. Standard training relies a lot on abstract "Hello World!" tutorials that fail to connect the employee to the core product, leading to early disengagement and high turnover. By ensuring that the hackathons or any other activity focuses on immediate and tangible capability is key. By accelerating confidence and shifting from compliance to curiosity, you could then create an initiative that will secure a talent pipeline and the desire to learn and collaborate in other group activities.

Internal quantum paper reading groups, where practitioners meet bi-weekly to discuss recent quantum computing preprints from arXiv,[14] serve a different but equally important function. They create a continuous learning signal that keeps quantum awareness current as the field evolves rapidly, build the habit of engaging with primary literature, and surface emerging techniques that may be relevant. As a low-cost intervention, one enthusiastic quantum champion can run a paper group that sustains quantum learning culture across a ten-to-twenty person community.

Knowledge transfer and institutional memory architecture

Here's a scenario that plays out in organizations across every industry: a quantum specialist joins, spends eighteen months developing deep expertise in variational quantum algorithms for the company's specific optimization domain, builds relationships with university partners, gets two production experiments running on IBM Quantum, and then gets a better offer from a national quantum lab and accepts it. With that departure, a significant fraction of the organization's quantum capability walks out the door.

This is by far not hypothetical. It's a pattern that repeats whenever organizations treat quantum expertise as a hiring problem rather than a knowledge management problem. The answer isn't to pay quantum specialists more (though you should; see the retention discussion in the skills section). The answer is to architect your quantum knowledge management such that the organization's quantum capability is embedded in systems, documentation, processes, and distributed expertise rather than residing primarily in individual heads. In the next section we'll cover some ways to manage and architect these as interconnected components.

Quantum knowledge management architecture

Effective quantum knowledge management requires four interconnected components:

1. ***Quantum Algorithm Implementation Library***: A structured internal repository of documented quantum circuit implementations, variational algorithm experiments, and quantum-classical hybrid structures with standardized documentation such as problem formulation, circuit design rationale, parameter choices, hardware results and error mitigation techniques applied, and business context. Think of this as your organization's quantum cookbook. A resource that allows a Tier 2 practitioner to understand, reproduce, and build on prior quantum work without needing to reconstruct context from the original developer.
2. ***Quantum Use Case Wiki***: A catalogued library of business use cases that have been evaluated for quantum suitability, organized by application domain (optimization, simulation, ML, cryptography, etc.) with structured assessments of quantum feasibility, expected timelines to quantum advantage, hardware requirements, and classical baseline performance. This wiki prevents repeated reinvention of the same problem framing and gives Tier 1 practitioners a curated entry point to quantum relevance in their specific domain.
3. ***Mentoring Pair Architecture***: Structured pairing of Tier 3 quantum specialists with Tier 2 target practitioners, with explicit mentoring accountabilities including joint project work, code review, and regular knowledge transfer sessions. The pairing should be formalized, time bounded, and tied to specific learning objectives for the Tier 2 mentee, not an informal "ask me anything" relationship that produces no systematic capability development.
4. ***Quantum Community of Practice Platform***: A dedicated internal community platform (Slack channel, Teams space, or dedicated community tool) where quantum practitioners across the organization share experiments, surface questions, post relevant papers, and connect with the external quantum developer ecosystem through shared links and community. The community of practice is the connective tissue that makes all other knowledge management investments more effective.

Each of the components within this architecture can be developed in parallel or in series, depending on the growth and needs of your organization. That being said, it's best to have the components at least in place so when the need presents itself, the team can move right away and not have to wait for everything to get set up. The less time lag, the better.

Key person risk mitigation

Let's go back to our earlier friend, who had just accepted a better job offer, for a moment to discuss key-person risk mitigation. Quantum knowledge concentration is a specific category of key-person risk that deserves explicit mitigation planning. In other words, what could we have done to keep our friend here with us? To do this you need to start by mapping your current quantum knowledge dependencies: which quantum capabilities exist primarily in one or two individuals? What would be lost organizationally if those people departed? Which university or vendor relationships are dependent on specific personal relationships rather than institutional agreements?

For each identified dependency, design a mitigation plan from the following list:

- ***Cross-training***: Explicitly assign a second practitioner to shadow and develop proficiency in the knowledge area. This is most effective when paired with joint project work rather than formal instruction.
- ***Documentation requirements***: Make structured documentation of quantum implementations and design decisions a standard deliverable for all quantum project work, not an optional extra.
- ***Succession planning***: For every Tier 3 specialist role, identify an internal candidate in active development for succession and track their development explicitly in performance management.
- ***Institutional relationship transfer***: For university and vendor partnerships, ensure that at least two organizational representatives are active in each relationship and that relationship documentation captures key contacts and history.

By applying these mitigation plans for each of the following, this should help mitigate the risk of key-person departure and provide you with some comfort that all you have done was not just train someone for a different company or, worse, a competitor. Let's now pull all these building blocks together and review the key critical skills we've learned in this chapter.

Critical skills for technical leaders

As I promised you at the beginning of this chapter, you now have the building blocks of a practical quantum workforce development plan tuned to where your organization is today. In this final section I want to share some critical skills that you can keep handy to ensure that you are keeping your team focused and growing. The five skills will serve as not only a review of this chapter but also provide you with the specific tasks that you as their leader will need to ensure that growth.

Skill 1: Quantum skills gap analysis

The ability to conduct a systematic, credible quantum skills gap analysis is foundational to every other workforce development decision you'll make. Without an accurate picture of where your workforce actually stands against the quantum skill requirements of your roadmap, training investments get misdirected, hiring specifications get inflated, and workforce development conversations with the C-suite lack the quantitative grounding needed to unlock budget.

A rigorous gap analysis combines three data sources: self-assessment surveys, manager calibration, and direct technical probing. The self-assessment survey establishes a baseline map of quantum awareness and competency claims across your technical population. It should be structured around the tier taxonomy competencies described earlier in this chapter, with specific, behaviorally anchored questions that ask about actual knowledge and experience rather than abstract confidence. For example, "Have you written a quantum circuit using Qiskit or a comparable SDK and run it on a quantum system?" is a better ask than "How confident are you in quantum programming?"

Manager calibration sessions are a critical quality check on self-assessment data. Managers of your Tier 2 target populations, engineering leads, AI team managers, and security engineering leads should be briefed on the quantum skills taxonomy and asked to assess the top two to five quantum capability development needs in their teams. This cross-referencing catches systematic over- and under-estimation in self-assessment and adds a perspective on organizational priority that individual contributors may not have.

The final output, a quantum skills gap report with breadth and depth gap quantification, build-vs.-buy-vs.-partner recommendations by skills area, and cost-per-competency estimates, becomes your investment case document. When you present this to your CHRO and CFO, you're not asking for a generic "training budget." You're presenting a specific, quantified capability gap with a costed remediation plan and a timeline. That specificity is what converts workforce development conversations from "that sounds nice" to "here's the budget."

Skill 2: Learning program design and evaluation

Designing quantum learning programs that produce measurable competency outcomes, not just training completion certificates, requires instructional design skills adapted to quantum subject matter. The specific challenge of quantum is that competency is genuinely difficult to assess superficially: a learner can memorize the definitions of superposition and entanglement and answer multiple-choice questions correctly without having any ability to formulate a quantum problem or write a functional quantum circuit. Designing assessment instruments that distinguish genuine competency from surface familiarity is a skill in itself.

Start with clear, tier-appropriate learning objectives written at the right level of Bloom's taxonomy.[15] Tier 1 objectives are primarily at the knowledge and comprehension levels: "Describe the difference between classical bits and qubits" or "Identify three categories of quantum computing applications." Tier 2 objectives rise to application and analysis: "Implement a Variational Quantum Eigensolver circuit in Qiskit for a given Hamiltonian" or "Analyze a business optimization problem and assess its suitability for QAOA formulation." Tier 3 objectives reach synthesis and evaluation: "Design a quantum error mitigation strategy for a specific hardware noise model" or "Evaluate the resource requirements of competing quantum algorithm approaches for a given problem size."

Assessment design should match the objective level. Knowledge and comprehension objectives can be assessed with quizzes and short written responses. Application and analysis objectives require actual coding exercises run against quantum simulators or hardware. Synthesis and evaluation objectives require project-based assessments where learners tackle genuine (or genuinely modeled) business problems with quantum approaches. The learning science principle here is simple: you cannot assess higher-order competencies with lower-order instruments.[16]

Skill 3: University and ecosystem partnership management

Academic partnership management is a distinct professional skill that differs meaningfully from managing commercial vendor relationships. Academic timelines, incentive structures, and success metrics are fundamentally different from industry norms, and technical leaders who approach university partnerships with purely commercial expectations consistently underperform compared to those who learn to operate effectively in academic contexts.

The most important cultural translation to make when engaging academic partners is around time horizons. A sponsored research agreement with a quantum faculty member will typically take six to twelve months from contract signing to first substantive research outputs. PhD students whose research you're funding will produce theses on academic schedules, usually three to five years from enrollment to graduation. Internship pipeline benefits from academic partnerships accumulate over multiple annual cohorts. If you're expecting quarterly deliverables and commercial-pace outcomes, you will be perpetually frustrated, and your academic partners will be frustrated by your frustration. Build academic timelines into your partnership expectations from the outset.

IP negotiation is the area where academic partnerships most commonly stall. Faculty are protective of their ability to publish, graduate students need research theses they can present at conferences, and universities have technology transfer offices that will assert institutional IP rights on any research funded with university resources.

The successful navigation strategy is to separate publication rights:

- ***Freely granted***: researchers must be able to publish free from commercialization rights
- ***Negotiable:*** you can typically obtain exclusive or co-exclusive licenses for specific applications within your domain

Working through a university's technology transfer office early in partnership structuring, rather than discovering IP constraints after research is complete, saves an enormous amount of time and goodwill.

Ecosystem partnership management, engaging with quantum open-source communities, national quantum initiatives, and quantum developer conferences, amplifies your talent visibility and knowledge access beyond what bilateral university agreements can achieve. Contributing to open-source quantum projects, even at modest levels – fixing documentation, submitting tutorials, sponsoring hackathons – builds organizational reputation in quantum developer communities in ways that attract curious, self-motivated talent who are often the most valuable quantum practitioners to recruit. The Quantum Open-Source Foundation (QOSF), Unitary Foundation (formerly the Unitary Fund), and the open-source communities around Qiskit, PennyLane, and Cirq are all worth engaging as ecosystem partners, not just as software resources.

Skill 4: Talent acquisition strategy for quantum specialists

Recruiting quantum specialists is categorically different from recruiting conventional software engineers, and applying conventional talent acquisition playbooks to quantum hiring produces predictably poor results. The reason is that the talent pool is small, globally distributed, academically oriented, highly mobile, and specifically sensitive to the quality of the quantum work environment you offer, and I don't mean just the compensation package.

The first imperative to consider is accurate role specification. Inflated requirements, such as the infamous "five years of experience in a two-year-old technology" problem, are chronic in quantum job postings. Requiring a PhD for every quantum role is both inaccurate – many Tier 2 roles are well within the capability of strong MS graduates – and counterproductive, as it narrows your candidate pool unnecessarily and signals to the market that you haven't done your quantum workforce homework. The suggestion here is to write role specifications based on the actual Tier 2 or Tier 3 competencies required for the role, with an honest assessment of which competencies are "must-have" versus "trainable." The competency framework in this chapter gives you the vocabulary to do this precisely.

Technical interview design for quantum roles requires more investment than most organizations put in. A generic coding interview will not effectively assess quantum algorithm development capability. Your interview process for Tier 3 roles should include a take-home quantum problem: a real or realistically modeled optimization or simulation problem from your domain that the candidate is asked to formulate as a quantum circuit, implement in the SDK of their choice, and present with design rationale. This format assesses the full competency profile, problem formulation, circuit implementation, SDK proficiency, and communication, and simultaneously signals to the candidate that the work at your organization involves serious quantum problems, not toy exercises.

Retention strategy for quantum specialists deserves as much attention as acquisition. The levers that matter most, based on surveys of quantum professionals, are: access to interesting problems (quantum specialists leave when they run out of challenging quantum work), research time and publication permissions (quantum PhDs overwhelmingly value the ability to maintain connection with the research community), conference and community participation (attendance at quantum conferences is a significant retention factor), and visible career development within the organization (quantum specialists need to see a path to senior technical leadership, not just management). Structuring these elements explicitly in quantum specialist role definitions, "Quantum Research Engineer with 20% dedicated research time and annual conference allocation", makes your offer substantially more competitive than compensation alone.

Skill 5: Quantum circuits and learning environment development

All the training architecture, certification pathways, and partnership programs in the world will underperform if the organizational culture treats quantum computing as a niche curiosity for specialists rather than a strategic capability that matters to the whole technical organization. Building a quantum learning culture, one that normalizes quantum curiosity, celebrates quantum experimentation, and makes it safe to be a beginner, is the multiplier that makes every other workforce development investment more effective.

Psychological safety is the foundational condition. Quantum is hard. People who encounter it for the first time frequently feel confused, intimidated, and worried that they're not "quantum smart enough." If your organizational culture punishes visible struggle or treats quantum competency as a marker of elite status, you will get exactly one cohort of learners and then a silent drop-off as the rest of the technical population quietly concludes that quantum is for other people. Creating a culture where it's normal to say "I don't understand this quantum concept yet; can someone explain it?" and where that question gets a helpful answer rather than a condescending response is the prerequisite for broad quantum literacy development. [17]

Leadership modeling is disproportionately powerful here. When a CTO or CIO visibly participates in internal quantum learning activities, takes an IBM Quantum Learning module, attends the quantum hackathon, or asks a question in the quantum Slack channel that demonstrates genuine engagement with the learning, it sends an unmistakable organizational signal that quantum learning is valued at every level, including the top. You don't need to become a quantum expert. You need to be a visible quantum learner. That's a very different bar, and it's achievable for any senior technical leader willing to invest two to four hours per month in visible quantum engagements.

Incentive systems for quantum learning culture operate at multiple levels. Formal incentives include certification premiums, career advancement requirements, and recognition in performance reviews. Informal incentives, such as those that drive sustained engagement, include peer recognition in team meetings, quantum "wins of the week" highlights in internal newsletters, and the social satisfaction of being part of a community that's working on something genuinely exciting and frontier. The quarterly quantum hackathon, where teams present their quantum experiments, creates visibility for quantum work, celebrates quantum learning publicly, and generates social proof that quantum is a real and valued organizational priority.

Finally, remember that quantum culture is a multi-year development, not a one-time intervention. The organizations that sustain quantum learning cultures over the three-to-five-year horizon needed to build genuine quantum capability are those that treat culture development as an ongoing program with regular investment, new hackathon themes, evolving paper reading group curricula, and updated certification incentives, rather than a launch event followed by hope. The compound returns on a well-sustained quantum learning culture are significant: each new cohort of quantum learners becomes a resource for the next, and the organization's collective quantum knowledge compounds year over year.

The quantum workforce development maturity model

To synthesize the frameworks covered in this chapter, I will provide you with an integrated Quantum Workforce Development Maturity Model that allows technical leaders to assess their organization's current state and plan progressive capability development.

Maturity Level	Description	Skills Taxonomy Status	Training Architecture	University Partnerships	Knowledge Management	Culture Indicators
Level 1: Aware	Quantum is on the radar, but workforce development is unstructured	No formal taxonomy Quantum skills not mapped to roles	Ad hoc: individuals self-directing quantum learning independently	None or early informal contacts	No structure documentation; knowledge in individual heads	Quantum learning is niche and individual No organizational signal
Level 2: Initiating	First structured quantum workforce investments begin	Tier 1-2 taxonomy defined Initial skills gap survey complete	Selected Tier 1 training deployed First certification incentives established	1-2 university conversations initiated Internship program design	Initial quantum use case wiki begun Some documentation standards	CTO visible as Quantum Learner First hackathon run Quantum Slack channel is active
Level 3: Developing	Systematic quantum workforce development in progress across key roles	Full three-tier taxonomy Gap matrix maintained Hiring specs updated	Tier 1 broadly deployed Tier 2 training for priority roles QCoE established	1-3 active university partnerships with internship pipelines National initiative engagement	Algorithm implementation library Mentoring pairs Community of practice active	Quantum literacy expected of technical hires Certification in career laddering Regular hackathons

Maturity Level	Description	Skills Taxonomy Status	Training Architecture	University Partnerships	Knowledge Management	Culture Indicators
Level 4: Advancing	Quantum workforce capability embedded as an organizational competency	Taxonomy updated with quarterly quantum skills market scan Workforce gap regularly reassessed	Tier 2 broadly deployed Tier 3 specialist development pipeline active Custom domain curricula	3+ university partnerships Sponsored research producing a recruitment pipeline Multi-institutional NQI engagement	Comprehensive knowledge architecture Succession plans for all Tier 3 roles External community contribution	Quantum culture self-sustaining Learner communities generating their own programming External quantum employer brand visibility
Level 5: Leading	Quantum workforce development is a strategic organizational capability and market differentiator	Skills taxonomy co-developed with National Quantum Initiative Shared externally as thought leadership	Internal quantum curriculum externally recognized Practitioners contributing to open-source quantum SDKs	Strategic university partnerships with IP frameworks Faculty affiliates Joint curriculum programs	Open-source contributions to quantum knowledge ecosystems External publications from internal quantum team	Cited as a quantum employer of choice Attracting talent proactively Quantum learning culture embedded in organizational identity

Table 6.5: Quantum Workforce Development Maturity Model

As with other models and frameworks, use this as a guide to get you started, but do remember to treat this and all other frameworks as living documents. They should be dynamic and adaptable to your specific needs and/or roadmaps. Once you have a well-designed system, you can very easily repeat or adapt it to other domains or organizations. Recalling something that was said to me by my mentor, "Don't underestimate the value of being the first in and the first to finish, as the only difference between the quick and the dead, is speed."

Summary

Phew! That was quite a bit of content. In all, I hope that it will put you at ease by highlighting some key points to consider and maybe even removing some preconceived notions on developing quantum talent in your organization. Just remember that the quantum talent shortage is not a future problem. It's the present constraint on how quickly organizations can move from quantum awareness to quantum value. The frameworks, models, and strategies presented in this chapter are designed to address that constraint systematically, not through wishful thinking about the talent market improving, but through deliberate organizational action to build quantum capability from within.

We've covered a lot of ground. The three-tier quantum skills taxonomy gives you the vocabulary to have precise conversations about quantum workforce requirements, distinguishing the broad Tier 1 literacy your whole technical organization needs from the domain-specific Tier 2 proficiency your highest-leverage practitioners require and the deep Tier 3 specialization your quantum center of excellence demands. The training architecture frameworks help you sequence learning investments effectively, choose external providers wisely, and build the internal quantum champions network that accelerates learning beyond what formal programs alone can achieve.

University partnerships, approached with the right expectations and structures, are your most reliable path to deep quantum talent over multi-year horizons. The IP negotiation guidance, internship pipeline design, and national quantum initiative engagement frameworks give you the practical mechanics to turn academic relationships from interesting conversations into genuine recruiting and research advantages. Certifications, embedded in compensation and career progression systems, create the extrinsic motivation structure that sustains quantum skill development through the inevitable dips in enthusiasm that characterize any multi-year learning journey.

Knowledge transfer architecture ensures that quantum expertise becomes an organizational asset rather than a key-person risk. The algorithm implementation library, quantum use case wiki, mentoring pair architecture, and community of practice platforms work together to distribute quantum knowledge systematically across the organization and protect it from the talent mobility that is endemic in quantum specialty markets.

Finally, quantum culture, psychological safety, visible leadership modeling, incentive systems that celebrate quantum curiosity and contribution, and the sustained programmatic investment that prevents culture from being a launch event rather than a long-term condition, are the multipliers that make all other investments more effective.

The companies that win the quantum talent race, the JPMorgan Chases, Airbuses, and Quantinuums of their industries, are not doing so because they found a secret quantum talent pool that others missed. They're winning because they started earlier, built more deliberately, and sustained the investment longer than organizations that treated quantum workforce development as something to figure out after the technology matured. The technology is maturing now. The time to start building is already behind us, but today remains the earliest opportunity available. Don't waste it.

In the next chapter, we turn from workforce capability to implementation practice, moving from the teams you've built to the quantum experiments they'll run and the frameworks for advancing quantum projects from proof-of-concept to production-scale deployment.

Further reading

1. `https://www.mckinsey.com/capabilities/tech-and-ai/our-insights/tech-forward/enabling-the-next-frontier-of-quantum-computing`
2. `https://doi.org/10.17226/25196`
3. `https://www.weforum.org/stories/2025/11/upskilling-quantum-talent/`
4. `https://quantum.cloud.ibm.com/learning/en`
5. `https://learn-xpro.mit.edu/quantum-computing`
6. `https://www.bcg.com/publications/2023/enterprise-grade-quantum-computing-almost-ready`
7. `https://www.airbus.com/en/innovation/digital-transformation/quantum-technologies`
8. `https://www.congress.gov/bill/115th-congress/house-bill/6227/text`
9. `https://www.quantum.gov/wp-content/uploads/2021/10/2021_NSTC_ESIX_INTL_TALENT_QIS.pdf`
10. `https://qt.eu/about-quantum-flagship/`
11. `https://arxiv.org/pdf/2201.02773`
12. `https://www.jpmorganchase.com/careers/explore-opportunities/students-and-graduates`

13. https://www.deloitte.com/us/en/insights/topics/emerging-technologies/quantum-computing-futures.html
14. https://arxiv.org/list/quant-ph/new
15. https://en.wikipedia.org/wiki/Bloom's_taxonomy
16. https://www.scirp.org/reference/ReferencesPapers?ReferenceID=1506705
17. https://www.wiley.com/en-us/The+Fearless+Organization%3A+Creating+Psychological+Safety+in+the+Workplace+for+Learning%2C+Innovation%2C+and+Growth-p-9781119477266

7

Prototyping and Proof-of-Concept Development

Let's be honest about what most quantum "pilots" are: expensive theatrical performances staged for executive audiences. A vendor brings their team on-site, runs some circuits on a 50-qubit system, shows a colorful Bloch sphere visualization, and everyone nods judiciously about the quantum future. Months later, the organization spent a few hundred thousand dollars and has learned essentially nothing actionable. The quantum prototype as organizational performance art is, unfortunately, a well-established genre.

Well, fear not! This chapter is your antidote to that. The distance between quantum theoretical promise and realized organizational value is bridged by rigorous prototyping and proof-of-concept (PoC) development, not by theater. For technical leaders, the prototype phase is where strategic quantum intent meets engineering reality: where vendor claims are stress-tested, algorithmic assumptions are validated or invalidated, and the true complexity of hybrid quantum-classical integration is encountered firsthand, often with some humbling surprises.

At the time of this writing, the quantum prototype landscape is materially different from even a few years ago. Hardware quality has improved substantially; error rates on leading superconducting and trapped-ion systems have dropped by orders of magnitude since 2020.[1, 2] Simulation tools have matured into genuine engineering-grade development environments. And the quantum algorithm research community has produced a clearer-eyed picture of where near-term advantage is genuinely achievable versus where it remains speculative. This means rigorous prototyping is now both more tractable and more consequential than ever before: tractable because you can run meaningful experiments, consequential because the gap between organizations that prototype intelligently and those that don't is beginning to translate into real competitive differentiation.

This chapter provides a practitioner-level guide to designing, executing, and evaluating quantum computing pilots and quantum-AI hybrid experiments. We will cover vendor selection criteria grounded in technical performance metrics, development methodologies adapted for the unique constraints of NISQ-era quantum systems, and success metric frameworks that produce decision-relevant feasibility frameworks that culminate in a defensible, evidence-based go/no-go decision on whether to proceed to full development or pursue alternative solution architectures.

By the end of this chapter, you will have the tools to run quantum pilots that generate genuine strategic intelligence. The benchmark for success is not "we ran quantum circuits," but rather "we now know, with evidence, whether quantum computing represents a viable path to competitive advantage for this specific problem, and we explain exactly why." That's the standard we're building toward.

One more thing before we get into it, and this one's for the readers who don't build circuits for a living: yes, parts of this chapter go deep. Error rates, circuit depth, gate fidelities, the works. If that's not your world, simply skim those sections with a clear conscience. However, please don't skim the whole chapter on the assumption that it's only "technical jargon." The company spotlights shared in this chapter were written for anyone, and the closing discussion of data readiness is the single most consequential section here for all non-technical leaders. If you read nothing else in this chapter, read those two things. They're where the strategic decisions actually get made, and they're the parts you'll likely be accountable for long after the vendor's fancy Bloch sphere slides have been forgotten.

We'll cover the following topics:

- Vendor selection criteria for quantum prototyping partnerships
- Quantum development methodologies for hybrid experiments
- Quantum simulation tools and early-stage application development
- Success metrics and prototype evaluation frameworks
- The Go/No-Go feasibility framework for development progression

Vendor selection criteria for quantum prototyping partnerships

Here's a scenario that plays out with remarkable regularity during the quantum vendor selection process: a technical team receives RFP responses from three quantum computing vendors, spends two weeks comparing qubit counts and press releases, and then selects the vendor with the largest system because "more qubits must be better." The prototype subsequently fails to produce useful results, and everyone is puzzled about why.

The qubit count fixation is the original sin of quantum vendor evaluation. It's the quantum equivalent of selecting a database vendor based solely on the size of their server room. What matters is not how many qubits a system has, but how well those qubits perform on the specific computational problem you are trying to solve, and that depends on a constellation of technical characteristics that most vendor evaluation frameworks do not adequately capture. [3]

Technical evaluation dimensions

A rigorous quantum vendor evaluation begins with the technical performance characteristics of the hardware itself. The key metrics and their practical implications are outlined in the framework below:

Technical Metric	What It Measures	Why It Matters for Prototyping	Red Flag Thresholds
Qubit Count	Total addressable quantum register size	Sets a ceiling on problem size	<50 qubits for optimization problems requiring >40 logical variables
Gate fidelity	Accuracy of single- and two-qubit operations	Directly determines circuit depth achievable before noise dominates results	<99.5% 1Q fidelity <99% 2Q fidelity for algorithms requiring >10 layers
T1/T2 Coherence Times	How long qubits maintain a quantum state (microseconds)	Sets practical circuit depth limit; Insufficient coherence collapses results	<100μs T1 for superconducting <10 ms T1 for trapped-ion applications
Connectivity between qubits	Which qubits can interact directly without SWAP overhead?	Low connectivity requires costly SWAP gates, which dramatically increase circuit depth	Fewer than 3 nearest-neighbor connections per qubit for molecular simulation

Technical Metric	What It Measures	Why It Matters for Prototyping	Red Flag Thresholds
CLOPS (Circuit Layer Operations Per Second)	Throughput of hybrid classical-quantum execution	Determines practical runtime for variational algorithms requiring thousands of shots	<1,000 CLOPS makes variational algorithm prototyping economically impractical
Error Mitigation Toolkit	Available noise suppression and post-processing techniques	Determines whether usable signals can be extracted from noisy hardware results	No support for ZNE, PEC, or M3 calibration methods

Table 7.1: Technical Evaluation Dimensions Matrix

Beyond raw hardware metrics, the software stack quality is frequently the make-or-break factor in prototype development velocity. A system with slightly lower gate fidelity but a mature, well-documented SDK with active community support and responsive developer tooling will often deliver better prototype outcomes than a nominally higher-performance system wrapped in immature software.[4] Evaluate the SDK comprehensively: documentation quality, example library coverage for your application domain, compiler optimization depth, and the maturity of error mitigation implementations.

Commercial and strategic evaluation dimensions

Do also keep in mind that technical performance is necessary but not sufficient for vendor selection. The commercial structure of quantum prototyping engagements varies dramatically across vendors and has significant implications for IP ownership, result integrity, and transition to expanded development. This could be a landmine for most firms, particularly if during engagements you later learn that data or details are public domain or have legal issues due to vague terms on handling and determining who owns what.

Dimension	Key Evaluation Questions	Risk Factors to Probe
PoC Engagement Structure	• Is the prototype scoped as a paid engagement or bundled cloud access? • Who owns the circuit designs and results?	• Vague IP terms that transfer ownership of prototype artifacts • Lack of results confidentiality provisions

Dimension	Key Evaluation Questions	Risk Factors to Probe
Reference Customer Access	• Can you speak with two or three organizations that have executed comparable prototypes? • What were their results?	• Vendors who cannot provide references for your application domain • Sanitized testimonials that avoid performance specifics
Roadmap Credibility	• Is the hardware improvement roadmap specific, with engineering milestones, or marketing-grade aspiration? • How has historical execution tracked against prior roadmaps?	• Roadmaps that promise fault-tolerant qubits within "3-5 years" without specifying error correction targets or physical qubit overhead estimates
Financial Stability	• What is the vendor's runway? • Have they secured Series B or later funding, or established revenue streams sufficient to maintain operations through your development timeline?	• Pre-revenue startups offering enterprise PoC engagements without a clear path to commercialization • Dependence on a single investor or grant program
Ecosystem and Partner Network	• What classical co-compute infrastructure (HPC, cloud GPU) is integrated with the quantum system? • What domain solution partners have built on the platform?	• Isolated quantum access without classical integration infrastructure • Thin partner ecosystem limits algorithm domain coverage

Table 7.2: Commercial and Strategic Evaluation Matrix

A structured vendor down-selection process for quantum prototyping should include a technical RFP with quantum-specific benchmark requirements, a structured PoC scoping session, and a reference architecture review. The RFP benchmark requirements are particularly important as they require vendors to execute a reference benchmark circuit on hardware (not just simulator) and report raw and error-mitigated performance data in a standardized format. Vendors who resist standardized benchmarking requirements are often concealing performance characteristics they know will compare unfavorably.[5]

Quantum development methodologies for hybrid experiments

Classical software development methodologies, even modern agile frameworks, were designed around a set of assumptions that quantum computing violates systematically. In classical development, you can run your code locally before deploying to production, your computational results are deterministic, and debugging means inspecting program state at any point. In quantum-classical hybrid development, your "production environment" is a supercooled dilution refrigerator you access via an API queue, your results are probabilistic distributions rather than deterministic outputs, and measuring quantum state destroys it. Needless to say, standard agile sprints require adaptation.[6]

Quantum-adapted sprint structure

A quantum-adapted sprint framework must accommodate three realities that have no classical analog: hardware access scheduling constraints, the iterative parameter optimization cycles of variational quantum algorithms, and the need to interleave classical simulation with hardware execution at appropriate development stages.

The following table breaks these down into sprint phases:

Sprint Phase	Duration	Primary Activities	Execution Environment	Gate Criteria
Algorithm Design	Week 1-2	Circuit architecture design, parameter initialization strategy, classical simulation of small instances	Classical simulator (exact state vector)	Circuit produces correct output on noiseless simulator for 6-8 qubit test instances
Noise-Realistic Simulation	Week 3-4	Noise model calibration from hardware specs, noise-realistic simulations, error mitigation strategy selection	Noise-realistic simulator (Qiskit Aer, Cirq, etc.)	Algorithm maintains >70% of noiseless performance under the target hardware noise model

Sprint Phase	Duration	Primary Activities	Execution Environment	Gate Criteria
Hardware Validation	Week 5-6	Transition to actual hardware, shot budget calibration, error mitigation implementation, and tuning	Quantum hardware (reserved access sessions)	Hardware results within 15% of noise-realistic simulation predictions
Optimizing and Benchmarking	Week 7-8	Parameter optimization, baseline comparison, performance characterization across problem sizes	Hardware + classical co-compute	Performance gap to classical baseline measured with statistical significance
Integration Prototype	Week 9-10	API integration testing, data pipeline validation, latency profiling, error handling robustness	Full hybrid stack (quantum + classical API layer)	End-to-end latency <target threshold under realistic load, error handling covers all failure modes

Table 7.3: Quantum-Adapted Sprint Structure Matrix

Hardware access scheduling deserves special attention because it has no classical analog. Quantum hardware systems are accessed via cloud queues with significant wait times, which could span hours during peak demand, or via reserved-time access arrangements with correspondingly higher cost. Your sprint planning must explicitly account for hardware access time in the development schedule rather than treating hardware execution as instantaneous as a local compiler invocation. Teams that learn this lesson early on avoid the scramble of discovering their "two-week hardware validation phase" takes four weeks because of queue delays.[7]

Quantum debugging and circuit validation practices

Debugging quantum programs requires a fundamentally different mental model than classical debugging. You cannot simply add a print statement in the middle of a quantum circuit, as reading qubit state collapses the superposition you are trying to preserve. Quantum debugging instead relies on a set of specialized techniques that provide indirect access to circuit behavior without destroying the quantum state of interest.[8]

Circuit visualization tools, available in Qiskit, Cirq, and PennyLane, are the first line of debugging, enabling teams to inspect circuit structure, gate decompositions, and qubit connectivity mappings before any execution. State tomography provides partial quantum state characterization through repeated measurements in multiple bases, enabling reconstruction of the density matrix for small subsystems. Noise model fitting, using techniques like randomized benchmarking and gate set tomography, characterizes the actual noise environment experienced by a circuit and enables realistic performance modeling before full-scale hardware runs.[9]

Version control practices for quantum development require adaptations beyond standard Git workflows. Quantum circuit definitions, parameter initialization histories, optimization convergence logs, and hardware calibration data all represent distinct artifact types that must be tracked, versioned, and associated with experimental results. Teams that treat quantum development with the same version control discipline as classical software development, committing circuit designs, parameter sets, and execution logs together with result data, create institutional memory that dramatically accelerates iterative prototype refinement.

Quantum simulation tools and early-stage application development

Now, the good news about current quantum simulation tools is that they are genuinely excellent. The bad news is that there are a lot of them, their performance characteristics differ substantially by application domain, and choosing the wrong one creates technical debt that can be surprisingly expensive to unwind. This section will provide you with a practical orientation to the major simulation frameworks and the application development patterns relevant to each.

Simulation framework comparison

The following table provides an overview of the various quantum simulators and some specifications for you to consider when selecting your ideal simulator provider. Do note that these were based on specifications available at the time of this writing. It's worth checking the latest documentation of each every so often to ensure that you are up to speed with the latest developments and advancements.

Framework	Primary Developer	Max Practical Qubits (exact sim)	Standout Capability	Best Fit Application Domains
Qiskit Aer	IBM	~30 qubits (statevector) ~50 qubits (MPS, stabilizer)	Realistic noise model integration with IBM hardware calibration data Mature error mitigation library	Combinatorial optimization (QAOA), general circuit simulation with IBM hardware noise models
Cirq + qsim	Google	~30 qubits (statevector) GPU-accelerated to ~38	High-performance statevector simulation Native integration with Google quantum hardware	Algorithm research, Google hardware targeting, high-performance simulation needs
PennyLane	Xanadu	~25 qubits (default.qubit) Larger with Lightning backends	Differentiable quantum circuit framework enabling automatic gradient computation Hardware-agnostic interface	Quantum machine learning, variational algorithms, hybrid optimization with ML frameworks
CUDA-Q	NVIDIA	GPU-limited 30+ qubits at high speed on H100	GPU-accelerated simulation Native CUDA integration for classical-quantum hybrid	High-throughput simulation for organizations with NVIDIA GPU infrastructure Chemistry simulation

Framework	Primary Developer	Max Practical Qubits (exact sim)	Standout Capability	Best Fit Application Domains
Amazon Braket SDK	Amazon	~34 qubits (SV1 simulator) TN1 for 50+	Cloud-managed simulation with seamless transition to multiple hardware backends (IonQ, Rigetti, OQC)	Multi-hardware prototyping, organizations with AWS infrastructure

Table 7.4: Simulation Framework Comparison Matrix

The performance envelope of quantum simulators is governed primarily by memory requirements for exact state vector simulation, which scale exponentially with qubit count. For example, a 30-qubit simulation requires approximately 8GB of RAM, while a 40-qubit simulation requires approximately 8TB. This is why simulator selection matters enormously for the prototype development cycle; teams routinely discover mid-prototype that their chosen simulator cannot faithfully represent their target circuit size on available compute infrastructure.[10]

Application development patterns by quantum domain

Quantum application development is not a uniform activity. The engineering complexity, prototype development timeline, and near-term advantage potential vary substantially by application category. Understanding these differences is essential for prototype scoping and timeline estimation. The following subsections will cover the general domains and their associated algorithms.

Combinatorial optimization: QAOA and variational approaches

Combinatorial optimization represents the most tractable near-term quantum application domain, with the Quantum Approximate Optimization Algorithm (QAOA) serving as the primary algorithmic framework. QAOA maps optimization problems onto quantum circuits through a parameterized ansatz structure, with problem-specific cost and mixer operators. The appeal is real, as many industrially relevant optimization problems, such as routing, scheduling, portfolio optimization, and molecular docking, map naturally onto the QAOA framework.[11]

The prototype development timeline for a QAOA application typically spans 6-10 weeks for an experienced quantum engineering team where 2 weeks are set for problem mapping and classical baseline establishment, followed by 3-4 weeks for circuit design, simulation, and parameter optimization development, and finally 2-3 weeks for hardware validation and integration prototyping. The critical challenge here is that QAOA's practical advantage over well-tuned classical solvers like simulated annealing and branch-and-bound remains an open research question for problem sizes accessible to NISQ hardware, a reality that prototype success metrics must honestly confront.[12]

Quantum Machine Learning: kernel methods and variational classifiers

Quantum machine learning (QML) is the quantum application domain with the largest gap between theoretical promise and demonstrable near-term practical advantage. Quantum kernel methods, which use quantum circuits to compute kernel functions for support vector machines on classical data, have attracted significant research attention because they offer a clear mathematical framework for potential quantum advantage.[13]

Variational quantum classifiers (VQC), which use parameterized quantum circuits as function approximators analogous to neural network layers, face a severe practical challenge known as the barren plateau problem, where gradient magnitudes vanish exponentially with circuit width for random initialization strategies, making optimization intractable for circuits of the depth needed to outperform classical methods on real data.[14] If you're considering creating prototypes in QML, then it's recommended that you should include careful investigation of whether barren plateau dynamics are present before investing significant hardware time.

Quantum chemistry simulation: VQE for molecular properties

Quantum chemistry simulation is arguably the application domain with the clearest long-term quantum advantage pathway and the most technically demanding near-term prototype requirements. The Variational Quantum Eigensolver (VQE) algorithm estimates ground-state energies of molecular Hamiltonians by minimizing energy expectation values over a parameterized quantum state. Even for industrially relevant molecules such as those relevant to drug discovery, materials design, and catalyst development, representing the electronic structure Hamiltonian requires more qubits than current NISQ hardware can handle with sufficient fidelity.[15] However, much of that has changed recently since advancements in both error mitigation and novel hybrid quantum-classical architecture have discovered utility in some cases where quantum systems reduce the processing time. This is often referred to as Quantum Utility.[16]

For near-term prototyping, VQE development is most productive when focused on small molecular fragments such as H2, LiH, and BeH2, which serve as test cases for algorithm development and hardware validation, rather than attempting to simulate target molecules directly on current hardware. Organizations with genuine quantum chemistry research programs should think of current prototyping work as algorithm and workflow development investment that positions them to exploit fault-tolerant hardware when it arrives, rather than expecting production-ready performance from NISQ implementations.

Success metrics and prototype evaluation framework

One of the most reliable predictors of a failed quantum prototype is the absence of pre-defined success criteria. When prototype evaluation criteria are left undefined until after results are generated, motivated reasoning reliably produces an interpretation that confirms whatever the team was hoping to find. If the results look good, the quantum approach is validated. Conversely, if they look bad, then the hardware was the problem. Both interpretations are unfalsifiable, and neither produces decision-relevant intelligence.

The solution is straightforward in principle and requires discipline in practice: define your success metrics before you design your circuits, before you touch a simulator, and certainly before you access quantum hardware.

Quantum prototype success metrics framework

The following three-category metric framework provides a structured approach to properly evaluate success metrics and prototypes.

Metric Category	Specific Metric	Measurement Approach	Interpretation Guidance
Technical Performance	Solution quality relative to classical baseline Approximate Ratio (AR)	Run equivalent problem instances on quantum prototype and best-available classical solver Compute ratio of objective function values	AR > 0.95 suggests competitive performance AR < 0.80 indicates a significant quality gap requiring explanation
	Circuit execution fidelity (state fidelity or expectation value error)	Compare hardware expectation values against noise-realistic simulation predictions Compute absolute error	Errors within 15% of noise model predictions suggest implementation correctness Larger derivations warrant noise model recalibration
	Optimization convergence rate (iterations to target energy/cost)	Track objective function improvement rate per 1,000 circuit executions (shots) across the optimization trajectory	Slow convergence often indicates barren plateau effects Compare classical simulation convergence as a diagnostic

Metric Category	Specific Metric	Measurement Approach	Interpretation Guidance
Resource Efficiency	Shot budget efficiency (result quality per 1,000 shots)	Track objective function improvement rate per 1,000 circuit executions (shots) across the optimization trajectory	Diminishing returns onset before budget exhaustion suggests optimization parameter tuning opportunities
	Classical co-compute overhead (fraction of runtime on classical resources)	Profile wall-clock time distribution across quantum execution, classical parameter update, and data transfer phases	Classical overhead >80% of runtime indicates quantum component is not computationally bottlenecking the workflow
	Qubit utilization (active qubits as a fraction of available qubits)	Measure the fraction of available qubits used in the compiled circuit Track SWAP overhead introduced by compilation	High SWAP overhead (>30% of gates) suggests a connectivity mismatch requiring alternative hardware targeting
Integration Readiness	API latency under realistic load (95th percentile end-to-end response time)	Load test quantum API integration at expected production request rates Measure end-to-end latency distribution	P95 latency exceeding application SLA threshold indicates integration architecture redesign is needed
	Data pipeline throughput (input encoding and output encoding rate)	Benchmark data encoding (classical to quantum format) and measurement decoding throughput at production data volumes	Encoding/decoding throughput bottleneck can eliminate quantum performance advantages entirely
	Error handling robustness (graceful degradation on hardware failure)	Inject hardware failure conditions (queue timeouts, calibration errors, decoherence events) and evaluate application-layer response	Production systems must fall back gracefully to classical computation on quantum hardware failures

Table 7.5: Quantum Prototype Success Metric Framework

Controlled comparison methodology is as important as metric selection. A common prototype evaluation error is comparing quantum results on a complex, production-scale problem instance against a poorly tuned or deliberately weak classical baseline. The incentive to make quantum look good by selecting an unfair classical baseline is real and must be explicitly guarded against. Classical baselines should use the best available solver for the problem category, with tuning effort comparable to the quantum optimization effort, at problem sizes that are directly comparable.

Statistical validity is also non-negotiable for quantum experimental data. Because quantum measurements are probabilistic, performance metrics are inherently noisy estimates. Reporting a single optimization run result as a prototype conclusion is scientifically invalid. You will need multiple independent runs with confidence intervals. A minimum of 20-30 independent optimization runs with bootstrap confidence interval estimation is a reasonable standard for QAOA-type experiments.

Company spotlights: quantum prototyping in practice

Across sectors as diverse as automotive manufacturing, financial optimization, and aerospace engineering, corporate quantum computing programs are maturing from curiosity-driven prototypes into methodologically credible industrial experiments. BMW Group, JPMorgan Chase, and Airbus each illustrate how disciplined program design, not speculative hype, determines the real acceleration of enterprise learning. BMW's structured approach to problem decomposition and its multi-vendor benchmarking demonstrate how applying quantum methods to solvable, bounded subproblems enables meaningful empirical progress without overstating capability.

Similarly, JPMorgan Chase's "simulate before you execute" workflow and hybrid quantum-classical integration architecture show how careful scoping and transparent performance framing convert prototypes into actionable inputs for technology investment decisions.

Airbus' Quantum Computing Challenge takes this rigor public, defining explicit classical baselines and publishing cross-platform results to promote reproducibility and grounded evaluation across the broader ecosystem. While their application domains differ, all three organizations converge on a common strategic principle: credible quantum prototyping is not about chasing hardware novelty but about designing disciplined, benchmarked, and transparent learning loops. For technical leaders, their programs offer replicable governance lessons: balance explorations across hardware modalities, publish comparative baselines, and treat quantum systems as modular optimizers within classical infrastructures. As quantum computing inches toward practical relevance, such disciplined prototyping cultures will distinguish early adopters who build cumulative advantage from those who burn cycles chasing demonstrations untethered from operational value.

BMW Group: Disciplined automotive optimization prototyping

BMW Group has emerged as one of the most methodologically rigorous corporate quantum prototyping practitioners in Europe, pursuing a portfolio approach that applies structured pilot discipline across multiple quantum application domains simultaneously. BMW's quantum computing program originally started as early as 2017, and they launched their quantum strategy in 2020.[17] Since then, they have expanded substantially through their participation as a key industry partner in the Munich Quantum Valley initiative,[18] and have focused primarily on combinatorial optimization problems embedded in automotive manufacturing and robotics, precisely the application domain where near-term NISQ hardware has some credible advantage potential.[19]

BMW's prototyping approach is notable for its explicit problem decomposition discipline. Rather than attempting to quantum-compute entire vehicle production scheduling problems, which involve thousands of variables and would dwarf any available quantum hardware, BMW's teams identify specific computational subproblems that are both practically significant and amenable to quantum treatment. For example: paint shop sequencing optimization with 20-40 binary variables,[20] assembly line job scheduling subproblems, and supplier network configuration under uncertainty. This decomposition discipline is what allows BMW to run meaningful quantum experiments rather than aspirational demonstrations.[21]

Their vendor evaluation process is equally instructive. BMW has worked with multiple quantum hardware providers including IBM Quantum,[22] Quantinuum,[23] and D-Wave,[24] using a comparative prototyping approach that evaluates each hardware modality on equivalent problem instances with standardized benchmarking methodologies. This multi-vendor approach serves both evaluation and risk management purposes by not committing exclusively to any single hardware provider; BMW maintains optionality as the quantum hardware landscape evolves. Their published prototype results have been notably honest about performance limitations, distinguishing between cases where quantum approaches showed genuine promise and those where classical solvers remained superior on current hardware.[25]

The key lesson from BMW's quantum prototyping program is that industrial quantum prototyping credibility is built through methodological rigor, not optimistic result interpretation. Their willingness to report both promising and disappointing prototype results, with clear attribution of limiting factors such as hardware noise, problem size constraints, and algorithm convergence issues, has made their published findings genuinely informative for the broader quantum computing community. For technical leaders designing their own prototyping programs, BMW's problem decomposition discipline and multi-vendor evaluation approach represent a practically adoptable template.

JPMorgan Chase: Financial optimization and quantum-classical portfolio optimization

JPMorgan Chase's quantum computing research team, operating out of their Global Technology Applied Research group,[26] has conducted some of the most technically rigorous financial quantum prototyping work published by any corporate quantum research program. Their prototyping focus spans portfolio optimization, options pricing simulation, and fraud detection pattern recognition, application domains selected based on explicit assessment of computational structure amenability to quantum speedup rather than quantum novelty appeal.[27]

JPMorgan's development methodology illustrates several quantum prototype best practices that broader organizations can emulate. Their team maintains a standing quantum algorithm research group that develops and evaluates algorithm approaches in advance of hardware execution, running computational experiments first on classical simulators to characterize algorithm behavior before committing hardware shot budgets. This "simulate before you execute" discipline dramatically improves hardware execution efficiency. Their early work in quantum amplitude estimation (QAE) on derivative pricing simulation represents a particularly clear example of disciplined prototype scoping: a specific classical Monte Carlo simulation subroutine, not the entire pricing system, was identified as a quantum replacement target, enabling focused technical evaluation.[27]

The quantum portfolio optimization prototyping program is instructive in its honest treatment of current hardware limitations. JPMorgan's published research explicitly characterizes the qubit count and gate fidelity requirements for quantum portfolio optimization to outperform classical quadratic programming solvers and honestly notes that current NISQ hardware does not meet those requirements for industrially relevant portfolio sizes. Rather than overselling current results, their published work frames prototype outcomes in terms of trajectory such as: "here is where the algorithm performs today," "here is what hardware improvement is needed for practical advantage," "here is our assessment of when that hardware will be available."[28] This temporal framing converts prototype results into genuine investment decision inputs.

JPMorgan's quantum prototyping program also demonstrates effective management of the quantum-classical integration challenge. Their hybrid portfolio optimization architecture explicitly designs the quantum component as a plug-in optimizer within a larger classical workflow, with well-defined API contracts, fallback behavior, and performance SLAs. This integration-first design mindset, treating the quantum component as a replaceable module within a classical architecture rather than a standalone quantum system, significantly reduces integration complexity and makes the prototype transition to expanded development more tractable.[29]

Airbus: Aerospace quantum prototyping with industrial rigor

Airbus' quantum computing efforts, coordinated through their Central Research and Technology division and the Airbus Quantum Computing Challenge, represent one of the most structured industrial quantum prototyping programs in the aerospace sector. Airbus has approached quantum computing with characteristic aerospace engineering discipline: defining specific design requirements, executing structured technical feasibility assessments, and maintaining honest evaluation criteria. Their application focus, aircraft taxi path optimization, computational fluid dynamics acceleration, and composite materials discovery, reflects a deliberate selection process that evaluated dozens of potential quantum applications against technical feasibility and business impact criteria before committing prototyping resources.[30] The Airbus Quantum Computing Challenge, launched in 2019 and producing several prototype engagements with quantum startups and university research groups, provides an unusually transparent window into structured quantum PoC evaluation. Airbus published explicit problem statements with quantified classical baseline performance data, enabling challenge participants to design experiments with clear comparison targets. This clarity in baseline specification, knowing what "better than classical" means quantitatively before prototype execution begins, is a discipline that many corporate quantum programs fail to apply but that dramatically improves the decision-relevance of prototype outcomes.

Their aircraft taxi path optimization prototyping program is particularly instructive for combinatorial optimization application development. The problem involves scheduling aircraft movements on airport taxiways to minimize total taxi time and fuel consumption, a combinatorial optimization problem with natural mapping onto QUBO (Quadratic Unconstrained Binary Optimization) formulations amenable to quantum annealing and gate-based QAOA approaches. Airbus has prototyped multiple solution approaches across quantum annealing hardware (D-Wave), gate-based quantum computing (IBM, IonQ), and classical GPU-accelerated solvers (NVIDIA), using a controlled comparison methodology that enables genuine cross-platform performance evaluation. Their published conclusion is that gate-based quantum approaches show promise for problem decomposition below 50 qubits but do not currently outperform tailored classical solvers at operationally relevant problem scales. This is the kind of honest, evidence-grounded finding that prototype programs should aspire to produce.[31]

For European technical leaders seeking a culturally adjacent model for industrial quantum prototyping, Airbus' program provides a directly applicable template. Their structured challenge format enables external prototyping resource engagement without full in-house quantum engineering capability. Their explicit baseline specification discipline creates evaluation clarity. And their multi-vendor, multi-modality comparison approach provides hedged learning across the quantum hardware landscape rather than commitment to a single technology bet.

The Go/No-Go feasibility framework for development progression

Now that we are a bit more familiar with how just a handful of companies develop and manage their quantum prototypes, let's focus on what the results of those prototypes ultimately tell us... Go or No-Go.

The go/no-go decision is the moment when quantum prototype work transforms from a learning exercise into an investment commitment. Done well, it's a disciplined synthesis of technical evidence, economic analysis, organizational capability assessment, and risk judgment that produces a defensible recommendation. Done poorly, it's a foregone conclusion, either "quantum enthusiast bias" from engineering teams that have fallen in love with the technology or "quantum skepticism bias" from finance functions that dismiss evidence of genuine potential, dressed up in analytical language.

The six-dimension Go/No-Go feasibility framework

There are six dimensions you can use to help you identify whether the results from your prototype are a go or no-go. The following Go/No-Go Feasibility Framework presented here is designed to structure the deliberation process in a way that surfaces evidence honestly across all relevant dimensions and produces a recommendation grounded in the specific prototype results rather than prior beliefs about quantum computing. The hope here is to help take the *emotion* out of some of the decision-making processes, though human nature does have its needs here and there.

Dimension	Core Evaluation Question	Evidence Sources	Go Threshold Indicators	No-Go Threshold Indicators
Technical feasibility	Does the quantum approach demonstrably outperform, or credibly project to outperform, classical alternatives at target scale?	Approximation ratio data, convergence analysis, scaling extrapolation from prototype results	AR > 0.95 at prototype scale Favorable scaling projection to target scale within hardware roadmap	Persistent quality gap vs. classical baseline Unfavorable scaling projection Noise-dominated results
Hardware Readiness	Is quantum hardware with production-required performance available or on a credible near-term roadmap?	Vendor hardware roadmaps, error correction timeline analysis, published qubit performance trajectories	Production-grade hardware available now or on a specific <18-month roadmap with milestone evidence	Production performance requires hardware that is more than 3 years away on optimistic roadmaps No milestone evidence
Integration Feasibility	Can the quantum component be integrated into existing system architecture without prohibitive engineering complexity?	API latency benchmarks, data pipeline throughput tests, error handling robustness assessment	Integration prototype meets SLA thresholds Clear API contract design Manageable data format conversion requirements	Latency requirements incompatible with quantum hardware round trip Data encoding bottlenecks eliminate performance advantages

Dimension	Core Evaluation Question	Evidence Sources	Go Threshold Indicators	No-Go Threshold Indicators
Economic feasibility	Do projected quantum performance gains justify development and operational costs at realistic production volumes?	Quantum cloud compute costs, project development headcount estimates, performance-to-cost ratio analysis at scale	NPV positive at 3-5 year horizon under conservative performance assumptions Cost/benefit ratio > 1.5x	NPV is negative under base-case assumptions Quantum compute costs are prohibitive at required shot volumes
Talent Feasibility	Does the organization have, or credibly plan to acquire, quantum engineering capability for full development?	Current team capability assessment, hiring market analysis, vendor support scope, university partnership options	Core quantum team in place or hiring plan viable Vendor support covers identified capability gaps	No quantum engineering capability and 18+ month hiring timeline No vendor support sufficient to bridge the gap
Risk Tolerance	Are residual technical and timeline risks within the organization's acceptance threshold?	Risk register from prototype phase, probability-weighted timeline analysis, technical risk benchmarking	Identified risks are addressable within the project risk budget Worst-case timeline within planning horizon	Timeline risk extends beyond the strategic planning window Technical risks are irreducible without hardware advances

Table 7.6: Six-Dimension Go/No-Go Feasibility Framework Matrix

Scoring and decision logic

The six dimensions should each receive a score from 1 to 5, reflecting the strength of evidence for proceeding to development. A total score of 24 or above (averaging 4 per dimension) represents a strong go recommendation. Scores of 18-23 suggest conditional go, proceed with specified conditions or risk mitigations explicitly addressed. Scores below 18 indicate no-go, with the prototype findings redirected toward alternative solution architecture evaluation.

Critically, the framework enforces a veto rule: a dimension score of 1, meaning fundamental infeasibility, not merely weakness, triggers a no-go recommendation regardless of aggregate score. A quantum approach that scores perfectly on economic and talent dimensions but cannot demonstrate any quantum performance signal above the classical baseline (Technical Feasibility = 1) should not proceed to development. The dimensional scores are not an averaging exercise that permits fundamental feasibility failures to be washed out by organizational strengths.

Presenting go/no-go findings to executive sponsors requires packaging the framework output in a format that supports informed decision-making rather than simply communicating scores with a brief narrative for each dimension. The key assumptions underlying the go/no-go determination should be explicitly stated so decision-makers can evaluate their plausibility, as well as the specific conditions or evidence updates that would change the recommendation. This format respects executive intelligence and time constraints while ensuring that the reasoning is transparent enough to challenge.

Managing cognitive bias in feasibility assessments

Two cognitive biases reliably distort quantum feasibility assessments:

- ***Quantum enthusiasm bias***, common in engineering teams that have spent months immersed in quantum algorithm development and have significant ego investment in a positive outcome, manifests as selective attention to promising prototype results and motivated reinterpretation of disappointing ones.
- ***Quantum skepticism bias***, common in finance and risk functions that associate "quantum" with science fiction rather than engineering, manifests as dismissal of genuine quantum performance signals and reflexive preference for classical incumbents. Structuring the feasibility assessment as a cross-functional facilitated workshop, with explicit representation from both quantum-positive and quantum-skeptical stakeholders, and with pre-committed evaluation criteria, is the most effective mitigation. Independent technical review of the prototype results by a quantum expert with no stake in the outcome is also valuable where feasible.

Skills developed

As a technical executive leader, the following skills form a decision toolkit that turns quantum prototypes from hype-generating demos into evidence-generating experiments that you can act on. Quantum Prototype Scoping and Design ensures teams pick tractable subproblems with explicit success thresholds and resource limits, so you avoid multi-year "experiments" that were never winnable on current hardware and can instead make crisp go/no-go calls against pre-committed baselines. Technical Vendor Management for Quantum Engagements gives you the fluency to challenge vendor algorithms, structure IP and data-access terms in your favor, and separate genuine technical signal from commercial momentum when vendors push to expand after a "successful" PoC. Quantum Algorithms Performance Analysis equips your organization to distinguish hardware-noise failures from fundamental algorithmic limits, using disciplined statistical methods and shot-distribution analysis to avoid both false positives and false negatives in feasibility judgments. Feasibility Assessment Leadership turns raw technical data into cross-functional, bias-resistant decisions by convening skeptics and enthusiasts under pre-defined criteria and producing executive-ready recommendations that highlight assumptions and residual risks. Finally, Iterative Prototype Refinement builds that habit of logging hypothesis, changes, and outcomes so you can recognize barren plateaus, noise saturation, or integration bottlenecks early, and know when additional spend is still buying learning versus when a disciplined stop or pivot decision will create more value for the business problem than another optimization cycle. Together, these skills let you govern quantum exploration with the same rigor you apply to any other strategic technology bet, while still leaving room for upside if and when the hardware delivers on its promised curve.

Quantum prototype scoping and design

The most expensive quantum prototype failures are not hardware failures or algorithm failures; they are scoping failures. A quantum prototype scoped too broadly (attempting to quantum-compute an entire business process rather than a specific computation subproblem) will inevitably produce inconclusive results because the problem is not tractable on available hardware. A prototype scoped without clear success criteria will produce results that cannot be evaluated against a meaningful standard. Prototype scoping is where the intellectual work of quantum application development happens, and doing it well is a skill that requires explicit development.

Effective scoping begins with problem decomposition analysis: systematically breaking down the target business problem into computational subproblems and evaluating each against quantum amenability criteria. The questions to answer for each subproblem are: Does this subproblem have an exponentially large solution space that quantum superposition could efficiently explore? Does the subproblem map naturally onto a mathematical structure (QUBO, eigenvalue problem, sampling distribution) for which quantum algorithms have theoretical advantage? Is the subproblem of a size (in terms of required qubits) that current or near-term hardware can address with meaningful fidelity? A subproblem that answers yes to all three questions is a prototype candidate; one that answers no to any of them should be set aside for later hardware generations.

Success criteria definition is the second critical scoping skill. Before any circuit design begins, the prototype team must specify, in quantitative terms, what "success" means: what is the classical performance baseline, what is the minimum quantum performance threshold that would justify continued investment, and what is the target quantum performance level that would demonstrate a clear go recommendation. Writing these numbers down before prototype execution, and committing them as the evaluation standard, is what distinguishes prototype programs that generate genuine intelligence from those that generate confirmation bias with quantum aesthetics.

Resource constraint specification is the third component of effective scoping. A quantum prototype design that does not specify qubit budget, shot budget, hardware access time budget, engineering effort budget, and timeline is not a prototype design, it's a wish list. Explicit resource constraints force scoping realism and prevent the prototype expansion that is the most common execution failure mode: the team discovers their original scope is under-constrained and gradually expands it until the prototype has become a research program with no end date. Developing the discipline to hold prototype scope against resource constraints, and to surface scope-constraint conflicts early through transparent communication with executive sponsors, is an essential skill for technical leaders managing quantum prototyping programs.

Practical development of this skill begins with facilitated prototype scoping sessions that follow a structured agenda: 90 minutes for problem decomposition, 60 minutes for quantum amenability analysis of candidate subproblems, 60 minutes for success criteria quantification, and 45 minutes for resource constraint specification. Technical leaders who have facilitated five or more such sessions develop a reliable intuition for prototype scoping quality and the warning signs – vague success criteria, absent classical baselines, and underspecified qubit requirements – that predict prototype failure before it begins.

Technical vendor management for quantum engagements

Managing quantum technology vendor relationships through prototyping engagements is a distinct skill set from conventional enterprise IT vendor management. The asymmetry of quantum expertise between the vendor and the buyer organization, the novelty of the technology landscape, and the significant IP and commercialization implications of successful prototypes create management challenges that standard vendor governance frameworks are not equipped to handle. Technical leaders who develop effective quantum vendor management practices protect their organizations from the significant downside risks of poorly managed quantum engagements while maximizing the learning value of the prototype. This is much different from the usual IT technology contracts, which often come down to cost, whereas with quantum, it generally comes down to whether the engagement succeeds, at least for the foreseeable future.

Technical oversight of quantum PoC engagements requires the ability to review quantum algorithm design artifacts for soundness, even without deep quantum engineering expertise. A technical leader who understands the mathematical structure of QAOA, the role of ansatz depth in variational quantum algorithm performance, and the relationship between circuit depth and hardware noise can evaluate vendor-proposed algorithm designs for obvious deficiencies and motivated choices. This does not require the ability to design quantum circuits from scratch; it requires enough conceptual fluency to ask probing questions and recognize when answers are evasive. Developing this fluency through the conceptual frameworks in Chapters 5 and 6, combined with hands-on exposure to quantum simulator tools, is the most efficient path.

Prototype engagement contract terms require specialized attention to clauses that are standard in enterprise software contracts but carry unusual implications in quantum contexts. IP ownership terms deserve careful review: if a vendor's engagement structure transfers ownership of quantum algorithm designs to the vendor, the buyer organization is funding quantum IP development for the vendor's benefit. Result reporting standards should specify not just the metrics to be reported but the raw data formats required for independent validation, shot histograms, optimization convergence logs, and circuit definitions. Escalation pathways for technical disputes should identify a mutually agreed independent technical reviewer who can adjudicate disagreements about prototype result interpretation and should be in place ahead of time.

The transition from prototype to expanded development engagement is where vendor commercial dynamics become most significant. Vendors have strong incentives to structure prototype success criteria in ways that make expanded engagement inevitable, success metrics that always pass, or prototype scope that answers only the questions the vendor is confident about. Technical leaders who recognize these structural incentives and counteract them through independent success criteria definition and external technical review are far better positioned to make development progression decisions based on genuine prototype evidence rather than vendor commercial momentum. Running a staged commercialization negotiation, completing the technical go-no-go assessment before engaging on commercial terms for expanded development, is practical protection against this dynamic.

Quantum algorithm performance analysis

Interpreting quantum algorithm prototype results is genuinely difficult, and the difficulty is not merely technical, it's structural. Quantum computation is probabilistic, which means prototype results are noisy estimates of true algorithm performance, not definitive measurements. NISQ hardware introduces systematic error patterns that can masquerade as algorithmic signals. And the absence of a mature intuition for quantum algorithm behavior, which classical engineers develop over decades of working with deterministic systems, means that many prototype result anomalies are initially misattributed. Developing reliable quantum performance analysis skills requires explicit cultivation.

The foundational skill is reading shot distribution histograms. Every quantum computation on gate-based hardware produces a probability distribution over computational basis states, estimated through repeated circuit executions (shots). A clean optimization result should show probability concentrated on a small number of high-quality solution states; a noise-dominated result shows probability spread broadly across many states with little structure. Learning to recognize the visual signatures of good optimization, noise-induced performance degradation, and barren plateau dynamics in shot histograms is the quantum equivalent of learning to read stack traces. It becomes second nature with practice but requires intentional exposure initially.

Statistical analysis of quantum experimental data requires tools that go beyond the descriptive statistics most engineers are comfortable with. Bootstrap confidence interval estimation for quantum expectation values, sensitivity analysis for variational parameter optimization results, and hypothesis testing frameworks for quantum vs. classical performance comparisons are techniques that quantum prototype teams should apply routinely but frequently skip due to unfamiliarity. A practical starting point is requiring that all prototype performance reports include 95% confidence intervals on all key metrics, computed from independent replicate runs, as a condition for review. This requirement forces statistical practice and develops the intuition for what well-characterized quantum performance data looks like versus point estimates that may not be reproducible.

Perhaps the most important analytical skill for quantum prototype interpretation is distinguishing between performance limitations that reflect hardware noise and those that reflect fundamental algorithmic constraints. A QAOA optimization result that performs poorly because the circuit is too noisy to extract signals will improve as hardware quality improves; it's a NISQ limitation, not a fundamental feasibility problem. A QAOA result that performs poorly because the algorithm does not find good optimization trajectories for the problem structure represents an algorithmic issue that will not be resolved by hardware improvement alone. These two failure modes call for entirely different responses: hardware noise limitations justify conditional go decisions contingent on hardware improvement; algorithmic limitations require algorithm redesign or application domain pivoting. Developing analytical fluency to distinguish them is what separates technically credible feasibility assessments from superficial ones.

Feasibility assessment leadership

Leading a structured quantum feasibility assessment is a cross-functional facilitation challenge as much as a technical analysis challenge. The six-dimension framework presented in this chapter does the structure work of ensuring comprehensive coverage; the human challenge is ensuring that each dimension receives honest, evidence-grounded treatment from the relevant experts, and that the deliberation process is protected from the cognitive biases that reliably distort quantum technology assessments. Technical leaders who develop this facilitation competency become their organizations' most valuable quantum decision-making assets.

Effective feasibility assessment workshop design begins with participant selection that deliberately includes quantum skeptics as well as quantum enthusiasts. Financial analysts, along with risk managers, and domain experts are as important to your quantum team as the quantum engineers. They identify any risks, test assumptions, assess performance indicators vs. classical baselines. The workshop facilitator's role is not to advocate for a predetermined conclusion but to ensure that each stakeholder group engages substantively with the evidence and that their findings are recorded in a form that can be challenged and updated.

Pre-commitment to evaluation criteria before the workshop is a practice borrowed from *decision science* that dramatically improves assessment quality. When feasibility scores are defined and calibrated before the prototype results are known, motivated reasoning has far less opportunity to influence the evaluation. Workshop preparation should include distributing prototype result data to participants in advance, with a request that each participant score their assigned dimensions independently before the group deliberation and share their scores and reasoning at the workshop opening. This structure's process surfaces disagreements early and prevents social dynamics from suppressing minority viewpoints.

Presenting feasibility findings to executive sponsors is the culmination of the assessment process and requires a communication skill that is distinct from the analytical skill of conducting the assessment. Executives making go/no-go development decisions need three things: a clear recommendation, a concise rationale that explains the primary evidence supporting the recommendation, and explicit identification of the key assumptions that, if wrong, would change the recommendation. A 15-minute executive briefing that presents the rationale, recommendation, and key assumptions very clearly is much more valuable that a 90-minute report that reaches the same conclusion. Technical leaders who develop the ability to produce both comprehensive analysis and the executive summary translation develop credibility as quantum initiative leaders rather than quantum technology advocates.

Iterative prototype refinement

Quantum prototypes almost never converge on a validated performance result in a single development iteration. The algorithm-hardware-integration design space is three-dimensional and highly coupled; an algorithm improvement that increases circuit depth may outpace hardware coherence improvements, while an integration architecture change may expose new latency bottlenecks that constrain quantum advantage. Navigating this coupled design space efficiently requires iterative refinement skills that are partly algorithmic (knowing which design levers to pull and in what order) and partly disciplinary (knowing when to keep iterating versus when to pivot or stop).

The iterative refinement process should be structured around a prototype experiment log that tracks, for each development iteration: the specific design change made (algorithm modification, parameter initialization strategy, error mitigation technique, circuit optimization), the hypothesis that motivated the change, the observed performance change, and the interpretation of whether the hypothesis was confirmed. This experimental discipline creates institutional memory that prevents teams from repeating failed approaches, enables clear attribution of performance improvements to specific design changes, and provides the evidentiary basis for distinguishing systematic progress from performance noise.

Recognizing prototype failure modes is perhaps the most operationally important iterative refinement skill. Three failure modes are particularly common in NISQ-era quantum prototypes: barren plateau failures (optimization gradients too small to navigate effectively), hardware noise saturation (circuit depth has exceeded the hardware's noise-tolerance threshold, and further algorithm development produces diminishing returns), and integration bottlenecks (classical data encoding or post-processing overhead has grown to dominate the total workflow latency). Each failure mode has distinct diagnosis signatures in prototype performance data, and each calls for a different response: algorithm redesign, circuit compression, or integration architecture refactoring, respectively. Developing the diagnostic fluency to identify which failure mode is operative, rather than applying generic "try harder" optimization effort, is what distinguishes effective iterative prototype development from expensive wheel-spinning.

The most difficult iterative refinement decision is recognizing when continued iteration is no longer value-creating and a pivot or stop decision is warranted. Technical teams with significant investment in a prototype approach are structurally reluctant to call a no-go outcome, preferring to attribute underperformance to solvable implementation issues rather than fundamental feasibility constraints. Developing intellectual honesty to recognize the difference, and the organizational courage to communicate it clearly to the executive sponsors, is what distinguishes technical leaders from technical advocates. A disciplined prototype stop decision, backed by clear evidence and honest analysis, is a genuinely valuable outcome that redirects organizational resources toward approaches with higher probability of success. The goal is not to succeed at quantum prototyping; it's to succeed at the business problem, which sometimes means concluding that quantum is not the right tool for this problem at this time.

Summary

This chapter has transformed the quantum prototype from an exploratory exercise into a structured strategic intelligence-generation process. The vendor selection framework presented in the first section provides the technical evaluation criteria, gate fidelity, coherence times, CLOPS, error mitigation capability, SDK maturity, that produce rigorous vendor down-selection rather than the qubit-count theater that characterizes immature quantum vendor assessments. The quantum-adapted agile development methodology gives prototype teams the sprint structure, hardware scheduling discipline, and circuit validation practices needed to execute hybrid experiments with genuine engineering rigor.

The simulation tool landscape assessment equips technical leaders to select the right development patterns for combinatorial optimization, quantum machine learning, and quantum chemistry simulation. Crucially, the simulation section provides realistic timeline estimates and honest characterization of near-term advantage potential for each application category, the intellectual foundation for prototype scoping decisions that reflect engineering reality rather than quantum marketing.

The success metric framework's three-category structure: technical performance, resource efficiency, and integration readiness, ensures that prototype evaluations generate comprehensive, decision-relevant data rather than cherry-picked performance highlights. The controlled comparison methodology and statistical validity requirements guard against the systematic biases that routinely produce misleading prototype conclusions. And the six-dimension Go/No-Go Feasibility Framework culminates the chapter with a structured decision process that transforms prototype evidence into defensible investment recommendations – recommendations founded in technical, hardware, integration, economic, talent, and risk evidence rather than quantum enthusiasm or quantum skepticism.

The five skills developed across this chapter: prototype scoping and design, technical vendor management, quantum algorithm performance analysis, feasibility assessment leadership, and iterative prototype refinement, form an integrated competency set that compounds in value across successive quantum initiative cycles. Organizations that institutionalize these practices build genuine quantum development decision-making muscle; the ability to run quantum experiments that produce real learning, evaluate results with appropriate rigor, and make investment decisions that reflect evidence rather than aspiration.

The company spotlights – BMW Group's disciplined problem decomposition and multi-vendor evaluation, JPMorgan Chase's integration-first hybrid design discipline, and Airbus' structured challenge format with honest baseline specification – demonstrate that quantum prototyping rigor is not theoretical. Organizations across industries and geographies are executing structured quantum pilots that generate genuine strategic intelligence and are using that intelligence to make informed development progression decisions.

The go/no-go decision reached through the framework in this chapter is not an endpoint, it's a trigger for the next layer of organizational readiness. Organizations that receive a go recommendation on a quantum prototype immediately face a challenge that prototyping rarely surfaces: their data is not ready for quantum processing. The encoding structures that quantum algorithms require, the streaming workflows that hybrid quantum-classical systems demand, and the privacy-preserving computation architectures that regulated data environments necessitate are all materially different from the classical data pipelines that most organizations have invested decades in building.

The next chapter addresses this quantum data readiness gap directly, building on the hybrid system design principles encountered in prototype integration of quantum development methodologies for hybrid experiments, the application development patterns of quantum simulation tools and early-stage application development, and the integration feasibility dimension of the Go/No-Go Framework. Chapter 8 provides the data architecture framework that CDOs, CTOs, and data leaders need to ensure their organizational data assets are accessible, appropriately formatted, and compliantly managed when quantum processing capabilities come online. The prototype work of this chapter tells you whether quantum computing is worth pursuing for your problem; the data strategy work of Chapter 8 tells you whether your organization's data infrastructure is ready to realize that potential when quantum hardware reaches production readiness.

Further reading

1. `https://arxiv.org/abs/2106.10522`
2. `https://www.ibm.com/quantum/roadmap`
3. `https://www.ibm.com/quantum/blog/quantum-advantage-era`
4. `https://doi.org/10.1371/journal.pone.0208561`
5. `https://doi.org/10.1109/QCE53715.2022.00042`
6. `https://www.cambridge.org/highereducation/books/quantum-computation-and-quantum-information/01E10196D0A682A6AEFFEA52D53BE9AE`
7. `https://www.science.org/doi/10.1126/science.1231298`
8. `https://journals.aps.org/pra/abstract/10.1103/PhysRevA.100.032328`
9. `https://iopscience.iop.org/article/10.1088/1464-4266/7/10/021`

10. https://www.nature.com/articles/s41534-019-0196-1
11. https://arxiv.org/abs/1411.4028
12. https://www.nature.com/articles/s41598-019-43176-9
13. https://doi.org/10.1103/PhysRevLett.122.040504
14. https://doi.org/10.1038/s41467-018-07090-4
15. https://doi.org/10.1021/acs.chemrev.8b00803
16. https://www.ibm.com/quantum/blog/what-is-quantum-utlity
17. https://www.bmwgroup.com/en/news/general/2025/quantum-computing.html
18. https://www.munich-quantum-valley.de/
19. https://www.press.bmwgroup.com/global/article/detail/T0335292EN/cutting-edge-research-into-quantum-computing:-bmw-group-and-technical-university-of-munich-agree-to-create-an-endowed-chair-in-%E2%80%9Cquantum-algorithms-and-applications%E2%80%9D?language=en
20. https://arxiv.org/pdf/2109.07876
21. https://iotm2mcouncil.org/iot-library/news/connected-industries-news/quantum-computing-optimises-bmw-production
22. https://fuelcellsworks.com/2025/11/20/clean-technology/ibm-s-nighthawk-quantum-chip-revolutionizing-climate-sims-and-fuel-cell-tech
23. https://www.quantinuum.com/press-releases/bmw-group-airbus-and-quantinuum-collaborate-to-fast-track-sustainable-mobility-research-using-cutting-edge-quantum-computers
24. https://arxiv.org/pdf/2111.01622
25. https://doi.org/10.1109/QCE52317.2021.00019
26. https://www.jpmorganchase.com/about/technology/research/applied-research
27. https://doi.org/10.22331/q-2020-07-06-291
28. https://doi.org/10.1109/TQE.2020.3030314
29. https://doi.org/10.1063/5.0082975
30. https://www.airbus.com/en/innovation/digital-transformation/quantum-technologies
31. https://doi.org/10.1007/s11128-021-03405-5

8

Data Strategy for the Quantum Era

Here is a truth that most quantum computing conversations skip past too quickly: the quantum computer is only as useful as the data you can feed it. And right now, in most organizations, the data is in the wrong shape, stored in the wrong places, governed by the wrong policies, and protected by methods that a quantum adversary will eventually find laughable. That is the uncomfortable starting point for this chapter, and the reason why data strategy belongs at the center of any serious quantum readiness program.

Think of it this way. Imagine you spent years acquiring a Formula One racing car, only to discover that your pit crew has no training, your fuel is the wrong octane, and the track was designed for a bicycle. The car cannot perform until the supporting infrastructure catches up. In this example, quantum computers are the Formula One car, your data architecture is the pit crew, the fuel, and the track, and most organizations are just not ready.

Data is the substrate upon which quantum computational advantage is realized. The algorithms that produce quantum speedups, whether in optimization, machine learning, simulations, or cryptanalysis, require data inputs that are precisely encoded into quantum states. They must also be processed through circuits with tight resource constraints and integrated back into classical decision systems through carefully designed measurement and aggregation workflows. None of that integration happens automatically. It requires deliberate architectural work that begins long before a quantum processor is provisioned.

The goal of this chapter is to provide a comprehensive technical framework for CDOs, CTOs, and data architecture leaders navigating the transition to quantum-era data strategy. We'll cover quantum data encoding principles and their architectural implications; hybrid classical-quantum workflow design; quantum-aware data governance; privacy-preserving computation under quantum threat; and a structured data architecture readiness assessment methodology that produces a prioritized remediation roadmap. The chapter is designed to be immediately actionable. Every framework, assessment methodology, and governance template discussed here can be put to work in your organization today, without waiting for quantum hardware to appear on your network. Leaders who invest in quantum-aware data strategy now will avoid the costly, time-pressured retrofitting that unprepared organizations will face as quantum systems move toward production deployment.

Throughout, we will ground the discussion in real organizational examples from enterprises that have already begun this journey, because while the quantum era is not fully here yet, its data requirements are already knowable, plannable, and, with the right frameworks, entirely manageable.

Topics covered in this chapter include:

- Quantum data encoding: principles and architecture implications
- Hybrid classical-quantum data workflow architecture
- Data governance in quantum environments
- Privacy-preserving computation in quantum contexts
- Data architecture readiness assessment and transition planning
- Critical skills for quantum data strategy leadership

Quantum data encoding: principles and architectural implications

Before a quantum algorithm can touch your data, that data must be translated from binary or real-valued representations that classical computers understand into quantum state representations that quantum circuits can manipulate. This translation process, quantum data encoding, is one of the most consequential and underappreciated engineering decisions in quantum system design. Get it wrong, and your quantum circuit spends most of its resources just loading the data, eliminating any computational advantage before the algorithm even begins.[1]

There are four primary encoding schemes that technical leaders need to understand, each with distinct tradeoffs in qubit overhead, circuit depth, and preprocessing requirements. Think of choosing an encoding scheme like choosing a data serialization format for a distributed system; the choice propagates throughout the entire architecture, and changing it later is very expensive.

Basis encoding

Basis encoding is the most straightforward approach; classical binary strings are mapped directly to computational basis states. For example, the binary string '1011' becomes the quantum state $|1011\rangle$. It's computationally clean, requires no complicated state preparation circuits, and preserves the classical data structure transparently.[2]

However, the architectural limitation is scale. Encoding a dataset of N samples each with d binary features requires $N \times d$ qubits and a separate quantum circuit execution for each sample. For high-dimensional datasets, such as the kind that make quantum machine learning interesting in the first place, basis encoding rapidly becomes impractical. It's most appropriate for combinatorial optimization problems where the data is a compact binary representation of a solution space, not for high-dimensional numerical datasets.

Amplitude encoding

Amplitude encoding achieves something remarkable: a vector of 2^n real-valued numbers can be encoded into the amplitudes of an n-qubit quantum state. This exponential compression is the mechanism behind many of the theoretical quantum speedups in linear algebra and machine learning – a 1,024-dimensional data vector encoded in just 10 qubits![3]

The cost, however, is circuit depth. Preparing an arbitrary quantum state with amplitude encoding requires a state preparation circuit whose depth scales with the number of data dimensions, and on near-term quantum hardware with limited coherence times, that circuit depth may exceed what the hardware can faithfully execute. The architectural implication for data leaders is clear: amplitude encoding requires aggressive dimensionality reduction in classical preprocessing stages. Your feature engineering pipelines must be designed to produce compact, normalized representations that the state preparation circuit can handle within coherence budgets. This is not a future concern; it shapes how you design data preprocessing pipelines today.

Angle encoding

Angle encoding represents each data feature as a rotation angle in a parameterized quantum circuit, embedding the data directly into the gate parameters rather than the state amplitudes. One feature per qubit, with the feature value determining the rotation angle applied.[4] This scheme has become practically dominant in near-term quantum machine learning because it requires shallower circuits and is more compatible with the qubit counts and coherence times of current hardware.

The preprocessing implication of angles is normalization: data must be scaled to lie within the valid range of rotation angles, typically $[0, 2\pi]$, or $[-\pi, \pi]$. This places specific normalization requirements on your data preparation pipelines that differ from the standardization conventions of classical machine learning. Data pipelines that output z-scored features for classical models must be adapted, or parallel preprocessing branches created, for quantum execution paths.

Quantum random access memory (qRAM)

Quantum random access memory (qRAM) is the most ambitious encoding architecture: a quantum analog of classical RAM that can prepare superpositions over memory addresses, enabling quantum algorithms to query large classical datasets in quantum superposition.[3] In principle, qRAM enables certain quantum algorithms to access exponentially large datasets with logarithmic query complexity, the theoretical basis for quantum speedups in data-intensive search and optimization.

In practice, qRAM remains hardware limited. Fault-tolerant qRAM implementations require large numbers of physical qubits with low error rates that current hardware does not yet provide. The architectural significance for leaders is prospective: qRAM is the encoding architecture that enables quantum advantage for large-scale data-intensive applications. Organizations with data assets organized into structured, queryable repositories will be better positioned to exploit qRAM capabilities as hardware matures. Designing your data lakes and feature stores with clean, query-accessible schemes is a qRAM readiness decision even if qRAM hardware is years away.

Encoding selection framework

The following is an encoding selection framework matrix that lays out and maps the data type to the ideal encoding scheme and provides the overhead needed in both qubits and the preprocessing requirements. Finally included is a list of quantum problem types which would be ideal for each encoding scheme.

Data Type	Encoding Scheme	Qubit Overhead	Circuit Depth	Preprocessing Requirement	Best For
Binary/ combinatorial	Basis	High ($N \times d$)	Low	Minimal	Optimization, QUBO problems
Dense numerical vectors	Amplitude	Low ($\log_2 d$)	High	Dimension reduction, normalization	Linear algebra, QML (fault-tolerant)

Data Type	Encoding Scheme	Qubit Overhead	Circuit Depth	Preprocessing Requirement	Best For
Tabular/feature data	Angle	Medium (d qubits)	Low-Med	Normalization to angle range	Near-term QML, variational circuits
Large classical datasets	qRAM	Very high	Med	Structured, addressable storage	Data-intensive search (future)

Table 8.1: Encoding Selection Framework Matrix

The encoding decision is not merely a quantum engineering choice; it's a data architecture decision with upstream implications for schema design, preprocessing pipeline structure, and the computational budget allocated to data preparation. Leaders reviewing quantum application proposals should demand explicit documentation of encoding choices and their preprocessing requirements before approving engineering work, since encoding mismatches discovered late in development are expensive to fix.[5]

Hybrid classical-quantum data workflow

No serious practitioner in the quantum computing field today expects pure quantum workflows, at least not for the foreseeable future. The architecturally honest picture of quantum computing in production is a hybrid model: classical computers handle data ingestion, feature engineering, result aggregation, and downstream decision logic, while quantum processors execute the specific computational subproblems where quantum advantage is sought. This hybrid reality is not a limitation to apologize for; it's the architectural design pattern that makes quantum computing practically useful in the near term.[6] Recently, the Qiskit SDK introduced Qiskit Patterns, which provide a similar workflow between classical and quantum.[7]

Understanding hybrid workflow architecture is essential for data leaders because the integration boundaries between classical and quantum execution stages are where most of the engineering complexity and most of the data management risk live.

The three stages of hybrid workflow data management

Similar to the Qiskit pattern, you can simplify the hybrid workflow data management down to three stages: pre-processing, execution, and post-processing.

Stage 1: Classical preprocessing

The classical pre-processing stage is responsible for transforming raw organizational data into quantum-ready representations. This includes data cleaning and validation, feature selection to reduce dimensionality to within quantum circuit capacity, normalization and scaling to satisfy encoding requirements, and serialization into the data format required by the quantum execution API. For near-term systems using angle encoding, this stage typically includes a classical ML pre-processing pipeline that produces normalized feature vectors of the dimensionality the quantum circuit accepts.[8]

The architectural implication is that your classical data pipelines must be refactored to support quantum output paths alongside existing classical ML output paths. This is best handled through a preprocessing abstraction layer that can route data transformations based on the target execution environment, which could include: classical, quantum, or hybrid, without duplicating pipeline logic.

Stage 2: Quantum execution interface

The quantum execution interface manages the handoff between classical preprocessing systems and quantum cloud or hardware APIs. This includes job submission, which includes encoding circuits and submitting to the quantum execution queue; shot management: specifying the number of repeated measurement shots required to achieve the desired statistical precision; result streaming: collecting measurement outcomes from the quantum API as they become available; and error handling: managing hardware unavailability, job queue saturation, and shot budget exhaustion.

Job queue saturation is a practically significant operational risk that data architects often underestimate. Current quantum cloud platforms such as IBM Quantum, Amazon Braket, and Microsoft Azure Quantum are shared computing resources with variable queue depths that can introduce latency measured in minutes to hours rather than milliseconds. For latency-sensitive applications, architectural provisions such as job priority queueing, fallback classical execution paths, and quantum result caching are not optional engineering niceties; they are production reliability requirements.[9]

Stage 3: Result integration and post-processing

Quantum measurement produces probabilistic outcomes: for each shot, the quantum circuit returns a measurement on the computational basis, and the desired computational results must be statistically inferred from the distribution of outcomes across many shots. Classical post-processing aggregates these measurements into the expectation values, probability distributions, or discrete results that downstream classical decision systems consume.

The statistical nature of quantum measurement output has data quality implications that classical data engineers are often unprepared for. Unlike classical functions that return a deterministic result, a quantum circuit returns a probability distribution that must be adequately sampled, and the statistical precision of that sampling depends on shot count, which has direct cost and latency implications. Data quality monitoring frameworks for hybrid pipelines must include shot-adequacy validation checks alongside conventional data quality dimensions like completeness and freshness.

Hybrid workflow architecture patterns

In the following table, I've broken down each pattern and listed both the classical and quantum roles, where the integration points exist for each, and the primary use cases where the specified pattern would be ideal.

Pattern	Classical Role	Quantum Role	Integration Point	Primary Use Case
Variational Hybrid	Feature prep, loss function eval, parameter update	Parametric circuit execution	Parameter-gradient loop	QML, variational optimization
Quantum subroutine	Full pipeline except for one subproblem	Accelerated subproblem (e.g., sampling)	API call with serialized input	Portfolio optimization, drug discovery
Quantum-Augmented Streaming	Stream ingestion, downstream decisioning	Real-time quantum inference on micro-batches	Low-latency streaming API	Anomaly detection, financial signals
Quantum Batch Analytics	ETL, data lake management, result storage	Overnight batch quantum computation	Scheduled job submission	Scientific simulations, optimization

Table 8.2: Hybrid Workflow Architecture Patterns Matrix

Leaders reviewing hybrid workflow architecture proposals should evaluate three architectural health dimensions. First, coupling tightness: does the architecture create hard dependencies on quantum API availability that would cascade into classical system failures? Second, shot budget management: is shot count treated as a configurable resource parameter with monitoring and alerting, or hard-coded? Keep in mind that some quantum modalities vary in very large orders of magnitude in the speed of each shot, where some modalities clock in at around 100,000 shots/sec and others around 3 shots/sec. And finally, result determinism: does the downstream classical decision logic account for the probabilistic nature of quantum outputs, or does it assume deterministic responses? Proposals that fail on any of these dimensions carry hidden operational risk that will surface in production.[10] Now that we've covered the technical frontier, let's now shift toward the organizational frontier.

Data governance in quantum environments

If quantum data encoding is the technical frontier of quantum data strategy, data governance in quantum environments is the organizational frontier, and the one that most enterprises are least prepared for. Existing data governance frameworks were designed to address the risks of classical cloud computing: data residency and sovereignty in hyperscaler data centers, role-based access controls for distributed data systems, audit trails for cloud-hosted data processing, and compliance with regulations written before quantum computing existed as a practical technology. None of these frameworks adequately address the novel governance challenges that quantum cloud deployments introduce.

The fundamental governance challenge with quantum cloud computing is that submitting a job to a quantum cloud platform is a data disclosure event. When your preprocessing pipeline serializes a feature matrix and sends it to your vendor's platform for circuit execution, that data leaves your organizational perimeter and enters a shared computing infrastructure operated by a third party. For organizations in regulated industries such as financial services, healthcare, defense, or critical infrastructure, this is not a detail to be addressed in the vendor's standard terms of service. It's a material data governance decision that requires explicit analysis, documentation, and potentially regulatory notification.

Now, if you're a non-technical leader reading that last paragraph with a familiar sinking feeling, then you've likely already seen this movie: the compliance review nobody scoped, the six-week delay, the pipeline refactoring twice because someone asked the residency question too late. The good news here is, you don't need to understand circuit execution to prevent that. You just need to ask yourself five questions early on and keep asking yourself these questions until the answers stop being adjectives.

First, what specific data, at what level of granularity, physically leaves your perimeter when a job is run: the raw records, a derived feature map, or something abstracted beyond recognition?

Second, where does it land, in which legal jurisdiction, and who else has infrastructure-level access while it is at rest?

Third, which of your existing regulatory commitments: GDPR, HIPAA, sectoral rules, customer contracts, were written in language broad enough to cover this, and more importantly, which weren't?

Fourth, what would you tell a regulator or an enterprise customer if they asked you to describe this data flow tomorrow, and is that description written down anywhere today?

And fifth, the one that saves the most rework: can we run this pilot on synthetic or obfuscated data and still learn what we're trying to learn? Surprisingly often, the answer is yes, and it very nicely converts a governance problem into a scheduling problem.

Quantum-specific data classification

Most enterprise data classification frameworks use a three- or four-tier sensitivity model: public, internal, confidential, and restricted/secret, that maps to cloud deployment constraints – restricted data stays on-premises, confidential data goes to private cloud, regulatory restrictions such as ITAR, and so on. Quantum cloud deployment requires an additional classification dimension: quantum processing sensitivity, which captures whether a data asset's privacy guarantees are meaningfully degraded by processing on a shared quantum execution environment.

Leaders should extend their existing classification frameworks with a quantum processing sensitivity tag that carries three values. First, Quantum-Safe: no meaningful additional sensitivity from quantum cloud processing. Second, Quantum-Conditional: can be processed on quantum cloud under specific contractual or technical controls. Third, Quantum-Restricted: cannot be processed on quantum cloud without additional safeguards such as privacy-preserving preprocessing or dedicated quantum hardware tenancy.[11]

Data residency and sovereignty in quantum cloud

Quantum cloud providers currently offer varying levels of data residency assurance. IBM Quantum's enterprise agreements[12] include geographic region selection for job execution, while Amazon Braket's data handling is governed by AWS's standard regional isolation model.[13] Microsoft Azure Quantum is integrated with Azure's compliance frameworks, offering the most mature enterprise governance controls among major quantum cloud providers.[14] For organizations subject to GDPR,[15] HIPAA,[16] or sector-specific data residency requirements, the adequacy of these controls requires explicit legal analysis, and in some jurisdictions, the adequacy assessment must be documented before data is processed on quantum cloud platforms.

Quantum provenance and audit trail requirements

Maintaining traceable records of which data assets were processed through quantum execution environments, quantum provenance, is an emerging governance issue that few organizations have formally addressed. Quantum provenance records should capture: the data asset identifier and classification tier, the quantum execution platform and geographic region, the job submission timestamp and job identifier, the circuit specification and parameter values, the shot count and measurement outcomes, and the post-processing transformation applied to produce the result.

This level of audit detail may seem excessive for research experiments, but it's the governance standard that regulated industries will eventually be held to as quantum processing becomes operationally significant. Building provenance capture into your quantum execution interface architecture from the beginning, treating it as a required feature rather than an optional add-on, is far less expensive than retrofitting it into production systems under regulatory pressure.

Quantum data governance framework execution

The following table lists each governance domain and its associated classical framework and the current quantum gap. Included is the quantum extension required to remain compliant.

Governance Domain	Classical Framework Coverage	Quantum Gap	Quantum Extension Required
Data Classification	Sensitivity tiers based on data content	No quantum processing sensitivity tier	Add Quantum-Safe, Quantum-Conditional/ Quantum-Restricted tags
Data Residency	Cloud region selection, on-prem vs. cloud	Quantum cloud residency controls vary by vendor	Explicit residency analysis per quantum cloud provider
Provenance and Audit	Data lineage in ETL pipelines	Quantum job execution not captured in classical lineage	Quantum execution event logging in provenance records

Governance Domain	Classical Framework Coverage	Quantum Gap	Quantum Extension Required
Vendor Management	Cloud DPA, security assessments	Quantum-specific data handling terms absent from standard agreements	Quantum data handling is added to vendor agreements
Access Control	RBAC on data assets and pipelines	Quantum job submission as data access event not modeled	Quantum job submission permissions in access control model
Incident Response	Data breach notification procedures	No quantum-specific exposure scenarios in IR playbooks	Quantum data exposure scenarios in IR runbooks

Table 8.3: Quantum Data Governance Framework Extension

Closing these governance gaps requires cross-functional engagement that data leaders often find challenging: legal and compliance teams need to understand enough quantum technology to reason about regulatory implications; security teams need to model quantum execution as a data processing activity; and data stewards need updated classification guidance that includes quantum sensitivity tiers. The data governance extension process is fundamentally a change management challenge as much as a technical one.[17]

Privacy-preserving computation in quantum contexts

Privacy-preserving computation is the set of techniques that allow computationally useful operations on sensitive data without exposing the underlying data to the system performing the computation. This has become a cornerstone of responsible data strategy for organizations handling personal, health, financial, and other sensitive information. Techniques such as differential privacy, homomorphic encryption, and secure multi-party computation have enabled enterprises to share and analyze sensitive data with research partners, cloud services, and analytical systems while maintaining meaningful privacy protections. The uncomfortable news is that quantum computing puts some of these protections at risk, and the timeline for that risk is closer than most privacy professionals realize.[18]

The quantum threat to classical privacy-preserving methods

Differential privacy adds carefully calibrated noise to data or query outputs to prevent statistical re-identification of individuals. The calibration of that noise, how much noise is needed to achieve a given privacy guarantee, depends on assumptions about the computational capabilities of potential adversaries. Those assumptions were made for classical adversaries. Quantum algorithms for machine learning inference could potentially extract patterns from differentially private datasets with significantly fewer queries than classical adversaries, meaning that noise calibrations adequate for classical threat models may be insufficient against quantum-capable adversaries.[19]

Homomorphic encryption, which allows computation on encrypted data without decryption, currently relies on lattice-based cryptographic assumptions that are believed to be quantum-resistant. However, the performance characteristics of fully homomorphic encryption schemes make them impractical for large-scale quantum machine learning workloads, and hybrid classical-quantum attacks on specific scheme parameters cannot yet be fully ruled out. Organizations that have made long-term data sharing commitments dependent on homomorphic encryption should document the cryptographic scheme parameters in their privacy risk registers and establish review triggers for quantum cryptanalysis research developments.[20]

Secure multi-party computation protocols based on oblivious transfer and garbled circuits rely on one-way function assumptions that current quantum algorithms do not efficiently break. However, certain MPC protocols that incorporate classical public-key cryptography for setup phases use RSA or elliptic-curve primitives that are vulnerable to Shor's algorithm. These hybrid MPC protocols should be identified and their classical cryptographic dependencies mapped as part of any comprehensive cryptographic inventory, a topic that Chapter 9 covers in depth from the security perspective.

Quantum-native privacy-preserving approaches

The emerging field of quantum-native privacy-preserving computation offers approaches that leverage quantum mechanical properties, rather than classical computational hardness, as the basis for privacy guarantees. Three approaches are most relevant for enterprise leaders to track.

Quantum homomorphic encryption (QHE) extends homomorphic encryption to quantum data, enabling computations on encrypted quantum states. Theoretical constructions for QHE exist,[21] but practical implementations remain in early research stages with significant overhead. The enterprise relevance of QHE is prospective; as quantum data sharing scenarios emerge, where organizations share quantum-processed feature representations rather than raw data, QHE provides a privacy-preserving channel for those exchanges.

Quantum secure multi-party computation (QSMPC) uses quantum communication channels, particularly quantum key distribution infrastructure, to implement information-theoretically secure MPC protocols whose security does not depend on computational hardness assumptions. For organizations with access to QKD network infrastructure (currently available in certain European and Asian enterprise network environments), QSMPC represents a near-term privacy technology with provable security against quantum adversaries.[22]

Quantum differential privacy (QDP) extends differential privacy to quantum computation, providing privacy guarantees for quantum algorithms that process sensitive data. The theoretical framework for QDP has been established in recent academic work,[23] and while implementation tooling is nascent, the framework provides a path for organizations to make provable privacy claims about quantum applications that process personal data.

Privacy investment quantum-resilience assessment

Addressing each of these privacy technologies is not an easy task and should never be done without your security team. The following table provides a breakdown of each privacy technology and its current classical usage and quantum threat levels, resilience timeline, and the recommended action to consider. Of course, these timelines can change at any time; therefore, as a leader, you should always plan for the worst and hope for the best, but plan!

Privacy Technology	Current Enterprise Use	Quantum Threat Level	Resilience Timeline	Recommended Action
Differential Privacy	ML model training, analytics	Medium: calibration assumptions at risk	3–7 years	• Document noise calibration assumptions • Plan recalibration process

Privacy Technology	Current Enterprise Use	Quantum Threat Level	Resilience Timeline	Recommended Action
Homomorphic Encryption	Secure analytics, cloud data processing	Low-Medium: lattice-based variants are more resilient	5–10 years	• Audit for non-lattice scheme use • Prefer CKKS/BFV schemes
Classical MPC (RSA/ECC setup)	Data sharing consortia	High: classical crypto dependencies	3–5 years	• Inventory MPC protocols • Migrate public-key setup to PQC primitives
Tokenization/ Pseudonymization	PII protection in analytics	Low: not cryptographically broken by quantum	Not directly threatened	• Maintain • Watch for quantum ML re-identification research
QKD-based QSMPC	Emerging enterprise use in select markets	None: quantum-native	Forward-looking	• Evaluate for high-sensitivity data sharing use cases

Table 8.4: Privacy Investment Quantum-Resilience Assessment

The privacy posture assessment implied by this table is not a one-time exercise; it's an ongoing obligation. The quantum threat landscape for privacy-preserving computation is evolving rapidly, with new cryptanalytic results published regularly. Privacy teams should establish a quarterly review cadence for quantum-relevant cryptanalysis developments and maintain a living risk register for privacy technology dependencies with documented quantum-resilience assessments.[24] Let's now take a look at how a global financial firm balanced out governance and privacy while maintaining a forward-thinking approach.

Company spotlight: BBVA (Banco Bilbao Vizcaya Argentaria)

Spain's BBVA has emerged as one of Europe's most advanced financial institutions in quantum computing readiness, with a program notable for its integration of data governance and privacy considerations alongside algorithmic development, a balance that many quantum programs struggle to maintain. BBVA's quantum team has been systematically working through the data governance implications of quantum use cases in portfolio optimization, credit scoring optimization, currency arbitrage, and derivative evaluation adjustments since it started its quantum journey back in 2018, all while producing governance frameworks that treat quantum data handling as a first-class compliance concern.[25]

BBVA's governance approach is shaped by the European regulatory environment, GDPR, the European Banking Authority's cloud outsourcing guidelines, and Spain's national data protection framework, which collectively create a demanding compliance context for any cloud-based data processing, including quantum cloud. Rather than treating regulatory compliance as a blocker, BBVA's quantum program team worked proactively with their data protection officers and legal counsel to develop quantum-specific data processing assessments that map quantum cloud data handling to GDPR Article 28[26] (processor agreement) and Article 35[27] (data protection impact assessments) requirements.[28] By completing the regulatory integration work before any production quantum workloads were deployed, BBVA can move quickly from pilot to production when quantum hardware reaches adequate capability.[29]

The privacy dimension of BBVA's quantum strategy also stands out. Given that BBVA's quantum use cases involve customer financial data, among the most sensitive personal data categories under GDPR, the bank has invested in evaluating quantum-native privacy-preserving approaches as potential long-term complements to classical differential privacy and encryption methods. BBVA's quantum research publications have included theoretical analysis of quantum privacy strategy. The key lesson from BBVA's experience for peer organizations is that regulatory preparation and privacy strategy are not tasks to defer until quantum deployment approaches; the analysis work is sufficiently complex that it must begin during the research and pilot phase, when timelines are still generous.[30]

Data architecture readiness assessment and transition planning

Everything discussed in this chapter so far, encoding schemes, hybrid workflow architectures, governance extensions, privacy posture analysis, converges on a practical question that every technical leader eventually faces: how ready is my organization's data architecture for quantum processing, and what do I need to do about the gaps? This section provides the structured assessment methodology and transition planning framework to answer that question with precision.

DAQRA: four-domain assessment framework

The Data Architecture Quantum Readiness Assessment (DAQRA) framework evaluates organizational readiness across four domains, each of which maps to the major topics of this chapter. Think of it as a diagnostic tool, like an MRI for your data infrastructure, that reveals where you are sound and where you need intervention, before the quantum computing deployment pressure forces emergency surgery.

Domain	What is assessed	Key Indicators of Readiness	Common Gaps Found
Data Format and Schema	Capability of existing data representations with quantum encoding schemes	• Normalized numerical features • Schema documentation • Dimensionality profiles documented	• No feature normalization standards • High-dimensional schemas with no reduction strategy • Undocumented data types
Pipeline Architecture	Latency, throughput, and integration flexibility for hybrid workflow support	• Modules preprocessing • API integration capability • Streaming pipeline support • Monitoring coverage	• Monolithic ETL • No quantum API integration patterns • Batch-only pipelines • No shot-budget management

Domain	What is assessed	Key Indicators of Readiness	Common Gaps Found
Governance and Compliance	Coverage of governance	• Quantum classification tier defined • Vendor DPA reviewed for Quantum • Provenance capture design	• No quantum sensitivity classification • Standard cloud DPA only • No quantum provenance policy
Privacy Posture	Resilience of privacy-preserving computation against quantum-capable adversaries	• Privacy tech inventory compute • Quantum threat assessments per technique • Transition triggers defined	• No privacy tech inventory • No quantum threat assessment • DP calibration assumptions are undocumented

Table 8.5: DAQRA: Four-Domain Assessment Framework

Assessment scoring and maturity levels

Each domain is scored on a five-level maturity scale, producing a domain-specific maturity score and an aggregate Quantum Data Readiness Index (QDRI) that supports executive communication and benchmarking.

Maturity Level	Score	Description	Typical Profile
Level 1: Unaware	1	• No quantum-specific consideration in data architecture decisions	• Organizations with no active quantum program
Level 2: Aware	2	• Quantum requirements documented, but no architectural changes initiated	• Organizations in the early quantum awareness phase

Maturity Level	Score	Description	Typical Profile
Level 3: Planning	3	• Quantum readiness gaps identified • Remediation roadmap in development	• Organizations with active quantum pilot programs
Level 4: Understanding	4	• Active architectural remediation underway • Quantum integration tested in pilot	• Organizations with production-oriented quantum programs
Level 5: Ready	5	• Data architecture fully supports hybrid quantum workflows with governance and privacy coverage	• Organizations with production quantum deployments

Table 8.6: Assessment Scoring and Maturity Levels

The remediation roadmap: sequencing quantum data architecture transitions

The DAQRA assessment produces a domain-specific maturity profile that drives a prioritized remediation roadmap. The sequencing principle is risk-weighted urgency: governance and privacy posture gaps carry the highest near-term organizational risk, e.g., regulatory and reputational exposure and should be addressed first, regardless of quantum hardware timeline projections. Pipeline architecture modernization and data format standardization are medium-urgency activities that can be sequenced as part of broader data modernization programs. Schema-level encoding optimization is a longer-horizon activity that can be timed to quantum hardware availability.

Horizon	Timeframe	Priority Actions	Key Deliverables
Immediate	0–6 months	• Governance gap closure • Privacy tech inventory • Quantum vendor DPA review	• Quantum classification policy • Privacy risk register • Vendor assessment

Horizon	Timeframe	Priority Actions	Key Deliverables
Near-Term	6–18 months	• Pipeline modularization • Quantum API integration patterns • Provenance capture design	• Hybrid pipeline architecture • Quantum execution interface spec • Provenance schema
Medium-Term	18–36 months	• Feature store quantum readiness • Dimensionality reduction strategy • Quantum data preprocessing pipelines	• Quantum-ready feature engineering library • Encoding selection guidelines
Long-Term	36+ months	• Full DAQRA Level 5 readiness • Production hybrid workflow deployment • qRAM readiness planning	• Production quantum data infrastructure • qRAM transition roadmap

Table 8.7: Sequenced Transition Roadmap

The transition roadmap is not a quantum-specific project; it's a data strategy evolution that produces value in classical contexts while building toward quantum readiness. Pipeline modularization reduces operational complexity regardless of quantum timelines. Feature store investment improves classical data operations while positioning for quantum encoding efficiency. Governance framework extensions improve regulatory posture across all cloud computing contexts. This dual-value principle is critical for securing organizational investment in quantum data readiness: every near-term action should deliver measurable classical data management improvement alongside quantum readiness progress.[31]

Company spotlight: JPMorgan Chase

JPMorgan Chase's quantum computing program is one of the most mature among global financial institutions. It offers a compelling case study on how a large enterprise can approach quantum data architecture readiness at scale, without waiting for production-ready quantum hardware to drive the investment case. JPMorgan's quantum program, housed within its Global Technology Applied Research group,[32] has been systematically building the data infrastructure, governance frameworks, and talent capabilities required for quantum advantage realization since 2019, with published research demonstrating practical quantum algorithms for derivatives pricing, portfolio optimization, fraud detection, and risk simulation. [33]

What distinguishes JPMorgan's approach from many corporate quantum programs, among many other things, is its rigorous integration of data architecture work with quantum algorithm development. JPMorgan researchers have published extensively on the data-processing needs of quantum finance algorithms. Their work on feature selection, normalization, and reduction of dimensionality guides the bank on how to prepare quantum circuits based on financial time-series data. The research-to-architecture translation process means that JPMorgan's data engineering teams are not guessing at quantum processing requirements; they are implementing specifications derived from the bank's own quantum research program.[34]

Critical skills for quantum data strategy leadership

The critical skills developed in this chapter represent a coherent capability set that no single prior discipline fully equips technical leaders for. Data architecture experience provides structural intuition, quantum computing literacy provides the encoding and circuit depth awareness, governance expertise provides the policy development capability, privacy technology knowledge provides the threat modeling foundation, and executive communication skill provides the stakeholder alignment capability. What's new and synthesized here is the combination, in other words, the ability to integrate quantum-specific technical knowledge into each of these leadership functions simultaneously. Leaders who develop all five skills will be equipped not just to execute quantum data strategy, but to lead it across their organizations, translating between quantum engineering teams, governance, and compliance functions, executive leadership, and external regulators and vendors with equal fluency. The rest of this section will break these skills down for you.

Quantum data architecture design

The first and most technically grounded skill is the ability to design data architecture that accommodates quantum processing requirements while maintaining backward compatibility with existing classical data consumers. This skill begins with a deep working knowledge of quantum data encoding schemes, not at the level of circuit implementation, but at the level of architectural implication. A leader with this skill can look at an organization's current feature store schema and immediately identify which features would require preprocessing modification for angle encoding, which high-dimensional feature sets would need dimensionality reduction for amplitude encoding, and which data access patterns encode requirements into data architecture decisions; this is the core competency.

Developing this skill requires deliberate exposure to quantum algorithm papers and technical documentation, specifically with the goal of executing data requirements rather than understanding quantum gate operations. A useful exercise is to select three quantum simulation or optimization algorithms relevant to your industry and trace the data pipeline implications of each: what preprocessing is required, what normalization constraints apply, what dimensionality limits bind the algorithm, and what format does the quantum execution API expect as input? Repeating this exercise across multiple algorithms builds the architectural intuition required to evaluate quantum application proposals from engineering teams or external consultants.

In practice, leaders with this skill serve as a quality control layer between quantum research teams, who may optimize for algorithmic elegance, and data engineering teams, who must implement operationally sustainable pipelines. A quantum researcher might propose an amplitude-encoded quantum ML approach without fully accounting for the state preparation circuit depth on near-term hardware. A leader with quantum data architecture design skill recognizes this as an architectural risk and redirects toward angle encoding with a dimensionality reduction preprocessing stage. This kind of early architectural intervention prevents expensive discovery-and-rework cycles in quantum application development.

Building this skill in your organization also means developing a shared architectural vocabulary for quantum data design, documented encoding selection guidelines, preprocessing specification templates, and data interface contract standards for classical-quantum boundaries. Without this vocabulary, every quantum application project begins architectural discussions from scratch, duplicating effort and producing inconsistent integration patterns across the organization's quantum application portfolio.

Hybrid workflow data pipeline engineering oversight

Overseeing the engineering of hybrid classical-quantum data pipelines requires technical leadership skills at the intersection of distributed systems architecture, streaming data processing, API design, and quantum execution management. The leader with this skill can review a hybrid pipeline architecture proposal and identify the failure modes that will surface in production, not by performing the engineering analysis themselves, but by knowing which questions to ask, which risks to probe, and which design patterns signal architectural health versus hidden fragility.

The specific failure modes most relevant to hybrid pipeline oversight are those that emerge from the quantum-classical boundary: job queue saturation, which occurs when quantum hardware demand exceeds supply, introducing unbounded latency; shot budget exhaustion, which is when sampling precision requirements are not adequately specified, producing statistically unreliable results; result non-determinism propagation, which occurs when probabilistic quantum outputs are consumed by classical systems that assume deterministic responses; and API dependency cascades, when quantum cloud API unavailability propagates failures into classical pipeline stages that lack fallback logic. A leader who can probe for these failure modes in architecture reviews provides substantial risk reduction value, independent of their ability to code solutions.

Developing this oversight skill requires building a mental model of what "production quality" means for hybrid quantum pipelines, informed by the operational characteristics of quantum cloud platforms. IBM Quantum's System Two and IBM Quantum Network documentation, Amazon Braket's developer guide, and Microsoft Azure Quantum's service level documentation all provide operational parameters, queue depths, job latency distributions, and hardware availability windows that should inform pipeline architecture decisions. Leaders who have internalized these operational parameters can evaluate whether a proposed architecture is appropriately designed for the reliability and latency characteristics of actual quantum cloud services.

This skill also encompasses the monitoring and observability dimensions of hybrid pipeline operations. Classical data pipeline monitoring, tracking throughput, latency, error rates, and data quality metrics, must be extended for quantum integration points to capture shot adequacy rates, quantum job latency distributions, circuit fidelity estimates, and quantum API error rates. Leaders should be able to specify the monitoring instrumentation requirements for hybrid pipelines and evaluate whether proposed monitoring architecture provides adequate operational visibility into both classical and quantum execution stages.

Quantum-aware data governance framework development

Extending enterprise data governance frameworks to cover quantum computing contexts requires a distinctive combination of technical literacy, policy development capability, regulatory interpretation skill, and cross-functional stakeholder management. The leader with this skill knows not only what governance extensions are needed, the quantum classification tiers, the provenance requirements, the vendor assessment protocols, but also how to develop them through the organizational processes that give governance policies legitimacy and enforceability.

The technical foundation of this skill is the ability to identify governance gaps systematically by applying quantum deployment scenarios against existing policy coverage. A practical methodology is to select three representative quantum use cases: a quantum ML application using customer data, a quantum optimization job running on a quantum cloud platform, and a quantum simulation using proprietary research data, and trace each through the organization's existing data governance policies, identifying every point where existing policy language is inadequate, ambiguous, or silent about quantum-specific considerations. This scenario-based gap analysis produces a concrete, defensible inventory of governance extensions required, which is more persuasive to governance stakeholders than abstract claims about quantum governance gaps.

The regulatory interpretation dimension of this skill is increasingly important as quantum-relevant regulatory guidance accumulates. NIST's post-quantum cryptography standards have direct governance implications for data protection requirements; sector-specific guidance from the European Banking Authority, the FDA's digital health frameworks, and defense acquisition regulations are beginning to address quantum computing scenarios. Leaders with this skill can translate regulatory guidance, which is often written in general terms that require interpretation for specific organizational contexts, into concrete governance policy specifications that satisfy regulatory intent while remaining operationally practical for the data engineering teams who must implement them.

Cross-functional alignment is frequently the hardest dimension of this skill. Data governance extensions require buy-in from legal to approve policy language, compliance to assess regulatory adequacy, security to align with security architecture, data stewardship to implement classification and handling procedures, and in some organizations, procurement to execute vendor agreement modifications. Leaders who develop facilitation and negotiation skills alongside their technical and policy development capabilities will close quantum governance gaps significantly faster than those who attempt to drive governance changes through technical authority alone.

Privacy impact assessment for quantum contexts

Conducting privacy impact assessments for quantum computing use cases requires analytical skills that account for novel privacy threat vectors that most privacy professionals have not yet been trained to evaluate. The Privacy Impact Assessment (PIA) process is well-established in most large organizations. It is a structured process for identifying personal data in scope for a proposed processing activity, evaluating the adequacy of proposed protections, and documenting residual risks for organizational acceptance. What is new in the quantum context is the threat model: the classical adversary assumption that underlies most privacy protection adequacy analyses must be supplemented with a quantum adversary analysis.

The practical skill here is the ability to interrogate privacy protection adequacy claims using quantum threat model lenses. When a proposed quantum ML application claims that differential privacy guarantees adequately protect the personal data in the training set, a leader with this skill asks: for what adversary model is that differential privacy calibration adequate? Has the epsilon parameter been analyzed against quantum inference attack scenarios, or only classical adversaries? These questions do not require the leader to perform the cryptographic analysis themselves; they require sufficient fluency to identify when the analysis has been done rigorously and when it has been assumed away.

Developing this skill requires building familiarity with the quantum privacy research landscape. Specifically, the growing body of work on quantum attacks on classical privacy mechanisms, quantum differential privacy theory, and quantum-secure multi-party computation. This familiarity does not require deriving theorems; it requires knowing which threat models have been formally analyzed, which remain open research questions, and which claims of quantum-resistant privacy rest on informal assumptions rather than proven results. This distinction, between formal quantum-security proofs and informal assertions of quantum resilience, is the analytical foundation of rigorous quantum privacy impact assessment.

In organizational practice, leaders with this skill serve as the bridge between privacy counsel and quantum engineering teams, translating quantum privacy research findings into terms that data protection officers and regulators can evaluate, and translating regulatory privacy requirements into quantum-technical constraints that engineering teams can implement. This bridging function is particularly valuable in GDPR-regulated environments, where data protection authorities may begin requiring quantum-specific risk analysis in PIAs as quantum computing capabilities become more prominent in public discourse.

The bridging function is worth dwelling on, because it's easy to read it as a job description and conclude that someone else has this covered. However, it's much better understood as a set of questions that must be distributed rather than a person who has to be hired. The CTO can tell you whether the epsilon parameter was calibrated against a quantum adversary model, and whether the claim rests on a formal proof or an informal assertion. However, the CTO cannot tell you whether the resulting residual risk is one the organization can defend in a regulatory proceeding and really shouldn't be asked to. That is the General Counsel's judgement, and it turns on things the CTO has no visibility into: the representations already made in your privacy notices, the indemnification language in your enterprise agreements, the posture your data protection authority has taken with peer institutions. Meanwhile the COO owns the question nobody assigns until it's too late. If this protection is judged inadequate eighteen months from now, what must be unwound, and how long does that take? Model retraining, deletion obligations, customer notification, pulling a deployed system back out of production. Those are operations problems, not privacy problems, and they are almost always discovered in the wrong order.

This gives each of you a different version of the same conversation. If you're a General Counsel, the question is not "*is this adequately protected*," it's "*show me the adversary model you calibrated against and tell me what it assumes an attacker cannot do.*" Assumptions are where liability lives, and the PIA's residual risk section is where they should be written down in language a regulator could read. If you're the COO, ask what the rollback path looks like if the assumption breaks, and ask for it in weeks rather than in principle. And if either answer arrives as a reassurance rather than a document, you have learned something useful about how rigorously the analysis was done.

Data readiness roadmap communication

The most strategically impactful skill in this chapter is also the least technically intensive (funny how that seems to almost always be the case): the ability to communicate quantum data architecture readiness findings and transition roadmaps to diverse stakeholder groups with the precision and persuasiveness required to secure organizational investment. Every assessment methodology, governance framework, and privacy analysis discussed in this chapter ultimately produces information that must be communicated to decision-makers who will allocate resources, approve policy changes, and accept or reject residual risks. The leader who cannot translate deeply technical quantum data architecture findings into compelling strategic language leaves those findings stranded in technical documentation, where they influence nothing.

The core competency of this skill is tiered communication: the ability to produce quantum data readiness artifacts calibrated to specific audiences without losing the essential content across tiers. An executive summary for the board conveys the strategic risk exposure from quantum data readiness gaps and the investment required to close them, in business impact language. A governance briefing for the legal and compliance leadership conveys the specific regulatory exposure points and the policy interventions required. A technical specification for the data engineering team conveys the precise architectural changes required, with enough details for implementation. All three artifacts must be internally consistent, consistent with each other and with the underlying assessment findings, and produced by a single leader who can hold all three levels of abstraction simultaneously. It's a big ask, but a necessary one.

Developing this skill requires practice with real quantum readiness communication scenarios, ideally in facilitated executive briefing simulations or structured stakeholder presentations. Leaders can develop the executive communication tier of this skill by practicing the translation exercise: take a technical finding from a DAQRA assessment, for example, say that the organization's existing differential privacy calibration assumptions do not account for quantum inference attacks. Then draft a three-sentence board-level version, a one-paragraph compliance team version, and a technical specification version. Comparing these three versions against colleagues' independent drafts reveals where the translation loses precision or gains unhelpful jargon, and iterative refinement builds the translation fluency required for real stakeholder communications.

The facilitation dimension of this skill, including running cross-functional data readiness review sessions that align engineering, governance, legal, and business stakeholders on quantum data transition priorities, is equally important, and even harder to develop through individual practice. Leaders should seek opportunities to facilitate multi-stakeholder quantum readiness conversations even before formal DAQRA assessments are complete, using emerging quantum governance gaps or privacy posture questions as discussion prompts that build stakeholder familiarity with quantum data concerns and organizational alignment on response priorities.

Summary

This chapter has delivered the technical framework and organizational methodology that data architecture leaders need to prepare their organizations for the quantum processing era, not at some theoretical future point, but in the practical near term, with actions that can begin immediately and deliver value along the way.

We began with quantum data encoding, the translation layer between classical data representations and quantum processing environments, establishing that encoding selection is an architectural decision with deep implications for preprocessing pipeline design, qubit resource requirements, and circuit execution feasibility. The four primary encoding schemes – basis, amplitude, angle, and qRAM – each suit different data types and application contexts, and leaders who build encoding literacy into their quantum application review processes will prevent costly architectural mismatches before they reach engineering.

We then examined hybrid classical-quantum workflow architecture, establishing that production quantum value is delivered through carefully engineered integration patterns, not standalone quantum systems, and that the classical-quantum data boundary is where most of the engineering complexity and operational risk lie. Pipeline modularity, quantum API integration patterns, shot budget management, and probabilistic result handling are not optional design considerations; they are production reliability requirements that must be specified in hybrid workflow architectures before engineering begins.

The data governance and privacy sections addressed the organizational risks that accumulate when quantum cloud deployments proceed without governance framework extensions and privacy posture analysis. Quantum-specific data classification, provenance requirements, vendor assessment protocols, and privacy technology transition planning are governance obligations that cannot wait for production quantum deployments to force the issue. As the BBVA spotlight illustrated, the most quantum-ready organizations are those that integrated governance and privacy work into their quantum programs from the earliest research phases, not just those that treated governance as a deployment prerequisite to be addressed at the last moment.

The DAQRA framework provides a structured, four-domain assessment methodology that produces a prioritized quantum data architecture remediation roadmap. In essence, it is a direct bridge between quantum strategy aspiration and data engineering execution. Leaders who complete DAQRA assessments will emerge with a clear picture of their organization's quantum data readiness position, a sequenced action plan for closing gaps, and the stakeholder communication artifacts required to secure the investment needed to execute that plan.

Organizations that complete this data architecture transition will be equipped with the data foundation required to realize quantum computational advantages when production-ready quantum systems become available. Competitors who have not made this investment will face a different, and much harder, challenge: executing architectural remediation under time pressure, with quantum hardware available but data infrastructure unprepared, governance frameworks inadequate, and privacy posture unanalyzed. In the quantum era, data architecture readiness is not a supporting function. It's a source of competitive advantage, or for those who delay, a source of competitive disadvantage.

The data governance and privacy analysis work developed in this chapter creates a direct bridge to the security-critical challenges addressed in Part 3 of this book. Throughout this chapter, we have repeatedly encountered the cryptographic substrate beneath quantum data strategy, the TLS connections securing quantum API calls, the encryption protecting data in transit to quantum cloud platforms, and the classical public-key primitives embedded in privacy-preserving computation protocols. These cryptographic dependencies are not abstract concerns; they are the encryption systems that Shor's algorithm will render obsolete when quantum hardware reaches sufficient scale, and the "harvest now, decrypt later" attack model means that data transmitted over those systems today may be exposed to adversaries collecting ciphertext for future decryption.

The following chapters take this cryptographic threat head-on, providing the strategic roadmap for migrating enterprise cryptographic infrastructure to post-quantum resistant standards. If this chapter has shown you where your data lives and how it needs to move through quantum processing environments, the next chapters will show you how to ensure that the cryptographic protections securing that data remain intact against quantum-capable adversaries. Together, this chapter and the following chapters form the complete quantum transition without creating unacceptable data or security exposure along the way.

Further reading

1. `https://doi.org/10.1038/nature23474`
2. `https://doi.org/10.1007/978-3-030-83098-4`
3. `https://doi.org/10.1103/PhysRevLett.100.160501`
4. `https://doi.org/10.1038/s42254-021-00348-9`
5. `https://doi.org/10.1098/rspa.2017.0551`
6. `https://doi.org/10.7566/JPSJ.90.032001`

7. https://quantum.cloud.ibm.com/docs/en/guides/intro-to-patterns
8. https://doi.org/10.1038/nature23474
9. https://doi.org/10.1063/5.0082975
10. https://doi.org/10.22331/q-2018-08-06-79
11. https://www.enisa.europa.eu/sites/default/files/2026-01/ENISA%20Threat%20Landscape%202025_v1.2.pdf
12. https://www.ibm.com/support/customer/csol/terms/?id=i126-9989&lc=en
13. https://aws.amazon.com/about-aws/global-infrastructure/regions_az
14. https://learn.microsoft.com/en-us/azure/quantum/
15. https://gdpr-info.eu/
16. https://www.hhs.gov/hipaa/index.html
17. https://www.weforum.org/reports/quantum-computing-governance-principles
18. https://doi.org/10.1109/MSP.2018.3761723
19. https://arxiv.org/html/2512.15286v1
20. https://www.nist.gov/pqc
21. https://doi.org/10.1038/s41534-020-00340-8
22. https://arxiv.org/html/2501.10083v1
23. https://doi.org/10.1109/JSAC.2025.3568046
24. https://www.enisa.europa.eu/publications/enisa-threat-landscape-2025
25. https://www.bbva.com/en/bbvas-journey-to-be-quantum-ready/
26. https://gdpr-info.eu/art-28-gdpr
27. https://gdpr-info.eu/art-35-gdpr/
28. https://www.bbva.com/en/bbva-getting-ahead-new-data-protection-regulations/
29. https://www.bbva.com/en/innovation/bbva-runs-successful-trial-of-distributed-quantum-simulation-in-the-cloud/
30. https://www.bbva.com/en/innovation/bbva-joins-the-international-alliance-to-shield-financial-systems-against-quantum-cybercrime/
31. https://doi.org/10.1140/epjqt/s40507-021-00091-1
32. https://www.jpmorganchase.com/about/technology/research/applied-research

33. https://arxiv.org/abs/1905.02666

34. https://doi.org/10.22331/q-2020-07-06-291

Subscribe to Deep Engineering

Join thousands of developers and architects who want to understand how software is changing, deepen their expertise, and build systems that last.

Deep Engineering is a weekly expert-led newsletter for experienced practitioners, featuring original analysis, technical interviews, and curated insights on architecture, system design, and modern programming practice.

Scan the QR or visit the link to subscribe for free.

https://packt.link/deep-engineering-newsletter

Part 3

Quantum-Safe Security Transformation

You've assessed your infrastructure, built your quantum-capable teams, and ran your first pilots. Now comes a parallel imperative that can't wait for the rest of the roadmap to mature. It's time to secure everything you're building against the most consequential cryptographic threat in modern computing history.

Part III is where quantum readiness becomes quantum survival. The chapters ahead are written for the security leaders who will be held accountable when the question shifts from "when will quantum break our encryption?" to "why weren't we ready?" This means the CISOs navigating cryptographic inventories that span thousands of systems, the security directors trying to sequence migrations without grinding operations to a halt, and the risk managers who need to explain quantum exposure to a board that has never heard of Shor's algorithm. If that sounds familiar, then keep reading.

Across the following chapters, you'll work through the four pillars of quantum-safe security transformation, and long-term architectural resilience. You won't find abstract warnings here. You'll find migration prioritization frameworks grounded in real regulatory timelines, threat assessment tools calibrated to your industry's specific exposure, deployment methodologies that protect business continuity, and governance structures built to outlast any single leadership tenure.

Think of this section as your quantum security transformation playbook. Each chapter builds on the last. You'll move from understanding what's vulnerable today, to assessing who the adversaries are and when they'll be capable, to executing migration without disrupting the business, and finally to building an architecture adaptive enough to evolve with whatever the next decade brings.

He harvest-now, decrypt-later threat means the clock is already running. The chapters ahead give you the frameworks to move with urgency, not panic.

This part of the book includes the following chapters:

9

Post-Quantum Cryptography Migration

Before we begin, let's be direct about something that many security teams have been quietly hoping would remain someone else's problem a little longer: it isn't. The cryptographic systems that protect your organization's most sensitive data, the public-key infrastructure underlying your TLS connections, your digital signatures, your VPN tunnels, and your certification authorities, were all designed to resist an adversary with classical computing resources. Quantum computers executing Shor's algorithm at scale will make those defenses obsolete. Not theoretically. Not eventually. Systematically, and on a timeline that your most sensitive data may not survive without action today. With that timeline advancing faster than anticipated, so must your defenses.

Here's the scenario that should keep security leaders awake: an adversary, let's say it's either a sophisticated nation-state, a well-resourced criminal organization, or a future threat actor, is not waiting for quantum computers to be ready before starting to work on your data. The harvest-now-decrypt-later (HNDL) attack model is elegantly simple and already operational. Collect encrypted data today, at scale, at relatively low cost. Store it. Decrypt it when quantum capability matures. For any data your organization holds that will still be sensitive in ten to fifteen years: strategic plans, personal health records, financial instruments, government communications, intellectual property, etc., that window has already been opened. The vault is being filled. The future key is being forged.

But fear not, this chapter is your operational response to that reality. This chapter will deliver a comprehensive strategic roadmap for post-quantum cryptography (PQC) migration, built on the finalized NIST PQC standards released in 2024 and calibrated to the real-world cryptographic complexity of enterprise security environments. You will emerge from this chapter with command of the migration planning frameworks, risk prioritization methodologies, implementation sequencing tools, and regulatory alignment strategies required to lead a systematic, operationally sound transition to quantum-resistant cryptographic systems.

The skills embedded throughout this chapter will sharpen both your technical acumen and your organizational leadership capacity. You will develop the ability to scope and lead cryptographic inventory programs that produce actionable asset registers, not just discovery artifacts gathering dust in a folder. You will learn to interpret NIST PQC standards well enough to guide your engineering teams toward correct algorithm selections and to challenge vendor implementations that deviate from guidance. You will build migration risk assessment and prioritization capabilities that let you defend sequencing decisions to CFO and board audiences in risk reduction terms. You will learn to systematically assess the PQC readiness of your vendor ecosystem, because your migration is only as fast as your slowest critical dependency. And you will develop the regulatory compliance program management skills to keep your organization on the right side of hardening regulatory timelines from Washington, Brussels, and London simultaneously.

PQC migration is not technology refresh. It's a multi-year enterprise transformation program that requires the full weight of security leadership to execute successfully. This chapter gives you the strategic and technical foundation to lead it. Topics include:

- Current Cryptographic Vulnerabilities and the Quantum Threat to PKI
- NIST Post-Quantum Cryptography Standards: Technical Overview and Adoption Framework
- Cryptographic Inventory and Asset Classification
- Migration Prioritization and Sequencing Frameworks
- Implementation Timelines, Resource Planning, and Regulatory Alignment
- Competencies for PQC Migration Leadership

Current cryptographic vulnerabilities and the quantum threat to PKI

Before you can build a migration plan, you need to understand precisely what is broken and what is not. The quantum threat to cryptography is real and technically specific, and conflating which algorithms are immediately threatened with which require only parameter adjustments is one of the most common and costly sources of migration planning errors. Let's look at this a bit deeper to understand the full context about this.

The existential threat to current public-key cryptography comes from Shor's algorithm, published by mathematician Peter Shor in 1994.[1] Shor's algorithm solves two computational problems that underpin the security of essentially all deployed public-key cryptography: integer factorization, which is the basis of RSA security, and discrete logarithm computation over finite fields and elliptic curves, which is the basis of Diffie-Hellman key exchange and Elliptic Curve Cryptography. A sufficiently large, fault-tolerant quantum computer running Shor's algorithm could break RSA-2048 and ECC-256 in hours or days, which are problems that would currently require billions of years for any classical computer.[2, 3]

The scope of what falls under this threat is vast. TLS 1.3, which protects virtually all internet traffic, uses asymmetric key exchange (ECDH or DHE) to establish session keys and digital signatures (RSA or ECDSA) for certificate authentication. Public-Key Infrastructure (PKI), the system of certificate authorities, digital certificates, and trust hierarchies that enables trusted identity on the internet and within enterprise networks, is built entirely on RSA and ECC. VPNs, code signing, email encryption (S/MIME, PGP), SSH authentication, and digital document signing all rely on quantum-vulnerable asymmetric algorithms.

The picture is more nuanced for symmetric cryptography. Grover's algorithm,[4] another quantum algorithm, provides a quadratic speedup in searching unstructured databases. Applied to symmetric key search, this effectively halves the security level of symmetric algorithms. AES-128 drops to the security equivalent of AES-64, which is generally considered insufficient for long-term secrets, while AES-256 drops to AES-128 security, which is acceptable for any use case. SHA-256 hash collision resistance similarly degrades, though SHA-384 and SHA-512 retain adequate security margins. The mitigation is parameter adjustment. For example: doubling the key lengths in most cases, rather than wholesale algorithm replacement.[5, 6, 7, 8]

The harvest-now, decrypt-later threat model

The Harvest-Now, Decrypt-Later (HNDL) attack model is the reason PQC migration is an urgent present-day operational requirement, not a future contingency plan. The model exploits the asymmetry between the cost of capturing encrypted data (low, today) and the anticipated capability to decrypt it (high, but achievable in the future). An adversary needs only to intercept and store encrypted traffic now; the decryption work can happen years later when cryptographically relevant quantum computers (CRQCs) exist.

The intelligence community has been explicit about this threat. In 2022, the NSA's Cybersecurity Information Sheet on CNSA 2.0 noted that nation-state adversaries with long-term strategic intelligence interests had both motivation and the technical capacity to conduct large-scale encrypted data collection operations.[9] Subsequent threat intelligence from CISA and allied agencies has reinforced this assessment without specifying operational details.

The quantitative pressure this creates depends on two variables: the sensitivity duration of your data such as how long it needs to remain confidential, and the estimated timeline to

Cryptographically Relevant Quantum Computers (CRQC) availability. For data that must remain confidential for ten or more years, financial records with long-term regulatory retention requirements, personally identifiable health information, government classified communications, long-lived intellectual property, critical infrastructure control systems, etc., the HNDL threat is operative today. Mosca's theorem formalizes this: if X is the time until a CRQC exists and Y is the time required to complete PQC migration, an organization where X < Y faces exposure.[10] Current estimates for CRQC timelines range from 8 to 20 years, with most expert consensus clustering around 10-15 years for cryptographically meaningful capability.[11, 12] PQC migration at enterprise scale typically requires 3-7 years for thorough execution. The math is not comfortable for organizations that have not started.

Which cryptographic components are threatened: a practical taxonomy

The following table will help you visualize and align each quantum threat to its level of urgency and mitigation approaches. This is based on the situation at the time of writing; always be sure your security team has a similar table or other form to track and update as development occurs or use this as a first-pass classification tool when taking inventory.

Cryptographic Category	Representative Algorithms	Quantum Threat	Urgency Level	Mitigation Approach
Public-Key Encryption & Key Exchange	RSA, ECDH, DHE, DH	Broken by Shor's Algorithm	Critical: Immediate	• Replace with PQC KEM (ML-KEM)
Digital Signatures	RSA-PSS, ECDSA, EdDSA	Broken by Shor's Algorithm	Critical: Immediate	• Replace with PQC signatures (ML-DSA, SLH-DSA)
Symmetric Encryption	AES-128, AES-256, ChaCha20	Weakened by Grover (halved key strength)	Moderate: Key size upgrade	• Migrate to AES-256 • Already deployed widely
Hash Functions	SHA-256, SHA-384, SHA-512	Collision resistance weakened by Grover	Low-Moderate	• Migrate to SHA-384/ SHA-512 for long-lived uses

Cryptographic Category	Representative Algorithms	Quantum Threat	Urgency Level	Mitigation Approach
PKI Certification Infrastructure	X.509 certificates (RSA/ECC)	Root/ Intermediate CA signatures vulnerable	Critical: Systemic	• Replace CA chain with PQC-signed certificates
TLS/SSL	TLS 1.3 (ECDH key exchange)	Key exchange and certificate auth vulnerable	Critical: Pervasive	• Hybrid PQC/ classical TLS • Full PQC migration
Code signing	RSA, ECDSA signatures	Broken by Shor's Algorithm	High: Long-lived artifacts	• Migrate signing infrastructure to PQC

Table 9.1: Cryptographic vulnerability taxonomy by algorithm category

NIST post-quantum cryptography standards: technical overview and adoption framework

In August 2024, the National Institute of Standards and Technology (NIST) published the first finalized post-quantum cryptography standards. It was the culmination of an eight-year global competition and evaluation process that began in 2016. For enterprise security teams, these publications represent the authoritative technical foundation for migration planning: the algorithms are specified, the security parameters are defined, the reference implementations are available, and the path from current cryptographic infrastructure to a quantum-resistant alternative is as clear as it has ever been.

The finalized NIST PQC standards

Understanding these standards at a sufficient level for migration leadership, not for implementing cryptographic code, but for making correct algorithm selection decisions, evaluating vendor implementations, and guiding engineering teams, is the essential technical grounding for PQC program leadership. What follows is that technically grounded overview:

Standard Name	Former Name	Use Case	Mathematical Basis	Security Levels	Performance Notes
FIPS 203: ML-KEM	CRYSTALS-Kyber	Key Encapsulation Mechanism (key exchange)	Module Lattice (MLWE)	Category 1, 3, 5	Fast Small keys/ciphertext Hardware friendly
FIPS 204: ML-DSA	CRYSTALS-Dilithium	Digital Signatures (general use)	Module Lattice (MLWE/MSIS)	Category 2, 3, 5	Fast signing/verification Moderate signature size
FIPS 205: SLH-DSA	SPHINCS+	Digital Signatures (hash-based, conservative)	Hash Functions (stateless)	Category 1, 3, 5	Slow signing Small public key Long-term conservative choice
FIPS 206: FN-DSA	Falcon	Digital Signatures (compact alternative)	NTRU Lattice	Category 1, 5	Compact signatures Complex implementation Hardware advantage

Table 9.2: Finalized NIST PQC standards (2024)

A few practical notes for migration leaders interpreting these standards. ML-KEM is the primary algorithm for everything currently using Diffie-Hellman or ECDH key exchange: TLS handshakes, VPN key establishment, encrypted messaging session initiation. ML-DSA is the general-purpose digital signature replacement for RSA-PSS and ECDSA, covering certificate signing, code signing, and document authentication. SLH-DSA is a conservative fallback option whose security rests on hash function security assumptions that are entirely independent of lattice problems, useful for high-assurance contexts where mathematical diversity provides additional defense in depth. FN-DSA (FALCON) produces compact signatures but has a more complex implementation profile that introduces side-channel risk if not implemented carefully; it is not recommended for initial deployment without specialized cryptographic engineering expertise.[13]

NIST security category levels: a decision framework

Each NIST PQC algorithm is available at multiple security levels, designated Category 1, Category 3, and Category 5. Understanding these categories is essential for making correctly calibrated algorithm selections for different data sensitivity requirements.

NIST Security Category	Classical Equivalent	ML-KEM Variant	ML-DSA Variant	Recommended Use Cases
Category 1	AES-128	ML-KEM-512	ML-DSA-44	• General commercial • Low-sensitivity • Performance-constrained systems
Category 3	AES-192	ML-KEM-768	ML-DSA-65	• Enterprise standard • Medium-sensitivity • Most organizational use cases
Category 5	AES-256	ML-KEM-1024	ML-DSA-87	• High-sensitivity • Classified • Long-lived secrets • National security systems

Table 9.3: NIST security category decision framework

For most enterprise use cases, ML-KEM-768 (Category 3) is the appropriate default for key encapsulation, and ML-DSA-65 (Category 3) for digital signatures. Organizations handling particularly sensitive long-lived data, financial records with decade-plus retention, healthcare information, strategic intellectual property, critical infrastructure control data, should evaluate Category variants.

The status of upcoming PQC standards

Just so you know, the NIST PQC standardization program did not conclude with the August 2024 publications. Several additional algorithm candidates are under evaluation, with particular interest in BIKE and HQC as additional key encapsulation mechanisms based on error-correcting codes, providing mathematical diversity from the lattice-based ML-KEM. Organizations in high-assurance environments should monitor NIST's ongoing standardization work, with additional standards expected in the not-so-distant future. Migration architectures designed with cryptographic agility, the ability to swap algorithmic implementations without system-wide re-architecture, will be positioned to incorporate new standards as they are finalized. A company leading this effort is IBM. Their researchers created 3 of the top 4 algorithms that were selected by NIST and have a team of security experts creating applications that can explore, advise, and remediate any risks related to quantum. Let's look a little deeper to get some insights for ourselves.

Company spotlight: IBM

IBM occupies a unique position in the post-quantum cryptography landscape: simultaneously a leading quantum computing hardware provider and one of the most aggressive enterprise organizations in deploying quantum-resistant cryptography to protect its own infrastructure and client services. IBM Research developed the CRYSTALS-Kyber (now ML-KEM) and CRYSTALS-Dilithium (now ML-DSA) algorithms that became two of the four finalized NIST PQC standards, giving the company both deep technical expertise in PQC implementation and a strong institutional commitment to accelerating enterprise adoption. The third algorithm, SPHINCS+ (now SLH-DSA), included IBM Research alongside collaboration with several industry and academic partners, and the fourth, FALCON (now FN-DSA), was developed by a researcher who has since joined IBM.[14]

IBM's PQC migration program is organized around what the company calls "cryptographic agility," the architectural principle that cryptographic algorithms should be modular, upgradeable components rather than hardwired dependencies in systems and protocols. IBM has been embedding PQC-ready cryptographic agility into its hardware security modules (HSMs), z/Series mainframe platforms, and cloud services since 2022, providing a migration path that does not require wholesale infrastructure replacement. IBM's z16 mainframe, launched in 2022, introduced integrated cryptographic accelerators capable of running both classical and PQC algorithms in hybrid mode, a design decision explicitly motivated by PQC migration planning.[15]

For security leaders evaluating IBM's approach as a migration model, the key lessons are threefold. First, the architectural investment in cryptographic agility made IBM's transition dramatically less expensive than a rip-and-replace approach would have been; modular cryptographic implementations allowed algorithm upgrades without system re-architecture. Second, IBM's decision to maintain hybrid classical/PQC operation during the transition period provided the backward compatibility required to serve clients not yet migrated, demonstrating that PQC transition does not require a "flag day" cutover. Third, organizations that began their post-quantum cryptography readiness work in 2022-2023 gave themselves a meaningful head start. They've had more time to identify where vulnerable cryptography exists, understand system dependencies, prioritize the areas that matter most, and build migration plans before deadlines and external pressure begin to compress the timeline. The advantage isn't that these organizations are already fully quantum safe, but that they have reduced uncertainty and built the knowledge, processes, and crypto-agility needed to move with greater confidence. Organizations that waited can still catch up, but they may have to do the same foundational work under tighter timelines and with less room for trial, adjustment, and learning.

Cryptographic inventory and asset classification

You cannot migrate what you cannot see. This is not a metaphor; it's the operational reality that derails PQC migration programs that skip or underinvest in the inventory phase. Cryptographic dependencies are embedded in modern enterprise technology estates at a depth and breadth that reliably surprises even experienced security architects. TLS is in your web applications, your internal microservices, your DevOps pipeline, your monitoring infrastructure, your code signing systems, your document management platforms, and your backup encryption implementations. IoT devices, industrial control systems, and embedded firmware have cryptographic implementations that predate any PQC awareness and may be effectively immovable without hardware replacement.

Building a comprehensive cryptographic asset register is a project leadership challenge as much as a technical challenge. It requires coordinating discovery workflows across multiple technical domains, application development teams, network operations, cloud engineering, identity and access management, and vendor relationship managers, without creating the operational disruption that comes from scanning production systems without preparation.

The cryptographic inventory discovery framework

The following Cryptographic Inventory Discovery Framework structures discovery across the six primary domains where cryptographic dependencies exist in enterprise environments.

Discovery Domain	What to Find	Primary Tools/ Methods	Key Outputs
Application Portfolio	Cryptographic libraries, TLS configurations, API authentication schemes, data encryption implementations	Static analysis (Cryptosense, Keyfactor, custom SAST rules), code repository scanning	Library inventory, algorithm usage map, deprecated algorithm flags
Network Infrastructure	TLS certificate grades, protocol versions, cipher suite configurations, VPN cryptographic parameters	Network scanners (Qualys SSL Labs API, testssl.sh, nmap scripts), passive traffic analysis	Protocol inventory, certificate expiry register, weak cipher report
Certificate Infrastructure (PKI)	CA hierarchy, issued certificates, certificate validity period, key sizes, signing algorithms	Certificate lifecycle management platforms (Venafi, Keyfactor), LDAP/AD queries, manual CA inventory	Certificate register, CA risk profile, expiry timeline
Cloud Environments	Cloud key management service configurations, S3/ Blob encryption settings, managed TLS endpoints, IAM signing algorithms	Cloud security posture management (CSPM) tools, cloud provider APIs, IaC scanning	Cloud cryptographic footprint, KMS key inventory, compliance gaps
IoT/OT/ Embedded Systems	Firmware cryptographic implementations, device certificate profiles, update signing mechanisms	Firmware analysis tools, device management platform queries, vendor documentation review	Device cryptographic profile, hardware constraint register, immovable asset list

Discovery Domain	What to Find	Primary Tools/ Methods	Key Outputs
Software Supply Chain	Third-party library cryptographic dependencies, open-source component versions, vendor-managed cryptographic services	Software composition analysis (SCA) tools (Snyk, Black Duck, OWASP Dependency-Check), SBOM analysis	Third-party cryptographic dependency map, vendor PQC readiness shortlist

Table 9.4: Cryptographic inventory discovery framework

Asset classification: the quantum vulnerability taxonomy

Data security relies on protecting various digital assets such as CRM databases, intellectual property, and financial records from unauthorized access, corruption, or theft throughout their lifecycle. Using tools like encryption, access controls, and regular backups to keep data private and reliable, which ensures that only the right people can see or change sensitive information. Raw discovery output is not actionable. The cryptographic asset register becomes the foundation for migration planning only when assets are classified by quantum vulnerability, data sensitivity, and migration urgency. The following taxonomy provides the classification structure:

Classification Tier	Asset Characteristics	HNDL Risk Level	Migration Priority
Tier 1: Immediately Threatened, High Sensitivity	• Asymmetric key exchange or signatures protecting data with >5-year confidentiality requirements (health records, financial data, IP, classified data)	Critical	Priority Wave 1: Begin Immediately
Tier 1: Immediately Threatened, Standard Sensitivity	• Asymmetric key exchange or signatures protecting data with <5-year confidentiality requirements (session tokens, transient traffic)	High	Priority Wave 2: Plan within 12 months

Classification Tier	Asset Characteristics	HNDL Risk Level	Migration Priority
Tier 2: Parameter Adjustment Required	• Symmetric encryption with <256-bit keys (AES-128) • SHA-256 used for long-lived integrity	Moderate	Priority Wave 3: Address during infrastructure refresh cycles
Tier 3: Not Materially Affected	• AES-256, SHA-384/512, sufficient parameterized symmetric systems	Low	Monitor for future algorithm research No immediate action required
Tier 4: Immovable Assets	• Hardware-constrained systems unable to run PQC algorithms (legacy embedded, certain IoT)	Variable	Risk acceptance, isolation, or hardware replacement program

Table 9.5: Quantum vulnerability asset classification taxonomy

Migration prioritization and sequencing frameworks

The cryptographic estate of a large enterprise typically contains thousands of individual systems, certificates, protocol endpoints, and data stores that rely on public-key cryptography. The operational reality is that you cannot migrate all of them simultaneously; you do not have the engineering resources, the vendor support, or the organizational change management capacity to execute everything at once. Migration prioritization is the science and art of deciding what goes first, what goes next, and what waits until later.

The multi-criteria prioritization framework below evaluates each inventoried cryptographic asset across four dimensions, producing a composite risk score that drives migration wave sequencing. The framework is designed to be defensible to CFO and board audiences, not just internally sensible to security teams, because the funding and executive commitment required for PQC migration programs at enterprise scale depends on priority decisions that non-technical audiences can understand and endorse.

Dimension	Scoring Criteria	Score 1 (Low)	Score 3 (Medium)	Score 5 (High)	Weight
Risk Exposure (HNDL)	Data sensitivity x confidentiality duration x threat probability	Transient, low-sensitivity data <1 year retention	Medium-sensitivity 1-10 year retention Standard threat profile	High-sensitivity >10 year retention Elevated threat profile	35%
Migration Complexity	Technical difficulty of replacing cryptographic implementation	Pure software library swap Well-supported algorithm replacement	Protocol co-evolution required Some hardware constraints Moderate vendor dependency	Hardware replacement required Deep embedded integration High vendor dependency No PQC support announced	25%
Operational Criticality	Business impact of migration-related downtime or performance degradation	Non-production Internal tooling Limited user impact	Customer-facing secondary systems Moderate revenue impact Contained blast radius	Core revenue-generating systems Mission-critical operations Broad organizational impact	25%
Regulatory Deadline	Compliance requirements governing migration timeline	No applicable regulatory guidance	Sector guidance published Voluntary compliance timeline indicated	Mandatory compliance deadline within 36 months Potential enforcement action for non-compliance	15%

Table 9.6: Multi-criteria migration prioritization framework

Computing composite prioritization scores across your cryptographic asset register, even a simplified version of this framework, transforms migration planning from an intractable "everything is a priority" conversation into a defensible sequencing discussion. The output is a migration wave structure that your CFO can understand: "We're spending the first migration budget portion on the systems where an adversary is most likely to have already captured encrypted data," your board can approve, and your engineering teams can execute against.

Migration wave structure: a typical enterprise sequencing

The following represents an enterprise PQC migration wave structure where the timelines are indicative; actual wave boundaries depend on organizational complexity, resource availability, and vendor support maturity.

Migration Wave	Timeline	Asset Categories	Key Activities	Success Criteria
Wave 1: Protect the Most Vulnerable	Year 1-2	Tier 1 high-sensitivity assets Internet-facing TLS endpoints Long-lived certificate authorities Code signing infrastructure	Hybrid PQC/classical TLS deployment CA hierarchy PQC signing PQC library integration for high-sensitivity applications	100% of Tier 1 high-sensitivity assets migrated Hybrid TLS deployed on all internet-facing endpoints
Wave 2: Systematic Enterprise Migration	Year 2-4	Tier 1 high-standard-sensitivity assets Internal PKI Enterprise applications VPN infrastructure	Full PQC certification issuance VPN cryptographic migration Enterprise application library updates IAM/MFA cryptographic updates	>80% of quantum-vulnerable enterprise systems migrated All new deployments PQC-first
Wave 3: Infrastructure Refresh and Legacy	Year 3-5	Tier 2 parameter adjustments Legacy systems on planned refresh cycles IoT/OT where hardware replacement is planned	AES-256 migration for AES-128 deployments SHA-384 adoption IoT device firmware updates where supported	All Tier 2 parameter adjustments complete Legacy systems decommissioned or isolated
Wave 4: Residual and Immovable	Year 4-7	Tier 4 immovable assets Deep embedded systems Hardware-constrained devices	Risk acceptance documentation Network isolation controls Hardware replacement procurement and deployment	All residual assets formally risk-accepted or isolated No unmanaged Tier 1 exposure remaining

Table 9.7: Enterprise PQC migration wave structure

Hybrid deployment: cryptographic agility in practice

A critical misconception about PQC migration is that it requires a clean cutover, disabling classical cryptography and enabling PQC simultaneously. This is neither architecturally necessary nor operationally realistic for most enterprise environments. Hybrid deployment strategies, which run PQC algorithms alongside classical algorithms in a combined key exchange or signature operation, provide quantum protection while maintaining backward compatibility with systems not yet migrated.[16] If I could rename the move to post-quantum cryptography, I would call it PQC expansion or PQC extension. These terms just feel more realistic because they describe what we are doing, building onto our current security, not throwing it away.

In practice, hybrid TLS combines ECDH key exchange with ML-KEM key encapsulation, deriving the session key from both operations. An attacker would need to break both the classical and the quantum-resistant algorithm to compromise the session. Providing, of course, immediate quantum protection even before the full migration is complete. Google, Cloudflare, and major browser vendors deployed hybrid ECDH+ML-KEM in TLS 1.3 for experimental use as early as 2023, with broader rollout ongoing following the NIST standard finalization back in 2024.[17] Let's now look at an example of how this PQC expansion worked out in a real scenario.

Company spotlight: Thales Group (France)

Thales Group, the French aerospace, defense, and digital security conglomerate with operations across more than 68 countries, represents one of the most comprehensive European approaches to enterprise PQC migration. As a major provider of cryptographic hardware (HSMs), identity and access management solutions, and defense communications systems to NATO member governments and critical infrastructure operators, Thales occupies a position where PQC readiness is simultaneously a product development imperative and an internal security requirement for the sensitive data the company handles on behalf of government and defense clients.[18]

Thales launched its quantum-safe initiative in 2021, establishing an internal PQC Center of Excellence that coordinates migration activities across its Luna HSM product line, CipherTrust data security platform, and SafeNet authentication infrastructure.[19] The company's strategic approach centers on hardware security module modernization, recognizing that HSMs sit at the root of trust for enterprise PKI and that quantum-vulnerable HSMs represent systemic risk regardless of software-layer migration progress. Thales's Luna HSMs with PQC support, launched in 2023, provide hardware-accelerated ML-KEM and ML-DSA operations, enabling enterprise customers to begin migrating their certificate authority roots to quantum-resistant algorithms without replacing broader heightened sensitivity to quantum intelligence threats and the EU's parallel policy push through ENISA's quantum cryptography guidance.

For security leaders drawing lessons from the Thales approach, several elements are transferable to enterprise migration programs. First, Thales's recognition that HSMs are the strategic linchpin, the point where migration investment delivers maximum leverage across the entire cryptographic estate, offers a practical prioritization heuristic. That is, wherever your root of trust lives, that is where PQC migration delivers the highest return on investment. Second, Thales's product and internal migration programs are deliberately synchronized, meaning the engineering expertise developed in building PQC-capable products directly accelerates the internal migration, reducing the net costs of both initiatives. Third, Thales's engagement with French national cybersecurity agency ANSSI and EU-level ENISA policy processes has positioned the company's migration timeline in deliberate alignment with emerging EU regulatory requirements, a compliance-forward approach that enterprise security leaders in regulated European industries should replicate.

Implementation timelines, resource planning, and regulatory alignment

A PQC migration program at enterprise scale is not a project; it's a program. The distinction matters operationally. Projects have defined beginnings and ends, singular deliverables, and bounded resource commitments. Programs are sustained, multi-year organizational commitments comprising dozens of interdependent projects, evolving resource requirements, and ongoing governance structures. CISOs who approach PQC migration as a project will find themselves perpetually restarting incomplete inventory feeds, incomplete prioritization, underfunded operations, which produces inadequate resource planning, which then creates migration delays, all of which compound into escalating regulatory risk.

Program Phase	Duration	Key Deliverables	Critical Dependencies	Resource Profile
Phase 1: Foundation	Months 1-12	Cryptographic asset Risk classification Vendor PQC readiness assessment Regulatory requirement mapping Initial Wave 1 migration plan	Executive sponsorship Security engineering capacity for discovery Vendor engagement framework	2-4 FTE security engineers 0.5 FTE program manager Vendor engagement budget
Phase 2: Wave 1 Migration	Months 6-30	Hybrid TLS deployment CA hierarchy PQC migration High-sensitivity application library migration Code signing infrastructure migration	Finalized NIST standards (available) PQC-capable certificate management platform Vendor library availability	4-8 FTE security/platform engineers Dedicated PKI specialist 1 FTE program manager
Phase 3: Systematic Migration	Months 18-54	Enterprise application migration VPN PQC transition Internal PKI full migration AES-256 parameter upgrades IoT/OT migration where feasible	Wave 1 completion Mature PQC library ecosystem Vendor product support across enterprise application portfolio	6-12 FTE across security, platform, and application engineering 1-2 FTE program management
Phase 4: Completion and Sustaining	Months 42-84+	Legacy system decommission or formal risk acceptance Immovable asset isolation PQC-first standard embedded in architecture review Sustaining governance	Program wave completion Updated technology acquisition standards Regulatory compliance validation	2-4 FTE sustaining 0.5 FTE compliance/audit support Ongoing vendor management

Table 9.8: PQC migration program timeline and resource profile

As you may have noticed in the previous table, the timelines overlap between phases. This is to reflect the iterative execution of each phase. Resource profiles are indicative for a mid-sized enterprise of approximately 5-20K employees and will scale with organizational complexity.

The regulatory landscape: what compliance requires and when

PQC migration is not purely a risk management choice; it's increasingly a regulatory compliance requirement. The regulatory landscape across major jurisdictions is evolving rapidly, and security leaders in regulated industries face the challenge of managing migration complexity while meeting hardening deadlines from multiple regulatory bodies simultaneously.

The following table summarizes the evolving PQC regulatory landscape and the requirements organizations may need to navigate across multiple jurisdictions. For leaders, such as yourselves, this is also an important planning signal: quantum-safe migration will require more than a technology roadmap; it will need coordinated budgeting, operating expense planning, procurement decisions, and investment prioritization across the business. CFOs and other executive leaders should begin accounting for these costs early, particularly where overlapping regulatory deadlines could create competing demands for funding and resources. Organizations that plan ahead will have more flexibility to spread investments over time, while those who wait may face compressed timelines, higher costs, and fewer implementation options.

Jurisdiction / Regulator	Key Requirement	Target Timeline	Affected Organizations	Documented Requirements
NSA-CNSA 2.0[20]	National Security Systems must transition to CNSA 2.0 algorithms (ML-KEM, ML-DSA, SLH-DSA) for software and firmware updates Full transition for all systems	2025-2033 phased by system type	NSS operators Defense contractors Cleared industry	System-by-system migration plans POA&M submissions Annual progress reporting
OMB M-23-02[21] / CISA PQC Guidance	Federal civilian agencies to inventory cryptographic systems Prioritize PQC migration for high-value systems Align with NIST standards	Inventory complete Migration 2025-2030 per OMB	ALL US federal civilian agencies Significant federal contractors	Cryptographic inventory submissions Migration roadmap documentation Annual status reports
DORA (EU Financial Sector) [22]	ICT risk management requirements implicitly require quantum risk in threat modeling PQC readiness expected in supervisory assessments	Ongoing Evolving supervisory guidance	EU financial entities ICT third-party providers	ICT risk assessments Resilience testing documentation Third-party PQC assessment evidence

Jurisdiction / Regulator	Key Requirement	Target Timeline	Affected Organizations	Documented Requirements
ENISA / EU Cybersecurity Act[23]	Member state guidance on PQC migration Critical infrastructure operators expected to implement ENISA quantum risk mitigation recommendations	2024-2027 national implementation guidance	EU critical infrastructure operators Essential service providers	Risk assessment documentation Implementation timeline reporting
UK NCSC PQC Guidance[24]	Organizations should begin PQC migration planning immediately Priority for long-lived sensitive data and critical national infrastructure	No hard deadline Risk-based urgency	UK government CNI operators Regulated financial services	Risk-based migration documentation Supply chain PQC assessments
US Financial Regulators (OCC, FDIC, FRB)[25]	Emerging supervisory expectations for quantum risk management PQC readiness expected in technology risk examination	Supervisory examinations beginning 2024-2025	US banks, broker-dealers, financial market infrastructure	Quantum risk assessment evidence Migration roadmap Board-level risk reporting

Table 9.9: Regulatory landscape summary

If your organization has operations in multiple jurisdictions, it must coordinate migration timelines across overlapping regulatory requirements. It's also good to ensure that you follow any updates should timelines, regulations, or audit processes change; you also want to be sure that your organizational leads keep you aware of any changes.

Regulatory compliance program management for PQC

Understanding what all the regulatory compliance requirements are is one thing. However, managing them is another beast altogether as each jurisdiction will come with its own range of challenges. Managing PQC regulatory compliance across multiple jurisdictions simultaneously requires a compliance program management capability that goes beyond standard regulatory tracking. This of course is not an unusual scenario for global financial institutions, multinational corporations, or technology companies with US federal contracts. The challenge is not just knowing what each regulator requires; it's synthesizing overlapping, sometimes inconsistent requirements into a unified migration program structure that satisfies all relevant obligations without creating duplicative compliance overhead.

Two practices distinguish well-managed PQC compliance programs from reactive ones. First, regulatory requirement mapping should be a living document, updated at least quarterly as guidance from NSA, CISA, ENISA, and sector-specific regulators evolves. What was voluntary guidance in 2023 has become expected practice and will become examination-tested compliance in today's world. Second, migration program milestones should be explicitly mapped to regulatory obligation dates, creating documented traceability between what your migration program is doing and what each regulator expects; examiner communication is dramatically easier when this mapping exists. Next, we'll see how one of the largest global institutions managed its way through one of the most heavily regulated industries, finance.

Company spotlight: JPMorgan Chase

JPMorgan Chase, with trillions of dollars in assets and cryptographic infrastructure spanning retail banking, investment banking, payment processing, and global custody operations across more than 60 countries, represents one of the most consequential enterprise PQC migration programs underway in the global financial sector. The bank's quantum security program, which has been publicly described in investor and regulatory communications since 2022, reflects both the genuine complexity of PQC migration at global banking scale and the specific regulatory pressures of US systemically important financial institutions.[26, 27]

JPMorgan Chase's approach to PQC migration is built around what its technology leadership describes as "crypto-agility at scale," the systematic replacement of hardwired cryptographic implementations with abstracted, upgradeable cryptographic services that can be updated without application-layer re-architecture.[28] The bank began its cryptographic inventory program in 2021, cataloging cryptographic dependencies across an application portfolio spanning tens of thousands of systems, and began hybrid PQC deployment in select high-priority environments in 2023. The bank has also been an active participant in standards development, contributing to NIST PQC evaluation processes and co-authoring industry guidance through the Financial Services Information Sharing and Analysis Center (FS-ISAC) on quantum risk management for financial institutions.[29]

JPMorgan Chase's experience offers several hard-won lessons for enterprise security leaders. Experiences such as the following. First, the sheer size and complexity of the cryptographic inventory exercise to determine the scope of cryptographic dependencies embedded in legacy trading systems, messaging infrastructure, and third-party integrations significantly exceeded initial estimates, validating the principle that cryptographic inventory must be completed before meaningful migration planning can begin. Second, the bank's engagement with US financial regulators, including participation in Treasury and FS-ISAC working groups on quantum risk, provides its compliance team early visibility into examination expectations, therefore enabling the bank to structure its migration documentation around the specific evidence formats that examiners are developing, rather than retrofitting documentation to examiner expectations after the fact.[30] Third, the supply chain PQC assessment program has created constructive pressure on the vendor ecosystem to accelerate PQC support timelines.[31, 32]

Competencies for PQC migration leadership

In essence, there are two competencies that you need to focus on for PQC migration. The first is understanding the NIST PQC standard interpretation and application, and the second is preparing your vendor and supply chain PQC readiness assessment. Let's dig into each of these individually.

NIST PQC standard interpretation and application

In practice, this manifests in three high-value leadership behaviors. First, when an engineering team or vendor proposes a specific algorithm selection for a use case, you should be able to evaluate whether it's consistent with NIST guidance. For example, does key exchange use ML-KEM or a NIST-approved alternative? Does the digital signature scheme match the security category level appropriate for the data being protected? Is the implementation derived from a NIST-validated reference implementation? Second, when a vendor proposes a "quantum-safe" solution using non-NIST algorithms such as proprietary lattice schemes or other unvetted alternatives, you should recognize this as a compliance and interoperability risk that requires documented justification. Third, you should be able to translate NIST security category designations into plain language for CFO and board audiences. For example, Category 3 is "appropriate for the vast majority of our commercial data protection needs, equivalent to AES-192 classical security," therefore connecting technical parameter choices to risk-management language that decision-makers can understand.

Vendor and supply chain PQC readiness assessment

Your organization's PQC migration will proceed at the pace of your slowest critical vendor. This is not hypothetical; enterprise cryptographic infrastructure is deeply dependent on third-party products and services whose cryptographic implementations you do not control. Certificate management platforms, HSMs, network security appliances, cloud providers, identity management systems, application development frameworks, and end-user productivity tools all contain cryptographic implementations that must be migrated. If your certificate management platform does not support PQC certificate issuance, you cannot migrate your VPN encryption. If your SaaS applications use non-upgradeable cryptographic libraries, you have a migration dependency that only the vendor can resolve.

The structured vendor PQC readiness assessment process begins with the identification of your cryptographically critical vendors, those whose products sit in your Tier 1 or Tier 2 migration priority categories. For each critical vendor, a formal PQC readiness questionnaire should be issued covering: current algorithm inventory and quantum vulnerability assessment, PQC algorithm integration roadmap with specific product release dates, NIST standard compliance commitment, and contractual willingness to include PQC migration milestones in SLAs and renewal terms.

Vendor PQC Readiness Dimension	Maturity Level 1 (Early)	Maturity Level 2 (Developing)	Maturity Level 3 (Advanced)	Your Action
Awareness & Assessment	Vendor is aware of algorithm threat but has not begun assessment	Vendor has completed internal cryptographic inventory Risk assessment in progress	Vendor has published quantum risk assessment and customer guidance	Request formal PQC roadmap commitment
Product Roadmap	No PQC product roadmap published	PQC roadmap in development No committed dates	PQC-capable product releases committed with specified dates aligned to NIST standards	Escalate to account executive Include PQC roadmap in contract renewal conditions
Standards Compliance	Vendor proposes proprietary or pre-standard quantum-safe algorithms	Vendor tracking NIST process Planning NIST alignment	Vendor product roadmap explicitly aligned to FIPS 203/204/205/206	Reject non-NIST implementations for enterprise deployment Document compliance risk
Customer Migration Support	No customer migration guidance or tooling available	Migration guidance documentation available Professional services beginning to develop PQC capability	Dedicated PQC migration support Tooling available Customer advisory resources in place	Engage migration support resources early Participate in beta programs to accelerate access

Table 9.10: Vendor PQC readiness assessment maturity framework

Summary

OK, that was quite a lot and we're just one chapter in Part 3 here. Let's just take a breath and look at where we have traveled so far. We opened with an uncomfortable truth: the cryptographic infrastructure protecting your most sensitive data is already under a harvest-and-store attack by adversaries planning for quantum capability that may arrive within a decade. We haven't speculated about that threat; we've analyzed it technically, framed its timeline pressure mathematically through Mosca's theorem, and connected it to the operational urgency that should drive our migration planning calendar today.

We've grounded your migration planning in the finalized NIST PQC standards, ML-KEM, ML-DSA, SLH-DSA, and FN-DSA, providing the algorithm selection guidance, security level decision framework, and implementation direction your engineering teams need. We've built out a comprehensive cryptographic inventory methodology covering six discovery domains, a quantum vulnerability classification taxonomy that distinguishes immediate threats from parameter adjustments from resilient components, and an asset register structure that supports defensible prioritization.

The multi-criteria migration prioritization framework translates raw inventory data into actionable migration wave sequencing, weighted by harvest-now-decrypt-later exposure, migration complexity, operational criticality, and regulatory deadlines, that you can defend to CFO and board audiences as a risk-reduction investment decision rather than a technical exercise. The migration wave structure takes that prioritization output and builds it into a realistic, phased program timeline with resource profiles calibrated to organizational scale.

The regulatory landscape analysis has given you visibility into the hardening compliance environment across US federal agencies, EU financial services, UK critical infrastructure, and NATO national security systems, a compliance calendar that your migration program must be aligned to, not retrofitted against. And three company spotlights, IBM's cryptographic agility architecture, Thales's European defense-sector HSM migration leadership, and JPMorgan Chase's financial-scale systematic migration program, have illustrated what successful PQC migration programs look like in practice across different organizational contexts and industry sectors.

The skills you developed throughout this chapter, cryptographic inventory leadership, NIST standard interpretation, migration risk assessment and prioritization, vendor supply chain readiness assessment, and regulatory compliance program management, provide the competency foundation for leading PQC migration as a major enterprise program, not a technology refresh managed beneath the awareness threshold of executive leadership. PQC migration requires executive sponsorship, multi-year engineering resource commitment, vendor ecosystem management, and regulatory coordination that simply cannot succeed without security leaders who can operate credibly at the executive and board level on these issues.

Organizations that complete PQC migration before cryptographically relevant quantum computers emerge will protect the confidentiality of their most sensitive data and maintain the trust of customers, partners, and regulators who depend on their cryptographic integrity. The organizations that defer will face the worst possible outcome: a race against quantum capability maturation with an incomplete migration, exposed data that cannot be retroactively protected, and regulatory examiners asking pointed questions about why warning signs were visible years in advance and action was not taken.

This chapter has equipped you with the migration roadmap and tools to execute PQC transition as a disciplined enterprise program. But executing a migration program without a continuously updated understanding of the threat environment it's designed to counter is navigating by an outdated map. This is where the next chapter comes in. There we will expand the aperture from migration execution to threat intelligence, providing comprehensive quantum threat landscape analysis, adversary capability assessment, and industry-specific vulnerability analysis that transforms PQC migration from a reactive compliance exercise into a dynamically calibrated strategic security investment.

In the next chapter you'll learn who the threat actors are and what quantum investments they are making, how to interpret CRQC timeline projections from credible sources without being misled by either alarmism or complacency. You'll also learn which industries face the most acute quantum vulnerability profiles and why, and how to build continuous risk monitoring frameworks that keep your threat assessments current as the quantum technology landscape evolves faster than any static briefing can capture. The next chapter provides the threat intelligence foundation that makes every migration prioritization decision in this chapter sharper, every regulatory alignment argument more credible, and every board conversation about quantum security investment more compelling. So, let's take a deep breath and get right to it!

Further reading

1. `https://arxiv.org/abs/quant-ph/9508027`
2. `https://doi.org/10.1038/nature23461`
3. `https://doi.org/10.1109/MSP.2018.3761723`
4. `https://doi.org/10.1145/237814.237866`
5. `https://doi.org/10.6028/NIST.FIPS.203`
6. `https://doi.org/10.6028/NIST.FIPS.204`

7. https://doi.org/10.6028/NIST.FIPS.205
8. https://doi.org/10.6028/NIST.FIPS.206
9. https://media.defense.gov/2022/Sep/07/2003071836/-1/-1/0/CSI_CNSA_2.0_FAQ.PDF
10. https://doi.org/10.1109/MSP.2018.3761723
11. https://www.ibm.com/thought-leadership/institute-business-value/report/quantum-decade
12. https://www.enisa.europa.eu/publications/post-quantum-cryptography-current-state-and-quantum-mitigation
13. https://doi.org/10.6028/NIST.FIPS.206
14. https://newsroom.ibm.com/2024-08-13-ibm-developed-algorithms-announced-as-worlds-first-post-quantum-cryptography-standards
15. https://www.hpcwire.com/off-the-wire/ibm-unveils-ibm-z16-quantum-safe-system-for-real-time-ai/
16. https://datatracker.ietf.org/doc/draft-ietf-tls-hybrid-design/
17. https://blog.chromium.org/2023/08/protecting-chrome-traffic-with-hybrid.html
18. https://cpl.thalesgroup.com/resources/encryption/post-quantum-cryptography-solutions-white-paper
19. https://cpl.thalesgroup.com/data-protection
20. https://media.defense.gov/2022/Sep/07/2003071836/-1/-1/0/CSI_CNSA_2.0_FAQ.PDF
21. https://www.whitehouse.gov/wp-content/uploads/2022/11/M-23-02-M-Memo-on-Migrating-to-Post-Quantum-Cryptography.pdf
22. https://eur-lex.europa.eu/legal-content/EN/TXT/PDF/?uri=CELEX:32022R2554
23. https://digital-strategy.ec.europa.eu/en/policies/cybersecurity-act
24. https://www.ncsc.gov.uk/whitepaper/next-steps-preparing-for-post-quantum-cryptography
25. https://www.congress.gov/crs-product/R44918
26. https://thequantuminsider.com/2025/10/13/jpmorganchases-1-5-trillion-security-and-resiliency-initiative-includes-investments-in-quantum/

27. https://www.jpmorganchase.com/ir/annual-report
28. https://www.jpmorgan.com/technology/news/firm-establishes-quantum-secured-crypto-agile-network
29. https://www.fsisac.com/
30. https://www.fsisac.com/newsroom/fs-isac-urges-global-coordination-for-migration-to-post-quantum-cryptography-in-financial-services
31. https://www.jpmorganchase.com/content/dam/jpmc/jpmorgan-chase-and-co/investor-relations/documents/events/2023/jpmc-investor-day-2023/global-technology.pdf
32. https://www.nccoe.nist.gov/sites/default/files/2021-10/6-Yassir-NIST-%2020200819-8.pdf

10

Quantum Threat Landscape and Risk Assessment

Okay, here we go. As mentioned at the beginning of the previous chapter, with the uncomfortable truth that you are almost certainly already a target of quantum-era attacks. Not because adversaries have quantum computers today, they don't, at least not ones capable of breaking your encryption. But the attack has already started. Right now, sophisticated nation-state actors are systematically vacuuming up encrypted data from financial institutions, healthcare archives, government agencies, and critical infrastructure operators, not to read it today, but to decrypt it tomorrow, when quantum hardware finally arrives. The attack vector has a name, which we've already learned: Harvest Now, Decrypt Later (HNDL). And it means that the quantum threat is not waiting politely in the future for your migration timeline to catch up with it. As you may well know, cyber attacks are an ongoing operational reality, where most incidents go undetected. However, it's worth noting that the financial and strategic stakes have escalated to enterprise-level exposure, and threat actors possess unprecedented compute capabilities. Businesses can no longer treat extortion payouts as a standard cost of doing business, because the risk exposure and financial stakes are too high.

For CISOs, security directors, and risk management leaders, this reality reshapes the entire framing of quantum security. It's not a problem you can defer until quantum computers are commercially available. By that point, the data your organization encrypted five, ten, or even fifteen years ago, such as patient records, financial transactions, classified communications, and intellectual property, could already be in adversary hands, just waiting to be unlocked. The question isn't whether to prepare. The question is how intelligently and urgently you prepare, given genuine uncertainty about the exact timing of quantum hardware milestones. In this case, this asymmetrical approach cannot result in CISOs "kicking the can down the road" to the next CISO. The investment will need to be ongoing for the organization to survive.

This chapter is designed to give you the analytical foundations and practical tools to answer that question rigorously. In fact, consider these as two parts where the first part we cover who/what are the threats, and the second part covers what to do next. We'll begin with a structured assessment of who the adversaries are, mapping nation-state quantum programs in China, the United States, Russia, and the EU alongside the emerging commercial threat landscape. We then tackle the timeline question head-on, not with false certainty but with a scenario-based planning framework that lets you make rational security investments across a range of quantum development timelines. From there, we go deep on industry-specific vulnerability analysis, because the quantum threat looks very different depending on whether you lead security for a bank, a hospital, a power grid, or a software company. Finally, we'll end with the operational infrastructure you need to keep your threat assessment current: continuous monitoring architectures, threat intelligence integration models, and risk quantification methodologies that translate quantum uncertainty into the financial language your board understands. This chapter also looks at how quantum risk shows up in the boardroom, where technical probabilities alone aren't enough. The discussion focuses on translating quantum risk into the financial and business terms board members use to weigh priorities, allocate capital, and decide what action to take.

The takeaway for you embedded throughout this chapter will meaningfully enhance both your technical acumen and your business effectiveness. Quantum threat intelligence analysis gives you the ability to critically evaluate the stream of quantum hardware claims and research publications, distinguishing genuine capability advances from vendor marketing noise. Scenario-based quantum risk planning equips you to structure security investments that are robust across multiple possible futures, avoiding both premature overinvestment and dangerous complacency. Industry vulnerability assessment leadership enables you to translate generic quantum frameworks into the specific risk language of your sector. Risk quantification and board communication bridges the gap between technical security analysis and financial governance. And threat intelligence program design ensures you have a sustainable, institutionalized capability for monitoring quantum threat evolution rather than relying on periodic briefings that go stale the moment they're delivered.

Quantum readiness, done well, is fundamentally an intelligence discipline. It requires the same analytical rigor, source evaluation, and calibrated judgement that characterize effective threat intelligence in any domain. The difference is that the threat environment is evolving faster than almost any previous cybersecurity challenge, the technical landscape is more opaque, and the stakes, for some organizations, are existential. This chapter is your analytical starting point.

This chapter will cover the following main topics:

- Quantum threat actor landscape and capability assessment

- Quantum attack timeline projections and scenario analysis
- Industry-specific quantum vulnerability
- Company spotlights: quantum security in practice
- Continuous quantum risk monitoring and threat intelligence integration
- Quantum risk quantification and enterprise risk integration
- Core analytical and leadership competencies

Quantum threat actor landscape and capability assessment

Understanding who's building quantum computers, and why, is an important first step in assessing your organization's quantum risk. The threat landscape isn't one-size-fits-all. It's different actors having very different resources, motivations, capabilities, and timelines, which means they won't pose the same level of risk to every organization. Treating them all as equally threatening can lead to poor decisions, much like treating every cybersecurity threat, from a small criminal group to a well-funded nation-state, as if it posed the same risk to the business.

Mapping the adversary ecosystem

The threat actor landscape can be organized into three tiers: nation-state programs with sustained multi-billion-dollar quantum development investments; sophisticated criminal enterprises and non-state actors with growing access to quantum cloud resources; and the future democratized threat enabled by commercial quantum-as-a-service availability. Each tier has different implications for your organization's quantum security planning horizon.

Nation-state quantum programs: the primary threat

Before going into details, I want to make sure one thing is perfectly clear. Nation-state security threats touch everyone everywhere, making the reality of cyber threats a global problem where no country is safe from hidden digital weak spots. Unknown zero-day flaws are the scariest part of this landscape because no one has fixed them yet. This reality leads directly to a secret dilemma: if a government finally cracks encryption, would they ever actually tell the world, or would they keep it hidden to maintain their silent advantage?

China: the most consequential adversary

China's quantum program represents the most strategically significant quantum threat for most organizations in the Western private sector and government. The Chinese Communist Party's 14th Five-Year Plan (2021-2025) allocated an estimated $15.3 billion to quantum research and development, and that figure covers only publicly disclosed investments, excluding classified programs.[1] China's quantum ambitions are explicitly dual-use: the same quantum sensing, communication, and computing capabilities that advance civilian scientific goals are directly applicable to quantum cryptanalysis and signals intelligence.

China's quantum computing program has produced genuine hardware achievements. Researchers at the University of Science and Technology of China demonstrated Jiuzhang 2.0, a 113-photonic-qubit system, and Zuchongzhi 2.0, a superconducting qubit system, with performance claims exceeding Google's Sycamore processor on specific benchmark tasks.[2] While these demonstrations remain far from cryptographically relevant capability, they signal serious technical depth. More consequentially, China's investment in quantum communications, including a 2,000-kilometer quantum-encrypted fiber network linking Beijing and Shanghai,[3] and quantum satellite experiments extending quantum key distribution to intercontinental ranges,[4] demonstrates strategic prioritization of quantum as a national security technology.

For security leaders, the FBI has been explicit about China's strategic intentions: the PRC is engaged in what the Bureau describes as a "well-resourced and systematic campaign" to acquire quantum-relevant intellectual property, targeting academic institutions, corporate research programs, and government contractors involved in quantum technology development.[5] Organizations with quantum R&D assets, sensitive national security-relevant data archives, or intellectual property with long-term strategic value should treat China as the primary quantum threat actor for HNDL risk assessments.

United States: competitor and security reference

The United States operates the most advanced ecosystem of quantum research institutions, private sector quantum hardware programs, and quantum security policy infrastructure in the world. US federal quantum R&D budgets have grown substantially since the passage of the National Quantum Initiative Act in 2018, with the FY 2025 budget request having reached approximately $998M across agencies including NIST, NSF, DOE, DOD, and DHS.[6] Private sector investment from IBM, Google, Microsoft, IonQ, and dozens of startups adds several billion dollars annually to the US quantum ecosystem.[7]

For security leaders, the US program matters as both a security framework reference and an intelligence source. NIST's Post-Quantum Cryptography standardization program, which published its first PQC algorithm standards in August 2024, represents the most authoritative international benchmark for quantum-safe migration. DARPA's Quantum Benchmarking Initiative, which enlisted multiple firms in 2025 to evaluate whether quantum prototypes are on a practical path toward utility-scale systems by 2033, serves as a leading indicator of timeline credibility assessment.[8]

Russia: constrained but engaged

Russia's quantum program is real but significantly resource-constrained relative to Chinese and American efforts. The Russian government established the National Quantum Laboratory (NQL) under the state nuclear corporation Rosatom, with an initial goal of producing a 100-qubit quantum computer. However, the ongoing war in Ukraine, economic sanctions, and associated supply chain disruptions have substantially limited Russia's ability to acquire the specialized equipment and materials needed for advanced quantum hardware development. [9]

Despite these constraints, Russia's signals intelligence services retain sophisticated cyber capabilities and strategic motivation to acquire quantum-relevant capabilities and data. Organizations in defense, critical infrastructure, and government sectors should not discount Russia as a quantum threat actor for HNDL risk assessments, even if near-term Russian quantum hardware development timelines are longer than Chinese equivalents. Russia's March 2023 agreement with China to deepen scientific and military technology cooperation, including in quantum technology areas, adds a further complication to clear threat actor attribution.[10]

European Union: security-oriented investment

The European Union's quantum program is primarily oriented around economic competitiveness, technological sovereignty, and defensive security rather than offensive cryptanalysis applications. The EU Quantum Flagship initiative represents a €1 billion, ten-year commitment to quantum technology research and infrastructure, with explicit security applications including the EuroQCI (European Quantum Communication Infrastructure) initiative aimed at building a quantum-encrypted communication network across EU member states.[11]

For security leaders, the EU's regulatory posture is at least as consequential as its research program. The European Commission's April 2024 recommendation urging member states to adopt a harmonized roadmap to post-quantum cryptography, and the EU's NIS Cooperation Group June 2025 roadmap urging completion of risk assessments and beginning of PQC migrations by 2026, targeting full transition of critical systems by 2030, creates compliance-driven migration timelines for organizations operating in EU markets.[12] Organizations with EU operations should treat EU regulatory alignment as a quantum security migration forcing function independent of threat timeline uncertainty.

The emerging commercial threat: quantum-as-a-service

The nation-state threat is concerning but relatively bounded: most organizations are not primary targets of nation-state quantum cryptanalysis programs. The more broadly concerning long-term threat is the democratization of quantum cryptanalytic capability through commercial quantum cloud access, the Quantum-as-a-Service (QaaS) threat model.

As quantum hardware approaches commercial accessibility, the barrier to quantum-enabled attacks will drop dramatically. A financially sophisticated ransomware operation, a state-sponsored criminal enterprise, or a well-capitalized fraud ring could, in a future where cryptographically relevant quantum computing (CRQC) is commercially available, rent quantum decryption capability by the hour. This is precisely the threat model that makes HNDL attacks rational today: adversaries who cannot yet afford quantum hardware are positioning to exploit commercial quantum access when it arrives. The financial services sector, healthcare organizations managing decades of patient records, and technology companies with valuable encrypted IP archives face the most acute QaaS threat exposure.

The following table provides a structured threat actor comparison across the dimensions most relevant to organizational quantum risk assessment.

Threat Actor	Investment Level	Primary Motivation	HNDL Threat	Key Target Sectors
China (PRC)	$15.3B+ (5yr plan)	Cryptanalysis, IP theft, military supremacy	High: Active now	Defense, Finance, Healthcare, Tech, Critical Infrastructure
United States	~$998M federal FY25 + billions private	Defense, economic leadership, PQC standardization	Framework setter	Internal use NIST/NSA set global standards
Russia	Moderate, sanctions-constrained	Signals intelligence, critical infrastructure disruption	Medium: Limited by sanctions	Government, Defense, Critical Infrastructure

Threat Actor	Investment Level	Primary Motivation	HNDL Threat	Key Target Sectors
European Union	€1B Flagship + national programs	Sovereignty, defensive security, economic competitiveness	Low: Defensive orientation	Regulation driver Compliance deadline setter
Criminal/ QaaS (Future)	Rental model: near-zero barrier	Financial fraud, ransomware, IP theft	High (2035-2045): Democratized access	Finance, Healthcare, Any sector with long-lived encrypted data

Table 10.1: Quantum threat actor landscape assessment matrix

Quantum attack timeline projections and scenario analysis

Here is the thing about quantum timeline projections: anyone who gives you a precise date for "Q-Day," which is the moment a cryptographically relevant quantum computer can break RSA-2048 in a practical timeframe, is either exceptionally confident or not paying careful enough attention to the actual science. The development trajectory of quantum hardware involves deeply uncertain engineering challenges in error correction, qubit coherence, fabrication yield, and system integration that make point forecasts essentially unreliable. These three factors are aligning somewhat quickly as of late. Fabrication yields are rapidly advancing, qubit coherence is advancing, and error correction is improving greatly towards fault tolerance. However, integration forecasting is still somewhat unreliable.

The honest case for scenario planning

The Global Risk Institute's Quantum Threat Timeline Report, produced annually with evolutionQ since 2019, illustrates this uncertainty precisely and illustrates something else besides: the uncertainty itself moves. The 2024 edition, synthesizing 32 expert judgements, put the probability of a CRQC breaking RSA-2048 in 24 hours by 2034 at 17–34%.[42] The 2025 edition, published 9 March 2026, revised that ten-year window to 28–49%, and rated a CRQC within fifteen years likely at 51–70%.[43] The optimistic bound moved fifteen points in a single survey cycle. A 28–49% range is not imprecision, it's intellectual honesty, but a range that shifts that far in twelve months is telling you something the range alone doesn't. The distribution is most definitely not stationary.

Two things moved it, and neither is the one you'd expect. The first is that manufacturing stopped being the constraint: imec has fabricated transmon qubits on a 300 mm CMOS pilot line with coherence times exceeding 100 μs,[44] IBM reports that shifting fabrication to 300 mm doubled its development speed while increasing chip complexity tenfold,[45] and in May 2026 IBM and the Department of Commerce announced Anderon, a pure-play quantum foundry backed by $1 billion in CHIPS incentives and $1 billion of IBM cash.[46] But wafer yield governs how many devices you can build, not how good they are, and fidelity is what drives error-correction overhead. Industrialization didn't shorten the road; it concentrated the remaining uncertainty in the parameters a fab cannot fix. The second mover is pure mathematics. Gidney's 2019 estimate for RSA-2048 was 20 million noisy qubits over eight hours; his 2025 revision put it at under a million in less than a week, on identical hardware assumptions, via approximate residue arithmetic, yoked surface codes, and magic state cultivation.[47] No qubit was added anywhere. The target isn't fixed, and it's under active attack by people who publish.

Which is why the honest answer to "what constitutes a CRQC" depends on the layer you measure. Willow is the clearest picture of where the physical layer actually sits: 105 physical qubits realizing a single distance-7 surface code memory, logical error suppressed by 2.14 ± 0.02 per two-unit distance increase, beyond break-even by a factor of 2.4.[48] Historic, the first proof that adding qubits can make a logical qubit better rather than worse. Also, one logical qubit, against Google's own estimate that current error rates may demand a thousand physical qubits per logical one.[49] Regulators have already repriced that gap. NSM-10 framed the 2022 objective as mitigating quantum risk "as is feasible by 2035";[50] Executive Order 14412, signed 22 June 2026, replaced the aspiration with dates, PQC key establishment across federal high-value assets by 31 December 2030, digital signatures by 31 December 2031, with a proposed FAR rule extending the 2030 obligation to contractors.[51] That five-year compression reflects no new certainty about hardware. It concedes the old deadline was calibrated against a distribution that has since moved and may move again. If you're still planning to 2035, you're planning toward a date your own regulator has abandoned. So, if the threat date cannot be fixed, what does a defensible plan look like? Several plans, held at once, with explicit triggers for moving between them.

Three-scenario quantum timeline framework

The following three-scenario framework provides the planning architecture for quantum security investment decisions. Each scenario reflects a distinct set of assumptions about the pace of quantum hardware progress and translates to different migration urgency levels for different data sensitivity categories.

Scenario	Nation-State CRQC	Commercial Access	Key Assumptions	Migration Urgency
Optimistic (Accelerated Progress)	2030-2033	2038-2042	Rapid error correction breakthroughs No fundamental physics obstacles Sustained investment acceleration DARPA QBI validates utility-scale by 2033	Immediate: Critical data assets require quantum-safe protection now HNDL attacks on highest-sensitivity archives are the primary near-term risk PQC migration should be at full operational pace
Central (Current Trajectory)	2033-2037	2042-2048	Steady but non-linear hardware progress Error correction overhead remains significant challenge China achieves first-mover capability US close behind	High: Long-lived sensitive data (10+ year confidentiality requirements) must begin migration now PQC migration planning and piloting underway HNDL risk immediate for highest-value data categories
Conservative (Delayed Progress)	2037-2045+	2048-2055+	Fundamental engineering obstacles persist longer than expected Fault-tolerant logical qubits prove harder to scale than current projections Significant setbacks in at least one major program	Moderate: Begin cryptographic inventory, PQC pilot deployments, and standards alignment immediately, HNDL risk real for highly sensitive data Migration can proceed at measured pace without crisis-level urgency

Table 10.2: Three-scenario quantum attack timeline framework

Key technical milestones as scenario indicators

Rather than waiting passively for experts to revise timeline forecasts, effective quantum risk monitoring programs track specific technical milestones that serve as leading indicators of scenario trajectory. Security leaders should monitor the following milestone categories as quantum hardware progress signals:

- Logical qubit counts: The number of fault-tolerant logical qubits demonstrated by leading programs (IBM, Google, Quantinuum, IonQ, D-Wave) is the most direct indicator of CRQC proximity. Track milestone announcements in IBM's Quantum Development Roadmap,[15] Google's published roadmap,[16] and DARPA's Quantum Benchmarking Initiative progress reports.[17]
- Physical qubit error rates: Physical error rates below approximately 10^{-3} per gate operation are generally required for a practical error correction overhead ratio. Announcements of error rate improvements from major quantum hardware programs signal progress toward fault tolerance.
- Coherence time milestones: Qubit coherence times (how long qubits maintain their quantum state) directly count computational depth. Milestone announcements showing sustained improvement in coherence times signal hardware maturation.
- Research preprint publications: arXiv.org's quant-ph category contains leading-edge quantum algorithm and hardware research.[18] Publications demonstrating improved Shor's algorithm implementations, error correction methods, or compilation efficiency can meaningfully shift timeline assessments.

Data sensitivity and longevity: calibrating HNDL urgency

The appropriate migration urgency depends critically on the intersection of your timeline scenario assessment and the sensitivity and longevity characteristics of your organization's data assets. A useful heuristic: if the confidentiality requirements for a specific data category extend beyond the earliest plausible date for CRQC availability (approximately 2030 under the Optimistic scenario), that data category faces HNDL exposure today.

Data Category	Confidentiality Horizon	HNDL Risk Today	Migration Priority
Classified national security communications	Indefinite / 25+ years	Critical	Immediate: migrate now regardless of timeline scenario

Data Category	Confidentiality Horizon	HNDL Risk Today	Migration Priority
Long-term patient health records / Genomic data	70+ years (lifetime)	High	Immediate for new data Prioritized migration for legacy archives
Financial transaction records / Banking archives	10-30 years regulatory	High	Urgent for records with 10+ year retention Immediate for highest-value transaction archives
Intellectual property / Trade secrets	Product lifecycle (5-20 years)	Moderate-High	Prioritize based on competitive value and product lifecycle horizon
Short-lived transactional / operational data	< 5 years	Low	Plan migration as part of standard system refresh cycles

Table 10.3: Data sensitivity and HNDL risk calibration matrix

Industry-specific quantum vulnerability

Quantum threats are not industry-agnostic. A hospital's quantum vulnerability profile looks nothing like a payment network's, which looks nothing like a defense contractor's. The data assets, regulatory frameworks, system architectures, and threat actor interests that characterize each sector create fundamentally different quantum risk configurations. Generic "your encryption is vulnerable" threat briefings are insufficient for the industry-specific prioritization that effective quantum security strategy requires.

This section profiles five high-exposure sectors with significant exposure to emerging security risks. For each sector, the focus is on the information security leaders need to make informed decisions about where to prioritize resources. This includes the most important vulnerable categories, the regulatory compliance requirements that create migration forcing functions, and the quantum threat actor interests that calibrate risk severity. Together, these factors provide a practical way to assess risk and determine where action may be needed the most.

Financial services: the most immediate and complex exposure

Financial services organizations face what is arguably the most acute quantum vulnerability profile of any commercial sector. The combination of high-value transaction data with long regulatory retention requirements, cryptographically secured payment protocol infrastructure, and intense nation-state adversary interest creates a three-dimensional quantum exposure that demands the most urgent and sophisticated response.

The HNDL threat for financial services is not theoretical. Transaction records, interbank communications, derivative pricing models, customer financial histories, and credit risk data are systematically archived under 7-30 year regulatory retention requirements, precisely the longevity profile that makes them valuable HNDL targets today. The Post-Quantum Financial Infrastructure Framework submitted to the SEC in 2025 noted that major financial institutions process transactions through 15,000+ cryptographic endpoints, all potentially vulnerable to HNDL attacks that are actively underway.[19]

Beyond archived data, financial services face quantum threats to the live cryptographic infrastructure underpinning payment network integrity. RSA and elliptic curve cryptography protect TLS sessions, digital signatures on transactions, and the certificate infrastructure that validates bank identities. A CRQC capable of rapidly compromising these would not merely decrypt historical data, it would undermine the real-time integrity of payment systems. Central bank digital currency regulators are beginning to address this proactively.

The regulatory landscape is tightening rapidly. The G7 Cyber Expert Group, co-chaired by the US Treasury and Bank of England, has urged financial authorities to establish quantum governance processes and PQC migration action plans.[20] In the EU, NIS2 Directive transposition requirements,[21] which broadened mandatory cybersecurity standards to financial market infrastructure by October 2024, will increasingly intersect with PQC migration mandates.[22] The US Quantum Computing Cybersecurity Preparedness Act mandates full cryptographic inventories by 2027.[23]

Healthcare: long-lived data, long-term consequences

Healthcare organizations manage some of the longest-lived sensitive data in any sector. A genomic sequence captured today could remain medically relevant for a patient's entire 70-plus-year lifetime. Mental health records, HIV status, genetic disease markers, and reproductive health information create deeply personal quantum vulnerability, if HNDL adversaries successfully collect and later decrypt this data, the harm to individuals would be permanent and irreversible.

The healthcare sector's quantum vulnerability is amplified by two structural factors: legacy system prevalence and medical device security constraints. Many healthcare organizations operate electronic health record systems and medical device platforms that were architected without cryptographic agility, meaning the path to post-quantum cryptography is not a simple algorithm swap but a complex system modernization challenge. Medical devices with 10-15 year operational lifecycles, deployed in clinical settings where interruption for software updates carries patient safety risk, represent particularly difficult quantum migration targets.

HIPAA's "minimum necessary" and data protection standards do not yet explicitly address post-quantum cryptography, but the regulatory trajectory is clear. Organizations handling genomic data, increasingly valuable for precision medicine applications, face particular scrutiny. The convergence of genomic data with identity information creates quantum-era biosecurity risks that extend beyond individual patient privacy to population-level health intelligence concerns that nation-state adversaries would find extremely valuable.

Government and defense: the highest-stake exposure

Government and defense organizations managing classified information face the most acute quantum threat of any sector, and in many cases, they are already in migration mode. The US National Security Memorandum 10 (NSM-10), signed in May 2022,[24] establishes an explicit mandate for federal agencies to migrate to quantum-resistant cryptography, with NSA's Commercial National Security Algorithm Suite (CNSA 2.0)[25] requiring phased PQC migration for national security systems between 2024 and 2033.[26]

The HNDL threat for government and defense is the most serious in the ecosystem. Communications classified at the secret and top-secret levels that were encrypted and transmitted years or decades ago may already have been collected by adversary signals intelligence programs. The US intelligence community's assessment is that nation-state adversaries, primarily China, are prioritizing HNDL collection of national security-relevant communications, strategic planning documents, and technical intelligence on sensitive defense programs.[27]

For defense contractors and cleared organizations in the defense industrial base, the quantum threat extends beyond their own data to the security of classified programs they support. Defense contractors operating under DFARS[28] and CMMC[29] cybersecurity requirements should anticipate PQC compliance requirements being incorporated into future contract requirements and begin proactive migration planning to avoid being disqualified from sensitive defense work due to quantum-inadequate cryptography posture.

Critical infrastructure: authentication and control system integrity

Critical infrastructure sectors, energy, water, transportation, telecommunications, face a quantum vulnerability profile that differs fundamentally from data-centric sectors. The primary concern is not long-lived data archive exposure but the integrity of authentication and communication systems that protect industrial control systems and SCADA networks. A CRQC-enabled adversary that could forge digital signatures or decrypt control system communications in real time could manipulate physical infrastructure in ways that cause catastrophic operational consequences.

The challenge for critical infrastructure operators is the operational technology (OT) environment. Industrial control systems and SCADA networks often run on hardware and software with operational lifetimes measured in decades, updating these systems requires scheduled maintenance windows and carries plant safety risks, and the cryptographic protocols embedded in industrial communication standards are not designed for algorithmic agility. Critical infrastructure organizations must begin quantum vulnerability assessments of their OT environments now, with the recognition that remediation will require longer lead times than equivalent IT environment transitions.

Technology companies: intellectual property at risk

Technology companies face a quantum threat that is less immediately intuitive but strategically significant: the long-term security of encrypted intellectual property archives. Source code repositories, patent applications, algorithm documentation, product roadmaps, and trade secrets encrypted today and stored for compliance or historical reference purposes could become accessible to quantum-capable adversaries in the future. For companies with strong intellectual property moats, where competitive advantage depends on the secrecy of proprietary algorithms, materials formulations, or product architectures, HNDL risk against IP archives is a genuine strategic threat.

Technology companies also face quantum vulnerability through their customer-facing cryptographic infrastructure, code signing certificates validating software integrity, and API authentication keys protecting customer data, all potentially vulnerable to quantum-enabled attacks. As the companies that build and operate the cryptographic infrastructure that other sectors depend upon, technology companies carry a systemic responsibility for quantum-safe transition that extends beyond their own risk posture to the ecosystem security of their customers.

The following industry-specific vulnerability heat map provides an at-a-glance view of sectors most exposed to quantum-era cyber risks. It assesses the relative threat from HNDL attacks, risks to live operational systems, regulatory pressure, and legacy OT/IT constraints, while identifying likely primary threat actors. Use this table as a starting point, rather than a static assessment. Your organization should regularly update its sector profile based on evolving threat intelligence, cryptographic dependencies, regulatory requirements, critical assets, and technology modernization progress.

Sector	HNDL Risk	Live System Risk	Regulatory Pressure	Legacy OT/IT Challenge	Primary Threat Actor
Financial Services	Critical	High	High (G7, NIS2, DORA)	Moderate	Nation-states Future QaaS criminal actors
Healthcare	Critical	Moderate	Moderate (HIPAA evolution)	High (legacy devices)	Nation-states (genomic intelligence) Future QaaS actors
Government / Defense	Critical High	High	Critical (NSM-10, CNSA 2.0)	Moderate-High	China Russia (primary) All state actors
Critical Infrastructure	Moderate	Critical	Growing (CISA directives)	Critical (decade-long OT cycles)	China Russia (strategic disruption)
Technology Companies	High (IP archives)	High (customer infra)	Moderate (ecosystem responsibility)	Low-Moderate	China (IP theft) Nation-state broadly

Table 10.4: Industry-specific quantum vulnerability heat map

Company spotlights: quantum security in practice

The following company spotlights illustrate how global financial institutions and critical-technology leaders are turning quantum strategy into a real-world capability. JPMorgan Chase, Thales, and HSBC demonstrate complementary approaches, from post-quantum cryptography and quantum key distribution to quantum-safe infrastructure, secure financial products, and enterprise-wide readiness. Each illustrates that quantum resilience is becoming a strategic business imperative rather than solely a future compliance concern.

JPMorgan Chase: building the quantum-secured financial network

JPMorgan Chase, the largest US bank by assets,[30] has moved beyond quantum risk assessment into genuine implementation, making it one of the most instructive examples of what proactive quantum security leadership looks like in a systemically important financial institution. The bank's quantum security program reflects exactly the kind of strategic, multi-layered approach that the threat landscape demands: combining post-quantum cryptography with quantum key distribution, operating in hybrid deployment architectures, and building institutional capability rather than waiting for the threat to crystallize.

The bank's most significant public demonstration is the deployment of a high-speed quantum-secured, crypto-agile network (Q-CAN) in Singapore, linking data centers over existing fiber with PQC-enabled key exchange. Lori Beer, Global CIO at JPMorgan Chase, described the strategic intent explicitly: "We are preparing a dual demonstration strategy that incorporates both post-quantum cryptography and QKD. This deployment of a high-speed quantum-secured crypto-agile network could enable novel security features beyond secure key exchange."[31] The Singapore deployment demonstrated that QKD can support high-speed private networks in production-level financial services environments, taking quantum security out of the laboratory and into operational infrastructure. Earlier work with Toshiba and Ciena on a metropolitan QKD network operating at 800 Gbps demonstrated real-time eavesdropping detection for banking data over standard fiber.[32]

The key lessons from JPMorgan Chase's approach are methodological as much as technical. First, the bank did not wait for NIST standards finalization to begin implementation, it operated in hybrid mode, testing and deploying PQC alongside existing cryptography while standards evolved. Second, it explicitly chose a crypto-agile architecture that allows algorithmic updates without infrastructure replacement. Third, it treated quantum security as a technology leadership opportunity, the Singapore QKD deployment was presented at the 2024 Optical Fiber Communication Conference, demonstrating that quantum security capability is also a competitive and reputational asset in financial services contexts.

For security leaders in financial services and other high-stakes sectors, JPMorgan Chase's experience offers a practical template: start with a cryptographic inventory, identify the highest-value data communication assets for early migration, deploy hybrid PQC/classical implementations to build operational confidence, and architect for crypto-agility so that future algorithm updates are routine rather than disruptive. The quantum-secured network deployment is not the destination; it's the beginning of a continuous cryptographic modernization program.

Thales: Europe's quantum-safe infrastructure champion

Thales, the French defense and technology conglomerate, represents the most comprehensive European example of an organization that has positioned quantum security as a core business capability rather than a compliance obligation. With more than €4 billion invested in R&D in 2024 alone, spanning cybersecurity, quantum technologies, and defense electronics, and operations across 68 countries, Thales sits at the intersection of the quantum threat landscape and the quantum security solution ecosystem.[33]

Thales's quantum security engagements span multiple dimensions. On the standards side, Thales researchers co-authored the FALCON digital signature algorithm, one of NIST's selected post-quantum cryptography candidates, giving the company deep technical insight into PQC implementation characteristics that most practitioners lack. The company participates in NIST's National Cybersecurity Center of Excellence Migration to PQC Project, contributing products for interoperability testing. It's a member of EuroQCI, the EU-wide quantum communication infrastructure project, and sits on multiple PQC consortiums in North America and Europe including RESQUE, the Post-Quantum Cryptography Alliance, and the PKI Consortium.[34]

The operational demonstration that most directly illustrates Thales's practical capabilities came in early 2026, when the company demonstrated remote deployment of post-quantum cryptography on SIM and eSIM cards to enhance 5G network security without replacing devices or interrupting service. This crypto-agile over-the-air update capability directly addresses one of the most challenging aspects of quantum migration: how to upgrade cryptography into billions of deployed devices at scale. The demonstration's significance extends well beyond telecommunications, any sector with large, deployed device populations facing quantum migration challenges (healthcare devices, industrial control systems, IoT infrastructure) should study the Thales approach as an architectural model.[35]

The business lesson from Thales is strategic positioning: the company has made quantum security readiness a differentiator in its defense and government contracts, a product line driver in its cybersecurity business, and a research priority that strengthens its technical credibility across its entire customer base. The EU's growing regulatory requirements for PQC migration, with the NIS Cooperation Group targeting full critical system transitions by 2030, directly benefit organizations like Thales that are ahead of the migration curve. For European organizations considering quantum security investment, Thales demonstrates that proactive quantum engagement is not just risk management but business development strategy.

HSBC: from gold tokenization to quantum-safe banking infrastructure

HSBC's quantum security journey is particularly instructive because it spans both the cryptographic defense dimension, protecting existing banking infrastructure, and the quantum opportunity dimension, using quantum-generated cryptographic keys to strengthen new financial products. The bank has moved through multiple phases of quantum engagement, each building organizational capability and technical confidence for broader deployment.

In 2024, HSBC made headlines with two distinct quantum security demonstrations. In the first, the bank piloted quantum-safe cryptography for tokenized assets, using PQC algorithms including CRYSTALS-Dilithium signatures to secure the transfer of digital tokens representing physical gold on its distributed ledger platform, achieving 1,000 transactions per second with Dilithium signatures and receiving Financial Conduct Authority regulatory sandbox approval.[36] In the second, HSBC used QKD alongside PQC in a simulated €30 million foreign exchange trade, becoming the first bank to trial quantum-safe protection of a trading terminal. The bank also joined PayPal in a working group on quantum-safe cryptography for payments, signaling a collaborative rather than proprietary approach to financial sector quantum security standards.

The partnership with Quantinuum, using Quantinuum's Quantum Origin platform, which deploys quantum-computing-generated entropy to strengthen classical cryptographic keys, illustrates an approach that is immediately deployable without waiting for PQC migration to be complete. By deploying quantum-strengthened key generation on existing classical infrastructure, HSBC added a quantum security layer to current operations while longer-term PQC migration work continues. This pragmatic "defend now, migrate continuously" approach is accessible to organizations that feel paralyzed by the scope of full PQC migration.[37]

HSBC's quantum program offers three key implementation insights for security leaders in financial services and beyond. First, start with specific high-value use cases, tokenized assets, trading terminal security, rather than attempting system-wide migration. Second, use regulatory sandbox environments to test quantum-safe implementations before full deployment, building regulatory confidence alongside technical confidence. Third, approach quantum security collaboratively, HSBC's willingness to share its experiences publicly and urge others to "move forward together" reflects a recognition that financial sector quantum security is a collective challenge where industry-wide progress serves all participants. Organizations that wait for competitors to solve the problem first will find themselves behind regulatory and technical curves when quantum security requirements become mandatory.

Continuous quantum risk monitoring and threat intelligence integration

If you conduct a comprehensive quantum threat assessment today, file the resulting report, and revisit it in three years, you will find it has aged badly. The quantum threat landscape evolves on timelines measured in months, not years. Hardware milestone announcements, research preprints demonstrating improved quantum algorithms, intelligence community reassessments of nation-state program progress, and new NIST standards guidance all have the potential to materially change your organization's quantum risk posture. Quantum risk assessment is not a project; it's an ongoing discipline.

Why point-in-time assessments are insufficient

The continuous quantum risk monitoring framework in this section organizes monitoring activity across four domains, each with distinct source types, monitoring frequencies, and escalation triggers. The framework is designed to integrate into existing threat intelligence platforms and security operations workflows rather than requiring dedicated quantum-specific infrastructure.

Monitoring Domain	Key Sources	Monitoring Frequency	Escalation Triggers
Hardware Progress Monitoring	• IBM Quantum Roadmap • Google Quantum AI blog • Microsoft Azure Quantum • arXiv.org quant-ph • DARPA QBI progress reports • Nature/Science publications	• Weekly scan • Monthly synthesis report	• Logical qubit count doubles in any major program • Physical error rates fall below 10^{-3} • Major hardware vendor announces accelerated roadmap • Independent replication of claimed breakthroughs

Monitoring Domain	Key Sources	Monitoring Frequency	Escalation Triggers
Adversary Intelligence Monitoring	• Intelligence Community assessments • NSA/CISA advisories • FBI alerts • NATO CCDCOE publications • Academic research on nation-state quantum programs • Classified feeds (for cleared organizations)	• Weekly scan • Immediate escalation on significant developments	• IC timeline assessment revisions • Nation-state quantum program announcements of major capability milestones • New HNDL attack evidence or attribution • Adversary quantum workforce or facility expansion signals
Standards and Research Monitoring	• NIST PQC project website • IETF working group publications • ETSI Quantum Cryptography Technical Committee • Academic cryptanalysis preprints • Vendor security advisories on PQC implementation	• Weekly for NIST/ IETF • Ongoing for arXiv preprints	• New NIST PQC standard finalization or deprecation • Cryptanalytic attack against selected PQC algorithm • IETF RFC publication for PQC protocol integration • Regulatory deadline announcements

Monitorin g Domain	Key Sources	Monitoring Frequency	Escalation Triggers
Incident and Threat Actor Monitoring	• Threat intelligence platform feeds • ISAC sharing networks • CISA advisories • FBI flash reports • Dark web monitoring for encrypted data exposure • Incident response partner intelligence	• Continuous • Daily review of high-priority alerts	• Incident with suspected quantum-relevant data exfiltration patterns • Evidence of systematic HNDL data collection • Operations • Quantum-capable threat actor infrastructure expansion • Sector-specific data breach patterns suggesting HNDL targeting

Table 10.5: Continuous quantum risk monitoring framework, four-domain architecture

Integrating quantum intelligence into existing platforms

The most practical approach to quantum threat intelligence integration is not building a dedicated quantum monitoring team or platform but extending existing threat intelligence infrastructure to incorporate quantum-relevant sources and taxonomy. Most enterprise threat intelligence platforms and Governance, Risk, and Compliance (GRC) systems can accommodate quantum threat intelligence with modest configuration changes.

For threat intelligence platforms, the key integration steps are: establishing a quantum threat actor profile taxonomy that maps nation-state quantum programs to existing threat actor tracking; creating quantum hardware milestone watch lists that trigger analyst attention when specific milestones are reported; configuring quantum-relevant keyword monitoring across existing open-source intelligence feeds (academic publication RSS, government announcement monitoring, vendor blog tracking); and establishing a quantum threat intelligence report template for regular distribution to security operations, risk management, and executive audiences.

For GRC systems, quantum risk integration requires establishing a quantum risk taxonomy entry with defined risk factors, likelihood drivers, and impact categories; configuring quantum risk indicators that feed into existing risk scoring and reporting frameworks; and establishing a quantum key risk indicator (KRI) dashboard that provides board-level visibility into quantum risk status without requiring deep technical knowledge. Standard GRC platforms including ServiceNow GRC,[38] Archer Technologies (formerly RSA Archer),[39] and MetricStream[40] can accommodate quantum risk taxonomy entries using existing framework extensibility features.

Calibrating intelligence products for different audiences

A single quantum threat intelligence report serves no audience well. Security operations teams need tactical indicators and monitoring guidance. Risk management leaders need quantified risk metrics and migration progress tracking. Executives and boards need strategic context and decision-support framing. Designing your quantum threat intelligence production workflow to serve all three audience types with appropriately calibrated content is essential for organizational quantum risk governance effectiveness.

Audience	Format	Frequency	Key Content Elements	Distributions
Security Operations	Technical alert / Advisory	As-needed / weekly	Specific monitoring indicators New sources to add Technical milestone details Adversary capability updates with operational relevance	SOC leads Cryptography engineers Architecture team
Risk Management / CISO	Monthly risk update	Monthly	Scenario trajectory assessment Migration program status Risk metric updates Regulatory landscape changes Emerging threat developments requiring strategy adjustments	CISO Risk committee CTO Compliance leads
Executive / Board	Quarterly risk dashboard + Annual deep dive	Quarterly + Annual	Quantum risk position vs. risk appetite Migration program progress and investment Peer/competitor posture benchmarking Regulatory compliance status Key strategic decisions required	Board Risk Committee CEO CFO General Counsel

Table 10.6: Quantum threat intelligence distribution matrix by audience

Quantum risk quantification and enterprise risk integration

Imagine walking into your board's risk committee and saying, "We face a significant quantum computing threat to our cryptographic infrastructure with a 17-34% probability of materialization by 2034." The room will nod thoughtfully, ask a few polite questions, and then return to the capital allocation decisions they came to discuss. The problem is not that board members don't care about quantum risk, it's that "17-34% probability" is not a risk management input. It's a technical probability. To function in board-level risk governance, quantum risk needs to be expressed in the financial metrics that risk committees actually use to make capital allocation decisions.

The translation problem: from technical threat to financial risk

Quantifying quantum risk in financial terms is genuinely challenging, the timeline uncertainty is substantial, the impact scenarios are severe, and the variables involved resist simple modeling. But "difficult to quantify" is not the same as "impossible to quantify," and the alternative, expressing loss dollars, consistently produces underinvestment. This section presents practical quantification methodologies that produce usable financial risk metrics without pretending to be more precise than the underlying data supports.

Probabilistic timeline modeling: converting uncertainty into distributions

The starting point for quantum risk quantification is converting the scenario-based timeline framework from a section on quantum attack timeline projections into a probability distribution over when cryptographically relevant quantum computing could emerge. Using the Global Risk Institute's expert survey results as calibration inputs, a 17-34% probability of CRQC by 2034 and approximately 79% by 2044, security leaders can estimate the likelihood of CRQC emergence across different time windows and connect those probabilities to the potential financial impact of compromise for specific data and system categories.[41]

For each time window, multiply the estimated probability of CRQC emergence by the potential loss associated with the affected assets. Summing those values produces an annualized expected loss estimate that can be compared with other cyber risk already competing for investment. The numbers will never be perfectly precise, but that isn't the goal. The goal is to create a credible, financially grounded estimate that leadership can use to make decisions.

This should be treated as a clear executive action item: calculate the organization's expected quantum-related loss and put that number on the first page of the investment case presented to the board. Boards may not need every technical detail behind the model, but they will understand the financial exposure, the cost of reducing it, and the decision being requested. That single figure can become the anchor for the broader discussion on funding, timing, and risk acceptance.

Scenario-based loss estimation for HNDL attacks

For organizations with high-value long-lived data assets, HNDL scenario analysis provides a more immediate financial risk quantification approach than timeline-dependent expected loss modeling. HNDL risk is current, if adversaries are collecting your encrypted data today, the financial exposure exists today regardless of CRQC timeline uncertainty.

A practical HNDL loss scenario framework estimates potential losses across three categories: direct financial losses (fraudulent transaction losses enabled by compromised payment system cryptography, IP theft value in terms of R&D investment and competitive revenue impact); regulatory and compliance losses (GDPR, HIPAA, and sector-specific regulatory penalties triggered by quantum-enabled data breach; class action settlement exposure for patient or customer data compromise); and reputational and business impact (customer attrition, brand value erosion, and partner confidence loss following a quantum-enabled breach). The following quantum risk quantification method selection table should provide some useful guidance.

Risk Quantification Method	What to Use	Key Inputs Required	Output Metric
Probabilistic Timeline Modeling	• Annual quantum risk portfolio comparison • Capital allocation discussions	• CRQC timeline probability distribution • Data asset inventory • Asset-specific loss estimates	• Annualized Expected Loss (AEL) • Loss Exceedance Probability (LEP) curve by data category

Risk Quantification Method	What to Use	Key Inputs Required	Output Metric
HNDL Scenario Loss Estimation	• Immediate board reporting • High-value data asset prioritization	• Encrypted data archive inventory • Regulatory penalty benchmarks • IP competitive value estimates • Incident cost benchmarks	• Scenario-specific loss range (low/base/ high) • Value at Risk (VaR) for HNDL scenarios
Migration Cost-Benefit Analysis	• PQC investment approval • Program prioritization decisions	• Migration cost estimates by system category • Risk reduction estimates per migration phase • Regulatory compliance cost avoidance	• Net Present Value (NPV) of migration program • Return on Security Investment (ROSI) by migration phase

Risk Quantification Method	What to Use	Key Inputs Required	Output Metric
Comparative Risk Benchmarking	• Portfolio risk context • Relative priority communication	• Existing cyber risk portfolio metrics • Industry metrics • Industry quantum readiness benchmarks • Peer organization posture intelligence	• Quantum risk rank within enterprise cyber risk portfolio • Relative gap to industry quantum readiness peer benchmark

Table 10.7: Quantum risk quantification method selection guide

Board-level quantum risk reporting design

The best quantum risk reporting for a board risk committee should be simple, visual, and easy to connect to the decisions the board already makes. Board members do not need a deep explanation of cryptographic tools or migration methodology. They need to understand what has changed, what the organization is doing about it, whether those actions are reducing risk, and what decisions may be needed next.

A useful way to think about the reporting is through three straightforward questions: What have we accomplished? What is it doing for the organization? And how is it making the organization safer?

- **Start with where the organization stands**: Rather than leading with technical activity, show the board how the organization's quantum risk position has changed since the last reporting period. If a cryptographic inventory is 60% complete, for example, explain what that means in practical terms: which critical systems have been reviewed, what vulnerabilities were uncovered, and which areas now have a migration plan. The board should be able to see progress, not just activity.
- **Show what is being protected**: Connect quantum-readiness work directly to the assets that matter most to the organization. That could include customer information, financial data, intellectual property, sensitive communications, digital identities,

operational systems, or critical infrastructure. This helps the board understand what its investment is actually protecting and why the work matters.

- **Connect risk to financial impact**: Whenever possible, translate quantum risk into financial and business terms that are already familiar to the board. Expected Loss, Value at Risk, Loss Exceedance Probability, potential business interruption, regulatory penalties, and remediation costs can help put quantum risk alongside other enterprise risks. The goal is not to create false precision, but to give decision-makers enough context to judge whether the level of investment matches the level of exposure.
- **Show whether the organization is getting safer**: A single risk score does not tell much of a story. Reporting should show the direction of travel. Is exposure decreasing, staying the same, or increasing? Metrics such as the percentage of critical systems inventoried, the number of high-risk cryptographic dependencies remaining, the percentage of priority systems with migration plans, and the number of key vendors assessed can help demonstrate whether current investments are reducing risk.
- **Explain how each action helps**: It should be clear why the organization is funding each major activity. Cryptographic discovery helps uncover vulnerabilities that might otherwise remain hidden. Crypto-agility makes future algorithm changes easier and less disruptive. Post-quantum migration helps protect long-lived sensitive information. Vendor assessments reduce third-party exposure. Updated procurement standards help prevent new vulnerable technologies from entering the environment. These connections make it easier for the board to see the value behind the work.
- **Tie progress to external deadlines**: Regulatory and standards milestones are important, but simply listing dates is not enough. The board should understand what needs to happen before those dates, how much time remains, and what could happen if the organization falls behind. This helps turn an abstract future deadline into a clear planning and accountability issue.
- **Be clear about what is still exposed**: Good reporting should also show where risk remains. Legacy systems, difficult-to-upgrade technologies, third-party dependencies, long-retention data, and systems with long replacement cycles may continue to create exposure even as other areas improve. The board needs a realistic picture of what has been addressed and what still needs attention.
- **End with the decisions that matter**: The report should make it easy for the board to see where its input is needed. That may include approving additional funding, accelerating a migration effort, changing procurement requirements, updating risk appetite, requiring vendors to demonstrate post-quantum readiness, or accepting a

defined level of residual risk. Where possible, each decision should include the expected benefit, cost, timing, and consequence of waiting.

Ultimately, a strong board report should allow a director to quickly answer a few simple questions: What has improved since the last report? What are the current investments protecting? Where are we still exposed? Are we moving fast enough? And what decision do we need to make next?

That is what turns quantum risk reporting from a technical update into something far more useful: a clear view of whether the organization is becoming more resilient and whether the investments being made are delivering real protection.

Core analytical and leadership competencies

The following takeaways represent the core analytical and leadership competencies built through engagement with this chapter's frameworks, case studies, and methodologies. These skills are practical, transferable, and immediately applicable to your organization's quantum security program. I've listed them here in compact chunks for your convenience.

Quantum threat intelligence analysis

Effective quantum threat intelligence requires critically evaluating a complex and often contradictory information environment. Vendor quantum hardware announcements are systematically optimistic, IBM's roadmap, Google's benchmark claims, and Microsoft's qubit announcements should all be evaluated against independent peer review, replication evidence, and third-party technical assessments before being used as planning inputs. A practical discipline: whenever you read a quantum hardware milestone announcement, ask three questions: Has this been independently replicated? What is the gap between this milestone and fault-tolerant logical qubit counts required for CRQC capability? And does this advance the capability of a threat actor who targets my organization? The answers to those three questions determine whether a headline-generating quantum announcement requires a strategy adjustment or simply a monitoring note.

Scenario-based quantum risk planning

The goal of scenario-based risk planning is not to pick the "right" timeline scenario but to design a security investment portfolio that provides acceptable protection under all three scenarios without overinvesting based on worst-case assumptions. A practical test: for each major quantum security investment your organization is considering, ask whether it delivers value under the Conservative scenario (long timelines). If an investment only makes sense under the Optimistic scenario, it may be premature. If it makes sense across all three scenarios, it is likely well-calibrated. Scenario planning workshops with executive and board audiences should explicitly surface the range of timeline uncertainty and build organizational shared understanding of why the uncertainty exists, not to create too much quantum anxiety, but to establish that rational action is possible and necessary regardless of which scenario proves correct.

Industry vulnerability assessment leadership

Leading a quantum vulnerability assessment for your industry requires more than applying a generic framework. It means bringing together the people who understand how your organization works, including its data, regulatory obligations, vendors, and operational constraints. A practical place to start is with a cross-functional quantum vulnerability working group that includes representatives from data governance, cybersecurity, compliance, enterprise architecture, procurement or vendor management, and operations. Each brings a different part of the picture: what information needs to be protected and for how long, which regulatory requirements apply, where vulnerable cryptography may be embedded, which third parties create dependencies, and how difficult particular systems may be to update or replace. This approach aligns with guidance from NIST and the Cybersecurity and Infrastructure Security Agency, which encourages organizations to identify their use of quantum-vulnerable cryptography, prepare cryptographic inventories, engage technology vendors, and examine supply-chain dependencies as part of preparing for post-quantum migration.[52, 53]

The goal of the working group should be to create an organization-specific quantum-safe exposure map, or PQC risk and dependency map. Rather than simply listing vulnerable algorithms, the map should connect critical systems and business processes to the cryptography they depend on, the sensitivity and expected lifetime of the data being protected, third-party and vendor dependencies, migration complexity, and the potential business impact of compromise. NIST's National Cybersecurity Center of Excellence specifically identifies understanding where quantum-vulnerable public-key cryptography is being used across hardware, software, and services as an important part of developing a prioritized migration roadmap.[52] The result is something much more useful to leadership than a technical inventory alone because it begins to answer not only what is vulnerable, but what matters most and where migration should begin.

Organizations don't have to start from scratch. Industry frameworks and sector-specific resources can provide a useful foundation. In financial services, for example, FS-ISAC has developed resources covering cryptographic infrastructure inventory, PQC risk modeling, cryptographic agility, and current and future-state planning.[54] These resources show how sector-level guidance can help organizations structure their own assessments, but they can't provide a complete picture of the systems, vendors, data, and dependencies inside any one company. That organization-specific layer is what turns an industry framework into an actionable business tool.

The same principle becomes even more important in environments where systems can't simply be patched or replaced. CISA's guidance for operational technology highlights the challenges that long equipment lifecycles, availability requirements, legacy systems, and upgrade limitations can create for PQC migration.[55] A hospital, financial institution, manufacturer, utility, government agency, and technology company may therefore reach very different migration priorities even when they're using some of the same cryptographic technologies. That's why understanding the operational context matters just as much as discovering the cryptography itself.

The complete quantum-safe exposure map should ultimately give leaders a clear view of your systems, your data, your dependencies, and your migration challenges. It should help answer a handful of practical questions: Where are we most exposed? Which information needs protection for the longest period of time? Which systems should be addressed first? Which vendors are we depending on to make the transition? What will be the most difficult or expensive to migrate? And where should we begin investing now rather than waiting? External reports and frameworks help establish what good preparation looks like. The internal exposure map turns that guidance into a prioritized plan that reflects the reality of your organization.

Risk quantification and board communication

The most important communication skill for quantum risk governance is the ability to translate between two very different languages: the technical language of quantum computing (qubits, error rates, Shor's algorithm) and the financial language of enterprise risk management (expected loss, value at risk, capital allocation). Security leaders who master this translation become effective quantum risk advocates in the boardroom. A practical starting point: take your existing cyber risk portfolio reporting format and add a quantum risk row with financial metrics calculated using the HNDL scenario loss estimation methodology from *Quantum risk quantification and enterprise risk integration* section. This approach leverages existing board familiarity with the reporting format while introducing quantum risk as a quantified, comparable risk category, rather than an exotic technical concern requiring a special briefing.

Threat intelligence program design for quantum monitoring

Designing a sustainable quantum threat intelligence monitoring program requires defining intelligence requirements before selecting sources and tools. Start with the questions your organization's quantum security decision-makers most need answered: What is the current trajectory on quantum hardware development timelines? Are there new signals of HNDL activity targeting our industry? Have NIST or other standards bodies issued guidance that changes our migration priorities? What is the current regulatory enforcement landscape for PQC requirements in our operating jurisdictions? Each of these intelligence requirements maps to specific source categories, monitoring frequencies, and analyst responsibilities. A program design that starts with requirements rather than sources is more likely to deliver actionable intelligence than one that monitors quantum news broadly and hopes something relevant surfaces.

Summary

This chapter has established the quantum threat intelligence and risk assessment architecture that enables security leaders to make dynamically calibrated, evidence-based quantum security investment decisions. The journey through this chapter has moved from threat landscape mapping to timeline scenario planning, industry-specific vulnerability analysis, continuous monitoring architecture, and board-level risk quantification, building a comprehensive analytical capability that transforms quantum threat awareness into operational security strategy.

The central insight running through each section is that quantum security demands the same analytical rigor as any mature threat domain. The adversaries are real and identifiable: China's $15.3 billion quantum program, Russia's constrained but engaged national program, and the emerging democratized threat of quantum-as-a-service. The attack vector, Harvest Now, Decrypt Later, is active today, making the urgency of quantum risk assessment immediate rather than speculative. The timeline uncertainty is genuine and should be engaged honestly through scenario-based planning rather than hidden behind false precision or dismissed through dangerous denial.

Industry-specific vulnerability analysis has shown that quantum threats manifest very differently across sectors, and that generic "your encryption is vulnerable" threat briefings are insufficient for the prioritization decisions that effective quantum security programs require. JPMorgan Chase's quantum-secured financial network, Thales's crypto-agile defense infrastructure and over-the-air PQC update capability, and HSBC's tokenized asset security program demonstrate that practical quantum security implementation is achievable today, organizations do not need to wait for quantum hardware to arrive to begin building quantum-safe cryptographic postures.

The continuous monitoring framework and risk quantification methodologies developed in this chapter ensure that quantum risk assessment does not become a static artifact but an evolving intelligence product that keeps pace with the rapidly advancing quantum technology landscape. Organizations that invest in quantum threat intelligence programs will be positioned to detect accelerating quantum hardware progress early, adjust migration priorities dynamically in response to evolving threat conditions, and maintain the board-level visibility and accountability required for effective quantum risk governance across multi-year security transformation programs.

The readiness posture built through this chapter: a living quantum threat assessment, a scenario-calibrated risk model, an industry-specific vulnerability map, a continuous monitoring program, and a board-ready risk quantification framework, is the essential analytical foundation for everything that follows. However, knowing your quantum risk exposure with precision is only half the challenge. The other half, how to actually reduce that exposure through operational security transformation, is the subject of the next chapter.

Chapter 11, Seamless Security Integration Strategy, addresses the operational dimension of quantum-safe security implementation that this chapter's threat assessment makes necessary. Understanding that your organization has critical quantum vulnerabilities across its financial archives, patient record systems, or classified communications infrastructure is one thing. Implementing post-quantum cryptography across those environments, while maintaining the service availability, system performance, and user experience that business operations depend upon, is an entirely different and equally demanding challenge. The next chapter provides the phased deployment methodologies, legacy system protection strategies, business continuity frameworks, and organizational change management approaches that translate the threat intelligence literacy developed here into operational quantum security transformation. The goal is not merely to know your quantum risk, it's to close it, systematically and without disruption.

Further reading

1. `https://www.heritage.org/big-tech/report/beating-china-the-race-quantum-supremacy`
2. `https://www.uscc.gov/research/vying-quantum-supremacy-us-china-competition-quantum-technologies`
3. `https://phys.org/news/2021-01-world-quantum-network.html`
4. `https://www.csis.org/analysis/understanding-chinas-quest-quantum-advancement`
5. `https://www.fbi.gov/news/stories/protecting-quantum-science-and-technology`
6. `https://www.quantum.gov/wp-content/uploads/2024/12/NQI-Annual-Report-FY2025.pdf`
7. `https://www.mckinsey.de/capabilities/tech-and-ai/our-insights/the-year-of-quantum-from-concept-to-reality-in-2025`

8. https://www.oecd.org/en/publications/an-overview-of-national-strategies-and-policies-for-quantum-technologies_5e55e7ab-en/full-report/component-4.html
9. https://www.heritage.org/big-tech/report/beating-china-the-race-quantum-supremacy
10. https://www.fbi.gov/news/stories/protecting-quantum-science-and-technology
11. https://digital-strategy.ec.europa.eu/en/library/quantum-europe-strategy
12. https://www.bis.org/publ/othp107.pdf
13. https://www.evolutionq.com/publications/quantum-threat-timeline-research-report-2024
14. https://doi.org/10.1116/5.0073075
15. http://ibm.com/roadmaps/quantum/2026/
16. https://quantumai.google/roadmap
17. https://www.darpa.mil/research/programs/quantum-benchmarking-initiative
18. https://arxiv.org/list/quant-ph/recent
19. https://www.sec.gov/files/cft-written-input-daniel-bruno-corvelo-costa-090325.pdf
20. https://home.treasury.gov/news/press-releases/sb035
21. https://eur-lex.europa.eu/eli/dir/2022/2555/en
22. https://www.bis.org/publ/othp107.pdf
23. https://www.congress.gov/bill/117th-congress/house-bill/7535/summary/55
24. https://www.congress.gov/crs_external_products/IN/PDF/IN11921/IN11921.3.pdf
25. https://media.defense.gov/2025/May/30/2003728741/-1/-1/0/CSA_CNSA_2.0_ALGORITHMS.PDF
26. https://doi.org/10.6028/NIST.IR.8547.ipd
27. https://www.uscc.gov/research/vying-quantum-supremacy-us-china-competition-quantum-technologies

28. https://www.federalregister.gov/documents/2025/09/10/2025-17359/defense-federal-acquisition-regulation-supplement-assessing-contractor-implementation-of
29. https://dodcio.defense.gov/cmmc/About/
30. https://www.usnews.com/banking/articles/biggest-banks-in-america
31. https://www.jpmorgan.com/technology/news/firm-establishes-quantum-secured-crypto-agile-network
32. https://www.jpmorganchase.com/newsroom/press-releases/2022/jpmc-toshiba-ciena-build-first-quantum-key-distribution-network
33. https://cpl.thalesgroup.com/blog/encryption/luna-hsm-pqc-quantum-safe-encryption
34. https://cpl.thalesgroup.com/resources/encryption/post-quantum-cryptography-solutions-white-paper
35. https://quantumzeitgeist.com/thales-post-quantum-cryptography/
36. https://www.isaca.org/resources/isaca-journal/issues/2025/volume-6/building-resilient-security-in-the-age-of-quantum-computing
37. https://www.quantinuum.com/press-releases/hsbc-and-quantinuum-explore-real-world-use-cases-of-quantum-computing-in-financial-services
38. https://www.servicenow.com/docs/r/xanadu/governance-risk-compliance/grc-risk-management-workspace/grc-risk-dashboards.html
39. https://www.archerirm.com/
40. https://www.metricstream.com/
41. https://globalriskinstitute.org/publication/2024-quantum-threat-timeline-report/
42. https://globalriskinstitute.org/publication/2024-quantum-threat-timeline-report/
43. https://globalriskinstitute.org/publication/quantum-threat-timeline-report-2025b/
44. https://www.nature.com/articles/s41586-024-07941-9

45. https://newsroom.ibm.com/2025-11-12-ibm-delivers-new-quantum-processors,-software,-and-algorithm-breakthroughs-on-path-to-advantage-and-fault-tolerance
46. https://newsroom.ibm.com/ibm-and-u-s-department-of-commerce-announce-americas-first-purpose-built-quantum-foundry
47. https://arxiv.org/abs/2505.15917
48. https://www.nature.com/articles/s41586-024-08449-y
49. https://research.google/blog/making-quantum-error-correction-work/
50. https://www.nsa.gov/Press-Room/News-Highlights/Article/Article/3020175/president-biden-signs-memo-to-combat-quantum-computing-threat/
51. https://www.whitehouse.gov/presidential-actions/2026/06/securing-the-nation-against-advanced-cryptographic-attacks/
52. https://www.nccoe.nist.gov/applied-cryptography/migration-to-pqc
53. https://www.cisa.gov/news-events/news/cisa-nsa-and-nist-publish-new-resource-migrating-post-quantum-cryptography
54. https://www.fsisac.com/knowledge/pqc
55. https://www.cisa.gov/resources-tools/resources/post-quantum-considerations-operational-technology

11

Seamless Security Integration Strategy

Most CISOs quietly carry a little confession: you can architect the most technically elegant quantum-safe cryptographic infrastructure in your industry, pass every compliance audit with flying colors, and brief your board on PQC migration progress with complete accuracy, and still watch the whole program come apart because a poorly executed deployment wave took down payment processing for six hours on Cyber Monday. Technical security excellence and operational implementation excellence are not the same skill. The most dangerous misconception in quantum-safe security planning is treating them as though they were.

This chapter is about the second skill set. You have spent the preceding chapters understanding what quantum-safe cryptography is, why the threat timeline matters, and what your cryptographic inventory looks like. Now we address the question that will ultimately determine whether your quantum-safe program succeeds or fails in practice. How do you actually deploy this, at enterprise scale, without destroying the operations you are trying to protect?

This is not a trivial question. Cryptographic infrastructure is the silent connective tissue of modern enterprise IT, woven into PKI systems, TLS termination layers, VPN concentrators, identity providers, API gateways, and application layer libraries in ways that make even experienced security architects blink when they see the dependency maps. When you touch cryptographic systems, you touch everything. That creates risk. Managing that risk, systematically, transparently, and with enough organizational confidence to actually execute, is the subject of this chapter.

We will walk through five interconnected domains. First, a three-phase deployment architecture that gives your program structure, decision gates, and rollback discipline. Second, protection strategies for the legacy systems that cannot be migrated, because in every enterprise, there are systems that will stubbornly resist migration longer than anyone planned. Third, a business continuity planning framework, calibrated specifically to the risk profile of cryptographic migrations. Fourth, the design principles of cryptographic agility, the architectural property that lets you swap algorithms without rearchitecting systems. And finally, a change management framework for the four stakeholder groups whose adoption determines whether your technical deployment creates lasting organizational capability or generates a compliance checkmark followed by organizational resentment.

By the end of this chapter, you'll have developed the skills that have value well beyond your quantum-safe program: quantum-safe deployment program management, legacy risk assessment and remediation planning, business impact analysis for cryptographic migrations, cryptographic architecture review, and security transformation change leadership. These are durable skills. The organization that learns to execute quantum-safe migration at scale becomes permanently better at security transformation, and that compounds value across every future program on your roadmap. Let's get started!

In this chapter we will cover the following topics:

- Phased deployment architectures for quantum-safe security
- Legacy system protection planning strategies during transition
- Business continuity planning for quantum-safe migrations
- Cryptographic agility architecture and long-term flexibility
- Change management and user adoption for quantum-safe security
- Competencies for quantum-safe implementation leadership

Phased deployment architectures for quantum-safe security

There is a tempting fantasy in enterprise IT transformation: the clean cutover. You pick a date, you flip a switch, the new system is live, and the old one is gracefully retired. Anyone who has ever managed a major cryptographic infrastructure migration has learned, sometimes painfully, that this fantasy does not survive contact with enterprise complexity. Dependencies you did not know existed surface on day one. Partner systems that were supposed to support the new protocol turn out not to. A line-of-business application built on a five-year-old library quietly breaks in ways that only manifest under production load.

The answer is not to plan better and try the clean cutover anyway. The answer is to architect your deployment in phases that are explicitly designed to discover and manage these surprises before they become incidents.[1]

The three-phase deployment model

A proven quantum-safe deployment architecture organizes migration activity across three sequential phases, each with distinct objectives, technical readiness gates, and rollback triggers. Think of it as a structured learning program where each phase teaches you something you could not have known in the previous one, and that knowledge improves the quality and confidence of subsequent phases.

Phase	Objective	Technical Readiness	Rollback Trigger
Phase 1: Parallel Deployment	• Deploy quantum-safe capabilities alongside classical systems using crypto-agile infrastructure	• PQC algorithm libraries validated in staging • Monitoring instrumentation active • Crypto inventory complete	• Any production service degradation > 1% attributed to PQC components
Phase 2: Hybrid Transition	• Activate PQC as primary mechanism for new data/ communications • Maintain classical backward compatibility	• Phase 1 stable for defined period • Partner interoperability confirmed • Rollback automation tested	• Partner interoperability failures • Performance degradation outside SLA • Anomalous cryptographic failures

Phase	Objective	Technical Readiness	Rollback Trigger
Phase 3: Full Migration	• Systematically retire classical cryptographic dependencies following validated partner transition	• All organizational and partner interactions confirmed transitional • Audit log of classical usage at zero	• Discovery of unmigrated classical dependencies • Regulatory compliance issues with retired algorithms

Table 11.1: Three-phase deployment model

The parallel deployment phase is where most of the technical discovery happens, and where your investment in crypto-agile infrastructure pays its first dividend. By running quantum-safe cryptographic capabilities alongside classical systems, you gain real-world performance data, identify unanticipated compatibility issues, and build operational familiarity with new cryptographic management procedures, all without bearing production risk.[2] Think of it as a dress rehearsal with live props, and a performance.

The hybrid transition phase is where organizational coordination becomes the dominant risk factor. You're now asking partner systems, internal applications, and customer-facing services to work with quantum-safe algorithms as the primary mechanism. The technical work is largely done; the challenge is ensuring that every integration point that touches your cryptographic layer has been tested, communicated, and confirmed. This phase tends to surface partner readiness gaps that were not visible during parallel operation.[3]

The full migration phase sounds like the finish line, but experienced practitioners describe it as the most operationally demanding. Retiring classical dependencies requires systematic discovery and confirmation that nothing, no overlooked microservice, no forgotten batch process, no third-party connector, is still relying on classical cryptographic paths. The investment in cryptographic inventory quality made early in your program is repaid here. Organizations that did cursory inventories discover their debts in Phase 3.

Deployment wave sequencing

Within each phase, deployment waves sequence specific systems for migration. The sequencing principle is straightforward in theory and genuinely difficult to execute in practice: migrate systems in order of ascending risk-continuity complexity, not in order of technical simplicity or team convenience. This means assessing each system on four dimensions: business criticality, cryptographic vulnerability severity, migration technical complexity, and operational change impact. Systems that are highly critical, technically straightforward to migrate, and carry lower operational change impact should lead deployment waves. Systems that combine high criticality with high migration complexity require separate risk planning and should not share waves with lower-risk workloads.[4]

Legacy system protection planning strategies during transition

Here's a reality that no quantum-safe migration plan survives without confronting straight on. You have systems in your environment that cannot be migrated to quantum-safe cryptographic algorithms within any timeline that matches your risk threshold. It's not because your team is not good enough, or because the technology doesn't exist, but because the system is a fifteen-year-old embedded controller with a vendor that went out of business, or a mainframe application whose cryptographic implementation is compiled into binary that nobody has the source code for, or a partner-managed platform where quantum-safe support has been promised for over a year and keeps slipping.

Legacy system quantum vulnerability is not an edge case; it's the norm at this point. According to a 2024 survey by the Cloud Security Alliance, 71% of respondents identified legacy system cryptographic dependencies as their most significant barrier to deploying advanced application authentication.[5] The question isn't whether you'll have legacy exposure during your transition. It's how you'll manage it.

Legacy quantum vulnerability triage

The best place to start is with a structured triage of your legacy estate. Not all legacy cryptographic exposure carries equal risk, and treating it as uniformly urgent leads to either paralysis or mis-prioritized investment. A four-dimension triage framework provides the structure needed to produce a defensible legacy risk register.

Triage Dimension	Assessment Criteria	High Risk Indicators	Lower Risk Indicators
Vulnerability Severity	Algorithm type, key length, implementation	• RSA-1024 or shorter • MD5/SHA-1 in active use • No PFS in TLS configurations	• ECDHE with P-256 or stronger • SHA-256 or better • Current TLS 1.3

Triage Dimension	Assessment Criteria	High Risk Indicators	Lower Risk Indicators
Data Sensitivity	Classification of data protected by the legacy cryptographic channel	• PII, financial records, trade secrets, regulated health data, long-lived secrets	• Non-sensitive operational data • Publicly available information
Migration Complexity	Technical feasibility and timeline for quantum-safe migration	• Binary-only implementation • Vendor unsupported • Embedded firmware • Mainframe assembly	• Active vendor • Documented API • Software-defined cryptographic layer
Remediation Cost	Resource requirements for interim protection vs. full migration	• Multi-year migration effort • Customer engineering required • No vendor roadmap	• Standard library update • Vendor patch available • Short migration timeline

Table 11.2: The four-dimension triage framework

Interim protection strategies

For systems that score high vulnerability with high migration complexity, three interim protection strategies provide meaningful risk reduction while longer-term remediation is underway.

Cryptographic proxy architectures interpose a quantum-safe cryptographic layer between legacy systems and their external communication channels. The legacy system continues using quantum-safe algorithms, translating at the boundary. This approach is architecturally elegant but requires careful implementation to ensure the proxy does not introduce new single points of failure or create cryptographic handoff vulnerabilities at the boundary.[6, 7] Think of it as giving your legacy system a quantum-safe bodyguard. The system does not change, but its exposure to the outside world is mediated by something much stronger.

Network segmentation reduces the attack surface exposure of unmigrated legacy systems by restricting their network reachability to the minimum required for operational function. The principle is simple: a legacy system that can only be reached by two internal applications has vastly lower quantum threat exposure than one accessible across your entire network perimeter. Segmentation does not solve the cryptographic vulnerability, but it dramatically reduces the likelihood and impact of exploitation.[8]

Data minimization is frequently the most cost-effective legacy protection strategy and the most consistently underutilized. If the data accessible through legacy cryptographic channels is minimized, through purging historical data, migrating sensitive data to quantum-safe protected stores, and limiting data exposure through legacy access paths, then the potential damage from future decryption is substantially constrained.[9]

Vendor and contractual strategies

For commercially supported legacy systems where quantum-safe migration depends on vendor product roadmaps, contractual and commercial strategies can accelerate support timelines. Security leaders who escalate quantum-safe requirements to vendor relationship management discussions, backed by documented risk assessments and coordinated with peer organizations, typically achieve faster roadmap commitments than those who rely solely on product feedback channels. Where vendor timelines are genuinely inadequate relative to organizational risk thresholds, contractual indemnification provisions, service level modifications, and, in extreme cases, vendor replacement programs provide escalation pathways.

Business continuity planning for quantum-safe migrations

The cryptographic systems you are migrating are not isolated security tools. They are load-bearing infrastructure. Your PKI issues the certificates that authenticate every TLS session on your network. Your VPN concentrators protect every remote worker's connection. Your identity provider uses cryptographic tokens to authenticate every application access request. When you migrate these systems and something goes wrong, and in enterprise migrations of this complexity, something always eventually goes wrong, the business impact is not contained to the security team. It radiates.

Business continuity planning for quantum-safe migrations therefore requires a different framing than traditional security project risk management. You are not managing the risk of a security control failure. You are managing the risk of foundational IT infrastructure disruption. The planning discipline is closer to data center migration planning than to security patch deployment, and the business impact analysis work that precedes each deployment wave is what makes the difference between a program that executed reliably and one that creates organizational trauma.[10]

The following framework provides you with a list of business impact analysis (BIA) components, along with each associated assessment, key questions to ask, and output.

BIA Component	Assessment Activity	Key Questions	Output
Dependency Mapping	Map cryptographic system to all dependent business processes	• Which business processes require this system to function? • What downstream systems depend on it?	Complete dependency registry with process owner attribution
RTO/RPO Definition	Negotiate recovery time and recovery point objectives with process owners	• What is the maximum tolerable outage duration? • What data loss is acceptable?	Documented RTO/RPO commitments by business criticality tier
Migration Window Design	Schedule migration activities within business continuity constraints	• When are the lowest-risk migration windows? • What advance notice do business stakeholders require?	Approved migration schedule with business stakeholder sign-off

BIA Component	Assessment Activity	Key Questions	Output
Rollback Criteria	Define quantitative trigger conditions for rollback activation	• What specific failure conditions require immediate rollback? • Who is authorized to trigger rollback?	Rollback decision matrix with named authorization levels
Communication Protocol	Design stakeholder notification workflows for planned and unplanned disruptions	• Who must be notified of migration windows? • What are the escalation paths for unplanned incidents?	Communication runbook with contact lists and message templates

Table 11.3: Business impact analysis framework for cryptographic migrations

Pre-migration validation environments

The most reliable protection against migration-induced service disruption is not a better rollback plan; it's a pre-migration validation environment that provides high-fidelity simulation of production migration sequences before production execution. This distinction matters more than most teams appreciate. A staging environment that does not replicate production load, production dependency topology, and production partner integration behavior will not surface the failure modes that cause production incidents. Investment in high-fidelity pre-migration validation environments, including realistic load generation, production-representative certificate hierarchies, and partner system simulators, pays back in reduced migration incidents and in the organizational confidence required to execute deployment waves without executive anxiety.[11]

Automated rollback mechanisms are the safety net beneath the pre-migration validation work. For each deployment wave, rollback automation should be designed, tested, and demonstrated to the executive sponsor before production migration execution begins. The ability to restore a cryptographic system to its pre-migration configuration within a defined recovery time objective, without manual intervention, transforms executive risk perception of deployment waves from existential to manageable. In practice, however, the existence of tested rollback automation means that rollbacks are rare, because teams that know they can roll back execute migration with more precision and less pressure-induced error.

Cryptographic agility architecture and long-term flexibility

Cryptographic agility is one of those architectural properties that sounds like a nice-to-have until you don't have it. Ask any security architect who has managed a migration away from SHA-1, or away from RSA-1024: the organizations that had abstracted their cryptographic dependencies behind well-defined interfaces executed those migrations in months. Those that had cryptographic algorithms compiled directly into application logic spent years, burned through engineering cycles, and in some cases never completed the migration, simply accumulating technical debt that sits in their legacy risk registers today.

With post-quantum cryptography, the argument for cryptographic agility is even stronger than in previous algorithm transition cycles. The post-quantum cryptographic landscape is still evolving. For example, NIST finalized ML-KEM and ML-DSA in 2024, but the research community continues evaluating additional candidates, and cryptanalytic progress, including recent results on some lattice-based schemes. What this means is that algorithm confidence levels will shift over time. An organization that hard-codes today's PQC algorithm selections into non-agile infrastructure will face the same migration challenge again within a decade. Cryptographic agility is not a hedge against uncertainty. It's a hedge against certainty, the certainty that the cryptographic landscape will continue to evolve.

The following cryptographic agility design patterns will provide some guidance on implementation actions and benefits, where each is based on the security system.

Security System	Agility Design Pattern	Implementation Approach	Operational Benefit
PKI Architecture	Algorithm-agnostic certificate profiles	• Certificate profiles define key usage and validity without encoding specific algorithm OIDs • CA hierarchy supports multiple simultaneous algorithm families	• Algorithm substitution without PKI rearchitecture • Multi-algorithm certificate hierarchies for hybrid operation

Security System	Agility Design Pattern	Implementation Approach	Operational Benefit
TLS Implementation	Negotiation-based algorithm selection	• TLS 1.3 extension support for PQC cipher suite advertisement • Server-side algorithm preference configuration independent of certificate type	• Rapid algorithm preference updates via configuration • Hybrid classical/PQC negotiation for backward compatibility
Key Management Systems	Algorithm-agnostic key storage schemas	• Key metadata schema separates key material from algorithm specification • Lifecycle workflows parameterized on algorithm family	• New algorithm support via metadata schema update • No key store rearchitecture for algorithm additions
Application Security Libraries	Cryptographic abstraction layers	• Application code calls abstract cryptographic service interfaces • Algorithm selection resolved at service layer • Application logic independent of cryptographic implementation	• Application migration from classical to PQC via service layer update • Zero application code modification required

Table 11.4: Cryptographic agility design patterns

Building the business case for cryptographic agility

One of the consistent challenges security leaders face is that cryptographic agility investments do not have a single, easily quantified threat scenario. The business case is probabilistic: the investment pays off if and when an algorithm substitution is required, and the magnitude of the payoff depends on what disruption the substitution would cause in the absence of agility provisions. The framing, while accurate, is often insufficient for budget committees that prefer single-scenario cost-benefit analysis.

The more effective business case construction presents cryptographic agility as insurance with identifiable policy terms. The premium is the incremental investment in agile architecture over non-agile implementation.[12] The claim scenario is any algorithm substitution event. The claim value is the cost of the non-agile migration: full application rearchitecture, extended deployment timelines, and the business disruption cost of operating with vulnerable cryptographic algorithms during the migration period. Organizations that experienced the SHA-1 deprecation cycles without agility provisions can often provide internal cost data for this scenario that makes the insurance premium calculation straightforward.

Change management and user adoption for quantum-safe security

Security programs fail for organizational reasons more often than they fail for technical ones. This isn't a comfortable truth for technically oriented security leaders, but it's consistently borne out by post-program retrospectives across enterprise security transformation programs of every type. A quantum-safe migration program is not primarily a cryptographic engineering project; it's an organizational change program that involves cryptographic engineering. The distinction isn't semantic. It changes what you measure, what you communicate, and where you spend leadership attention.[13]

Addressing user resistance early

One of the most difficult parts of any major migration is that the people you rely on most to make the change work may also be the ones most hesitant to embrace it. They often understand the current systems better than anyone else, help define test cases, identify operational risks, and know where implementation can go wrong. That makes early education and involvement especially important. Quantum-safe migration shouldn't be presented as a technical change being imposed on users, but as a business transition they're helping shape. When people understand why the change matters, how it affects their work, and where their experience is needed, resistance can become participation. The education discussed earlier in this book therefore isn't just about awareness. It's also a practical way to build trust, create internal champions, and gain the support needed to carry a complex migration through to completion.

The four stakeholder groups whose adoption behavior determines quantum-safe program success each require different change management approaches, different communication strategies, and different definitions of what adoption looks like. The following table provides a list of common change management approaches for each stakeholder group.

Stakeholder Group	**Key Change Impacts**	**Adoption Success Metrics**	**Change Management Approach**
Security Operations Teams	New cryptographic system management procedures Updated monitoring configurations Revised incident response protocols	PQC alert triage proficiency Time-to-acknowledge on PQC-related alerts Runbook compliance rate	Hands-on lab training on PQC systems management Updated runbooks delivered 4+ weeks before deployment Dedicated Q&A sessions with cryptographic engineers Parallel monitoring period with senior support available
IT Operations Teams	New deployment, configuration, and troubleshooting procedures for PQC components Certificate{ XE “quantum-safe security:user resistance, addressing” } lifecycle changes	Deployment success rate in staging Troubleshooting ticket resolution time Change control compliance	Scenario-based training on PQC component deployment Shadowing program with security engineers during early waves Updated configuration management documentation Clear escalation paths to cryptographic subject matter experts

Stakeholder Group	Key Change Impacts	Adoption Success Metrics	Change Management Approach
End Users	Authentication workflow changes Potential performance differences Client software upgrade requirements	Client upgrade completion rate Help desk ticket volume User satisfaction scores post-deployment	Advance notice of changes (4+ weeks) Clear explanation of what will change and what will not Automated upgrade tooling where possible Help desk briefing before deployment waves Visible leadership communication endorsing the migration
Partner Organizations	Protocol { XE "quantum-safe security:user resistance, addressing" }negotiation requirements Certificate chain changes Timeline coordination needs Interoperability testing requirements	Interoperability test completion rate Partner readiness confirmation before wave activation Time-to-resolve partner compatibility issues	Partner communication program starting 6+ months before wave activation Dedicated technical coordination resources for top-tier partners Written interoperability testing protocols Escalation pathways for partner compatibility issues Joint testing environment for critical integrations

Table 11.5: Change management framework by stakeholder group

Communication planning for quantum-safe migrations

The communication planning dimension of quantum-safe change management deserves specific attention, because it's where the "quantum" component of quantum-safe security creates a distinctive challenge. When you tell most end users and many IT professionals that you are upgrading your cryptographic infrastructure to protect against quantum computers, the mental model most people reach for involves a science-fiction scenario that feels simultaneously implausible and existential. Neither extreme is helpful for adoption.

Effective quantum-safe change communication frames the migration not as a response to an imminent threat but as a proactive infrastructure upgrade – the cryptographic equivalent of upgrading your building's lock system before the master key technology becomes publicly available, not after. This framing is accurate, avoids catastrophizing, and maps to a familiar mental model that most people can engage with without anxiety or dismissal. It also positions the organization's security leadership as competent and forward-thinking rather than reactive, a perception that builds organizational trust in the program and reduces resistance.[14]

For partner communication programs, the recommended approach begins six months or more before wave activation for critical integration partners, not sixty days. Partners have their own change control processes, their own engineering resource constraints, and their own program timelines. The organizations that achieve smooth partner transitions are those that treat partner readiness as a co-production challenge, working with partners to understand their constraints, providing technical resources that reduce the engineering burden of compatibility work, and establishing joint testing environments that make partner validation practical rather than theoretical.

Adoption monitoring and resistance management

Adoption metrics for quantum-safe programs should be instrumented before deployment waves begin, not after. The metrics that matter the most are: client software upgrade completion rates, help desk ticket volumes by category, partner interoperability test completion rates, and security operations alert triage proficiency scores. Each provides leading indicators of adoption friction that allow intervention before friction becomes program-threatening resistance.

As described earlier in this chapter, the most common form of resistance in quantum-safe programs is not explicit objection but passive delay. Teams that acknowledge the migration in steering committee meetings but do not actually prioritize the upgrade activities in their sprint planning. The diagnostic signal for this pattern is a growing gap between stated completion timelines and actual completion rates. The intervention is not pressure but resources. Most passive delay in quantum-safe migrations reflects genuine workload competition, not strategic obstruction. Leadership that responds to adoption gaps by providing dedicated migration resources – for example, temporary staffing, protected sprint capacity, and vendor professional services – consistently achieves better outcomes than leadership that responds with escalation and accountability messaging.

Preparing for quantum-safe security does more than address a new class of cryptographic risk. Done well, it also strengthens leadership, governance, and transformation capabilities that an organization can carry forward into future security initiatives.

Competencies for quantum-safe implementation leadership

The following list of competencies developed through quantum-safe security implementation leadership is not a list of quantum-specific capabilities. They are security transformation leadership capabilities that become permanently embedded organizational competencies, compounding value across every future security transformation program on your roadmap. Let's examine how these each develop through quantum-safe program execution.

Quantum-safe deployment program management

Enterprise-scale quantum-safe deployment programs are complex multi-workstream programs with cryptographic infrastructure risk profiles that differ materially from typical IT project risks. The program management competency that develops through quantum-safe execution includes establishing multi-tier governance structures: deployment team, workstream leads, steering committee, and board risk committee, with clear accountability, escalation pathways, and decision rights at each tier.

The specific program management discipline that quantum-safe programs develop most sharply is critical path management across workstreams with asymmetric risk profiles. A deployment wave that includes both a low-risk certificate authority update and a high-risk VPN concentrator migration requires sequencing and dependency management that treats these workstreams as fundamentally different risk objects, not interchangeable tasks on a Gantt chart. Leaders who develop this asymmetric risk management discipline in quantum-safe programs apply it with immediate value to subsequent infrastructure transformation programs of every type.

Program health review disciplines developed in quantum-safe programs, specifically the ability to provide accurate status visibility to board risk committees without either sanitizing risk or catastrophizing normal program complexity, are among the most transferable leadership skills the quantum-safe program develops. Board audiences for security programs are becoming increasingly sophisticated, and the credibility built through transparent, data-driven quantum-safe program reporting has durable value that extends well beyond the quantum-safe migration itself.

Legacy risk assessment and remediation planning

The legacy risk assessment competency developed through quantum-safe programs is the ability to conduct structured vulnerability triage that produces credible, actionable remediation plans under real-world resource and timeline constraints. This is fundamentally different from vulnerability assessment in isolation. It requires integrating technical severity scoring with business impact analysis, migration complexity estimation, and cost-benefit analysis into investment prioritization recommendations that hold up under CFO scrutiny.

The CFO's ability to translate cryptographic vulnerability into residual risk exposure in business terms is a capability that many technically oriented security leaders find challenging and that quantum-safe programs provide structured opportunity to develop. The leaders who emerge from quantum-safe legacy remediation programs with credible experience presenting risk-based investment cases to finance leadership have developed a professional capability that is persistently valuable across their careers.

Business impact analysis for cryptographic migrations

The business impact analysis competency developed through quantum-safe programs is the ability to map technical infrastructure dependencies to business process impacts with the precision required to make defensible scheduling and rollback decisions. This requires facilitation skills such as running BIA workshops with business process owners who may not understand cryptographic infrastructure, and analytical skills. Translating technical service disruption into business impact terms that process owners can validate is very important.

The pre-migration validation design discipline, specifically the ability to design test plans that provide statistically meaningful assurance of migration success before production deployment, is a transferable competency that improves the quality of all subsequent infrastructure migration programs. Organizations that develop this discipline through quantum-safe migrations execute future migrations with measurably lower incident rates.

Cryptographic architecture review

The cryptographic architecture review competency developed through quantum-safe programs includes the ability to evaluate proposed cryptographic implementation against multiple simultaneous criteria: algorithm selection appropriateness, key management design integrity, protocol interoperability, cryptographic agility provisions, and performance characteristics. This multi-criteria evaluation discipline, applied under time pressure to real implementation designs with real engineering trade-offs, develops technical judgement that is difficult to acquire through any other means.

The specific ability to identify architectural patterns that create unnecessary cryptographic lock-in – the PQC bolting anti-pattern discussed earlier, and its analogues in key management system design, certificate profile design, and application security library integration, is a diagnostic skill that directly prevents the accumulation of technical debt that will drive future migration costs. Security leaders who develop this pattern-recognition capability in quantum-safe program context apply it immediately to any subsequent architecture review where cryptographic implementation decisions are made.

Security transformation change leadership

The change leadership competency developed through quantum-safe programs is the ability to assess, design, execute, and monitor change management programs for complex, multi-stakeholder security technology transitions. The quantum-safe program develops this skill at high intensity because the stakeholder landscape: security operations, IT operations, end users, and partner organizations, requires genuinely different change management approaches executed simultaneously, with adoption monitoring that surfaces friction early enough to allow intervention.

The partner organization change management experience, coordinating quantum-safe transitions with external organizations that have independent governance processes, engineering resource constraints, and migration timelines, develops the diplomatic and coordination skills required for any security initiative that depends on partner ecosystem alignment. These skills are becoming increasingly central to CISO effectiveness as security programs increasingly extend beyond organizational boundaries, and the quantum-safe migration provides an unusually rich development environment for them.

Summary

The central message of this chapter is simple enough to state in one sentence: quantum-safe security excellence is only as valuable as your ability to implement it without disrupting the business operations it's designed to protect. Everything else in this chapter addresses what that requires in practice: how to execute the transition, where to invest, what to prioritize, how to balance risk against cost and operational impact, and how to build a roadmap that protects the organization while keeping the business moving.

The three-phase deployment structure – parallel deployment, hybrid transition, and full migration – provides the structural framework that makes enterprise-scale quantum-safe implementation manageable rather than overwhelming. By designing explicit readiness gates, rollback triggers, and deployment wave sequencing criteria within each phase, security leaders transform what might otherwise be a sprawling, indefinitely scoped migration program into a sequence of bounded, governed, and reversible operational steps.

Legacy system protection is the domain where program plans most frequently encounter reality. Cryptographic proxy architectures, network segmentation, and data minimization strategies provide near-term risk reduction for systems that cannot be migrated within acceptable timelines. The legacy risk triage framework, assessing vulnerability severity, data sensitivity, migration complexity, and remediation costs, produces the investment prioritization discipline required to make credible legacy remediation cases to finance leadership.

Business continuity planning for cryptographic migrations requires mapping cryptographic system dependencies to critical business processes with the precision to make defensible scheduling, rollback, and communication decisions. Pre-migration validation environments and automated rollback mechanisms are the operational infrastructure that gives executive sponsors the confidence to authorize deployment waves without existential anxiety.

Cryptographic agility architecture is the investment that makes quantum-safe migration a one-time learning event rather than a recurring cryptographic crisis. Organizations that build algorithm-agnostic PKI profiles, TLS negotiation extensions, key management schemas, and application security abstraction layers during their initial PQC migration create the architectural foundation for rapid, low-cost algorithm substitution across all future cryptographic transition cycles.

Change management is where technically excellent programs most frequently fail, and where leadership attention most reliably determines outcomes. Structured stakeholder engagement for security operations, IT operations, end users, and partner organizations, executed early, with adoption monitoring and genuine intervention resources, transforms cryptographic migration from an organizational disruption into a demonstration of security leadership capability.

The competencies developed throughout this chapter – deployment program management, legacy risk assessment, business impact analysis, cryptographic architecture review, and change leadership – are durable organizational competencies that compound value across every future security transformation program. Organizations that emerge from quantum-safe migration having genuinely developed these capabilities become permanently better at security transformation. That's the compounding dividend of treating quantum-safe migration as a leadership development program, not just a compliance exercise.

Finally, this chapter has equipped you with the operational tools to execute quantum-safe transitions with managed risk and sustained continuity. But implementation is only the beginning of the long game. The next chapter turns from the execution of initial quantum-safe transitions to the harder and more enduring challenge: building security architectures with genuine adaptive capacity. In other words, systems that evolve with the quantum technology landscape, respond to emerging cryptanalytic discoveries, and maintain quantum-safe postures across decades of technological change. Because, as important as it is to cross the initial PQC migration finish line, the organizations that truly win the quantum security race are those that build the architectural and organizational machinery to keep winning, long after the initial migration is complete.

Further reading

1. https://csrc.nist.gov/pubs/sp/1800/38/iprd-(1)
2. https://www.etsi.org/deliver/etsi_tr/103900_103999/103949/01.01.01_60/tr_103949v010101p.pdf
3. https://bidenwhitehouse.archives.gov/wp-content/uploads/2024/07/REF_PQC-Report_FINAL_Send.pdf
4. https://link.springer.com/rwe/10.1007/978-3-030-71522-9_386
5. https://cloudsecurityalliance.org/press-releases/2024/10/30/csa-finds-technical-debt-as-top-hurdle-to-identity-system-modernization
6. https://msendpointmgr.com/2026/01/21/zero-trust-for-legacy-systems-bridging-the-gap-without-compromising-principles/
7. https://www.cisa.gov/sites/default/files/2024-09/Strategy-for-Migrating-to-Automated-PQC-Discovery-and-Inventory-Tools.pdf
8. https://globalriskinstitute.org/publication/2023-quantum-threat-timeline-report/
9. https://doi.org/10.1109/MSP.2018.3761723
10. https://arxiv.org/html/2404.08231v2
11. https://cloudsecurityalliance.org/blog/2024/11/07/securing-staging-environments-best-practices-for-stronger-protection
12. https://doi.org/10.1016/j.infsof.2024.107604
13. https://hbr.org/1995/05/leading-change-why-transformation-efforts-fail-2
14. https://doi.org/10.1016/j.jmig.2007.07.001

12

Future-Proofing Your Security Architecture

Let's be honest about something that most quantum security roadmaps don't say loudly enough: finishing your post-quantum cryptography migration isn't the end of your quantum security story. It's actually just the end of the beginning.

Think about what typically happens after your organization completes a major company-wide change, such as strengthening how it protects sensitive information or asking employees to take one extra step to verify their identity before logging in. The transition may be a challenge at first, but over time this new approach would seem second nature. For example: using an Authenticator to verify login. However, once everyone has settled into the new approach, you as a leader cannot assume that the work is all done. Did those migrations end the need for ongoing security vigilance? Of course not. The threat landscape kept advancing. New attack techniques emerged. Regulatory requirements multiplied. And organizations that had treated those migrations as one-time projects found themselves scrambling again while organizations that had built adaptive security architectures simply adapted.

Quantum security is following the same pattern, only this time with higher stakes and a faster pace of underlying technological change. When the National Institute of Standards and Technology (NIST) finalized its first set of post-quantum cryptography standards in 2024, it marked a watershed moment that many organizations treated as permission to start their PQC migrations. What it also marks, if you're reading the signals correctly, is the beginning of a new era of cryptographic algorithm evolution that will continue for decades as quantum hardware capabilities advance, cryptanalytic techniques improve, and the relationship between classical and quantum computing matures in ways we can only partially anticipate today.

This chapter provides the architectural frameworks, monitoring mechanisms, partnership strategies, and governance structures that enable security leaders to build genuine adaptive capacity, not merely the appearance of future-readiness. You will develop five critical skills that directly improve your technical and business effectiveness: the ability to scan the quantum technology horizon systematically and translate emerging developments into actionable architectural guidance; the ability to continuously monitor your security architecture and adaptive responses; the competency to build and manage a portfolio of strategic quantum security partnerships; the skill to lead quantum-safe compliance programs across multiple simultaneous regulatory frameworks; and the ability to communicate compelling long-term quantum security vision narratives that sustain organizational commitment across leadership transitions and competing priorities.

These aren't abstract capabilities. They are the practical competencies that distinguish security organizations that stay ahead of the quantum threat curve from those that continuously play catch-up. For organizations that complete the transformation journey outlined across the previous 3 chapters of this book, they represent the difference between a security architecture that was quantum-safe this year and one that remains quantum-safe in 10 years and beyond. So, let's get moving and build that architecture!

In this chapter, we will cover the following topics:

- Emerging Quantum Security Technologies and the Evolving Defense Landscape
- Continuous Security Architecture Monitoring and Adaptive Response
- Strategic Security Partnerships for Quantum Resilience
- Quantum-Safe Compliance Frameworks and Audit Considerations
- Long-Term Security Architecture Vision and Governance

Emerging quantum security technologies and the evolving defense landscape

If you were to ask a room full of CISOs what quantum security means, the majority will correctly identify post-quantum cryptography as the central immediate priority. However, PQC is one instrument in a larger quantum security orchestra, and the instruments are beginning to tune up. Understanding what's coming, and when it will be ready for organizational deployment, is the first essential capability for future-proofing your security architecture.

Quantum key distribution: the promise, the practicality, and the path forward

Quantum Key Distribution (QKD) represents something genuinely remarkable in the history of cryptography. A key exchange mechanism whose security is guaranteed by the laws of physics rather than the assumed computational difficulty of mathematical problems. When two parties exchange a quantum key using protocols such as BB84 or its successors, any eavesdropping attempt disturbs the quantum states being transmitted, and that disturbance is detectable. The security guarantee is information-theoretic rather than computational, meaning it holds regardless of how powerful an adversary's computer is.[1, 2]

That sounds like the perfect answer to the quantum threat. So why isn't it your organization's primary quantum security solution today, you ask? The honest answer is that QKD's physics are elegant, but its engineering is hard. Current QKD deployments face several significant practical constraints that limit their near-term applicability for most enterprises:

- **Distance limitations:** Without quantum repeaters, which remain in early research stages, QKD transmission distances are constrained to roughly 100-150 km over fiber, or somewhat longer in experimental satellite-based deployments.[3, 4] This limits point-to-point QKD to metropolitan or campus network applications.
- **Infrastructure requirements**: QKD requires dedicated optical fiber channels or line-of-sight optical paths, specialized quantum optical hardware, and low-noise environments. It cannot be overlaid on existing IP network infrastructure without significant physical plant investment.[5]
- **Cost:** Enterprise-grade QKD systems currently cost hundreds of thousands of dollars per link, far exceeding the cost of PQC software implementations that provide comparable security for most applications.[6, 7]
- **Authentication dependency:** QKD solves the key distribution problem but not the authentication problem. It must be connected with classical or post-quantum authentication mechanisms to prevent man-in-the-middle attacks, making it a complement, rather than replacement, for PQC.[8]

Despite these constraints, QKD deployments are advancing in specific high-value contexts. The Chinese national quantum communication backbone spans over 4,600 km using trusted node architectures.[9] European quantum networks are developing under the EuroQCI initiative with planned integration into critical infrastructure by the late 2020s.[10] Banking and financial market infrastructure in countries including Japan, South Korea, and Switzerland have piloted QKD links for interbank communication.[11]

Architectural guidance for security leaders: QKD is not a replacement for PQC-based network security in the near term for most organizations. It's an appropriate investment for specific high-value, point-to-point connections where the cost of dedicated infrastructure is justified by the sensitivity of the data being protected and the availability of budget, typically in financial services, national security, and certain critical infrastructure applications. Track QKD capability advances, particularly the development of quantum repeaters and satellite QKD infrastructure, but don't divert resources from your PQC migration to pursue QKD before it's operationally mature for your use cases.

Quantum random number generation: a near-term upgrade worth pursuing

Here's a quantum technology with a very different near-term story: Quantum Random Number Generation (QRNG) is mature, commercially available, reasonably priced, and directly applicable to improving cryptographic security in systems you're operating today.

Classical computers are deterministic machines. Their pseudo-random number generators (PRNGs) produce sequences that appear random but are generated by deterministic algorithms seeded with initial values. For many cryptographic applications, high-quality PRNGs are adequate, but they are vulnerable to seed compromise, algorithm vulnerability, and, in theory, to an adversary with sufficient computational resources who can reverse-engineer the algorithm to predict outputs.[12]

QRNG devices generate truly random numbers from quantum mechanical processes, measuring photon arrival times, detecting vacuum fluctuations, or observing radioactive decay. These quantum processes are genuinely non-deterministic; their outcomes cannot be predicted even in principle by an adversary with unlimited computational resources.[13] For high-security cryptographic applications, key generation for long-lived certificates, seed values for critical HSMs, randomness for security tokens, QRNG provides a genuine security upgrade.

Commercial QRNG solutions are available from multiple vendors, including ID Quantique (now a company of IonQ),[14] Quantis (a division of ID Quantique),[15] and Cambridge Quantum Computing (now part of Quantinuum),[16] with hardware devices, PCIe cards, and cloud-accessible QRNG APIs available at price points accessible to enterprise security budgets. NIST has published guidance on QRNG evaluation and integration,[17] and ETSI has developed QRNG standards that provide evaluation frameworks for procurement decisions.[18]

The emerging quantum security research horizon

Beyond QKD and QRNG, the quantum security research community is developing a range of additional quantum-native security mechanisms that will progressively mature over the 5–15-year horizon. Security architects responsible for long-range architecture planning should have working awareness of these developments:

- **Quantum authentication protocols:** Quantum position-based authentication, quantum token protocols, and quantum biometric schemes are being developed as potential complements to classical multi-factor authentication mechanisms. While most remain in research stages, device-independent quantum authentication protocols have demonstrated proof-of-concept implementations.[19, 20]
- **Quantum digital signature schemes:** Quantum digital signatures provide information-theoretically secure signing mechanisms that, like QKD, derive their security from quantum mechanical properties rather than computational hardness. Experimental implementations using GHz photon sources have demonstrated practical quantum digital signature schemes, though infrastructure requirements remain a deployment barrier.[21, 22]
- **Quantum-secured distribution ledgers:** Research groups are exploring quantum-secured blockchain architectures that combine PQC signature schemes with QKD-based key distribution for high-assurance transaction validation. Several university research groups and consortia are active in this space.[23, 24, 25, 26]
- **Blind quantum computation:** Blind quantum computation protocols allow computations to be performed on quantum processors without the processor, or an eavesdropper, learning the input, outputs, or algorithm being executed. This has significant implications for quantum cloud computing security and the privacy-preserving use of quantum computing services.[27, 28]

Technology readiness assessment framework for emerging quantum security technologies

How should security architects assess emerging quantum security technologies against their organizational security portfolios? The following Technology Readiness Assessment Matrix provides a structured approach to evaluating emerging quantum security technologies against six key dimensions:

Technology	TRL-Level	Deployment Readiness	Use Case Fit	Cost Profile	Strategic Priority
PQC (FIPS)	9	Deployment-ready	Universal	Low (software)	Immediate
QRNG (hardware devices)	8-9	Production-ready	High-security key gen	Low-Medium	Near-term upgrade
QRNG (cloud API)	8	Production-ready	Distributed applications	Low	Near-term upgrade
QKD (metro fiber)	6-7	Pilot-ready for specific uses	High-value point-to-point links	High	Selective evaluation
QKD (satellite)	5-6	Research/pilot stage	Global high-security links	Very High	Long-range monitoring
Quantum Authentication	3-5	Research stage	Future MFA complement	TBD	Horizon monitoring
Quantum Digital Signatures	4-5	Early experimental	High-assurance signing	TBD	Horizon monitoring
Quantum-secured Blockchain	3-4	Conceptual/ Experimental	High-value transaction systems	TBD	Long-range monitoring
Blind Quantum Computation	4-5	Experimental demonstrations	Quantum cloud security	TBD	Long-range monitoring

Table 12.1: Technology Readiness Assessment Matrix. Technology Readiness Level (TRL) scale: 1=Basic research; 5=Technology validated in relevant environment; 9=Actual deployment proven in operational environment.

Continuous security architecture monitoring and adaptive response

Imagine trying to navigate a constantly shifting landscape while only looking at a map that was drawn three years ago. That's what security architecture management looks like without a systematic monitoring program. The quantum security landscape, including cryptographic algorithm security, quantum hardware capabilities, threat actor developments, and regulatory requirements, changes continuously. Organizations, including those in education and investment, that don't monitor these changes systematically will always be reacting to the developments that a more attentive competitor would have anticipated.

Designing and operating an effective quantum security architecture monitoring program is the second cornerstone of adaptive security posture, and it's more practical to implement than many security leaders assume.

The four monitoring domains

An effective quantum security monitoring program needs to track four independent domains simultaneously. Think of these as four rivers that all feed the same lake; changes in any one eventually affect all the others, and an alert navigator watches all four.

- **Domain 1, Cryptographic Algorithm Security Research:** This domain tracks the ongoing security analysis of deployed and candidate cryptographic algorithms, including post-quantum algorithms. The IACR (International Association for Cryptologic Research) ePrint archive[29] publishes cryptographic research preprints: CRYPTO,[30] EUROCRYPT,[31] and ASIACRYPT[32] conference proceedings contain the most rigorous peer-reviewed analyses. The NIST post-quantum cryptography project website[33] tracks official status changes for standardized and candidate algorithms. This domain requires the most specialized technical depth to monitor effectively; this is where academic partnership value is highest.
- **Domain 2, Quantum Hardware Capability Advances:** This domain tracks progress in quantum processor coherence times, error rates, qubit counts, and fault-tolerant computing milestones that affect the timeline for a cryptographically relevant quantum computer. Key sources include IBM Quantum roadmap[34] publications, Google Quantum AI[35] research papers, academic quantum computing journals, and DARPA quantum computing program[36] announcements. Commercial intelligence services from firms such as Inside Quantum Technology[37] and The Quantum Insider[38] provide curated monitoring for non-specialist security teams.

- **Domain 3, Threat Actor and Intelligence Developments:** This domain tracks indicators that nation-state or sophisticated criminal actors are advancing quantum computing capabilities or quantum attack techniques, as well as "Harvest Now, Decrypt Later" evidence from threat intelligence sources. CISA's Cybersecurity Advisories,[39] NSA/CSS Commercial National Security Algorithm (CNSA) guidance updates,[40] and sector-specific ISACs[41] with classified and sensitive threat intelligence sharing channels are primary sources.
- **Domain 4, Regulatory and Standards Evolution:** This domain tracks changes to quantum security requirements across relevant regulatory frameworks, NIST guidance updates, FIPS standard revisions, sector-specific regulatory guidance, and international standards development. Organizations operating across multiple jurisdictions need particular attention to divergences between US, EU, and Asian regulatory timelines.[42, 43]

The quantum security architecture monitoring dashboard

Translating continuous monitoring data into actionable security architecture visibility requires a structured dashboard framework. The following Quantum Security Architecture Monitoring Dashboard provides integrated visibility across the four monitoring domains and six key architectural status dimensions:

Dashboard Dimension	Key Indicators	Monitoring Frequency	Escalation Trigger	Primary Owner
Cryptographic Asset Coverage	% systems with quantum vulnerable crypto inventoried % with active migration plans	Quarterly	Coverage drops below 95% New system class discovered untracked	Security Architecture Lead
PQC Migration Progress	Migration milestones vs. plan By-system-class progress Risk-weighted completion %	Monthly	Milestone slip > 30 days High-critically system delayed	CISO / Program Manager
Cryptographic Agility Readiness	% systems with with algorithm-agile architecture Brittle system count and risk ranking	Quarterly	New brittleness indentified in critical system Major acquisition lacks agility	Security Architecture Lead
Algorithm Security Status	NIST/IACR alert status for deployed algorithms Known attack capability timeline estimates	Continuous / Monthly review	Any credible attack on deployed PQC algorithm NIST guidance update	Crypto SME / CISO
Threat Intelligence Currency	Date of last QRNG/harvest threat assessment Nation-state capability assessment age	Monthly	Credible CRNL (Crypto-Relevant Nation-State Lab) capability advance Sector targeting intelligence	Threat Intelligence Lead
Regulatory Compliance Posture	Framework-by-framework compliance status Upcoming requirement deadlines Open findings	Quarterly / Pre-examination	New regulatory guidance issues Examination scheduled Finding unresolved > 90 days	Compliance Lead / CISO

Table 12.2: Quantum Security Architecture Monitoring Dashboard

Embedding quantum security in architecture governance processes

A monitoring program is only valuable if its outputs flow into governance processes that produce architectural decisions. Also worth noting that this approach is only as good as your organization's regular IT practices. The following quantum security checkpoints should be embedded into three core governance processes that most organizations already operate.

- **System Acquisition and Procurement:** Require vendors to disclose cryptographic dependencies for all system acquisitions, including software libraries, hardware security modules, communication protocols, and key management components. Map disclosed dependencies against quantum-vulnerable algorithm lists. Require contractual commitments to PQC upgrade availability and timeline. Evaluate vendor quantum security roadmaps as selection criteria alongside functionality and cost.[44]
- **Major Change Management:** Include quantum security impact assessment as a standard gate in major change review processes. Changes that modify key management systems, introduce new cryptographic dependencies, extend data retention periods, or alter cryptographic protocol configurations should require explicit sign-off on quantum security implications from the Security Architecture Review Board.
- **Vendor Onboarding and Third-Party Risk Management:** Incorporate quantum security questionnaire items into vendor security assessments. For clinical vendors handling sensitive data, require evidence of PQC migration plans and timeline commitments. Assess third-party quantum security posture as a component of supply chain risk scoring.[45]

Architecture Review Board: the quantum security governance heartbeat

Most organizations shouldn't try building their own quantum-security governance models. Instead, they should consider hiring experienced outside advisors to help establish a strong structure quickly, particularly as quantum risk becomes a competitor to other business priorities. The Security Architecture Review Board (SARB), or any comparable cross-functioning leadership group, could then turn insights into practical decisions regarding technology priorities, investments, and accountability. For example, industries such as finance, health care, aerospace and defense might already have more mature structures because the pressure and regulatory stakes are higher. However, every organization can use this forum to guide its quantum-security efforts as they're developing:

- **Quarterly Quantum Security Architecture Review:** A standing agenda item at SARB quarterly reviews that covers monitoring dashboard status, significant developments in any of the four domains, architecture adaptation decisions triggered by monitoring outputs, and migration program progress against plan.
- **Annual Quantum Security Architecture Assessment:** A comprehensive annual review of the quantum security architecture roadmap, including scanning inputs, technology readiness reassessments, threat capability updates, and 5-year roadmap revision.
- **Threshold-Triggered Emergency Reviews:** Defined criteria that trigger emergency SARB sessions outside the regular cadence, particularly relevant for significant cryptographic algorithm security developments, major quantum hardware capability announcements, or significant regulatory guidance changes.
- **Architecture Exemption Process:** A documented process for evaluating and time-limiting exemptions from quantum security architecture standards, particularly for legacy systems where immediate migration is technically infeasible. All exemptions should carry explicit risk acceptance, compensating controls, and expiration dates.

Strategic security partnerships for quantum resilience

Here's the truth that experienced CISOs know but that the security industry often underplays: you cannot build and maintain world-class security capability entirely in-house. The cyber threat landscape is too broad, too fast-moving, and too technically specialized for any single organization to achieve independent mastery across all relevant domains. Quantum security intensifies this reality by adding a dimension of physics and mathematics that extends well beyond the training of most enterprise security teams.

Strategic partnerships are not admissions of weakness. They are intelligent force multipliers. The organizations that maintain the most effective quantum security postures over the coming decade will be those that most skillfully assemble and manage portfolios of strategic partnerships that extend their capabilities, intelligence, and influence well beyond what they could build independently.

The quantum security partnership ecosystem

Four partnership types provide complementary and largely non-overlapping value to enterprise quantum security programs. A mature quantum security partnership portfolio should include elements of each:

Partnership Type	Primary Value Provided	Investment Required	Strategic Fit
Quantum Security Vendors	PQC implementation expertise, quantum-safe product roadmaps, implementation support capability, tooling and automation	• Commercial contracts • Relationship management	All organizations undertaking PQC migration
National Laboratories / Government Agencies	Cutting-edge research access, standards development participation, classified threat intelligence (for cleared orgs), validation services	• Relationship investment • Collaboration agreements • Potential CRADA for labs	Critical infrastructure, defense contractors, highly regulated sectors
Academic Research Institutions	Early access to cryptographic research, quantum attack technique developments, graduate talent pipeline, emerging tech proof-of-concepts	• Research funding, sponsored research agreements, student fellowship programs	Organizations with research capability and longer strategic horizon
Industry Consortia	Peer benchmarking, shared threat intelligence, collective standards advocacy, operational benchmarking, sector-specific guidance	• Membership fees • Staff time for active participation • Working group engagement	All organizations, particularly valuable for regulated sector participants

Partnership Type	Primary Value Provided	Investment Required	Strategic Fit
Peer Organization Information Sharing	Sector-specific implementation experience, common vendor intelligence, shared regulatory interpretation, incident response coordination	• Reciprocal sharing commitment • ISAC/ISO membership • Bilateral agreements	All organizations Most valuable within the same sector

Table 12.3: Four quantum security partnership ecosystems

National laboratory and governance agency partnerships

For security leaders unfamiliar with national laboratory engagement, the value proposition deserves specific elaboration. The U.S. national laboratory system, including NIST, Oak Ridge National Laboratory, Argonne National Laboratory, Sandia National Laboratory, and Pacific Northwest National Laboratory, represents a concentration of quantum computing and quantum security research capability without parallel in the private sector.[46] There are many, including me, who would go as far as referring to them as "national treasures."

NIST deserves particular attention for its central role in quantum security standards development. Beyond the headline PQC standardization work, NIST operates the National Cybersecurity Center of Excellence (NCCoE), which is actively developing practical implementation guidance, reference architectures, and migration tooling for PQC deployment in specific operational contexts, including financial services, telecommunications infrastructure, and federal agency environments.[47] Participation in NCCoE working groups provides organizations with direct influence over the practical guidance that will shape industry practice and regulatory expectations.

For private sector organizations seeking national laboratory partnerships, the Cooperative Research and Development Agreement (CRADA)[48] mechanism provides a structured vehicle for joint research activities, and many national laboratories operate industry partnership programs with more accessible entry points than full CRADA arrangements. For critical infrastructure operators, the Department of Energy's Cybersecurity, Energy Security, and Emergency Response (CESER) office and the National Nuclear Security Administration (NNSA) both operate partnership programs relevant to quantum security.[49]

Key industry consortia for quantum security leaders

Several industry consortia provide value for enterprise quantum security program leaders. The following are the most strategically important for security executives to evaluate:

- **ETSI Quantum Safe Cryptography (QSC) Working Group:** Develops technical standards, implementation guidance, and security evaluations for quantum-safe cryptography. Particularly valuable for organizations with European operations or European regulatory exposure. ETSI QSC standards are informing EU regulatory requirements through ENISA's work.[50]
- **Cloud Security Alliance (CSA) Quantum-Safe Security Working Group:** Provides cloud-specific quantum security guidance, implementation resources, and a practitioner community. The CSA's Quantum-Safe Security Working Group has produced practical guidance on cloud services provider PQC roadmaps and hybrid deployment architectures.[51]
- **FS-ISAC (Financial Services Information Sharing and Analysis Center):** For financial services sector participants, FS-ISAC provides sector-specific threat intelligence, quantum security working groups, and peer benchmarking on PQC migration progress. The FS-ISAC Quantum Computing Cybersecurity Threat Working Group has published sector-specific guidance.[52]
- **Health-ISAC:** For healthcare sector participants, Health-ISAC provides quantum security intelligence sharing relevant to healthcare data protection, medical device security, and HIPAA compliance implications.[53]
- **Industrial Internet Consortium (IIC) Quantum Security Task Group:** For industrial control systems and IoT-heavy environments, the IIC provides guidance on quantum security in operational technology contexts, a significantly different technical challenge than enterprise IT environments.[54]

Partnership portfolio management: from dormant relationships to active intelligence

Security leaders who've tried to build strategic partnerships know the frustrating pattern: organizations invest in establishing relationships, signing collaboration agreements, joining consortia, attending kickoff meetings, and then the relationships gradually atrophy as operational priorities crowd out strategic engagement. Months later, the partnership exists on paper but provides little actual value.

Avoiding this pattern requires treating the partnership portfolio with the same structured management rigor you'd apply to any other security program component. The following Partnership Portfolio Management Framework provides a sustainable engagement model:

Partnership Tier	Engagement Model	Minimum Engagement Cadence	Value Realization Mechanism	Portfolio Review
Tier 1: Strategic (2-3 partners)	Embedded relationship manager Joint projects Executive sponsor alignment	Monthly operational Quarterly strategic review	Joint research outputs Early advisory access Co-developed tooling	Annual strategic assessment Leadership review
Tier 2: Active (5-8 partners)	Designated relationship owner working group participation structure intelligence sharing	Quarterly touchpoints Working group meetings	Intelligence reports Benchmark data Standards influence Implementation guidance	Semi-annual value assessment
Tier 3: Monitoring (10+ partners)	Consortium memberships Mailing list subscriptions Conference attendance	Annual engagement Event-based interaction	Publication access Peer community Emerging opportunity identification	Annual membership ROI review

Table 12.4: Partnership Portfolio Management Framework

Quantum-safe compliance frameworks and audit considerations

The regulatory landscape for quantum security is in the same dynamic state as the technology landscape itself: the direction is clear. Specific requirements are still taking shape, and organizations that track the evolution systematically will have compliance advantage over those who wait for requirements to become fully explicit before beginning program development. Understanding the current state and likely trajectory of quantum security regulatory requirements and designing compliance programs that can adapt efficiently as requirements evolve is the fourth cornerstone of adaptive quantum security posture.

The regulatory landscape: a sector-by-sector survey

Quantum security requirements are emerging at different speeds and with different specificities across sectors. The following framework maps the current state and near-term trajectory across the major regulatory domains relevant to US and international enterprises:

Regulatory Domain	Current Quantum Security Requirements	Near-Tern Trajectory	Key Compliance Actions
Federal Agencies & Contractors (NIST, NSM-10)	NSM-10 (2022) mandates federal agency PQC migration CNSS Policy 15 applies to NSS NIST SP 800-208 and FIPS 203/204/205 define PQC standards	FISMA updates to incorporate PQC compliance Expanded contractor scope Likely FedRAMP PQC requirements for cloud services	Complete CNSA 2.0 transition planning Align FedRAMP-authorized services to PQC roadmap Monitor NIST SP 800-227 development
Financial Services (Fed, OCC, FFIEC)	No explicit PQC mandate Supervisory expectations for quantum risk in technology risk management frameworks OCC Bulleting 2023-17 mentions quantum as emerging technology risk	Likely formal quantum risk management guidance within 2-3 years Potential exam procedures for quantum risk management FFIEC expected to issue updated technology examination guidance[1]	Develop quantum risk management program documentation Brief examiners on program status proactively Engage with FS_ISAC quantum working group
Financial Services (EU-DORA, ECB)	DORA Article 6 includes ICT risk management requirements with emerging quantum security interpretation ECB cyber resilience oversight expectations increasingly include quntum horizon planning	EBA/ESMA/EIOPA supervisory guidance on quantum security expected Potential DORA regulatory technical standards on quantum-safe requirements	Conduct DORA-framed quantum ICT risk assessment Document quantum security in ICT risk management framework Engage with ECB and EBA guidance development

Healthcare (HHS/ HIPAA)	No specific HIPAA quantum security requirements HHS HICP voluntary cybersecurity practices do not yet explicitly address quantum	HHS OCR likely to address quantum security in HIPAA Security Rule updates currently in development[1]	Proactively assess ePHI encryption quantum vulnerability Develop PQC migration plan for ePHI systems Document risk management rationale
Critical Infrastructure (CISA)	CISA has issues quantum security alerts and guidance documents CISA Binding Operational Directive 23-02 sets PQC requirements for .gov Sector-specific agencies (SSAs) issuing sector-tailored guidance	Critical infrastructure sector-specific quantum security requirements expected via Sector Risk Management Agencies (SRMAs) TSA, MERC, CIP and other sector standards bodies likely to formalize requirements	Engage with sector SMRA on quantum security expectations Participate in CISA quantum security working groups Align to CISA CPRT (Cybersecurity Performance Goals) quantum recommendations
Defense Industrial Base (CMMC, DFARS)	DFAARAS clause 252.204-7012 Safeguarding requirements apply to CUI CMMC 2.0 does not yet explicitly incorporate PQC requirements but DoD CIO is developing updated crypto standards	DoD CIO quantum security policy development underway Likely CMMC 3.0 or interim DFARS updates to incorporate NSA CNSA 2.0 requirements for DoD contractors	Track NSA CNSA 2.0 transition timeline Prepare for DFARS contractual crypto requirements update Align CMMC documentation to incorporate quantum security controls

Table 12.5: Current state and near-term trajectory framework

Designing a unified compliance control framework

One of the most practically valuable compliance program design decisions is the choice between managing regulatory requirements independently. With separate control frameworks, evidence collections, and audit preparation for each regulatory domain versus building a unified control framework that addresses multiple regulatory requirements through common control implementations.

The independent approach is simple to design initially but becomes administratively unsustainable as regulatory requirements multiply. A large financial institution might face simultaneous quantum security examination expectations from varying groups such as: The Federal Reserve (for BHC oversight), the OCC (for national bank charter oversight), DORA (for EU operations), and FFIEC IT examination procedures (for combined examinations), plus CMMC requirements if it has defense contracts. Consider a cautionary note to firms who only look at the quarter-to-quarter game, yet do not play long ball well.

The unified framework approach requires more design investment upfront but scales dramatically better as requirements mature. The following Quantum Security Common Control Mapping provides a starting structure:

Common Control Domain	Control Examples	NIST CSF Mapping	Regulatory Framework Coverage
Cryptographic Asset Inventory	Maintain current inventory of all cryptographic algorithm deployments, key management systems, certificates, and cryptographic dependencies across the enterprise technology portfolio	ID.AM-2, ID.AM-3	NSM-10, NIST SP 800-57, FFEIC IT, DORA Art. 8, CMMC AC.3.022
Quantum Risk Assessment	Conduct annual quantum security risk assessment covering cryptographic vulnerability exposure, harvest-now-decrypt-later risk, timeline to travel, and residual risk acceptance documentation	ID.RA-1, ID-RA-3, ID-RA-5	NIST RMF, FFEIC IT, DORA Art. 6, HIPAA Sec. 164.308(a)(1)
PQC Migration Planning	Maintain documented PQC migration plan with risk-prioritized migration sequence, milestone schedule, resource allocation, and executive accountability	PR.IP-7, PR-IP-9	NSM-10, NIST NCCoE Migration Guide, DORA Art. 11
Cryptographic Agility Architecture	Document cryptographic agility requirements and implementation status across all security architecture domains Track brittle system inventory and remediation roadmap	PR.DS-2, PR.DS-6	NIST SP 800-131A, NSA CNSA 2.0, FedRAMP CM controls

Common Control Domain	Control Examples	NIST CSF Mapping	Regulatory Framework Coverage
PQC Implementation and Testing	Test and validate PQC algorithm implementations against NIST-approved algorithm specifications Maintain implementation test evidence and third-party validation records	PR.DS-5, DE.CM-8	FIPS 203/204/205 compliance, NIST CAVP testing requirements, FedRAMP CM-6
Quantum Security Monitoring	Operate continuous monitoring program covering algorithm security research, quantum hardware advances, threat intelligence, and regulatory changes Maintain monitoring records and response actions	DE.CM-1, DE.AE-3, RS.AN-1	FFEIC IT monitoring requirements, DORA Art.10, CMMC SI.3.218
Third-Party Quantum Risk Management	Assess and manage quantum security risk in the vendor and third-party ecosystem Maintain vendor PQC migration status documentation Include quantum security requirements in vendor contracts	ID.SC-2, ID.SC-4, RS.MI-3	FFEIC Third-Party Risk, DORA Art. 28/30, CMMC SR.3.169

Table 12.6: Quantum Security Common Control Mapping

Audit program design for quantum-safe security

As quantum security requirements mature from voluntary guidance to regulatory mandate, audit programs will progressively incorporate quantum security as a standard examination element. Preparing for this evolution, designing evidence collection, testing, and documentation approaches that support external audit and regulatory examination, is an investment that pays compound returns as examination intensity increases.

The following quantum security audit readiness framework addresses four dimensions of audit program design:

- **Evidence Architecture:** Design documentation and evidence collection systems that produce audit-ready materials as a byproduct of normal security operations, rather than requiring burdensome evidence assembly exercises prior to examinations. Cryptographic inventory tools that produce exportable reports, migration program dashboards with audit trail logging, architecture review board meeting minutes, and compliance mapping documentation updated on a rolling basis are all examples of evidence that should exist as operational artifacts rather than pre-audit emergency assemblies.
- **Testing Methodology:** Develop quantum security control testing procedures that validate both the existence and effectiveness of quantum security controls. For cryptographic controls, this includes algorithm implementation validation against NIST CAVP test vectors, key management procedure walkthroughs, and penetration testing components specifically targeting quantum-vulnerable cryptographic implementations. For governance controls, testing should include SARB meeting record review, roadmap milestone verification, and escalation process testing.
- **Documentation Standards:** Maintain documentation that clearly traces quantum security program decisions to risk assessments, regulatory requirements, and governance approval authorities. Audit examiners want to see a coherent decision trail that demonstrates that quantum security program design was deliberate and risk-informed, not ad hoc. This includes documented rationale for migration prioritization decisions, risk acceptance documentation for systems with delayed migration timelines, and executive and board-level oversight evidence.
- **Examiner Communication Strategy:** Don't wait for examiners to discover your quantum security program status. Instead, get ahead of examination cycles with proactive briefings that explain your program structure. Examiners who understand your program design are better positioned to evaluate it accurately. Examiners who encounter your program for the first time during examination will assess it against implicit frameworks that may not match your program's actual approach.

Long-term security architecture vision and governance

Everything we've discussed so far in this chapter, the technology monitoring framework, the adaptive architecture principles, the partnership portfolio, the compliance program, requires organizational commitment to sustain across years and decades of change. Technology cycles pass. Executive sponsors move on. Budget priorities shift. Geopolitical events reshape organizational priorities overnight. And the organizations that began investing in quantum security programs in 2020 or 2022 will face the risk, in 2033 and beyond, that the initial urgency that created their programs has dissipated before the programs have achieved their full adaptive maturity.

Preventing that degradation, building governance structures that sustain quantum security program momentum across the full multi-decade horizon of technological change, is the final challenge this chapter addresses. And having the ability to maintain momentum and make the program structural is what makes all this fundamentally a governance and communication challenge, not a technical one.

The quantum security architecture governance model

A durable quantum security governance model requires four structural components that, when operating together, create self-sustaining institutional commitment to quantum security adaptation:

- **Quantum Security Architecture Board (QSAB):** A standing governance body with defined membership, mandate, and decision authority responsible for quantum security architecture standards, roadmap approval, exception management, and regulatory compliance oversight. QSAB membership should include the CISO (chair), Security Architect Lead, CTO or CIO representative, Chief Risk Officer or representative, Legal/Compliance Lead, and rotating business unit representation. QSAB should meet quarterly at minimum, with emergency convening authority for threshold-triggered events. Critical success factor: the QSAB must have actual authority over cryptographic standards and migration program resources allocation, not merely advisory influence, to be effective.
- **Quantum Security Technology Roadmap:** A rolling five-year quantum security technology roadmap, reviewed and updated annually by the QSAB, that maps the organization's quantum security capabilities against projected threat, technology, and regulatory developments over the planning horizon. The roadmap should include current state architecture assessment, target state architecture by year, capability development initiatives with annual milestones, technology adoption decisions for

emerging quantum security technologies, and regulatory milestone alignment. Annual updates should be triggered by the monitoring framework's outputs and should include explicit tracking of the roadmap's accuracy. For example, comparing projections made three years prior against actual developments to improve forecasting discipline.

- **Quantum Security Investment Framework:** A multi-year quantum security investment commitment that maintains consistent resource allocation to quantum security capability development across business cycle fluctuations. This requires executive-level sponsorship to convert from annual budget discretion to a committed multi-year program investment. Similar to the transformation from project-based to program-based investment models that mature security organizations have adopted for security operations capabilities. The framework should define baseline annual investment floors, criteria for investment scaling in response to accelerating threat or regulatory developments, and governance approval requirements for investment scope changes.
- **Quantum Security Talent Strategy:** Organizations need a clear plan to grow, build, and retain quantum-security expertise. This goes beyond simply hiring cryptographic engineers and quantum-security architects. New roles will continue to emerge across the quantum ecosystem. These may include risk-management, legal, procurement, operational, and technical roles. Where each one can affect your organization's security posture.

A firm strategy combines university partnerships, targeted hiring, and internal training. It also includes knowledge-management practices that protect expertise when employees suddenly decide to depart or choose new roles. Staff turnaround can weaken even a well-designed program over time. Organizations that treat talent strategy as a foundational program component rather than an HR afterthought are more likely to sustain execution consistency than those relying on individual champions.

The quantum security architecture maturity model

Security leaders need a common framework for assessing their organization's quantum security program maturity and communicating program progress to boards and executive committees. The following Quantum Security Architecture Maturity Model provides a five-level framework that maps organizational capabilities across six dimensions:

Maturity Level	Cryptographic Inventory	Architecture Design	Monitoring Program	Partnership Ecosystem	Compliance Program	Governance Structure
Level 1: Aware	Ad hoc No systematic inventory	No quantum security consideration in design	No structured monitoring Reactive awareness	No strategic partnerships	Monitoring regulatory developments only	No quantum security governance body
Level 2: Initiated	Partial Inventory of high-criticality systems	PQC requirements stated but not enforced in governance	Basic monitoring of NIST/NSA publications	Initial vendor engagement No formal partnerships	Gap assessment completed Compliance roadmap drafted	CISO quantum security ownership Informal program
Level 3: Developing	Comprehensive inventory of IT systems OT in progress	Cryptographic agility standards defined Limited enforcement	Monitoring program operating for 3 of 4 domains Quarterly reviews	2-3 active partnerships Working group participation	Compliance control framework defined Multi-framework mapping	QSAB established Quarterly review cadence Roadmap v1.0

Level 4: Managed	Enterprise-wide inventory including OT and third-party systems	Crypto agility enforced in acquisition and change management Brittle system backlog managed	All 4 domains monitored Dashboard operational Escalation process tested	Active partnership portfolio across all 4 types Regular engagement cycles	Unified compliance framework operational Audit-ready evidence	QSAB fully operational Roadmap updated annually Investment framework in place
Level 5: Optimizing	Automated inventory with continuous discovery Real-time convergence metrics	Architecture automatically assessed for quantum security Agility metrics tracked	Continuous monitoring with automated alerting Adapting response tested	Strategic partnerships providing intelligence advantage Co-development activities	Compliance evidence automated Proactive regulator engagement Exception program	Governance integrated into enterprise architecture Talent strategy mature Succession planning active

Table 12.7: Quantum Security Architecture Maturity Model

Communicating the long-term quantum security vision

The most technically rigorous quantum security architecture is worthless if the organization doesn't sustain the commitment to build and maintain it. Long-term organizational commitment to multi-decade security programs requires more than logical argument. It requires a compelling narrative that connects the quantum security mission to organizational values, strategic priorities, and the people doing the work.

Developing and communicating an effective quantum security vision narrative is the fifth and arguably most underinvested skill in the quantum security leader's toolkit. Here are the principles that distinguish vision communications that sustain commitment from those that fade with the initial briefing cycle:

- **Connect to organizational identity, not just threat landscape:** "We need to do this, or we'll get hacked" creates urgency but not commitment. "This is what it means to be a trustworthy institution in the quantum era" creates identity alignment that survives the ebb of immediate threat anxiety. Frame quantum security as an expression of organizational values. Commitment to customer trust, stewardship of sensitive information, responsibility to stakeholders, rather than purely as threat response. Keep in mind that a reputation that has been built over decades can be damaged in a matter of minutes.
- **Make the long timeline an asset, not a liability:** Many executives experience quantum security timeline discussions as demotivating. If the serious threat is 5-10 years away, why prioritize it now? Reframe the timeline as an opportunity: organizations that build adaptive quantum security architectures over the next three to five years will navigate the quantum transition with manageable effort and sustained competitive advantage. Whereas organizations that wait will face the compressed, expensive, and operationally disruptive version of the same transition.
- **Translate technical progress into business outcome narratives:** Board members and executive committee members don't experience business outcomes. Develop translation narratives that connect technical quantum security progress to outcomes they do care about: reduced cyber insurance risk, maintained regulatory standing, competitive advantage in security-sensitive customer segments, reduced systemic risk in the event of cryptographic breakthrough.
- **Design vision communications for longevity, not just the current moment:** Quantum security vision documents and board presentations written in 2025 will still be in circulation in 2027 when the next executives join who weren't in the room for the original briefing. Design communications to be contextually durable. Grounding strategic rationale in principles rather than specific quantum computing capability

timeline estimates that will have changed and building the vision around organizational values that persist across leadership transitions.

Maintaining continuity through organizational change

Leadership transitions are the most common threat to long-term program continuity. The CISO who established the quantum security program leaves; the new CISO arrives with different priorities and a different threat model; the program loses its executive champion and begins to atrophy. This pattern is familiar enough to every security leader that it hardly needs documenting; what needs documenting is the governance design that prevents it.

Three practices provide the strongest protection against leadership-transition-induced program degradation:

- **Board-Level Embedding:** When quantum security governance is embedded in board-level committee charters such as Technology Committee, Risk Committee, Audit Committee, it acquires an accountability anchor that survives CISO transitions. Board members ask about quantum security program status regardless of which CISO presents. The program can't be quietly deprioritized without board-level visibility. Achieving this embedding is a multi-year organizational change effort, but organizations that accomplish it have fundamentally different program continuity than those relying solely on CISO championship.
- **Institutionalized Program Documentation:** Comprehensive, current program documentation: architecture roadmaps, compliance frameworks, partnership agreements, governance charters, and monitoring reports, all serve as organizational memory. This enables an incoming CISO to understand the quantum security program's state and rationale without a lengthy reconstruction effort. Organizations where quantum security program knowledge exists primarily in the heads of individual contributors are vulnerable to knowledge loss in ways that documented programs are not.
- **Succession Planning for Quantum Security Leadership:** Identify and develop two to three individuals within the security organization who have deep quantum security program knowledge and could serve as interim program leaders if the primary champion departed unexpectedly. This isn't about managing for attrition; it's about building organizational resilience that allows the program to sustain momentum through inevitable personnel changes without losing the institutional knowledge that makes the program effective.

A practical integration guide

So far, we've covered quite a bit, most of which has been woven into the frameworks and guidance provided. Now, let's explicitly surface everything to develop and apply each into your organization's context.

Emerging technology horizon scanning

Horizon scanning is not the same as following quantum computing news. It requires systematic monitoring of specific technical domains, evaluation frameworks for assessing claim credibility, and translation mechanisms that convert research insights into architectural implications. You can build this skill by the following:

- Establishing a structured quarterly reading practice covering IACR ePrint preprints, NIST PQC project updates, and the conference proceedings of at least one of CRYPTO, EUROCRYPT, or ASIACRYPT.
- Developing personal Technology Readiness Assessment competency for evaluating new quantum security technology claims. Learning to distinguish between research demonstrations, proof-of-concept deployments, and operationally ready solutions.
- Creating a quarterly horizon scanning brief for the Security Architecture Review Board that summarizes language, building organizational horizon scanning literacy alongside your own.
- Engaging with at least one academic partner or national connection who can serve as a technical translator. Helping you assess the significance of research developments you encounter in monitoring rather than requiring you to have research-level technical depth yourself. There are very few people that can read a quantum research paper, understand its technical significance, and clearly explain what it could mean for a specific industry. That combination of scientific depth and practical business insight is very rare. Those who can bridge both worlds serve as advisors or lead quantum-focused institutions. This is why having strategic partnerships with trusted advisors and universities is very important and provide a high value return in the long run.

Adaptive architecture design and governance

Adaptive architecture is a design philosophy that must be operationalized in specific technical and governance mechanisms. The following can help you develop the right skill which can map back to your organization's education plans:

- Conducting a Cryptographic Brittleness Assessment of your current security architecture, identifying components whose cryptographic dependencies are deeply embedded in application logic, hardware implementations, or protocol specifications in ways that make algorithm changes expensive and disruptive.

- Developing or adopting a Cryptographic Agility Design Standard that specifies how algorithm selection, key management, and cryptographic operation interfaces should be implemented across different architectural tiers to support future algorithm transitions with minimal disruption.
- Embedding cryptographic agility evaluation criteria into existing governance processes. Architecture Review Board checklists, vendor security assessment questionnaires, and major change review templates, so that agility assessment becomes a routine element of architecture governance rather than a special-purpose quantum security activity.

Strategic partnership development and management

Partnership development is a relationship management skill that requires sustained investment to produce value. Build your quantum security partnership portfolio through:

- Completing a Partnership Gap Analysis against the four partnership types identified earlier in this chapter. Which types are you missing entirely? Which existing relationships are dormant rather than active? What intelligence gaps does your current portfolio leave unaddressed?
- Beginning with the most accessible entry points for partnership types you don't currently have: ETSI QSC or CSA Quantum-Safe Working Group membership for consortium partnership; NIST NCCoE working group participation for government agency partnership; a sponsored research agreement or student fellowship program for academic partnership.
- Applying the Tier 1/2/3 engagement model to rationalize your existing partnership investments, ensuring that your highest-value partnerships receive Tier 1 engagement intensity and that lower-priority relationships are efficiently maintained at Tier 3 rather than receiving sporadic attention that provides neither value nor closure.

Quantum compliance program leadership

Compliance leadership in a rapidly evolving regulatory environment requires both current knowledge and structural adaptability. Develop this capability through:

- Building a regulatory tracking function. Even a simple spreadsheet-based process that monitors quantum security guidance and rulemaking across all relevant regulatory frameworks on a quarterly basis, with assigned responsibility for tracking specific frameworks based on staff expertise.

- Completing a Common Control Mapping exercise using the framework described earlier in this chapter as a template. Identifying the specific control implementation in your organization that addresses quantum security requirements across multiple regulatory frameworks. This mapping is the foundation of a unified compliance program.
- Establishing proactive regulatory engagement practice. Attending regulatory comment periods on quantum security guidance development, participating in NIST and CISA working groups, and briefing your primary examiners on your quantum security program status before rather than during examination cycles. Regulators respond better to organizations that engage constructively with guidance development than to those who appear only during compliance demonstrations.

Long-term security vision communication and organizational alignment

Vision communication is a craft skill that improves with deliberate practice. Develop your quantum security vision communication capability through:

- Drafting a Quantum Security Vision Narrative for your organization. A 1–2-page document that articulates the quantum security mission, strategic rationale, program structure, and long-term commitment in language accessible to senior non-technical executives and board members. Socialize the draft with two or three senior stakeholders to test comprehension and resonance before finalizing.
- Designing a Quantum Security Board Communication Calendar that schedules regular board-level quantum security briefings tied to meaningful program milestones and monitoring outputs, rather than briefing only when urgent developments rather than episodic crisis communication.
- Practicing quantum security narrative translation by developing specific bridge statements that connect quantum security technical developments to business outcomes for your organization's specific strategic context. Practice these translations with non-technical peers until they feel natural and don't require rehearsal.

Summary

In this chapter, we took a journey from the emerging frontier of quantum security technology to the long-horizon governance structures that sustain adaptive security posture across decades of change. Let's consolidate the key architectural elements you now have at your disposal.

You've seen that the quantum security defense landscape extends beyond PQC to include QRNG (a near-term, practical upgrade), QKD (a specialized, high-value point-to-point solution for specific contexts), and an emerging horizon of quantum-native authentication, signing, and privacy mechanisms that will progressively mature over the next 10-15 years. Your Technology Readiness Assessment framework enables you to evaluate emerging quantum security technologies against organizational context rather than reacting to vendor claims without structured evaluation criteria.

You've built the architecture of a continuous monitoring program. Covering cryptographic algorithm security, quantum hardware advancement, threat actor developments, and regulatory evolution. You've also observed how monitoring outputs flow into Architecture Review Board governance processes that produce adaptive architecture decisions rather than accumulating as unactioned intelligence. The Quantum Security Architecture Monitoring Dashboard provides the integrated visibility that enables proactive adaptation rather than reactive crisis response.

You've mapped the quantum security partnership ecosystem and developed a Partnership Portfolio Management Framework that keeps relationships active and value-producing rather than allowing them to decay into dormant connections that exist only in organizational charts.

You've navigated the evolving regulatory landscape across federal, financial services, healthcare, and critical infrastructure frameworks, and developed a Unified Compliance Control Framework approach that addresses multiple simultaneous regulatory obligations through common control implementations rather than duplicated parallel programs. The audit readiness framework ensures that compliance program investments produce examination-ready evidence as a byproduct of operational program activities.

And you've built the governance architecture! The Quantum Security Architecture Board, the rolling technology roadmap, the multi-year investment framework, and the talent strategy, that gives your quantum security program the institutional durability to persist through leadership transitions, business cycle pressures, and competing strategic priorities. The Quantum Security Architecture Maturity Model provides the common measurement framework that enables you to assess your program's current state and communicate progress to boards and executive committees in structured, consistent terms.

Together, these frameworks, partnership structures, compliance designs, and governance mechanisms constitute not just a quantum-safe security program, but a genuinely adaptive quantum security architecture. A living system capable of evolving intelligently in response to the continuing advances in quantum technology, cryptanalytic capability, and threat actor sophistication that will define the security landscape of the 2030s and beyond.

This chapter completes Part III of this book, dedicated to quantum security transformation. But the book's journey isn't finished! And in a meaningful sense, neither is yours as a quantum-informed leader.

Through Parts I, II, and III, the focus has been on the quantum technologies most immediately actionable for business, technology, and security leaders: quantum computing capabilities, infrastructure integration, and post-quantum cryptography. These are the instruments you need to play now. However, quantum computing exists within a much larger quantum technology orchestra that is tuning up in parallel, and other instruments are beginning to matter in ways that strategic leaders can no longer afford to ignore.

What I am describing is the topic for Part IV "The Quantum Ecosystem: Big Picture and Strategy," particularly Chapter 13, "The Quantum Technology Ecosystem: Sensing, Networking, and the End-to-End Vision." This takes you to that broader vantage point. It surveys the full spectrum of quantum technologies: quantum sensing, quantum networking, quantum distributed computing, quantum key distribution as a networking layer rather than merely a cryptographic tool, and advanced quantum communication architectures. Learning how they interconnect into an integrated quantum capability landscape that is greater than the sum of its parts! For the security architect who has just completed this chapter, Chapter 13 provides critical context: the QKD technology you've been tracking as a specialized cryptographic mechanism is also the foundational layer of the emerging quantum internet that will transform secure communications infrastructure over the next two decades. The quantum hardware capability advances you've been monitoring for their cryptographic threat implications are also enabling quantum sensing capabilities that will reshape threat detection, critical infrastructure protection, and intelligence collection in ways that security architects will need to understand and plan for. Understanding the full quantum technology ecosystem, how its components connect, how they're converging, and what the integrated end-to-end vision looks like in practice, is the strategic prerequisite for making investment decisions, shaping security architecture vision, and building organizational capabilities that remain relevant across the full arc of the quantum technology transition, not just its security chapter.

The adaptive security architecture you've built in this chapter is ready for what comes next. Let's make sure you are too.

Further reading

1. https://doi.org/10.1016/j.tcs.2014.05.025
2. https://doi.org/10.1364/AOP.361502
3. https://doi.org/10.1103/PhysRevLett.120.030501
4. https://doi.org/10.1038/s41586-020-2401-y
5. https://doi.org/10.6028/jres.114.010
6. https://arxiv.org/abs/2401.02303v1
7. https://doi.org/10.1145/3727505.3727528
8. https://www.amazon.science/blog/qkd-and-authentication-separating-facts-from-myths
9. https://doi.org/10.1038/s41586-020-03093-8
10. https://digital-strategy.ec.europa.eu/en/policies/european-quantum-communication-infrastructure-euroqci
11. https://www.idquantique.com/quantum-safe-security/quantum-key-distribution/
12. https://www.nist.gov/publications/statistical-test-suite-random-and-pseudorandom-number-generators-cryptographic
13. https://doi.org/10.48550/arXiv.1604.03304
14. https://www.idquantique.com/random-number-generation/overview/
15. https://www.idquantique.com/random-number-generation/products/quantis-qrng-pcie/
16. https://www.quantinuum.com/blog/introducing-quantum-origin
17. https://csrc.nist.gov/presentations/2024/nist-standards-on-random-numbers
18. https://www.etsi.org/technologies/quantum-key-distribution
19. https://doi.org/10.1007/s10623-015-0157-4
20. https://doi.org/10.1103/RevModPhys.94.025008
21. https://doi.org/10.1103/PhysRevLett.113.040502
22. https://doi.org/10.1103/PhysRevLett.117.190501
23. https://doi.org/10.1088/2058-9565/aabc6b

24. https://doi.org/10.3390/quantum1010002
25. https://thequantuminsider.com/2025/03/22/how-to-build-a-quantum-blockchain-researchers-test-a-blockchain-that-only-quantum-computers-can-mine/
26. https://doi.org/10.1016/j.cosrev.2025.100752
27. https://doi.org/10.1109/FOCS.2009.36
28. https://doi.org/10.1038/s41534-017-0025-3
29. https://www.iacr.org/eprint/
30. https://www.iacr.org/meetings/crypto/
31. https://www.iacr.org/meetings/eurocrypt/
32. https://www.iacr.org/meetings/asiacrypt/
33. https://www.nist.gov/pqc
34. https://www.ibm.com/roadmaps/quantum/
35. https://quantumai.google/
36. https://www.darpa.mil/research/programs
37. https://www.insidequantumtechnology.com/
38. https://thequantuminsider.com/
39. https://www.cisa.gov/news-events/cybersecurity-advisories
40. https://media.defense.gov/2022/Sep/07/2003071836/-1/-1/0/CSI_CNSA_2.0_FAQ_.PDF
41. https://www.nationalisacs.org/
42. https://www.nsa.gov/Cybersecurity/Post-Quantum-Cybersecurity-Resources/
43. https://www.enisa.europa.eu/publications/post-quantum-cryptography-current-state-and-quantum-mitigation
44. http://cloudsecurityalliance.org/artifacts/a-practitioners-guide-to-post-quantum-cryptography
45. https://doi.org/10.1109/MSP.2018.3761723
46. https://www.quantum.gov/wp-content/uploads/2024/12/NQI-Annual-Report-FY2025.pdf
47. https://nvlpubs.nist.gov/nistpubs/CSWP/NIST.CSWP.39.pdf

48. https://www.doi.gov/techtransfer/crada
49. https://www.energy.gov/ceser/cybersecurity
50. https://www.etsi.org/technologies/quantum-safe-cryptography
51. https://cloudsecurityalliance.org/research/working-groups/quantum-safe-security
52. https://www.fsisac.com/knowledge/pqc
53. https://health-isac.org/
54. https://www.iiconsortium.org/wc-security/
55. https://ithandbook.ffiec.gov/it-booklets/information-security
56. https://www.federalregister.gov/documents/2025/01/06/2024-30983/hipaa-security-rule-to-strengthen-the-cybersecurity-of-electronic-protected-health-information

Part 4

The Quantum Ecosystem: Big Picture and Strategy

You've built the infrastructure. You've developed the teams. You've secured the architecture. Now it's time to step back and see the full picture.

Part IV is where the individual pieces of quantum readiness come together into something larger. The chapters ahead are written for the executives, investors, policymakers, and senior technical leaders who understand that quantum is not a single technology to be adopted. It's an ecosystem to be built. And the decisions that will shape that ecosystem are being made right now, not in some distant future when the technology is mature and the competitive positions are already locked in.

Across these chapters, you'll move from understanding the full spectrum of quantum technologies as an integrated strategic landscape, to learning how to actively construct the partnerships, talent pipelines, and institutional frameworks that will define who leads the quantum era. These chapters are deliberately big picture. They are designed to give you the strategic altitude to see beyond any single quantum initiative and understand the compounding, interconnected nature of what is being built across research labs, government programs, and corporate strategy offices around the world.

You won't find implementation checklists here. You'll find ecosystem literacy that sharpens your investment instincts, partnership frameworks that extend your organization's quantum reach far beyond what it could build alone, and a talent pipeline architecture that treats quantum workforce development as the long-term competitive advantage it is.

Think of this section as your quantum horizon map. It's the strategic complement to everything that came before it. And it ends with a simple, urgent reminder: the organizations that will define the quantum era are making their foundational moves today, while the partnerships are still available, the talent is still recruitable, and the competitive positions are still open.

The window is open. The chapters ahead will help you decide what to do with it.

This part of the book includes the following chapters:

- *Chapter 13, The Quantum Technology Ecosystem: Sensing, Networking, and the End-to-End Vision*
- *Chapter 14, Building the Quantum Ecosystem*

13

The Quantum Technology Ecosystem: Sensing, Networking, and the End-to-End Vision

Let's be honest about something. When most executives hear the word "quantum," their mental image defaults to quantum computing, those shimmering spherical cryostats suspended above a forest of gold wires, the photogenic icon of a revolution that may or may not be just around the corner. And fair enough, quantum computing has commanded the lion's share of headlines, boardroom attention, and venture capital investment. The preceding chapters of this book gave it serious and deserved attention. But here, at the gateway to Part IV, it's time to pull back the lens and see the full picture. Because quantum computing is only one instrument in a much larger quantum technology orchestra, and limiting your strategic planning to computing alone is a bit like investing in a single section of an orchestra and being surprised when it can't play a symphony. Ok, ok, I'll try to go easy on the music analogies.

Quantum sensing, quantum networking, quantum distributed computing, quantum key distribution (QKD), and advanced quantum cryptography are each maturing on their own development trajectories, and critically, those trajectories are deeply interconnected. The maturation of quantum networking accelerates both distributed computing and QKD deployment. Advances in quantum sensing create demand for quantum-secure communication of sensor data. And quantum distributed computing becomes possible only once quantum networking infrastructure is sufficiently robust. These are not parallel stories running in separate lanes; they are chapters in a single convergent narrative, and the organizations that understand the whole story will be in a far stronger strategic position than those reading only selected chapters.

This chapter is your big-picture briefing. It covers what each quantum technology in the broader ecosystem actually is, why it matters, what the practical near-term applications look like right now, not in some indeterminate quantum future. How these technologies interconnect into an integrated end-to-end quantum solution architecture, which would eventually lead into an entangled solutions group of hybrid interconnected systems. Along the way, you'll develop five critical skills that will sharpen both your technical literacy and your strategic acumen. The ability to speak fluently about the full quantum ecosystem with investors and board members; to think in terms of integrated solution architectures rather than isolated technology bets; to differentiate technology maturity levels with the precision needed to time investment decisions correctly; to build compelling present-state and future-state use case narratives for organizational stakeholders; and to design cross-technology quantum investment portfolios calibrated to your industry context and strategic objectives.

By the end of this chapter, you'll understand not just what quantum technologies are coming, but which ones are already here, how they connect, and what an architecturally coherent quantum strategy looks like across the full spectrum. That understanding is the strategic prerequisite for Chapter 14, which addresses the equally critical question of how the quantum ecosystem gets built: through talent pipelines, university partnerships, and sustained institutional commitment. But first, let's meet the full orchestra.

This chapter will cover the following topics:

- Quantum sensing: Precision measurement at the limits of physics
- Quantum networking: Entanglement-based communication infrastructure
- Quantum distributed computing: Scaling quantum power across connected nodes
- Quantum key distribution and quantum cryptography: The provably secure communication layer
- The integrated end-to-end quantum solution: Technologies working in concert
- Quantum technology maturity assessment framework
- Cross-technology quantum investment portfolio design framework
- Quantum ecosystem skills: Integration and application

Quantum sensing: Precision measurement at the limits of physics

If you're looking for the quantum technology that offers the most unambiguous near-term business value, meaning the one where you can deploy it today, get real data, and demonstrate

ROI to your CFO before the year is over, then quantum sensing deserves your immediate attention. While quantum computing continues its journey toward fault-tolerant operation and quantum networking is still building metropolitan-scale infrastructure, quantum sensing has quietly crossed the threshold from research into commercial deployment across several industries. It's, in the vocabulary of technology readiness, already doing real work in the real world.

Quantum sensing exploits the extreme sensitivity of quantum mechanical states to their environment. Where classical sensors are fundamentally limited by thermal noise and electromagnetic constraints, floors defined by physics that engineers have been bumping against for decades, quantum sensors use those same quantum mechanical sensitivities as their working mechanism. A quantum gravimeter, for example, doesn't fight gravity gradient noise. Instead, it reads it with extraordinary precision. A quantum magnetometer doesn't struggle to detect faint magnetic fields; it uses the quantum states of atoms to detect magnetic field variations far below the threshold at which any classical instrument can operate.[1]

The primary quantum sensing modalities

Quantum sensing technology encompasses several distinct categories, each targeting different measurement domains:

- **Atomic clocks and quantum timekeeping:** Atomic clocks, already the backbone of GPS, telecommunication synchronization, and financial market timestamping, represent the most commercially mature quantum sensing technology. Next-generation optical atomic clocks now achieve precision roughly 100 times better than the cesium microwave standards currently in use,[2] with implications for navigation, geodesy, and distributed system synchronization that extend across virtually every industry.
- **Quantum magnetometers:** Operating on principles including atomic spin magnetometry and superconducting quantum interference devices (SQUIDs), quantum magnetometers detect magnetic field anomalies at sensitivity levels far exceeding classical instruments. Applications span brain imaging (magnetoencephalography, or MEG), cardiac diagnostics (magnetocardiography, or MCG), detection of buried ferromagnetic objects, and power grid anomaly detection.
- **Quantum accelerometers and inertial navigation systems (INS):** These devices enable GPS-independent positioning by measuring acceleration and rotation with quantum-mechanical precision. For maritime, aviation, and military applications where GPS denial is a strategic risk, quantum INS represents a critical resilience capability that is actively being developed by programs including the UK's National

Quantum Technologies Program and DARPA's Quantum-Assisted Sensing and Readout (QuASAR) initiative.[3]

- **Quantum-enhanced imaging:** By exploiting entangled photon pairs and quantum illumination techniques, quantum-enhanced imaging systems can achieve resolution and sensitivity beyond the classical diffraction limit, enabling applications in low-light security imaging, medical diagnostics, and remote sensing.[4]

Strategic implications of quantum sensing are distributed across a notably broad range of industries, which is precisely what makes it strategically distinctive. Unlike quantum computing, whose near-term advantages are concentrated in specific computational problem classes, quantum sensing touches defense and intelligence, healthcare, energy, agriculture, construction, financial markets infrastructure, and environmental monitoring.[5]

Present-day use case: Utility infrastructure mapping

Present Day, Quantum Gravimetry for Urban Infrastructure: A utility company partners with a quantum sensing technology provider to deploy quantum gravimeter survey teams ahead of urban construction projects. The gravimeters detect previously unmapped legacy pipe networks and subsurface voids with sufficient precision to avoid costly construction incidents, therefore reducing project delays by 30% and eliminating three significant infrastructure damage events in the first deployment year. Sensing data is processed through classical AI-driven signal pipelines that translate raw quantum sensor outputs into actionable infrastructure maps. This quantum-classical hybrid workflow is operating at commercial scale today, not in some future state.

Future State, Urban Quantum Sensing Networks: As quantum sensing matures, cities could deploy networks of quantum gravimeters at high-risk locations, including bridges, tunnels, rail corridors, water mains, utility routes, and areas prone to sinkholes. These sensors detect subtle changes in the gravitational field that can signal underground voids, water loss, soil movement, damaged tunnels, or other hidden conditions before they appear at the surface. Combined with asset records, inspection histories, weather data, and AI-based risk models, this information could help city teams identify where inspections and repairs are needed most. Quantum gravity sensing has already been demonstrated for detecting subsurface structures, including utility-sized tunnels beneath roads.[34]

This would not replace engineers or conventional inspections. It would instead give them earlier warning and a clearer view of risks that are difficult to see today. Instead of reacting after a road collapses or a water main breaks, cities could prioritize preventative work based on likely impact. The benefits would extend beyond public works, supporting better decisions in insurance, property valuation, development planning, transit expansion, and long-term resilience investments.

Quantum networking: Entanglement-based communication infrastructure

If quantum computing is the brain of the quantum technology ecosystem and quantum sensing is its nervous system, then quantum networking is the circulatory system. The infrastructure that connects everything else. And like the circulatory system, its importance is easy to underestimate precisely because its value shows up as the performance of everything that depends on it, rather than as a standalone capability.

Quantum networking transmits quantum states between physically separated quantum systems using entanglement and quantum teleportation. This is categorically different from classical networking, which transmits copies of information encoded in classical bits. The key word here is copies. Classical networks move data by copying it, which means a sufficiently capable adversary can, in principle, copy your data without leaving evidence. Quantum networking, by contrast, transmits quantum states that cannot be copied. This is due to the no-cloning theorem, a fundamental result of quantum mechanics, and any attempt to intercept or measure quantum states in transit inevitably disturbs them, making interception detectable.[6]

This is not merely a security feature; it's an architectural property of the technology. And it has implications that extend far beyond secure communication.

The building blocks of quantum network infrastructure

Building a quantum network requires infrastructure components that have no classical analog, which will eventually drive a whole new set of architectural and design principles:

- **Quantum repeaters:** Classical optical networks use repeaters to amplify signals over distance. Quantum states cannot be amplified without being measured, which would destroy the quantum information. Quantum repeaters instead extend the range of entanglement distribution by refreshing and extending entanglement through a process called entanglement swapping, without ever measuring the quantum states being transmitted.[7] Quantum repeater technology is the primary limiting factor for long-distance quantum networking today.
- **Quantum memory nodes:** Storing quantum states long enough to synchronize entanglement distribution across multiple network segments requires quantum memory devices that preserve quantum coherence on timescales of milliseconds to seconds. Several physical platforms, including rare-earth-doped crystals, atomic vapor

cells, and nitrogen-vacancy centers in diamond, are advancing toward the memory performance specifications required for practical quantum repeater networks.[8]

- **Quantum-optical interfaces:** Most quantum processors use matter-based qubits (superconducting circuits, trapped ions, or neutral atoms) that cannot directly transmit quantum states over optical fiber. Quantum-optical interfaces convert between matter-based and photonic quantum state representations, enabling quantum processors to connect to optical quantum networks, a critical integration requirement for the quantum internet.[9]

Current quantum networking deployments are already demonstrating metropolitan-scale feasibility. The Chicago Quantum Network, operated by Argonne National Labs and partners including Fermilab and the University of Chicago, provides a 124-mile quantum networking testbed over deployed fiber infrastructure.[10, 11] In Europe, the EuroQCI (European Quantum Communication Infrastructure) initiative is funding national quantum network deployments across all EU member states, with the goal of creating a pan-European quantum communication backbone by 2027.[12] In the UK, BT and partners have demonstrated quantum networking over deployed BT fiber infrastructure in London.[13] And China's QUESS satellite program achieved quantum key distribution over ground-satellite distances exceeding 1,200 kilometers,[14] extending quantum networking beyond the reach of any terrestrial fiber deployment.

The strategic significance of quantum networking extends well beyond secure communication, a point that deserves particular emphasis. Quantum networks are simultaneously the communication security infrastructure for the quantum era, the connective tissue that will link distributed quantum computers into large-scale quantum computing clusters, and the platform that will enable distributed quantum sensing arrays to correlate measurements in ways that isolated sensors cannot achieve. Investing in quantum networking is not a single-use investment; it's infrastructure with compounding strategic value across every quantum technology layer.

Present-day use case: Quantum-secured financial settlement

Present Day, QKD-Assisted Interbank Settlement: A financial services consortium operates a pilot quantum network connecting three metropolitan trading hubs over deployed fiber infrastructure. Entangled photon pairs generate quantum-secure session keys for interbank settlement communications, operating in parallel with classical TLS-encrypted channels. This hybrid model, quantum networking for highest-sensitivity transaction categories, classical infrastructure for volume traffic, extracts near-term quantum networking value without requiring full infrastructure replacement. The key operational insight and investment point: quantum and classical networks coexist; you do not need to replace the old to deploy the new.

Future State, The Quantum Financial Internet: A mature quantum internet connects financial institutions, central banks, and regulatory bodies across jurisdictions through multi-node quantum repeater networks, enabling quantum-secured distributed ledger protocols with mathematically provable transaction integrity guarantees. Real-time quantum-authenticated audit trails eliminate entire categories of financial fraud that classical cryptographic systems cannot fully prevent, creating regulatory and compliance value that may ultimately drive quantum network adoption faster than pure security considerations.

Quantum distributed computing: Scaling quantum power across connected nodes

Here's a constraint that anyone who has worked in enterprise IT will immediately recognize: the hardware you actually have is never quite big enough for the problem you actually need to solve. For quantum computing, this constraint is particularly acute. Today's quantum processors, even the most advanced commercially available systems, operate with qubit counts and error rates that limit them to specific problem classes. The large-scale fault-tolerant quantum computers that will deliver the most transformative computational advantages require qubit counts and error correction capabilities that current hardware cannot yet achieve.

Quantum distributed computing addresses this constraint by connecting multiple quantum processing nodes through quantum communication channels, enabling them to execute quantum algorithms as a single logically unified quantum computing resource. Think of it as a quantum computing cluster. Analogous to the distributed computing architectures that power classical cloud infrastructure, but with the additional challenge that quantum state distribution between nodes requires quantum networking infrastructure that preserves quantum coherence across the entire distributed system.[15]

Technical approaches to distributed quantum computing

Three primary technical approaches are being pursued for quantum distributed computing, at varying levels of maturity:

- **Circuit cutting:** This is the most immediately available approach. Large quantum circuits that exceed the qubit capacity of a single device are decomposed into smaller subcircuits, each executable on an available quantum processor. Classical post-processing reconstructs the results of the full circuit from the outputs of the subcircuits. Circuit cutting introduces classical overhead that partially offsets quantum advantage, but it enables quantum computation at scales not achievable on any single device today, making it practically useful for specific near-term applications in quantum chemistry, optimization, and machine learning.[16]

- **Entanglement-based distributed gate operations:** This approach uses shared entanglement between quantum processing nodes to execute two-qubit gate operations across physically separated processors, enabling genuinely distributed quantum computation without the classical reconstruction overhead of circuit cutting. This approach requires quantum networking infrastructure capable of distributing high-fidelity entanglement between nodes on demand. A requirement that is at the frontier of current quantum networking capability.[17]
- **Modular quantum computing architectures:** Rather than networking geographically separated quantum processors, modular architectures connect multiple quantum processor modules within a single system chassis using quantum interconnects. Essentially building a quantum compute cluster at chip or rack scale. IBM, Quantinuum, and several research groups are actively developing modular approaches as a near-term pathway to larger effective qubit counts without requiring metropolitan-scale quantum networking infrastructure.[18]

For technical executives planning infrastructure investments, the critical insight about quantum distributed computing is its relationship to quantum networking: the organizations that build quantum networking infrastructure today are simultaneously investing in the quantum distributed computing capability of tomorrow. Quantum network investments are not sunk costs against a single use case; they are foundational infrastructure assets whose value compounds as additional quantum technology layers, computing, sensing, and cryptography, are deployed on top of them.

Present-day use case: Pharmaceutical molecular simulation

Present Day, Cross-Platform Quantum Chemistry: A pharmaceutical company runs quantum chemistry simulations of candidate drug molecules across two quantum cloud processors simultaneously using classical circuit cutting techniques. The molecular simulation circuits exceed the qubit capacity of any single available device, but decomposition across two platforms enables simulation at scales not previously accessible. The approach has already accelerated identification of two promising drug candidates in an antibiotic-resistance therapeutic program, demonstrating that near-term quantum distributed computing, even with classical overhead, delivers meaningful scientific value today.

Future State, Consortium Quantum Drug Discovery Networks: A consortium of pharmaceutical companies operates a shared quantum distributed computing network connecting specialized processors at three research facilities, each optimized for different quantum chemistry simulation tasks. End-to-end quantum simulation of drug-protein interaction dynamics at biologically realistic scales, from electron structure calculation through protein folding, eliminates the classical approximation errors that currently limit computational drug discovery accuracy and compresses development timelines from years to months. One thing to note is that while this is all incredibly impressive, it's easy to fall into the trap of assuming that quantum networking can scale as easily and as smoothly as classical. This is not necessarily the case, particularly that of quantum computing, they are not apples to apples, likely more like apples to onions.

Quantum key distribution and quantum cryptography: The provably secure communication layer

There is a version of security, one that virtually all enterprise IT infrastructure currently depends on, that rests on a bet. The bet is that the mathematical problems underlying public-key cryptography (factoring large integers, computing discrete logarithms) are and will remain computationally capability, and quantum computers are specifically designed to win that particular bet, at least for the problem classes underlying RSA and elliptic curve cryptography.[19]

Post-quantum cryptography (PQC), covered in depth in Chapter 9, addresses this by replacing the bet: instead of relying on problems that quantum computers can solve efficiently, PQC relies on mathematical problems that concurrent quantum algorithms cannot solve. The security guarantee is still computational as it depends on the assumed hardness of the underlying mathematical problems, but the computational assumptions are quantum-resistant rather than merely classically hard.

Quantum key distribution (QKD) operates on an entirely different security model. QKD does not merely replace one computational assumption with another; it eliminates the computational assumption entirely. QKD security is guaranteed by the laws of physics rather than the assumed hardness of mathematical problems, a qualitatively different and fundamentally more robust security guarantee for use cases where even long-term computational security assumptions are considered insufficient.[20]

How QKD works, and why it matters

QKD protocols, most famously BB84[21] and E91,[22] distribute cryptographic keys between communicating parties using the quantum mechanical properties of individual photons or entangled photon pairs. The critical security property is this: any attempt by an eavesdropper to intercept or measure the photons being used to distribute the key inevitably disturbs those photons in ways that are detectable by the communicating parties. An eavesdropper cannot intercept and re-transmit quantum states without leaving detectable traces. This is not a design feature that could be worked around with better technology, it's a consequence of the quantum mechanical laws governing the universe. The security guarantee is information-theoretical rather than computational: even an adversary with unlimited computational power, including a fully operational cryptographically relevant quantum computer, cannot break QKD-protected communication without being detected.

This distinction matters enormously for organizations protecting data over 10-to-30-year timescales, critical infrastructure control systems, national security communications, central bank settlement infrastructure, and long-lived classified archives. For these use cases, the "harvest-now, decrypt-later" threat model, in which adversaries collect encrypted data today and decrypt it once cryptographically relevant quantum computers become available, represents a concrete, present-tense risk that QKD directly addresses by making even currently collected ciphertext cryptographically useless, because the keys used to encrypt it were generated and distributed via physics-guaranteed processes.

QKD and PQC: Partners, not competitors

A common misconception among executives encountering QKD for the first time is that it competes with post-quantum cryptography, that organizations must choose between them. This is wrong, and understanding why it's wrong is itself a strategically important piece of quantum ecosystem literacy.

PQC is the right near-term migration path for most enterprise cryptographic systems. It operates over classical communication infrastructure, is deployable as software updates, has been standardized by NIST, and provides quantum-resistant security appropriate for most enterprise use cases. QKD is appropriate for the highest sensitivity use cases. Cases where information-theoretic rather than computational security guarantees are required, and where the capital infrastructure investment in dedicated QKD hardware and fiber or satellite infrastructure is justified by the sensitivity of the communications being protected. Most enterprises will deploy PQC broadly and QKD selectively; national security agencies, central banks, and artificial infrastructure operators are likely to deploy both across their most sensitive communications.

Beyond key distribution: The broader quantum cryptography toolkit

QKD is the most mature and commercially deployed component of a broader quantum cryptography toolkit that includes quantum digital signatures (providing non-repudiation guarantees based on physics rather than computation), quantum secret sharing (distributing secrets across multiple parties such that only authorized subsets can reconstruct them), and quantum-secured multi-party computation (enabling multiple parties to jointly compute on private inputs without revealing those inputs to each other, with security guaranteed by quantum mechanical principles). These capabilities extend quantum mechanical security guarantees to a range of enterprise use cases. Use cases such as secure financial computation, privacy-preserving regulatory reporting, and distributed decision-making, that will become increasingly relevant as quantum networking infrastructure matures.

Present-day use case: Defense agency QKD network

Present Day, Metropolitan QKD for Classified Communications: A national defense agency deploys a metropolitan QKD network connecting its headquarters with three classified data centers over dedicated dark fiber. QKD-generated keys protect the most sensitive classified communications; classical encryption handles volume traffic on general network infrastructure. Commercial QKD hardware from established providers is integrated with existing key management infrastructure through standardized interfaces, allowing quantum-generated keys to be consumed by conventional encryption appliances without disrupting security operations center workflows. This hybrid integration model, quantum security where it matters most, classical security everywhere else, is the operationally realistic deployment pattern for near-term QKD adoption.

Future State, Satellite QKD for Allied-Nation Security Infrastructure: A satellite-based QKD network provides quantum-secure key distribution between government facilities across transcontinental distances, eliminating the fiber infrastructure constraint that currently limits QKD to metropolitan scales. Combined with quantum networking, the satellite QKD layer feeds a quantum-secured communication backbone connecting defense, intelligence, and critical infrastructure operators across allied nations, with security integrity guaranteed by physics against adversaries with arbitrarily advanced computational capabilities.

The integrated end-to-end quantum solution: Technologies working in concert

Now that we have toured each instrument in the quantum technology orchestra, it's time to hear them play together. Because the most important thing to understand about the quantum technology ecosystem is that its transformative potential is not additive. It's multiplicative. The capability of an integrated quantum solution, including sensing, networking, distributed computing, QKD, and quantum cryptography operating as interconnected layers of a coherent architecture, is not the sum of the capabilities of each component. It's qualitatively different from what any component can achieve in isolation.

Think of it this way: a quantum sensor that cannot securely transmit its data is strategically limited. A quantum network that has no quantum-sensing data to transmit and no quantum computing to process it is underutilized infrastructure. A quantum distributed computer that has no quantum-secure communication channels is vulnerable. Now, let's put everything together in a single workflow or pipeline. Sensing generating data, networking transmitting it with physics-guaranteed security, distributed computing processing it at quantum scale, QKD and quantum cryptography ensuring the integrity of every layer. Now you have something genuinely unprecedented: a measurement, communication, and computation architecture whose security guarantees extend from the physical sensor layer to the computational analysis layer, all grounded in the laws of physics rather than computational assumptions.[23, 24]

The integrated architecture model

The quantum-classical integration layer deserves its own place in the investment conversation. It's where quantum capabilities integrate with classical AI, machine learning, data engineering, workflow and cloud systems that turn technical output into business decisions. Quantum technologies rarely deliver themselves as a stand-alone tool. Its near-term value will come from hybrid workflows in which classical systems prepare data, guide quantum workloads, interpret results, and embed those results into operational processes. For many technical executives, this is encouraging news. Organizations that have invested in AI and data infrastructure are not starting from zero. They already have many of the capabilities needed to make quantum outputs useful, including data pipelines, model-development practices, scalable computing environments, governance, and teams that know how to operationalize analytics. The investment question isn't simply whether to fund quantum activities or pilots. It's whether to strengthen the integration layers that allow quantum and classical capabilities to work together and produce value. The following table provides a list of technologies, their functions, and maturity status for each layer.

Layer	Technology	Function in Integrated Architecture	Maturity Status
Physical Sensing Layer	Quantum Sensing (gravimeters, magnetometers, atomic clocks)	Generates high-fidelity measurement data from physical environments inaccessible to classical sensors	Commercial-Deployable Now
Communication Layer	Quantum Networking (entanglement, repeaters, quantum memory)	Transmits quantum states and distributes entanglement between nodes with physics-guaranteed security	Early Commercial, Metropolitan Scale

Layer	Technology	Function in Integrated Architecture	Maturity Status
Security Layer	QKD + Quantum Cryptography (BB84, E91, quantum signatures)	Protects all inter-component communication channels with information-theoretic security guarantees	Sensitivity Deployments
Computational Layer	Quantum Distributed Computing (circuit cutting, modular architectures)	Processes quantum data and executes optimization/ simulation algorithms beyond single-device capacity	Research-to-Pilot, Advancing Rapidly
Integration Layer	Classical AI + Data Processing	Translates quantum outputs into actionable intelligence Interfaces quantum and classical system components	Mature, Available Today

Table 13.1: Integrated Architecture Model

The integration dependency map

Understanding the dependency relationships between quantum technology layers is essential for sequencing investment decisions correctly. The following framework captures the key integration dependencies that determine which investments unlock which downstream capabilities:

Investment	Direct Capability	Unlocks Downstream	Sequencing Priority
Quantum networking infrastructure	Secure quantum communication channels	Distributed computing, distributed sensing, QKD at scale	High, Foundational enabler
QKD deployment	Physics-guaranteed key distribution	Quantum-secured multi-party computation, quantum-authenticated audit trails	High, Available now for sensitive use cases
Quantum sensing pilots	Precision measurements in target domains	Distributed sensing networks (requires networking layer)	Very High, Immediate ROI available
Circuit cutting tooling	Near-term distributed quantum computation	Full entanglement-based distributed computing (requires networking)	Medium, Advances rapidly
Quantum memory R&D partnerships	Extended entanglement range	Long-distance quantum networking and continental QKD	Medium, 3-5 years horizon
Quantum-classical AI integration	Actionable quantum outputs today	End-to-end quantum solution orchestration	Very High, Leverage existing AI capability

Table 13.2: Integration Dependency Map

Present-to-future use case: Integrated public safety security

Present Day, Public Safety Event Detection: Today, most security experts leverage metal detectors, cameras, access controls, and other technologies such as AI to monitor high-risk locations such as airports, schools, major public events, and transit hubs. In future deployments, quantum magnetometer arrays could add a more sensitive, passive layer of detection. By positioning them along selected zones, or entrances, they could identify unusual magnetic signatures associated with certain concealed metallic objects. AI systems could help security personnel distinguish a meaningful alert from your everyday usual activities by simply comparing signals with location, context, and other available data. This would support faster, more focused screening rather than replacing trained personnel, established processes, or tools. It's important to note that as QKD can help detect interception during the key exchange process, it doesn't authenticate the source of the sensor data or prevent spoofing on its own. Protecting against spoofed alerts will still require signed data, identity controls, and a layered cybersecurity architecture.[35]

Near-Term: Quantum distributed computing nodes at regional analysis centers process multi-sensor quantum data fusion algorithms correlating magnetometer, gravimeter, and quantum-enhanced imaging data streams. Threat characterization accuracy exceeds what any classical sensor fusion method can achieve.

Mature Quantum: A fully integrated quantum solution connects sensing networks, secure quantum communication infrastructure, and distributed quantum analysis computing into a coherent, provably secure, physically tamper-evident perimeter intelligence system, whose security integrity rests on the laws of physics from sensor to analysis.

Quantum technology maturity assessment framework

One of the most common and most expensive mistakes in quantum strategy is applying the wrong investment thesis to the wrong technology at the wrong maturity level. Investing in quantum distributed computing with the urgency appropriate to quantum sensing is a waste of resources. However, delaying quantum sensing investment because you're waiting for quantum computing maturity is a missed competitive opportunity. The quantum technology maturity differentiation requires a framework for making these distinctions systematically rather than impressionistically. In essence, investors need to keep watch for maturity changes in the landscape.

The following maturity assessment framework maps each major quantum technology across five dimensions: Technology Readiness Level (adapted from NASA's standard TRL scale),[25] Commercial Availability, Organizational Readiness Requirements, Investment Horizon, and Early-Mover Risk. Use this framework to calibrate your investment timing decisions for each quantum technology layer independently.

Technology	TRL (1-9)	Commercial Status	Org Readiness Needed	Investment Horizon	Early Mover Risk
Atomic Clocks / Quantum Timing	9	Mature Commercial	Standard Procurement	Immediate	Very Low

Technology	TRL (1-9)	Commercial Status	Org Readiness Needed	Investment Horizon	Early Mover Risk
Quantum Gravimeters	7-8	Commercial: Specialist Providers	Domain expertise + pilot planning	0-2 years	Low
Quantum Magnetometers	6-7	Early Commercial: Growing Provider Base	Domain expertise + pilot planning	0-2 years	Low
Quantum Inertial Navigation	6-7	Early Commercial: Defense Focus	Specialist Partnership	1-3 years	Low-Medium
QKD (Metro, Fiber)	7-8	Specialized Commercial	Cybersecurity + network ops	0-2 years (high-sensitivity)	Low
Quantum Networks (Metro)	5-6	Early Commercial: Testbeds	Network infrastructure team	2-4 years	Medium
QKD (Satellite)	5-6	Early commercial: Government Focus	Government partnership / Consortium	3-6 years	Medium
Circuit Cutting / NISQ Distributed	5-6	Pilot: Cloud Accessible	Quantum software team	1-3 years (pilots)	Medium
Modular Quantum Computing	4-5	Research-to-Pilot	Research partnership + talent	3-6 years	Medium -High

Technology	TRL (1-9)	Commercial Status	Org Readiness Needed	Investment Horizon	Early Mover Risk
Entanglement-Based Distributed Computing	3-4	Research Stage	University / Lab partnership	5-10 years	High

Table 13.3: Maturity Assessment Framework Map

Do keep in mind that the information based on creating the assessment, along with any frameworks, was originally documented at the time of this writing. It would be considered good practice to ensure that your teams are kept up to speed with the latest information and advancements as they become available so they can update the frameworks as needed.

Company spotlight: ID Quantique (IDQ)

Founded in 2001 as a spin-off from the University of Geneva, making it one of the world's oldest quantum technology companies, ID Quantique (IDQ) represents the European quantum technology ecosystem at its most commercially mature. Headquartered in Geneva, Switzerland, IDQ has spent over two decades building commercial products across quantum random number generation, quantum key distribution, and quantum sensing, amassing a customer base that spans telecommunications providers, financial institutions, government agencies, and defense organizations across more than 60 countries. In 2017, IDQ was acquired by SK Telecom, South Korea's largest wireless carrier, providing the capital and telecommunications industry relationships to accelerate commercial QKD deployment at carrier scale.[26] A strategic partnership model that illustrates how quantum technology companies can reach commercial scale through alignment with established infrastructure operators.

IDQ's QKD product provides commercial-grade QKD hardware that integrates with standard optical networking infrastructure and existing key management systems. The company's Quantis quantum random number generators[27] are deployed in financial market infrastructure, government systems, and cybersecurity applications requiring cryptographic-quality randomness that is physically unmanipulable rather than computationally approximated. In the quantum sensing domain, IDQ's single-photon detection technology[28] underpins quantum sensing and quantum communication systems for clients including national research programs and defense agencies across Europe and Asia.

The strategic lesson from IDQ's 20-plus year development arc is not an anomaly. It's the realistic timeline for quantum technology companies reaching genuine commercial scale, and partner selection should account for financial sustainability over that horizon. Second, IDQ uses an integration-first design for its products. They build QKD systems that plug directly into existing infrastructure and management systems. This avoids the need for a costly "full stack" replacement. Ultimately, this approach creates a blueprint for making quantum technology easier for enterprises to adopt within a mature ecosystem. Third, IDQ's acquisition by IonQ in 2025[29] illustrates the value of industry partnerships (which started with SK Telecom) for quantum network technology companies. Which is a model likely to replace across the quantum ecosystem as quantum networking technology matures toward carrier-grade deployment.

For European organizations evaluating QKD deployment, IDQ provides a particularly compelling proof point: quantum key distribution is not a future technology to be monitored from a distance. It's a commercially available product with a documented customer base, standards-compliant integration interfaces, and a two-decade track record of operational deployment. The barrier to piloting QKD in high-sensitivity communication contexts is organizational priority, not technology readiness.

Company spotlight: Toshiba Quantum Technology

Toshiba's quantum technology research program, headquartered at Toshiba Research Europe's Cambridge Research Laboratory in the UK, has been at the frontier of quantum communication research for more than 20 years. Toshiba made the organizational commitment to commercial deployment by establishing Toshiba Quantum Technology as a dedicated business unit focused on bringing QKD and quantum networking products to market.[30] This transition from research program to commercial business unit is strategically significant. It represents a major industrial corporation committing the capital and organization needed to move quantum tech from the lab into real-world infrastructure. Toshiba's massive manufacturing power and deep ties to government and finance provide a commercial head start that smaller startups simply cannot match.

Toshiba's quantum technology portfolio centers on its Multiplexed QKD system, which achieves industry-leading key generation rates by multiplexing multiple quantum channels on a single optical fiber. A critical capability for making QKD economically viable at enterprise scale, since higher key generation rates reduce the cost per bit of quantum-secured communication and enable QKD to protect higher-bandwidth communication streams. The company has demonstrated QKD over fiber distances exceeding 600 kilometers using a Twin-Field QKD protocol. A world record at the time of publication (2018) that directly addresses the distance limitation that has historically constrained QKD deployment to metropolitan-scale fiber networks.[31] Toshiba is also a participant in multiple UK national quantum network programs, including the UKRI-funded Quantum Communications Hub, giving the company a central role in shaping the UK's national quantum communication infrastructure architecture. [32]

Toshiba Quantum Technology's roadmap includes quantum network infrastructure products targeting telecommunications operators, a QKD-as-a-service model for enterprise customers, and quantum sensing products leveraging the company's expertise in single-photon detection. [33] Their diverse quantum technology portfolio positions the company to participate across multiple layers of the integrated quantum ecosystem rather than in a single technology vertical. For executives evaluating quantum partnerships, Toshiba Quantum Technology illustrates that the quantum ecosystem is increasingly populated not only by specialized quantum startups but by major industrial organizations with the manufacturing scale, standards relationships, and customer access to drive quantum technology deployment into mainstream infrastructure.

Cross-technology quantum investment portfolio design framework

Cross-Technology Quantum Investment Portfolio Design is arguably the most immediate practical skill developed in this chapter for senior executives accountable for technology investment decisions. The following framework provides a structured approach to designing a quantum investment portfolio calibrated to organizational industry context, strategic priorities, and technology maturity timelines.

The framework is organized around three portfolio tiers that correspond to different investment time horizons and risk-return profiles:

Tier 1: Foundational investments (Deploy now — 0-24 months)

These are the investments in quantum technologies at commercial readiness, where the risk-return calculus favors early deployment over continued monitoring:

Investment Category	**Technology**	**Industries with Highest Near-Term ROI**	**Investment Approach**
Quantum Sensing Pilots	Quantum gravimeters, magnetometers, atomic clocks	Energy, utilities, construction, defense, healthcare, financial markets	Vendor pilot contracts Outcome-based pricing where available
QKD for High-Sensitivity Communications	Commercial QKD hardware + fiber infrastructure	Defense, national security, central banking, critical infrastructure operators	Dedicated dark fiber + commercial QKD hardware Hybrid classical / quantum deployment
PQC Migration (complementary to QKD)	NIST-standardized PQC algorithms	All industries: foundational cyber hygiene	Software-layer migration Prioritize long-lived data and critical systems
Quantum-Classical AI integration	Classical AI systems designed to consume quantum outputs	All industries with quantum sensing or computing pilots	Internal capability building + partnership with quantum-ready AI vendors
Quantum Workforce Development	Training, partnerships, talent acquisition	All industries	University partnerships, online quantum education programs, specialist hiring

Table 13.4: Foundational Investments (Deploy Now – 0-24 months)

Tier 2: Strategic option investments (Build now, deploy at maturity, 2-5 years)

These are investments that position the organization to deploy quantum capabilities as they reach commercial readiness, without premature large-scale commitment:

Investment Category	Technology	Strategic Purpose	Investment Approach
Quantum Network Pilots	Metropolitan quantum networking testbed access	• Infrastructure readiness • Distributed computing and sensing preparation	• Consortium membership • Testbed access agreements • Standards body participation
Quantum Computing Access	NISQ cloud access + circuit cutting tooling	• Algorithmic capability development • Problem domain identification	• Cloud subscription + internal algorithm development team
QKD Satellite Readiness	Satellite QKD infrastructure partnerships	• Transcontinental quantum-secure communication preparation	• Government program participation • Consortium investment
Modular Quantum Computing Partnerships	Hardware partner relationships for modular QC roadmap	• Position for fault-tolerant quantum computing access	• Research partnership agreements • Quantum computing vendor contracts with roadmap commitments

Investment Category	Technology	Strategic Purpose	Investment Approach
Quantum Security Standards Participation	ETSI, ISO, NIST quantum security standards bodies	• Influence standards that will govern quantum network and QKD deployment	• Standards body membership • Technical expert secondment

Table 13.5: Tier 2: Strategic Option Investment (Build Now, Deploy at Maturity – 2-5 years)

Tier 3: Innovation option investments (Explore now, commit later, 5-10+ years)

These are small-scale investments in early-stage quantum capabilities that preserve option value and organizational knowledge without requiring large-scale commitment:

Investment Category	Technology	Strategic Purpose	Investment Approach
Entanglement-Based Distributed Computing Research	University research partnerships National lab programs	Early insight into distributed quantum computing architectures	Research grants co-funding University partnership agreements
Quantum Internet Architecture Research	Quantum repeater R&D Quantum memory research	Position for quantum internet infrastructure buildout	Research consortium participation Small equity investment in quantum networking startups
Quantum Sensing Network Architectures	Networked quantum sensor array research	Prepare for distributed sensing networks that require quantum networking	Applied research partnerships with sensing + networking providers

Investment Category	Technology	Strategic Purpose	Investment Approach
Advanced Quantum Cryptography Primitives	Quantum digital signatures Quantum MPC research	Explore quantum cryptography capabilities beyond QKD	Research partnership with academic quantum cryptography groups

Table 13.6: Tier 3: Innovation Option Investments (Explore Now, Commit Later, 5-10+ years)

The portfolio design principle underlying all three tiers is in sequencing. Investments in Tier 1 are not just immediate value generators; they are also capability-building investments. Investments that make Tier 2 deployments more successful by ensuring that your organization has the operational experience, technical talent, and vendor relationships required to deploy more complex quantum technologies as they mature. Organizations that begin with Tier 3 investments while skipping Tier 1 are accumulating research knowledge without operational experience. Organizations that focus exclusively on Tier 1 without Tier 2 strategic options risk being competitively disadvantaged when the next wave of quantum capabilities reaches commercial readiness. Having a balanced portfolio positions your organization to capture quantum value at each stage of the ecosystem's maturation.

The five quantum ecosystem skills: Integration and application

Throughout this chapter, five critical skills have been woven into the frameworks, use cases, and strategic discussions. Here is a consolidated integration of how each skill applies in practice, and how they compound when applied together.

Quantum ecosystem literacy for strategic decision-making

The ability to speak fluently about the full quantum technology ecosystem, not just quantum computing, is the foundation skill that enables all the others. In practice, this skill is exercised most often in executive and board communications such as: explaining to a CFO why a quantum sensing pilot belongs in the near-term capital plan; articulating to an audit committee why QKD and PQC are both necessary but serve different security tiers; communicating to a board the strategic logic of a quantum networking consortium investment when full commercial deployment is still two to four years away. The analogies and use cases in this chapter are explicitly designed to support these conversations, use them. The utility company and infrastructure mapping example translates quantum gravimetry into a language any CFO can evaluate; the financial services consortium QKD example frames quantum networking in the terms most relevant to banking executives. Ecosystem literacy is not about being able to derive the Schrodinger equation; it's about having the conceptual vocabulary and use case library to make quantum technology intelligible and compelling to non-specialist stakeholders.

Integrated solution architecture thinking

The integration dependency map and the maturity assessment framework are the primary tools for developing this skill. When evaluating a vendor proposal for a quantum solution, the first question is not "does this technology work?" but "what other technology layer does this assume or require, and are those layers at sufficient maturity to support the proposed architecture?" A QKD proposal that assumes fiber quantum network repeater infrastructure that doesn't yet exist in your geography is not a deployable solution, it's a future-state vision priced as a present-state product. Integrated architecture thinking allows you to identify these gaps before signing contracts, and to ask vendors the right questions about integration dependencies, fallback architectures, and maturity-sequenced deployment roadmaps.

Quantum technology maturity differentiation

The maturity assessment framework in this chapter operationalizes this skill as a practical decision support tool. Apply it by mapping each quantum technology relevant to your industry against its actual TRL and commercial availability status and then calibrating your investment posture accordingly. Quantum gravimeters in the energy and utilities sectors are at TRL 7-8 with commercial providers available; the investment thesis is "deploy now and learn." Entanglement-based distributed quantum computing is at TRL 3-4; the investment thesis is "maintain research visibility and option value through university partnerships." Conflating these maturity levels, treating research-stage technologies as deployment-ready, or treating commercially available technologies as too immature to pilot, is one of the most common and most costly quantum strategy errors.

Present-state and future-state use case development

Every use case in this chapter is structured as a two-part narrative: what is achievable today with current technology and current organizational capabilities, and what will become achievable as the ecosystem matures. This structure is deliberately designed to provide stakeholders with both a near-term investment rationale (the present-state use case) and a long-term strategic vision (the future-state use case). This ensures that quantum technology investment proposals do not rest entirely on future-state promises that require multiple technology layers to mature simultaneously. When developing use cases for your own organizational context, start with the present-state: what can you deploy with currently available quantum technology, within your current organizational and infrastructure constraints, and what measurable business outcome would it deliver? Then extend the future-state: what additional capabilities would become available as quantum networking, distributed computing, and advanced quantum cryptography mature, and how does the organizational capability you are building today position you to capture those future-state advantages?

Cross-technology quantum investment portfolio design

The three-tier portfolio framework provides the structural architecture for this last skill, but the skill itself is in calibrating the portfolio to your specific organizational context. Portfolio calibration requires three inputs: your industry's quantum technology relevance profile (which quantum technologies are most applicable to your specific business domain and competitive landscape), your current organizational quantum capability level (do you have quantum-aware technical talent, established quantum vendor relationships, relevant pilot program experience), and your strategic time horizon (how much of your competitive advantage depends on being a first-mover in quantum versus a fast-follower). Organizations in defense, financial services, and critical infrastructure should weigh Tier 1 investments more heavily, given the regulatory and competitive pressures that make early QKD and quantum sensing adoption strategically necessary. Organizations in pharmaceuticals and materials science should weigh Tier 2 quantum computing investments more heavily, given the domain-specific competitive advantage that quantum chemistry simulation will eventually deliver. Retail, logistics, and consumer-facing businesses have longer time horizons and should weigh Tier 3 research options more lightly while focusing on Tier 1 investment in quantum sensing applications relevant to supply chain and operational efficiency.

Summary

This chapter has expanded the strategic quantum lens from the focused domains of quantum computing, AI integration, and post-quantum cryptography to encompass the full quantum technology ecosystem that will ultimately deliver the most transformative quantum-enabled capabilities. Let's anchor the key insights before moving forward.

Quantum sensing is commercially available and delivers measurable business value today, where access and costs vary based on industry and domain. In infrastructure mapping, defense detection, medical diagnostics, and energy resources characterization, making it the quantum technology with the most immediate relevance for the broadest range of industries. Quantum networking is crossing the threshold from research to early-commercial deployment, with metropolitan-scale networks operational on multiple continents and the EuroQCI initiative building toward a pan-European quantum communication backbone. Quantum key distribution provides physics-guaranteed security for the highest-sensitivity communication use cases, and its relationship with post-quantum cryptography is complementary rather than competitive, both deployed, calibrated to the sensitivity of the use case. Quantum distributed computing is the architectural pathway from today's NISQ-era devices to tomorrow's fault-tolerant quantum computers, and organizations investing in quantum networking infrastructure today are simultaneously building the foundation for distributed quantum computing capability. And the integrated end-to-end quantum architecture: sensing, networking, distributed computing, QKD, and quantum cryptography operating as coherent, interdependent layers, is not a speculative future concept but an architectural destination that forward-looking organizations are already positioning themselves to reach.

The five skills developed in this chapter: quantum ecosystem literacy, integrated architecture thinking, technology maturity differentiation, present- and future-state use case development, and cross-technology portfolio design, are the strategic toolkit for making sound quantum investment and policy decisions across the full arc of the quantum technology transition, not only its most viable first act. Together, they enable leaders to move beyond single-technology quantum strategies toward quantum ecosystem strategies that position their organizations to capture compounding quantum value as successive technology layers reach commercial maturity.

One final framing before the transition to the next chapter: understanding the quantum technology ecosystem, as this chapter has endeavored to provide, is necessary but not sufficient for organizational quantum readiness. The quantum technology ecosystem described here will not materialize through market forces alone. It will be built, deliberately, collaboratively, and with sustained institutional commitment, by organizations and governments that understand something important: the distance between today's quantum research frontiers and tomorrow's quantum commercial infrastructure is measured not only in technology readiness levels and hardware performance benchmarks, but in talent, partnership architecture, and ecosystem investment.

That is precisely the terrain that the next chapter explores. The most important quantum capabilities of the 2030s are being shaped by decisions made in university research labs, government funding agencies, and corporate strategy offices right now. Building the talent pipelines, university partnerships, research-to-commercial pathways, and cross-disciplinary innovation ecosystems that will determine which organizations, institutions, and nations lead the quantum era, that's the work of Chapter 14. The ecosystem architecture this chapter has mapped is the destination; Chapter 14 provides the construction plan.

Further reading

1. `https://doi.org/10.1103/RevModPhys.89.035002`
2. `https://doi.org/10.1038/s41586-021-04349-7`

3. https://www.darpa.mil/research/programs/quantum-assisted-sensing-and-readout
4. https://www.sciencedirect.com/science/article/pii/S2950257825000228
5. https://quantumconsortium.org/publications/reports/
6. https://doi.org/10.1103/RevModPhys.74.145
7. https://doi.org/10.1038/35106500
8. https://doi.org/10.1080/09500340.2016.1148212
9. https://doi.org/10.1038/nphoton.2009.231
10. https://news.uchicago.edu/story/chicago-quantum-network-argonne-pritzker-molecular-engineering-toshiba
11. https://www.anl.gov/article/argonne-to-receive-new-funding-to-develop-quantum-networks
12. https://digital-strategy.ec.europa.eu/en/policies/european-quantum-communication-infrastructure-euroqci
13. https://asia.toshiba.com/press-release/english/bt-and-toshiba-launch-first-commercial-trial-of-quantum-secured-communication-services/
14. https://doi.org/10.1038/nature23655
15. https://doi.org/10.1109/MNET.001.1900092
16. https://doi.org/10.1103/PhysRevResearch.4.013091
17. https://doi.org/10.1126/science.aam9288
18. https://www.ibm.com/roadmaps/quantum/
19. https://doi.org/10.1109/SFCS.1994.365700
20. https://doi.org/10.1038/nphoton.2014.149
21. https://doi.org/10.1016/j.tcs.2014.05.025
22. https://doi.org/10.1103/PhysRevLett.67.661
23. https://doi.org/10.1002/9781118648919
24. https://www.oreilly.com/library/view/becoming-quantum-safe/9781394374328/
25. https://www.nasa.gov/directorates/somd/space-communications-navigation-program/technology-readiness-levels/
26. https://www.idquantique.com/id-quantique-sk-telecom-join-forces/

27. https://www.idquantique.com/random-number-generation/overview/
28. https://www.idquantique.com/long-distance-high-key-rate-qkd-with-clavis-xgr/
29. https://www.sec.gov/Archives/edgar/data/1824920/000095017025027713/ionq-ex99_2.htm
30. https://www.toshiba.eu/quantum/about/
31. https://doi.org/10.1038/s41586-018-0066-6
32. https://gtr.ukri.org/projects?ref=EP%2FT001011%2F1
33. https://www.toshiba.eu/quantum/
34. https://www.birmingham.ac.uk/research/perspective/quantum-technology-underground
35. https://www.nsa.gov/Cybersecurity/Quantum-Key-Distribution-QKD-and-Quantum-Cryptography-QC/

14

Building the Quantum Ecosystem

Ok, let's be direct with one another here. The quantum ecosystem described in the preceding chapters of this book will not materialize through market forces alone. It will not emerge spontaneously from a collection of well-funded startups, however clever their founders. It will not be conjured into existence by a single government program, however generously budgeted. And it will not be delivered by any one university research center, however brilliant its faculty. The quantum ecosystem, the interconnected web of research institutions, talent pipelines, industry partnerships, government programs, cross-disciplinary innovation structures, and commercial development pathways that will power the quantum economy of the 2030s, will be built. Deliberately. Collaboratively. And with the kind of sustained institutional commitment that characterizes every technology transition of genuine historical consequence. The distance between today's quantum research frontiers and tomorrow's commercial quantum infrastructure is not measured primarily in technology readiness. Quantum hardware is improving at rates that regularly surprise even quantum physicists. Quantum software frameworks are maturing. Cloud-based quantum computing access is democratizing experimentation. The binding constraints on quantum value realization, for organizations, industries, and nations, are talent, partnership architecture, and ecosystem investment. And unlike quantum hardware, those constraints respond directly to decisions that executives, policymakers, university leaders, and startup founders can make right now.

This final chapter delivers the actionable playbook for building the quantum ecosystem today, not as a future aspiration for when the technology matures, but as an immediate strategic program whose near-term milestones are achievable and whose long-term returns compound with each passing year. You'll leave this chapter equipped with skills that will elevate both your technical and business acumen: the ability to design and execute university quantum partnership strategies that deliver near-term value while building long-horizon talent relationships; the navigation competency to engage productively with national quantum initiative programs and government-funded research centers; the organizational design skills to build and lead cross-disciplinary quantum teams; the ecosystem mapping capability to strategically position your organization for maximum value creation as the quantum economy matures; and the talent pipeline architecture expertise to build a multi-stage quantum workforce development system from undergraduate intern through senior research director. These are not theoretical frameworks; they are operational capabilities grounded in the experience of organizations and institutions that are building the quantum ecosystem right now.

Drawing on the architecture of the U.S. National Quantum Initiative, the EU Quantum Flagship, the Chicago Quantum Exchange, IBM's university partnership network, and defense quantum programs from DARPA and AFRL, this chapter provides the structural models, governance frameworks, and strategic starting points needed to begin building today. The most important quantum capabilities of the 2030s are being shaped by decisions made in university research labs, government funding agencies, and corporate strategy offices right now. This chapter helps you understand those decisions.

In this chapter we will cover the following topics:

- University-Industry Quantum Partnership Model
- Government-Funded Quantum Programs as Ecosystem Anchors
- Cross-Disciplinary Quantum Ecosystem Development
- Defense and National Security Quantum Partnership Models
- Building the Quantum Talent Pipeline
- Critical Skills for Quantum Ecosystem Leaders

The university-industry quantum partnership model: structure and strategic value

If you have ever sat in a university cafeteria and tried to explain to a quantum physics PhD student why your company's supply chain optimization problem is genuinely fascinating, then you already have some intuition for what makes university-industry quantum partnerships work and what makes them fail. The gap isn't intellectual. Quantum researchers are among the most curious, capable people on the planet. The gap is structural. Without clear frameworks for how academic curiosity and industrial application meet, the partnership exists mostly on paper and delivers mostly disappointment.

Universities are the primary source of quantum talent, quantum research breakthroughs, and quantum technology proof-of-concepts. That makes them the most strategically important external partners for any organization building quantum capabilities. But that value is only realized when partnerships are structured with sufficient clarity of purpose, mutual benefit design, and operational discipline to sustain productive collaboration across the multi-year timelines quantum research genuinely requires.[1] A partnership agreement signed in Q1 that produces nothing useful by Q4 is not a failed partnership, it's an immature one. The organizations that extract genuine value from university quantum relationships understand that the investment horizon is measured in years, not quarters. Of course, this is simply a fundamental truth at this point, as no CFO will force this to change anytime soon.

The partnership spectrum: from transactional to transformational

University-industry quantum partnerships exist on a spectrum of integration depth, each tier delivering different value at different cost and complexity. Understanding where your organizational priorities map onto this spectrum is the first step in partnership strategy design.

Partnership Tier	Structure	Value Delivered	Time Horizon
Tier 1: Sponsored Research	Industry funds targeted research IP licensing rights Early access to outputs	Specific research outputs Provisional patents Proof-of-concept validation	12-24 months per project Renewable
Tier 2: Talent Pipeline Agreement	Structured internship/ coop programs Capstone project sponsorship Campus recruiting access	Pre-qualified talent pipeline Student project outputs Brand recognition in target programs	2-4 years Pipeline builds over time

Partnership Tier	Structure	Value Delivered	Time Horizon
Tier 3: Research Center Affiliate	Annual affiliate membership fee Access to center seminars, preprints, and researcher community	Intelligence on research frontiers Information recruitment relationships Network access	Annual Low commitment Broad access
Tier 4: Deep Integration Model	Co-located researchers Co-supervised graduate students Joint curriculum development Shared lab access	Deep talent pipeline Joint IP development Faculty co-investigators Research co-publication	5-10 years Requires dedicated partnership management resources
Tier 5: Strategic Alliance	Named research centers Endowed professorships Joint degree programs Governance participation	Institutional brand alignment Long-horizon co-development Top-tier talent access Policy influence	10+ years Anchor investment Board-level commitment

Table 14.1: University-Industry Quantum Partnership Spectrum

Most organizations building quantum capabilities for the first time should begin at Tier 1 or Tier 2, establishing a small number of focused sponsored research agreements to talent pipeline programs with universities whose research strengths align to their quantum priorities. Before attempting the resource intensity of deep integration models. The instinct to partner broadly and quickly is understandable, quantum is moving fast and the fear of missing out is real. Resist it. A Tier 4 partnership with two universities you have invested in properly will deliver more value than Tier 1 agreements with ten universities you manage hastily.[2]

Governance architecture: the difference between partnerships that work and those that look good in press releases

Partnership governance is not a compliance function; it's the operational infrastructure that determines whether the partnership delivers its intended value or deteriorates into a polite non-relationship characterized by annual check-in calls and recycled presentations. Effective university-industry quantum partnership governance requires four structural elements working in concert.[3]

First, a joint steering committee with genuine decision-making authority, not advisory authority, over research direction, IP disposition, and resource allocation. This committee should include faculty principal investigators and department chairs on the university side, and senior quantum strategy and business development leaders (not procurement or legal staff) on the industry side. Meeting quarterly is a minimum; monthly touchpoints via working groups are better.

Second, clear IP ownership frameworks established at the partnership's inception, not negotiated in the context of a specific breakthrough when stakes and emotions are both elevated. The standard framework for quantum research partnerships distinguishes background IP (each party owns what it brought to the partnership), foreground IP (jointly developed IP, with licensing terms specified in advance), and publication rights (specifying faculty rights to publish research results, with reasonable industry review windows typically of 30-60 days for patent filing preparation).

Third, student and postdoctoral researcher protocols covering confidentiality obligations, project participation rights, and thesis/dissertation publication rights. Graduate students are the primary research workforce in university quantum centers, and their engagement depends on confidence that participation in industry-sponsored research will not compromise their academic careers. Partnerships that fail to address this clearly lose their best researchers to competing opportunities.

Fourth, relationship continuity mechanisms that sustain partnership health through the inevitable disruptions of faculty sabbaticals, graduate student graduation cycles, and organizational leadership transitions. The most common cause of university-industry partnership deterioration is not disagreement, it's discontinuity. The partner relationship manager on the industry side changes; the key faculty collaborator goes on sabbatical; the corporate champion gets promoted to a role without quantum in the portfolio. Partnerships with no structural continuity mechanisms beyond personal relationships collapse under these conditions.[4]

Evaluating university quantum capability: a practical assessment framework

Not every research university with a quantum physics department is a valuable quantum partner for every organization. Effective partnership strategy requires honest assessment of the research-to-organizational-priority fit, the university's track record of productive industry engagement, and the depth of quantum talent being produced. The following framework provides a structured approach to target university identification.

Assessment Dimension	Key Indicators	Weighting (customize by org priority)
Research Strength Alignment	Faculty publications in target quantum domains Active NSF/DOE grants Quantum center/institute presence	High (30%)
Talent Production Depth	PhD and MS graduates per year in quantum-relevant fields Undergraduate quantum coursework availability Quantum-literate CS graduates	High (25%)
Industry Partnership Track Record	Existing corporate partners Technology transfer office effectiveness IP licensing revenue Startup spinout rate	Medium (20%)

Assessment Dimension	Key Indicators	Weighting (customize by org priority)
Geographic and Infrastructure Access	Proximity to organizational quantum facilities Access to quantum hardware (on-site or via national lab partnerships) Cleanroom and fabrication access	Medium (15%)
Engagement Appetite and Culture	Faculty openness to applied research Department chair support Prior positive industry partner references TTO responsiveness	Medium (10%)

Table 14.2: University Quantum Capability Assessment Framework

Company spotlight: IBM Research, university partnership as ecosystem architecture

IBM's quantum program is one of the strongest examples of a university-industry partnership operating at scale. The company has had a long and rich history of working with universities to turn research into practical capability and, ultimately, new industries. IBM has followed that path across several technology eras, from mainframes in the 1960s and 1970s to personal computing in the 1980s, and AI in the 2010s, and now quantum. It also requires sustained investment in software, partnerships, talent, manufacturing, and the system capabilities needed to move technology beyond the lab. Through the IBM Quantum Network, IBM brings together universities, research institutions, national labs, startups, and commercial partners to advance quantum research, software, hardware, and workforce development.[5] The network gives researchers access to systems and tools that help them explore applications IBM may not identify internally. It also helps create the talent pipeline that supports IBM's own quantum workforce and the broader ecosystem. A recent example is the recent installation of their IBM Quantum System Two at RIKEN's Center for Computational Science in Japan, where it operates alongside the Fugaku supercomputer. RIKEN is working with SoftBank, the University of Tokyo, and Osaka University to develop quantum and high-performance computing software, build a hybrid platform, and prepare these capabilities for future services.[34] For executives and investors, the RIKEN-IBM collaboration is an early signal that quantum computing may already be addressing scientific problems that even leading supercomputers struggle to solve. The team used quantum hardware and error-reduction software to model the behavior of advanced materials with results that classical approaches could not reliably reproduce.[35] Over time, this capability could shorten the path to new materials for faster electronics, more efficient energy technologies, and other high-value industrial applications. It also demonstrates that useful quantum progress will come from an ecosystem of hardware, software, supercomputing, and research partners, not from quantum hardware alone.

Strategic Approach: IBM provides network members with cloud access to its quantum computing systems, including its most advanced processors, alongside software development tools, training curricula, and a collaborative research community. University members contribute algorithm research, error mitigation techniques, quantum chemistry applications, and a continuous stream of quantum-trained graduates. IBM's research partnerships with MIT,[6] the University of Tokyo,[7] and ETH Zurich[8] represent deeper Tier 4-5 engagements, with co-located researchers, joint publications, and curriculum co-development. The partnership model is explicitly designed to grow the total quantum ecosystem, not merely to benefit IBM, a strategic logic grounded in the recognition that IBM's quantum business requires a large population of quantum-literate potential customers, partners, and employees that IBM cannot produce unilaterally.

Key Lessons and Implementation Insights: IBM's partnership architecture illustrates three principles critical for any organization building university quantum relationships at scale. First, standardized engagement models with tiered depth allow organizations to manage many partnerships simultaneously without creating custom governance overhead for each. Second, technology access as a partnership asset: providing university researchers with quantum hardware access they could not otherwise afford. This creates a reciprocal dynamic of genuine mutual benefit that sustains faculty engagement more effectively than grant funding alone. Third, community credibility and talent attraction that proprietary-only approaches cannot match.[9, 10]

For your organization: You may not be IBM. But the structural lesson translates directly. Identify what you have that universities want: cloud access, proprietary datasets, application domain expertise, hardware prototypes, or industry problem specifications, and design your partnership value proposition around that asset. The organizations that build the best university quantum partnerships are those that think hardest about what they bring to the relationship, not merely what they want to extract from it.

Government-funded quantum programs as ecosystem anchors

Here is a counterintuitive truth about government quantum programs: the organizations that treat them primarily as funding sources are the organizations that extract the least value from them. The organizations that treat them as ecosystem anchors, as structured access to talent networks, research infrastructure, collaborative frameworks, and technology roadmap intelligence that no market mechanism can provide, are the ones that emerge from government program engagement with durable competitive advantages.

National quantum initiatives represent the most significant ecosystem-building investments in quantum technology history. Understanding how to engage with them strategically is one of the most valuable capabilities any quantum leader can develop.[11]

The U.S. National Quantum Initiative: architecture and engagement points

The National Quantum Initiative Act of 2018 established the legislative framework for coordinated U.S. quantum investment across civilian research, defense, and workforce development.[12] In the years since, NQI-funded programs have created a network of research infrastructure, talent development programs, and industry engagement pathways that now constitute the backbone of the U.S. quantum ecosystem. The following are just a few examples:

Program / Center	Research Focus	Industry Engagement Pathway	Lead Institution(s)
Q-NEXT (DOE QIS Research Center)	Quantum networking, sensing, and communication Quantum materials	Affiliate membership Sponsored research Workforce development programs	Argonne National Lab / U. Chicago
QSC (Quantum Science Center)	Quantum materials, sensing, and computing with topological qubits	Industry fellowship program Collaborative research agreements	ORNL / Vanderbilt / U. Tennessee

Program / Center	Research Focus	Industry Engagement Pathway	Lead Institution(s)
C2QA (Co-design Center for Quantum Advantage)	Quantum error correction and fault-tolerant quantum computing	Computation User Program Workforce training Industry partnerships	Brookhaven National Lab / IBM
SQMS (Superconducting Quantum Materials and Systems)	Superconducting qubit coherence Quantum sensor development	Industry partner program Materials collaboration Prototyping access	Fermilab / Northwestern / NIST
QED-C (Quantum Economic Development Consortium)	Quantum supply chain Workforce development Standards and benchmarking	Consortium membership (open to all organizations) Working group participation Workforce tools access	SRI International (NIST-administered)
NSF Quantum Leap Challenge Institutes	Quantum simulation, sensing, and algorithm development	Industry affiliate programs Collaborative research Student fellowship co-sponsorship	Multiple university consortia (6 institutes)
DARPA Quantum Benchmarking Initiative	Quantum computer performance assessment Defense-relevant benchmarking	Direct industry participation (hardware/software benchmarking data contribution)	DARPA / multiple industry performers

Table 14.3: U.S. National Quantum Initiative: Key Programs and Industry Engagement Pathways

The international quantum program landscape: competitive context and partnership opportunity

The United States is not alone in recognizing quantum as a generational national priority, and the international quantum program landscape defines the competitive context within which both national quantum strategies and corporate quantum investments must be understood.

The European Union's Quantum Flagship, launched in 2018 with a flagship budget of EUR 1 billion over 10 years, has evolved into a comprehensive ecosystem development program spanning quantum computing, quantum communication, quantum sensing, and quantum theory.[13] The Flagship's industry engagement model is notably different from the U.S. approach. Rather than organizing primarily around national laboratory anchors, the EU Quantum Flagship has built its ecosystem around quantum technology companies, many of them European startups and scale-ups, as co-developers of the research agenda. This creates meaningful industry-university partnership structures within Flagship consortia that offer access points for international corporate partners.

The UK National Quantum Computing Centre (NQCC), established in 2021 as part of the UK National Quantum Strategy, represents a model of government-funded quantum infrastructure specifically designed to bridge the gap between university quantum research and commercial quantum application development.[14] The NQCC's co-location of quantum hardware development, software and algorithm research, and commercial application teams in a single physical facility creates cross-disciplinary collaboration conditions that most distributed programs cannot replicate. For international companies seeking to access UK quantum research communities, the NQCC's industrial partners program provides a structured entry point.

Japan's Moonshot R&D quantum program, with its 2050 goal of fault-tolerant quantum computers with a million physical qubits, represents the longest-horizon national quantum investment with the most explicitly technology-development-focused research agenda.[15] Canada's National Quantum Strategy and Australia's National Quantum Strategy complete the picture of allied nations that have made explicit, sustained national commitments to quantum leadership, and each represents both a competitive context and a potential collaboration opportunity for organizations building international quantum strategies.

Practical engagement: extracting value from government quantum programs

Understanding the programs is necessary but insufficient. The organizations that extract maximum value from government quantum program engagements do three things that their less sophisticated peers do not. First, they assign dedicated government program relationship management resources, not as a compliance or grant-writing function, but as a strategic partnership development function reporting to senior quantum leadership. Second, they approach program participation with a value-contribution mindset, actively contributing data, problem specifications, and benchmarking results rather than merely consuming program outputs. Programs designed around government research missions are more open to industry partners who enhance the program's value than to those who merely seek to extract it. Third, they invest in understanding the IP and publication governance frameworks that govern government-funded research, not to extract IP, but to understand what research assets are available for commercial licensing and what publication obligations create early intelligence access for research program participants.[16] Taken together, these are ambitious, and they often imply a sustained, hands-on operating model rather than a one-off engagement.

Cross-disciplinary quantum ecosystem development: from campus to commerce

There is a particular kind of meeting that happens regularly in quantum organizations, and it's a reliable indicator of organizational maturity. In the less mature version, the quantum physicists present their results to the business team, who nod politely and then ask questions that reveal they understood perhaps forty percent of what was said. In the more mature version, the quantum physicists and the business development team and the application domain expert and the legal counsel are all in the room together from the beginning, arguing productively about which problems are worth solving, what the solution architecture should be, and how the resulting capability can be deployed in a real commercial context. The difference between those two meetings is a cross-disciplinary quantum team design. Without a clear, organization-specific vision of which problems to solve, these structures can feel like momentum without direction. This in turn usually serves as a good indicator to take a step back and identify where the earlier efforts had failed before picking up the pieces.

The most transformative quantum applications will emerge at the intersection of quantum physics and domain expertise. That intersection requires organizational and institutional structures that bring quantum physicists into sustained, productive collaboration with computer scientists, domain specialists, business strategists, legal experts, and policy professionals.[17] Building those structures: inside organizations, inside universities, and across the ecosystem, is the core challenge of quantum ecosystem development.

The Chicago Quantum Exchange: a model for cross-disciplinary ecosystem architecture

The Chicago Quantum Exchange (CQE) has become one of the most instructive models of cross-disciplinary quantum ecosystem development at the regional level. The CQE connects the University of Chicago, Argonne National Laboratory, Fermilab, the University of Illinois

Urbana-Champaign, Northwestern University, Purdue University, and the University of Wisconsin-Madison, alongside an industry partner network of more than 30 companies, through shared research infrastructure, joint faculty appointments, and affiliate programs that provide structured access to the Exchange's research community.[18]

What distinguishes the CQE from a simple research consortium is its explicit commitment to the full pathway from quantum research to commercial quantum application. The CQE's quantum-to-business development pipeline includes not just research funding and talent programs but dedicated commercialization support for quantum technology startups, industry problem-specification programs that connect corporate partners' quantum application needs with CQE research teams, and quantum policy engagement programs that position CQE faculty and industry partners as informed voices in national quantum policy discussions. For industry partners, the CQE affiliate program provides access to pre-competitive research results, early recruitment relationships with graduate students, and the kind of informal research network access that no formal agreement can replicate.[19]

The three-stage commercialization pathway: from research to market

The journey from a promising quantum physics result to a deployable commercial quantum application is rarely a straight line, but it's not random either. Organizations and ecosystems that successfully navigate this journey typically traverse three distinct stages, each with its own institutional requirements, failure modes, and success criteria.

Stage	Key Activities	Institutional Requirements	Common Failure Modes
Stage 1: Research Validation	Proof-of-principle experiments Theoretical framework development Performance characterization on controlled problems	University lab access National quantum center collaboration Peer review Grant funding	Over-claiming performance Ignoring noise and error effects Insufficient domain problem specification

Stage	Key Activities	Institutional Requirements	Common Failure Modes
Stage 2: Applied Proof-of-Concept	Industry problem mapping Quantum algorithm design for real data Hybrid classical-quantum pipeline development Benchmarking vs. classical baselines	Cross-disciplinary team (physicists + domain experts) Cloud quantum hardware access Industry data access Applied research funding	Physics-first problem framing Missing domain expertise Underpowered classical baselines Premature scale-up ambition
Stage 3: Commercial Development	Product architecture design Customer co-development Production quantum access negotiation Regulatory and compliance mapping Go-To-Market strategy	Product management Legal and IP counsel Business development Dedicated quantum engineering team Commercial quantum hardware contracts	Talent transition from research to product roles IP ownership disputes Premature productization Quantum hardware availability constraints

Table 14.4: The Three-Stage Quantum Commercialization Pathway

Important to note regarding Stage 3, the commercialization push at this stage still needs to be managed through an incubation-style business development model. That way the effort is treated as a deliberate path to learning and capability formation, and not as a one-to-one substitute for a fully market-ready product in the organization's broader portfolio.

Designing cross-disciplinary quantum teams: organizational architecture for innovation

The organizational design of cross-disciplinary quantum teams is one of the most consequential, and most underappreciated, elements of quantum strategy execution. The instinct in many organizations is to organize quantum teams around technical function: quantum hardware engineers in one group, quantum software developers in another, quantum algorithm researchers in a third. This structure is efficient for technical depth development but is poorly suited to cross-disciplinary quantum application development, which requires frequent, low-friction collaboration across technical and non-technical boundaries.

The most effective cross-disciplinary quantum teams for application development organize around quantum application domains rather than technical functions. A quantum logistics optimization team might include a quantum algorithm researcher, a classical optimization specialist, a supply chain domain expert, a software engineer for classical-quantum hybrid systems, a business development professional familiar with the target customer segment, and a legal advisor with quantum IP expertise. This structure creates the conditions for genuine cross-disciplinary collaboration from the earliest stages of application development, not the downstream-review model where physicists develop and business/legal staff respond.

For universities designing quantum graduate programs with cross-disciplinary structures, the implication is clear: quantum PhD programs that produce graduates with deep physics expertise and no understanding of computational complexity, industry application domains, or professional communication norms are producing talent that is technically impressive but commercially underutilized.[20] The programs that will produce the quantum workforce the industry needs are those that embed quantum physics training within cross-disciplinary structures that develop domain knowledge, professional skills, and collaborative competency alongside quantum technical depth.

Company spotlight: Pasqal, European quantum computing's cross-disciplinary commercialization model

Pasqal, the French quantum computing company spun out of the Institut d'Optique and the work of Nobel Prize winner Alain Aspect's research group, represents one of the most instructive European examples of the research-to-commerce pathway in quantum computing.[21] Founded in 2019 with origins in CNRS-funded atomic physics research, Pasqal has developed neutral atom quantum processors that have attracted partnerships with EDF (energy optimization), BASF (materials simulation), and a growing roster of financial services firms exploring quantum portfolio optimization applications. As of 2026, Pasqal is entering a new phase of development with new financing worth over €340 million in anticipation of going public,[22] and employs over 200 staff across Paris, Massy, Amsterdam, and its expanding North American operations.

Strategic Approach: Pasqal's cross-disciplinary commercialization model explicitly bridges the gap between cutting-edge quantum physics (its neutral atom architecture requires deep expertise in atomic physics, laser systems, and cryogenic engineering) and commercial application development. The company employs quantum physicists, quantum software engineers, domain specialists in chemistry and optimization, and dedicated industry partnership teams that co-develop application use cases with enterprise customers. This cross-disciplinary structure is institutionalized in Pasqal's collaboration with French grandes ecoles, including Ecole Polytechnique and CentraleSupelec, through joint research programs and curriculum co-development that feed Pasqal's talent pipeline.[23] Pasqal's participation in the EuroHPC Joint Undertaking as an industrial partner provides both research collaboration access and visibility in the European quantum policy community.[24]

Key Lessons and Implementation Insights: Pasqal illustrates three principles with direct applicability to organizations building quantum capabilities in Europe and beyond. First, deep university-lab origin does not constrain commercial ambition, the organizations most capable of commercializing quantum research are often those with the deepest research DNA, because they understand both what is physically possible and where the boundaries of current capability genuinely lie. Second, cross-national expansion (Pasqal's simultaneous presence in France, the Netherlands, and North America) allows quantum companies to access the most relevant talent and customer communities for specific application domains without concentrating all ecosystem risk in a single geography. Third, EuroHPC engagement provides not just research funding but ecosystem positioning as a recognized European quantum leader, a positioning that supports talent recruitment, customer credibility, and policy influence simultaneously.

Defense and national security quantum partnership models

Defense quantum programs occupy a unique position in the quantum ecosystem: they represent simultaneously the most urgent near-term application domain, where quantum sensing, cryptography, and optimization have clear mission-critical value, and the most resource-intensive source of quantum ecosystem investment available to organizations willing to navigate the compliance requirements that defense engagement entails. For those who dismiss defense quantum partnerships as bureaucratically burdensome, it's worth noting that the internet, GPS, touchscreens, and voice recognition, technologies that now constitute the infrastructure of modern life, all trace their foundational investments to exactly this model. [25] The question isn't whether the complexity is real. It's whether the value justifies it. For many quantum organizations, it does.

DARPA's quantum programs: structure and industry engagement model

DARPA's Quantum Benchmarking Initiative represents a model of defense-industry quantum partnership that is worth studying carefully. Unlike traditional defense research programs that fund specific hardware or algorithm development goals, the Benchmarking Initiative is designed to develop rigorous, application-relevant performance metrics for quantum computers. Which is a public good for the entire ecosystem that also happens to serve defense needs for honest assessment of quantum computing progress. Industry quantum hardware and software developers participate by contributing benchmarking data, gaining access to rigorously characterized performance comparisons and defense application requirement specifications that would be difficult to obtain through any other channel.

DARPA's ONIQD (Optimized with Noisy Intermediate-Scale Quantum devices) program funded applied quantum algorithm development for combinatorial optimization problems with direct defense relevance. For example, logistics, scheduling, and materials discovery, while generating openly publishable algorithmic advances that enriched the commercial quantum algorithm community.[26] This dual-benefit structure, where defense-funded quantum research generates both classified capability development and openly publishable commercial-relevant science, is the hallmark of the most valuable defense quantum programs from an ecosystem perspective.

Navigating ITAR, export control, and classification requirements

The compliance framework governing defense quantum partnership opportunities because of compliance complexity are making a strategic error; the compliance requirements are substantial but manageable for organizations that invest in the appropriate legal and regulatory infrastructure. The key frameworks governing defense quantum work are ITAR (International Traffic in Arms Regulations), which restricts the export of defense-related technologies in the involvement of foreign nationals in defense-classified research;[27] EAR (Export Administration Regulations), which governs dual-use quantum technologies; and the security clearance framework, which determines who can access classified quantum research results and facilities.[28]

For organizations considering defense quantum engagement for the first time, the practical starting point is not a classified program but a DARPA Broad Agency Announcement (BAA) response or an Air Force SBIR/STTR application.[29] These programs provide structured entry into the defense quantum ecosystem without immediate classified work requirements, building the organizational track record and cleared-personnel infrastructure that deeper defense engagement requires over time. The Air Force Research Laboratory (AFRL) Information Directorate has developed university partnership models for quantum networking and quantum sensing research that are explicitly designed to produce both defense capability outputs and publishable academic research, an arrangement that sustains faculty engagement precisely because it does not require choosing between academic and defense career paths.[30]

For policymakers: designing defense quantum investment portfolios

The most effective defense quantum investment portfolios balance classified capability development, where defense needs are genuinely distinct from commercial applications, with dual-use research investments whose commercial spillover accelerates the broader quantum ecosystem. Historically, the most valuable returns on defense quantum investment have come from the dual-use tier: DARPA's foundational investments in quantum error correction and quantum algorithm development have generated both defense-relevant capabilities in the commercially applicable science that underpins today's quantum computing industry.

Policymakers designing defense quantum investment portfolios should resist the temptation to classify too broadly. Classified research programs are more expensive to administer, produce fewer publicly available outputs, and attract smaller talent pools than unclassified programs. The appropriate classification threshold for defense quantum work is genuine national security sensitivity, quantum cryptanalysis capabilities with adversary intelligence value, quantum sensor designs with classified performance characteristics, quantum networking architectures for classified communication systems, not quantum research that is commercially relevant but not genuinely sensitive. Overclassification reduces the ecosystem spillover value to defense quantum investment without providing meaningful security benefit.[31]

Building the quantum talent pipeline: from student projects to commercial quantum workforce

Here is the workforce challenge stated plainly: there are not enough quantum-trained professionals to meet the demand that will exist when quantum computing reaches commercial maturity, and by the time that demand fully materializes, the organizations that did not invest in talent pipeline architecture years earlier will find themselves unable to compete for the limited supply of experienced quantum talent at any price they are willing to pay. The quantum talent shortage is not a future problem. It's a present one, and it's intensifying. McKinsey Global Institute estimated in 2021 that demand for quantum computing professionals alone could reach 4,000 positions in the United States by 2030, against a supply trajectory that falls far short of that number without sustained workforce development investment.[32]

The most durable competitive advantage in the quantum economy will be organizational mastery of the talent pipeline. By having the ability to continuously attract, develop, and retain quantum-capable professionals from entry-level quantum software engineers through seasoned quantum research directors. And unlike quantum hardware, which requires billions of dollars of capital investment to develop, talent pipeline architecture is accessible to organizations of nearly any size that commit to building it seriously.

The quantum talent pipeline architecture: stage-by-stage design

To build a talent pipeline, you'll need an architecture that traverses through phases while the technology evolves around it. This way you can ensure that the talent pipeline not only stays current but remains aligned with the pipeline stage personas. The following stage-by-stage design should help you get started.

Pipeline Stage	Target Talent Profile	Engagement Program Design	Conversion Metrics
Stage 1: Undergraduate Intern/Co-op	Junior/Senior undergraduates in physics, CS, EE, math with quantum coursework	10-12 week summer programs Project work in real quantum application teams (not administrative roles) Mentorship by senior quantum staff Technical presentation to senior leadership	Return offer rate Full-time conversion rate Academic program recommendation frequency
Stage 2: Graduate Research Sponsorship	MS and PhD students in quantum computing, quantum physics, quantum information science	Thesis research co-sponsorship Quarterly site visits to industry facilities Joint publication opportunities Industry-defined research problem exposure	Post-graduation offer acceptance rate Thesis-to-application relevance Faculty relationship depth
Stage 3: Postdoctoral Fellowship	Recent PhDs seeking applied research experience Quantum physicists transitioning to industry	2-3 year industry postdoc programs with publication rights, conference attendance, and academic collaboration maintenance Clearly defined transition pathway to permanent role	Permanent conversion rate Research output quality Peer network expansion

Pipeline Stage	Target Talent Profile	Engagement Program Design	Conversion Metrics
Stage 4: Entry-Level Quantum Professional	Quantum software engineers, quantum algorithm developers, quantum research scientists (0-4 years experience)	Structured onboarding with quantum domain orientation Internal quantum community Publication and conference support Quantum certification pathway Quantum project rotation program	18-month retention rate Promotion to mid-level Internal publication rate Quantum certification completion
Stage 5: Senior Quantum Specialist / Director	Experienced quantum researchers, quantum engineering directors, quantum program leads (5+ years)	Research leadership autonomy Faculty adjunct appointment support External advisory board participation Internal quantum strategy influence Competitive compensation benchmarking	3-year retention rate Recruitment success rate University partnership depth Quantum community reputation

Table 14.5: Quantum Talent Pipeline Architecture, Stage-by-Stage Design Framework

Just as important, don't think only in terms of academic quantum roles. The talent pipeline should also cover the practical, engineering, and facility-facing jobs that make quantum systems usable in the real world. For example, as quantum hardware scales, you'll need specialized electrical work (power distribution, grounding, cabling), HVAC and cooling technicians (to support dilution refrigeration or other temperature-control needs), and HVAC/plumbing integration (to keep water or coolant systems reliable and safe). You'll also want people for facilities maintenance and upgrades. These include roles such as commissioning engineers, reliability technicians, safety and compliance specialists, and technicians who can keep everything running day-to-day while hardware and infrastructure evolve. You'll also want support engineers in the mix, people who can triage and resolve issues your clients report. If you only hire senior developers, you may end up with a gap when defects or usage problems show up in production. Who handles those reports quickly, stabilizes the system, and reduces downtime and cost while the team works on deeper fixes?

Retaining quantum talent in industry environments

The most common cause of quantum talent departure from industry organizations is not compensation. It's professional identity erosion, where researchers feel their work is disconnected from the publishing, presenting, and community collaboration engagements that originally made them recognizable and identified as quantum professionals. When competitive confidentiality is managed in ways that take away those professional developmental growth and visibility channels, people don't just lose a benefit, they lose the sense of who they are professionally. Quantum researchers are trained in academic environments where publishing, presenting at conferences, collaborating openly with peers, and maintaining active intellectual community engagement are core professional activities. Industry environments that strip away those professional development elements in the name of competitive confidentiality systematically undermine the professional identity of their quantum workforce, and then express surprise when their best quantum talent returns to national laboratories or universities.

The quantum organizations that successfully retain top talent recognize that professional development investment is not a nice-to-have benefit, it's a retention strategy with measurable ROI. Programs that support quantum staff in maintaining academic publishing activity, attending and presenting at quantum conferences, maintaining adjunct faculty or visiting researcher appointments at university partners, and participating in industry standards bodies and quantum consortia create the professional ecosystem conditions that quantum researchers need to thrive in industry settings. Quantum researchers who feel intellectually vibrant and professionally connected are far less likely to leave than those who feel intellectually isolated, even at significantly lower compensation levels.

National quantum workforce policy: the lever policymakers control

For policymakers, the quantum talent shortage represents both the most consequential near-term risk to national quantum competitiveness and the domain where policy interventions have the clearest, most direct leverage. The NSF Quantum Education and Workforce initiative, the DOE Quantum Graduate Fellowship program, and the growing portfolio of quantum curriculum standards initiatives represent meaningful interventions, but they address the pipeline at its narrowest point (graduate-level quantum training) while leaving the pipeline's upstream sections largely unaddressed.

The quantum talent pipeline begins at K-12, where the physics, mathematics, and computer science foundations that make quantum education possible are either built or neglected. Changing curriculum is a difficult and slow process, but there are practical ways to ease topics in without waiting for a textbook refactor to occur. For example, similar to how coding and cybersecurity modules were gradually incorporated through teacher training, elective courses, and the many hands-on programs, quantum concepts can be introduced through short problem sets, lab demonstrations, and age-appropriate modules that connect to existing math and programming standards. National quantum literacy programs for secondary students, introducing the conceptual foundations of quantum mechanics, quantum computing, and quantum cryptography at an age-appropriate level, represent multi-decade investments in quantum workforce depth. Such initiatives require policy commitment measured in election cycles rather than fiscal years. Furthermore, international talent policy is critical. Quantum expertise is globally distributed, making the free flow of talent necessary. Immigration frameworks that restrict international specialists from building careers represent an unforced competitive disadvantage, which no amount of domestic development can fully offset.[33]

Critical skills for quantum ecosystem leaders

The following skills described in this section are not abstract competencies. They're operational capabilities that translate the strategic framework in this chapter into organizational action. Each skill maps directly to the frameworks, tools, and models presented earlier, and each includes practical examples drawn from the organizations and programs featured in this chapter.

University partnership strategy development

What it is: The ability to design and execute university quantum partnership strategies that deliver measurable near-term value while building the long-horizon talent and research relationships that constitute sustainable quantum competitive advantage.

What it requires: Conducting university quantum capability assessments using the framework described in Table 14.2 to identify target partners with research strengths aligned to organizational quantum priorities. Structuring partnership agreements that navigate the IP, publication rights, and student protocol considerations described earlier in the chapter on building internal organizational infrastructure. Dedicated partnership management roles, student project intake processes, and faculty engagement protocols are required to sustain productive university relationships over multi-year timeframes. Evaluating partnership portfolio health using metrics that capture both near-term deliverables and long-horizon relationship indicators.

Practical Application: Begin by applying the assessment framework from Table 14.2 to three to five target universities. Score each on the five assessment dimensions, weight the dimensions by your organizational quantum priorities, and rank the universities by total weight score. Contact the technology transfer office and relevant department chair at your top-ranked university to request an initial partnership scoping conversation. Bring a specific quantum research question or talent need, not a generic partnership inquiry, to maximize the probability of a substantive response. Set a ninety-day goal of advancing from initial conversation to a Tier 1 sponsored research agreement or Tier 2 talent pipeline agreement.

Business acumen impact: Leaders who develop university partnership strategy skills build one of the most defensible long-run competitive advantages available in the quantum economy. University partnerships compound in value over time. Where each year of productive partnership deepens faculty relationships, expands student project contributions, and strengthens the organizational reputation that attracts the next generation of quantum talent. Organizations without this capability will find themselves recruiting from a talent pool that their partnership-invested competitors have been shaping for years.

Government program engagement and navigation

What it is: The ability to identify, engage, and extract maximum strategic value from national quantum initiative programs, DOE National Quantum Information Science Research Centers, DARPA programs, and NSF Quantum Leap institutes.

What it requires: Mapping the government quantum program landscape against organizational quantum priorities using the framework in Table 14.3 as a starting point. Structuring industry participation proposals that articulate clear mutual benefit for both the organization and the program. Managing ongoing participation to extract maximum value from research community access, infrastructure sharing, and network relationships. Understanding the IP and publication frameworks governing government-funded research and the compliance requirements governing defense quantum program participation.

Practical application: Identify one government quantum program from Table 14.3 whose research focus most directly aligns with your organizational quantum priorities. For QED-C, join as a consortium member (open to all organizations, fees are modest) and identify one working group to participate in actively. For DOE quantum user facilities, submit a quantum computer user program proposal for access to national lab quantum hardware for a specific applied research project. For a DARPA program, request a technical exchange meeting with the program manager to understand current research focus and industry participation opportunities. The goal in the first twelve months is active participation in at least one government quantum program, not passive affiliation.

Business acumen impact: Government program engagement builds intelligence access. Early visibility into quantum research trajectories, performance benchmarks, and application domain requirements that's not available through market mechanisms. Organizations engaged in QED-C working groups, for example, shape the quantum workforce standards, benchmarking frameworks, and supply chain development priorities that will govern the commercial quantum market. That isn't just a research benefit, it's a standards-shaping competitive advantage with direct business value.

Cross-disciplinary quantum team design and leadership

What it is: The organizational design and leadership ability to build and lead cross-disciplinary quantum teams that productively integrate quantum physicists, software engineers, domain specialists, business developers, and legal professionals.

What it requires: Designing team structures organized around quantum application domains rather than technical functions. Creating productive interfaces between technical and non-technical quantum team members. Facilitating the shared vocabulary development that effective cross-disciplinary collaboration requires. Managing the interpersonal dynamics of cross-disciplinary teams through the professional culture differences that arise when physicists, engineers, business developers, and lawyers must collaborate on high-stakes problems.

Practical application: If you're building a quantum application team for the first time, resist the instinct to hire only quantum physicists and defer domain specialist and business development hiring until later. The pathway illustrated in Table 14.4 demonstrates clearly that Stage 2 (Applied Proof-of-Concept) is the stage where most quantum business value is first demonstrated. It requires domain expert co-development from the beginning, not from downstream review. Structure your first quantum team around a specific application problem (not a general quantum research mandate) and hire the full cross-disciplinary team needed to take that problem through Stage 2 before expanding scope.

Business acumen impact: Cross-disciplinary quantum team design is the capability that separates quantum organizations that prototype from those that commercialize. The graveyard of quantum business is littered with technically impressive quantum research results that never found a commercial home because no one on the team understood the commercial context well enough to bridge the gap. Leaders who master cross-disciplinary team design build the organizational capability to convert quantum physics achievements into quantum business outcomes.

Quantum ecosystem mapping and strategic positioning

What it is: The ability to construct and maintain a comprehensive map of the quantum technology ecosystem, including, but not limited to, technology developers, research institutions, government programs, industry applications, and talent pools, and to use that map for strategic organizational positioning.

What it requires: Identifying key ecosystem actors, relationship patterns, and ecosystem gaps relevant to organizational quantum priorities. Using ecosystem maps to identify strategic positioning opportunities including anchor tenant roles in emerging quantum clusters, co-founding roles in quantum industry consortia, and early mover positions in quantum application categories where ecosystem infrastructure is not yet established. Communicating ecosystem positioning strategy to board and investor audiences in ways that convey long-term competitive moat value.

Practical application: Build your first quantum ecosystem map by identifying, for each of the five program categories in Table 14.3, which program your organization currently has an active relationship with and which represents the most valuable untapped engagement opportunity. Add to this map the top three universities in your geographic region or research priority domain, the two to three quantum hardware and software vendors you use or are evaluating, and the one or two industry consortia (QED-C, Quantum Industry Canada, QuIC in Europe) most relevant to your sector. The resulting map will almost certainly reveal relationship gaps, white space in your ecosystem architecture, that represent specific, actionable partnership development priorities for the next twelve months.

Business acumen impact: Ecosystem mapping transforms quantum strategy from an abstract capability to investment into a concrete relationship and positioning program with measurable milestones. Organizations that maintain active ecosystem maps are better positioned to identify partnership opportunities before competitors, anticipate technology availability timelines more accurately than those relying solely on vendor roadmaps, and represent their quantum strategy credibly to board members and investors who want to understand how the organization is positioned relative to the broader quantum competitive landscape.

Quantum talent pipeline architecture and management

What it is: The integration of university partnership management, professional development program design, and quantum workforce retention strategy into a coherent, actively managed multi-stage talent development system.

What it requires: Defining the quantum talent pipeline stages relevant to organizational quantum workforce requirements using the framework illustrated on Table 14.5. Designing engagement programs and incentive structures appropriate for each pipeline stage. Measuring pipeline health using metrics that provide early warning of talent supply constraints and conversion rate deterioration. Engaging constructively with university faculty, department chairs, and graduate program directors as genuine strategic partners rather than transactional recruiting contacts. Representing organizational quantum talent needs effectively in national quantum workforce policy discussions.

Practical application: Audit your current quantum talent pipeline against the five stages illustrated in Table 14.5. For each stage, answer three questions: Do we have an active engagement program? What are our conversion metrics for this stage? What is our retention rate for talent that successfully converts? The audit will almost certainly reveal that most organizations have reasonable Stage 4 and 5 infrastructures (traditional HR programs) but weak or nonexistent Stage 1-3 infrastructure (the upstream university engagement stages that build the pipeline's long-run health). The audit outcome becomes the starting point for a twelve-month pipeline development program focused on building the stages with the most severe gaps.

Business acumen impact: Quantum talent pipeline architecture is the investment with the longest lead time and the highest compounding return in the quantum economy. The organization that begins building its Stage 1 and Stage 2 university engagement programs today will have a materially deeper pipeline of experienced quantum talent in five years than any organization that waits for commercial quantum maturity to begin talent development. In a market where quantum talent is already scarce and will become significantly more scarce, that pipeline depth is a genuine and durable competitive moat.

Chapter summary: building the quantum ecosystem starting now

This chapter delivered the actionable ecosystem-building playbook that transforms quantum strategic intent into organizational and institutional action. Let's wrap things up here by consolidating the key structural insights into a single executable framework.

Ecosystem Building Domain	Near-Term Actions (0-12 months)	Long-Term Value (3-7 years)
University Partnerships	Conduct university capability assessment Establish first Tier 1 or Tier 2 partnership Deploy joint steering committee governance structure	Sustained talent pipeline IP co-development Research co-publication Faculty engagement depth
Government Program Engagement	Join QED-C Identify one DOE/NSF program aligned to quantum priorities Submit first user program proposal Attend NQO industry briefings	Research community access Intelligence on quantum technology trajectories Standards-shaping influence Dual-use research access
Cross-Disciplinary Team Design	Define first quantum application problem Build cross-disciplinary team organized around that problem Advance through Stage 1-2 commercialization pathway	Organizational capability for quantum application commercialization Cross-disciplinary quantum innovation culture Commercial quantum application portfolio

Ecosystem Building Domain	Near-Term Actions (0-12 months)	Long-Term Value (3-7 years)
Defense Partnership (if applicable)	Build ITAR/EAR compliance infrastructure Respond to open DARPA/AFRL BAAs in relevant quantum domains Develop cleared domains Develop cleared-personnel baseline	Defense quantum program participation Access to classified performance benchmarks Dual-use technology development Mission-critical quantum application positioning
Talent Pipeline Architecture	Audit current pipeline against five-stage framework Launch Stage 1 or Stage 2 university engagement program Implement retention investment for current quantum staff	Durable quantum talent competitive advantage Reduced recruiting cost Organizational quantum knowledge depth Workforce development ROI

Table 14.6: Quantum Ecosystem Development, Near-Term Actions and Long-Term Value

The organizations and governments that invest in quantum ecosystem development now establishing university partnerships, engaging with national quantum initiative programs, building cross-disciplinary quantum teams, and constructing talent pipelines that extend from campus to career, will shape the quantum technology landscape of the 2030s rather than adapt to it. The quantum ecosystem does not build itself. It's built by leaders who understand that the most important quantum decisions of the next decade are being made right now, in the partnership agreements being signed, the research programs being funded, and the students being mentored in quantum labs around the world.

You have the frameworks. You have the models. You have the practical starting points. You have the five skills that will distinguish the quantum ecosystem builders from the quantum ecosystem observers. The next step is not a meeting or a task force or a consulting engagement. Far from it. The next step is a phone call to a university quantum center director, a QED-C membership application, a conversation with your most promising quantum intern about what a full-time role might look like. Small actions, taken consistently, build the ecosystem infrastructure that nothing else can provide.

Those who act today will not merely participate in the quantum era. They will define it.

Book summary: Quantum Readiness for Leaders: key takeaways and a call to action for the quantum era

First, it's good to keep in mind one very important thing. We have done this before.

In the early 1970s, the personal computer was a hobbyist's curiosity, a machine that required its operator to understand assembly language, hand-wire circuit boards, and tolerate frequent, unexplained crashes. Corporate executives dismissed it. Investors called it a toy. Established technology companies, some of the largest and most profitable in the world, looked at early microprocessors and saw no credible threat to their mainframe empires. They were wrong, spectacularly and permanently. Within a decade, the personal computer had not merely disrupted the technology industry, it had restructured the global economy, redefined what it meant to work, communicate, and create, and rendered entire categories of organizational capability either commonplace or obsolete.

The leaders who thrived were not those who had predicted the personal computer's precise trajectory, no one did that accurately. They were the leaders who recognized the transition early enough to act, who built organizational capabilities and partnerships during the years when the technology was still rough and the business models still uncertain, and who entered the era of PC ubiquity already equipped to compete rather than scrambling to catch up. The quantum transition is our generation's version of that moment. The technology is rough. The business models are still uncertain. The timelines are contested. And the leaders who will define the quantum era are making their foundational decisions right now.

Key takeaways for every reader

Across fourteen chapters and four strategic sections, **Quantum Readiness for Leaders** has delivered a comprehensive, practitioner-calibrated guide to the most consequential technology transition of the coming decade. Whether you engaged with every chapter or focused on the parts most directly relevant to your role, the essential takeaways are these:

- Quantum is not a single technology, it's an ecosystem. Quantum computing, quantum sensing, quantum networking, quantum key distribution, and quantum cryptography are interconnected technology layers that individually deliver significant value and collectively enable capabilities no classical technology can approach. Strategic quantum readiness requires awareness of the full ecosystem, not mastery of any single component.

- The timeline is compressed by threats you cannot see. The harvest-now-decrypt-later attack model means that adversaries may already be collecting your most sensitive encrypted data today, storing it for decryption when cryptographically relevant quantum computers arrive. Post-quantum cryptography migration is not a future project; it's a current operational imperative for any organizations with long-lived sensitive data and adversaries with the resources to act on long-horizon intelligence collection strategies.
- Talent is the primary constraint. Quantum hardware is becoming accessible through cloud services. Quantum software frameworks are maturing rapidly. The binding constraint on quantum value realization, for organizations, industries, and nations, is the availability of quantum-literate professionals at every level of the workforce, from quantum algorithm developers through quantum-aware executives. Investment in quantum talent development, university partnerships, and quantum workforce pipelines is the highest-leverage quantum investment most organizations can make today.
- Infrastructure investment decisions made today have decade-long implications. Cryptographic architectures, data pipeline designs, and computing infrastructure decisions being made in current IT investment cycles will either accelerate or constrain quantum integration as quantum technologies mature. Leaders who embed quantum-readiness criteria into today's infrastructure decisions and the costly retrofitting that unprepared organizations will face under time pressure.
- Ecosystem partnership is not optional, it's strategic infrastructure. No single organization will develop all the quantum capabilities it needs in isolation. The organizations that will lead the quantum era are those that build the right university partnerships, government program relationships, industry consortium memberships, and vendor ecosystems now, creating collaborative networks whose collective intelligence, talent production, and research output far exceed what any organization can generate independently.
- Policy shapes the quantum landscape. For policymakers, the decisions being made today about quantum research funding, export control frameworks, quantum workforce development programs, PQC migration mandates, and international quantum cooperation agreements will determine whether national economies are quantum leaders or quantum followers in the 2030s. The window for foundational policy investment is open now and will not remain open indefinitely.

Continue your quantum journey: your mentor in the months and years ahead

Congratulations! Reading this book was a significant investment of your time and attention, and it represents exactly the kind of strategic commitment that separates quantum-ready leaders from those who are still waiting for quantum to become obvious before they engage. But a book, by its nature, is a snapshot, a carefully constructed view of the quantum landscape as it stands today, with the best available projection of where it's heading. The quantum landscape, of course, does not hold still.

New quantum hardware milestones will be announced. New post-quantum cryptography standards will be finalized and updated. New national quantum strategies will be published. New industry partnerships will reshape the ecosystem. New research breakthroughs will compress timelines or reveal new obstacles. And new policy decisions: on export controls, on workforce development, on international quantum cooperation, will open and close strategic windows. Staying ahead of all of this, in real time, with the depth and relevance required to make sound decisions, is a genuine and ongoing challenge.

That is precisely why I write *AI & Quantum Decoded* at `substack.com/@aiquantumrobert`. A resource designed to do what a book structurally cannot: keep you current as the landscape moves and translate that currency into action. The distinction that matters most is not between those who know quantum is important and those who do not. By now, most serious leaders know it is. The distinction that will define competitive outcomes is between those who know what is changing and those who also know how to respond to it. That second half, the frameworks, the implementation milestones, the decision-ready analysis, is what the publication is built around.

The content spans the full range of this book's readership. Developers and IT professionals will find technical deep-dives, code-level guidance, and hands-on coverage of the latest tools and research. Executives, investors, policymakers, and startup founders will find strategic frameworks, policy analysis, and the kind of context that makes new developments immediately actionable rather than merely interesting. Whatever your role and wherever you are in your quantum journey, the goal is the same: not just to inform you about what is emerging, but to equip you to lead through it.

The quantum era belongs to those who act now

History does not reward the organizations and leaders who waited for certainty before acting on transformative technology transitions. It rewards those who developed the judgment to act decisively under uncertainty, who invested in capabilities before they were obviously necessary, built partnerships before they were obviously valuable, and developed talent before it was obviously scarce. The personal computer generation of leaders who built that judgement became the architects of the information economy. The internet generation of leaders who built it became the architects of the digital economy. The leaders building quantum today will become the architects of systems whose full dimension we cannot yet fully predict, but whose foundational structures we are shaping this very moment. Similarly, it's like laying down the foundation and framing of a new house or building before anyone can see the final interior design. You can't see what the room will look like, however the choices you make early on determine whether the whole structure will have the functionality, strength, and readiness to grow.

You have read this book because you already understand that quantum is not a technology story for physicists and engineers alone. It's a leadership story, about the decisions that executives, investors, and policymakers make when the technology is still emerging, the standards are still forming, the talent is still scarce, and the competitive landscape is still being shaped. Those decisions are yours to make. The frameworks, tools, and strategic perspectives in these pages are your foundation.

The quantum era is not coming. It's already here, in the research labs and startup offices and national quantum centers where the capabilities of the 2030s are being built right now. The question isn't whether your organization will be part of it. The question is whether you will help build it or inherit whatever others have built in your absence.

So at least for now, when that article lands on your desk with the headline, "A demonstration of quantum advantage in...", and it will, you won't need to scramble for context, summon a consultant, or wait for someone else to tell you what it means for your organization. You will already know. More importantly, you'll already know what to do next.

Keep in mind, that's not a small thing. That's precisely the kind of preparedness that turns a technology transition from a threat into an opportunity, and from an opportunity into a competitive advantage that compounds with every decision you make from this point forward.

And let's not forget: that demonstration of quantum advantage may not come from a competitor's press release or a research lab's announcement. It may come from your own organization, because you chose to act while others were still deliberating.

The quantum future is yours to build. Start now.

Welcome to Quantum!

Further reading

1. `https://doi.org/10.1109/MCSE.2017.29`
2. `https://compete.org/reports/`

3. https://www.researchgate.net/publication/42437138_Best_Practices_for_Industry-University_Research_Collaborations
4. https://doi.org/10.17226/25196
5. https://www.ibm.com/quantum/ibm-quantum-network
6. https://newsroom.ibm.com/2023-05-21-IBM-Launches-100-Million-Partnership-with-Global-Universities-to-Develop-Novel-Technologies-Towards-a-100,000-Qubit-Quantum-Centric-Supercomputer
7. https://www.ibm.com/quantum/blog/japanese-quantum-ecosystem
8. https://www.prnewswire.com/news-releases/ibm-releases-a-new-blueprint-for-quantum-centric-supercomputing-302711715.html
9. https://www.ibm.com/new/announcements/ibm-is-recognized-as-the-current-company-to-beat-in-a-2025-gartner-report-on-quantum-computing
10. https://www.gartner.com/en/documents/7247830
11. https://www.quantum.gov/
12. https://www.congress.gov/bill/115th-congress/house-bill/6227
13. https://qt.eu/media/pdf/Strategic-Reseach-and-Industry-Agenda-2030.pdf
14. https://uknqt.ukri.org/
15. https://www.jst.go.jp/moonshot/en/program/goal6/
16. https://www.sri.com/wp-content/uploads/2023/11/QTMR-Final-Report-of-Needs-Capabilities-and-Gaps-v5.pdf
17. https://doi.org/10.48550/arXiv.2106.10522
18. https://chicagoquantum.org/about/members
19. https://chicagoquantum.org/about/partners
20. https://doi.org/10.17226/26850
21. https://www.pasqal.com/
22. https://www.pasqal.com/newsroom/pasqal-is-entering-a-new-phase-of-development-with-new-financing-expected-of-at-least-e340-million-in-anticipation-of-its-public-listing/
23. https://www.pasqal.com/newsroom/centralesupelec-and-pasqal-a-partnership-at-the-heart-of-quantum-computing-to-further-accelerate-the-future-of-quantum-technology/

24. https://www.pasqal.com/newsroom/pasqal-drives-europes-quantum-industrialization-with-the-integration-of-two-qpus-into-europes-first-hybrid-hpc-quantum-infrastructure/
25. https://doi.org/10.2307/20032161
26. https://www.darpa.mil/program/optimization-with-noisy-intermediate-scale-quantum-devices
27. https://www.pmddtc.state.gov/ddtc_public?id=ddtc_kb_article_page&sys_id=24d528fddbfc930044f9ff621f961987
28. https://www.bis.gov/regulations/ear
29. https://www.darpa.mil/work-with-us/communities/small-business/sbir-sttr-overview
30. https://www.afrl.af.mil/RI/
31. https://files.gao.gov/reports/GAO-25-106856/index.html
32. https://www.mckinsey.com/capabilities/tech-and-ai/our-insights/quantum-computing-funding-remains-strong-but-talent-gap-raises-concern
33. https://www.quantum.gov/wp-content/uploads/2024/12/NQI-Annual-Report-FY2025.pdf
34. https://www.r-ccs.riken.jp/en/outreach/topics/20250701-2/
35. https://newsroom.ibm.com/2026-07-30-ibm-and-qedma-demonstrate-quantum-advantage,-modeling-physics-beyond-classical-capabilities-through-trusted-quantum-computation

15

Unlock Your Exclusive Benefits

Your copy of this book includes the following exclusive benefits:

DRM-Free PDF Version

Download DRM-free PDF and ePub copies of this book.

7-Day Packt Library Access

Get 7-day unlimited access to 8,000+ books and videos. No credit card required.

Available for first-time Packt+ trial users only.

Next-Gen Reader Access

Read this book on Packt Reader with progress sync, dark mode and note-taking.

Follow the guide below to unlock them. The process takes only a few minutes and needs to be completed once.

Unlock this Book's Free Benefits in 3 Easy Steps

Step 1

Keep your purchase invoice ready for *Step 3*. If you have a physical copy, scan it using your phone and save it as a PDF, JPG, or PNG.

For more help on finding your invoice, visit `https://www.packtpub.com/en-us/unlock?step=1`.

> Note
>
> **Note**: If you bought this book directly from Packt, no invoice is required. After *Step 2*, you can access your exclusive content right away.

Step 2

Scan the QR code or go to `packtpub.com/unlock`.

On the page that opens (similar to *Figure 15.1* on desktop), search for this book by name and select the correct edition.

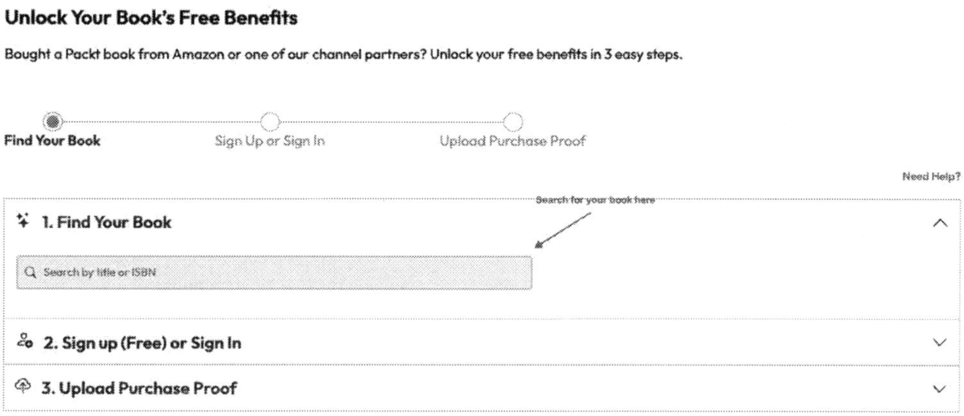

Figure 15.1: Packt unlock landing page on desktop

Step 3

After selecting your book, sign in to your Packt account or create one for free. Then upload your invoice (PDF, PNG, or JPG, up to 10 MB). Follow the on-screen instructions to finish the process.

Need Help

If you get stuck and need help, visit `https://www.packtpub.com/unlock-benefits/help` for a detailed FAQ on how to find your invoices and more. This QR code will take you to the help page.

Note

Note: If you are still facing issues, reach out to `customercare@packt.com`.

Other Books You May Enjoy

If you enjoyed this book, you may be interested in these other books by Packt:

Dancing with Qubits

Robert S. Sutor

ISBN: 978-1-83763-675-4

- Explore the mathematical foundations of quantum computing
- Discover the complex, mind-bending concepts that underpin quantum systems
- Understand the key ideas behind classical and quantum computing
- Refresh and extend your grasp of essential mathematics, computing, and quantum theory
- Examine a detailed overview of qubits and quantum circuits
- Dive into quantum algorithms such as Grover's search, Deutsch-Jozsa, Simon's, and Shor's
- Explore the main applications of quantum computing in the fields of scientific computing, AI, and elsewhere

Learn Quantum Computing with Python and IBM Quantum

Robert Loredo

ISBN: 978-1-80324-480-8

- Get familiar with the features within the IBM Quantum Platform
- Create and visualize quantum gates and circuits
- Operate quantum gates on qubits using the IBM Quantum Composer
- Install and run your quantum circuits on an IBM Quantum computer
- Discover Qiskit and its many features such as the Qiskit Runtime
- Get to grips with fundamental quantum algorithms and error mitigation techniques to help you get started
- Understand the new era of quantum utility and how this moves us closer towards quantum advantage

Packt is searching for authors like you

If you're interested in becoming an author for Packt, please visit `authors.packt.com` and apply today. We have worked with thousands of developers and tech professionals, just like you, to help them share their insight with the global tech community. You can make a general application, apply for a specific hot topic that we are recruiting an author for, or submit your own idea.

Share your thoughts

Now you've finished *Quantum Readiness for Leaders*, we'd love to hear your thoughts! Scan the QR code below to go straight to the Amazon review page for this book and share your feedback or leave a review on the site that you purchased it from.

https://packt.link/r/1806388758

Your review is important to us and the tech community and will help us make sure we're delivering excellent quality content.

Subscribe to Deep Engineering

Join thousands of developers and architects who want to understand how software is changing, deepen their expertise, and build systems that last.

Deep Engineering is a weekly expert-led newsletter for experienced practitioners, featuring original analysis, technical interviews, and curated insights on architecture, system design, and modern programming practice.

Scan the QR or visit the link to subscribe for free.

`https://packt.link/deep-engineering-newsletter`

Index

D

E

Made in United States
Orlando, FL
04 November 2026

90204516R00267